the
cricinfo
guide to

international
cricket
2009

edited by
**steven
lynch**

THE CRICINFO GUIDE TO INTERNATIONAL CRICKET 2009
Edited by **Steven Lynch**

Published by John Wisden & Co Ltd
© John Wisden & Co Ltd, 2008

"Cricinfo" is the registered trademark of Cricinfo UK Ltd
www.cricinfo.com

John Wisden & Co Ltd
13 Old Aylesfield, Golden Pot, Alton, Hampshire GU34 4BY

ISBN: 978-1-905625-15-4

1 3 5 7 9 10 8 6 4 2

Typeset in Mendoza Roman and Frutiger by Typematter, Basingstoke
Printed and bound in Great Britain by Clays Ltd, St Ives plc

Distributed by Macmillan Distribution Ltd

CONTENTS

About Cricinfo 4

Introduction 5

How to use Statsguru 6

Player index by country 8

Player profiles A-Z **10**

Ireland 210

Kenya 212

The Netherlands 214

Scotland 216

Zimbabwe 218

NEW Coaches 220

Umpires and Referees 223

Test match records 230

One-Day International records 232

NEW Twenty20 International records 234

Australia records 236

Bangladesh records 240

England records 244

India records 248

New Zealand records 252

Pakistan records 256

South Africa records 260

Sri Lanka records 264

West Indies records 268

International schedule 2008-09 272

ABOUT CRICINFO

Cricinfo is, by a distance, the world's No. 1 cricket website. It is also a triumph of passion and entrepreneurship. It began as a lark in 1993, when a group of cricket-besotted expatriates working in the United States created a software application that allowed similarly obsessed fellow fans to submit cricket scores from remote locations. Soon, what started as a form of social networking had turned into a serious business.

Ten years, a few million users, and a dotcom rollercoaster ride later – during which the site sponsored a women's World Cup and the English County Championship – Cricinfo merged with its main rival, Wisden.com, to produce a site of unmatched depth and breadth. Cricinfo not only covers every ball bowled in international cricket, but does so with a distinct and independent voice.

It is a voice now heard by more people around the world than ever before. Cricinfo is accessed by over seven million users every month. The site's worldwide reach, authority and brand recognition are unrivalled in online cricket – thanks in part to its editorial motto, which is not merely to report on what matters to cricket, but to make sense of it by bringing to bear a unique global perspective that is not the preserve of the traditional media.

The site's database is fully searchable and incorporates the full Wisden archive, dating right back to the first Almanack in 1864. There's a comprehensive records section, profiles for every current first-class player, and also **Statsguru**, an interactive query tool that allows users to set their own parameters while searching for statistics relating to every one of the 3000 international and 45,000 first-class cricketers to have played the game (more details on page 6).

Live scores and informed ball-by-ball text commentary continue to be the heart of the site, but they are supplemented by in-depth match reports, analysis and comments from a dedicated and talented editorial team across the world, and some of the most credible voices in world cricket – among them Ian Chappell, Geoffrey Boycott, Tony Greig, Michael Holding, David Lloyd, Sanjay Manjrekar and Kumar Sangakkara. These experts are the backbone of Cricinfo's audio service, which was launched in 2006 and offers match analysis, panel discussions and interviews.

A new section, Cricinfo Magazine, bringing together a wide range of feature content, from interviews to columns to bite-sized articles, was launched in 2008. The site's roster of popular blogs features players as well as top cricket writers. Cricinfo also has its own Fantasy League, which has been a huge hit. And mobile content is another fast-growing area.

During 2007, Cricinfo was taken over by ESPN. The acquisition provides the site with access to better technology and more sophisticated multimedia content – as in the case of Cricinfo TV, the new video service.

From here, the Cricinfo story can only get bigger and better.

INTRODUCTION

Welcome to the third edition of the **Cricinfo Guide to International Cricket**, which brings you details – in words and pictures, facts and figures – of 200 players, taken from the well-stacked database of Cricinfo, the world's largest single-sport website. The main addition this year is the inclusion of records for the latest form of the international game – Twenty20 matches. The stats section for each player has been expanded to include his T20 record, while overall records can be found towards the back of the book. The other innovation is a section on the coaches of all the Test-playing countries (this can be found near the umpires and referees). We have also found new photographs of most of the players featured.

The main pages feature a photo of each player, with a concise summary of his career, then mix some unusual facts with statistics for Tests, one-day and Twenty20 internationals and first-class matches. There is also a selection of records (both country-by-country and overall), a rundown on the players from the leading non-Test-playing nations, and a handy guide to the coming year's international fixtures. We have tried to include every player likely to appear in international cricket in 2009 – but, like all selectors, we will undoubtedly have left out someone who should have been included. Details of anyone who managed to escape our selectorial net can be found on Cricinfo.

Many of the profiles are edited and updated versions from Cricinfo's player pages, for which I must thank the site's current editorial staff, especially Sambit Bal (my successor as the site's global editor), Martin Williamson and Andrew Miller, and several former colleagues and contributors to the Cricinfo and Wisden websites, notably Kamran Abbasi, Tanya Aldred, Lawrence Booth, Simon Briggs, Tony Cozier, Tim de Lisle, Cris Freddi, Rabeed Imam, Lynn McConnell, Neil Manthorp, Rob Smyth, Anand Vasu and Telford Vice. Thanks are also due to Christopher Lane and Scyld Berry of Wisden, the designer Ray Rich, the *Wisden Cricketer's* art director Nigel Davies (who designed the cover), Cricinfo's stats editor S. Rajesh, and Travis Basevi, the man who built Cricinfo's searchable database, Statsguru. The majority of the photographs are from Getty Images, apart from a few reproduced by kind permission of the International Cricket Council, and some specially shot for Cricinfo.

The statistics have been updated to **September 12, 2008**, the end of the international season in England. The figures have been taken from Cricinfo and include, for the first time in published form, the number of boundaries hit by each batsman in international cricket. The abbreviation "S/R" in the batting tables denotes runs per 100 balls; in the bowling it shows the balls required to take each wicket. A dash (–) in the records usually indicates that full statistics are not available (such as details of fours and sixes, or balls faced, in all domestic matches). Individual figures for players who have appeared for more than one side in official internationals include the additional matches, details of which are given in the player's "Facts" box. These matches are excluded in the national records sections, which explains any differences in the figures for the players concerned.

And finally, I couldn't have managed without the support of my wife Karina and our son Daniel, who was born on Shane Warne's birthday last year. May his first ball in an Ashes Test be just as good.

Steven Lynch
September 2008

GO FIGURE ... THE NEW IMPROVED STATSGURU

Australia is usually considered the toughest country for touring batsmen. The pitches are generally bouncy and help the fast bowlers, while the Aussies have, for the last 20 years or so, had the world's best bowling attack. A few visiting top-order batsmen have conquered the conditions there, but most of those have preferred the relatively friendly conditions of Adelaide and Sydney to Brisbane, Perth and Melbourne, where the bounce and seam movement offer a much tougher test.

This statement would ring true to any cricket fan, but how do you prove it? Until recently, the only options would have been to rope in a professional statistician, or examine every scorecard for every match on every ground. The first option requires at least a nodding acquaintance with a member of a rare tribe; the second requires a lot of free time.

Now, though, a much simpler option is available at the click of a mouse. The new improved **Statsguru**, Cricinfo's stats engine, is more powerful than the earlier version; even better, it remains absolutely free. The database covers every single Test, one-day and Twenty20 international yet played, and the scope of analysis is far greater than was available before.

The new Statsguru can handle general queries about batting, bowling and fielding, by players or by teams. Want to find a list of those who have scored more than 1000 runs in Tests in England since 1970? Or what about the aggregate runs scored by each team in the 2000s? Or the bowlers with the lowest averages in innings in which they have taken five-fors? The new Statsguru whips up answers to that sort of thing, and much much more.

To go back to our initial query, let's find out the average runs per wicket of overseas teams at Sydney and Adelaide since 1990, and compare that to Brisbane, Melbourne and Perth. And to refine the idea a little further, let's only look at the top seven batsmen and leave the tailenders out of it. On the Statsguru home page, select "Tests", then "batting", then move to the advanced filter. Select the "away" option, then Adelaide Oval from the grounds dropdown, and add Sydney to the query as well. Put in the required date, select "1-7" in the "batting position" filter, and "overall aggregate" in "group figures by". Submit the query, and you'll find that the average runs per wicket for top-order visiting batsmen on these two grounds is 35.63 – but repeat the process for the other three grounds and the average is more than seven runs lower at 28.30.

If you tweak the "group figures by" filter to "individual players", and change the "result qualification" to four or more innings, up comes a list of batsmen who have performed exceptionally at one set of venues but not the other. Plenty of big names are among those who have been hugely successful at Sydney and Adelaide, but not at Brisbane, Melbourne and Perth. The contrast is particularly stark for Brian Lara: five 50-plus scores, including two double-centuries, from 15 innings at Adelaide and the SCG, but only 417 runs from ten Tests at the other three:

Batsman	Adelaide and Sydney			Brisbane, Melbourne, Perth			Difference
	Tests	Runs	Avge	Tests	Runs	Avge	
Michael Vaughan (E)	2	401	100.25	3	232	38.66	+61.59
Sachin Tendulkar (I)	8	952	86.54	8	570	38.00	+48.54
Brian Lara (WI)	8	994	66.26	10	417	23.16	+43.10
Michael Atherton (E)	5	490	54.44	9	306	17.00	+37.44
VVS Laxman (I)	6	765	69.54	5	316	35.11	+34.43
Rahul Dravid (I)	6	624	69.33	5	325	36.11	+33.22
Nasser Hussain (E)	4	429	61.28	6	360	30.00	+31.28
Graham Gooch (E)	4	428	53.50	5	243	24.30	+29.20
Gary Kirsten (SA)	6	579	52.63	3	119	23.80	+28.83

Meanwhile, some lesser-known names have the opposite stats, with better averages at the supposedly tougher venues:

| Batsman | Adelaide and Sydney | | | Brisbane, Melbourne, Perth | | | |
	Tests	Runs	Avge	Tests	Runs	Avge	Difference
Mark Ramprakash (E)	2	146	36.50	4	347	57.83	−21.33
Shaun Pollock (SA)	5	202	28.85	4	192	48.00	−19.15
Hansie Cronje (SA)	4	253	31.62	2	141	47.00	−15.38
Sourav Ganguly (I)	6	302	27.45	5	394	43.77	−16.32
Carl Hooper (WI)	4	194	27.71	5	298	37.25	−9.54
Graeme Hick (E)	3	138	27.60	4	275	34.37	−6.77
Shiv Chanderpaul (WI)	3	176	29.33	5	286	35.75	−6.42

Another cricket truism is that it's difficult for overseas fast bowlers to perform on the subcontinent, where the typical pitch lacks pace and bounce, added to which is the heat at many venues. So which overseas fast bowler has conquered all these hurdles and been among the wickets?

Again Statsguru can now give you the answer. Clicking on the "view" option on the advanced-filter page for Test bowling allows you to select the teams for the bowlers, opponents, host countries and much more. Select pace bowlers, submit the query, and you'll find Shaun Pollock on top of the list for Tests in India, Pakistan, Bangladesh, Sri Lanka and Sharjah, with 60 wickets, although his fellow South Africans Allan Donald and Dale Steyn have better averages:

Player	Tests	Wkts	Avge	S/R	5wi	10wm
Shaun Pollock (SA)	17	60	23.18	56.8	2	0
Glenn McGrath (A)	16	58	25.96	60.3	1	0
Jason Gillespie (A)	13	51	22.86	49.9	1	0
Matthew Hoggard (E)	14	50	28.22	59.2	1	0
Makhaya Ntini (SA)	18	48	34.52	66.8	0	0
Heath Streak (Z)	17	48	32.56	73.3	1	0
Dale Steyn (SA)	9	46	21.58	34.5	3	0
Courtney Walsh (WI)	10	40	23.72	51.9	3	0
Andrew Flintoff (E)	12	39	29.61	66.7	0	0
Allan Donald (SA)	9	36	20.33	48.5	1	0

There's much more to Statsguru than just batting and bowling outputs, though. There's also the unique partnership option, which offers plenty of stats on stands for each wicket, each team, and each pair. Which opening pair, for example, has most often offset the disadvantage of losing the toss in helpful bowling conditions in one-dayers? Try the advanced filter in the ODI partnership option, choose the relevant options (lost toss, batting first, partnership for first wicket, at least 15 stands), and you find that Australia's David Boon and Geoff Marsh averaged 53 in the 19 innings when they opened the batting after Australia lost the toss and were put in; overall, they averaged only 40.03 per partnership. Sachin Tendulkar and Sourav Ganguly averaged 43.73 after losing the toss and batting first, but overall their average went up to 49.32.

If all this numbers talk has got you going, then here are some more questions to test your understanding of Statsguru. With which player has Rahul Dravid scored the most runs in Tests? How much does he average in partnerships with VVS Laxman? And which team has won the most Tests after losing the toss?

I'll leave you with the most monumental stat of all: in 1886 Tests to September 2008, 1,834,235 runs have been scored for the loss off 57,711 wickets, at an overall average of 31.78. What about finding out the corresponding numbers for ODIs? Happy hunting!

S. Rajesh
Cricinfo statistics editor

PLAYER INDEX

AUSTRALIA
Bollinger, Doug................................... 20
Bracken, Nathan................................. 24
Casson, Beau..................................... 29
Clark, Stuart 33
Clarke, Michael................................... 34
Haddin, Brad 62
Hayden, Matthew................................ 66
Hilfenhaus, Ben 67
Hodge, Brad 68
Hopes, James 70
Hussey, David 73
Hussey, Michael................................. 74
Jaques, Phil 78
Johnson, Mitchell 82
Katich, Simon 88
Lee, Brett 94
McGain, Bryce 96
Marsh, Shaun................................... 102
Noffke, Ashley.................................. 124
Ponting, Ricky................................... 141
Ronchi, Luke.................................... 151
Siddle, Peter 169
Symonds, Andrew 184
Tait, Shaun..................................... 185
Voges, Adam 199
Watson, Shane.................................. 202
White, Cameron................................ 203

BANGLADESH
Abdur Razzak 11
Aftab Ahmed.................................... 13
Dhiman Ghosh.................................. 40
Dolar Mahmud.................................. 43
Farhad Reza..................................... 48
Habibul Bashar 61
Junaid Siddique 83
Mahmudullah 99
Mashrafe Mortaza.............................. 107
Mohammad Ashraful 113
Mushfiqur Rahim 119
Nazimuddin 122
Raqibul Hasan.................................. 149
Shahadat Hossain 161
Shahriar Nafees 163
Shakib Al Hasan 164
Syed Rasel 183
Tamim Iqbal 186

ENGLAND
Ambrose, Tim 14
Anderson, James................................ 16
Bell, Ian.. 17
Bopara, Ravi 21
Bresnan, Tim 26
Broad, Stuart 27
Collingwood, Paul............................... 35
Cook, Alastair 36
Denly, Joe 39
Flintoff, Andrew 51
Harmison, Steve 64
Hoggard, Matthew.............................. 69
Mascarenhas, Dimitri 106
Panesar, Monty................................. 130
Patel, Samit 133
Pattinson, Darren 136
Pietersen, Kevin 139
Prior, Matt 145
Shah, Owais 160
Sidebottom, Ryan 170
Strauss, Andrew 180
Swann, Graeme 182
Tremlett, Chris 191
Vaughan, Michael 197
Wright, Luke 204

INDIA
Chawla, Piyush 32
Dhoni, Mahendra Singh 41
Dravid, Rahul 44
Gambhir, Gautam............................... 55
Ganguly, Sourav................................. 56
Gony, Manpreet 60
Harbhajan Singh 63
Jaffer, Wasim 76
Karthik, Dinesh 87
Khan, Zaheer.................................... 89
Kumar, Praveen 91
Kumble, Anil 92
Laxman, VVS 93
Ojha, Pragyan 127
Patel, Munaf 132
Pathan, Irfan 134
Pathan, Yusuf 135
Raina, Suresh 146
Sehwag, Virender 159
Sharma, Ishant................................. 165
Sharma, Rohit 166
Singh, RP 172
Sreesanth, S 178
Tendulkar, Sachin 189
Uthappa, Robin 194
Yuvraj Singh 208

NEW ZEALAND
Elliott, Grant 47
Flynn, Daniel.................................... 52
Franklin, James 53
Fulton, Peter.................................... 54
Gillespie, Mark 59
Hopkins, Gareth 71
How, Jamie...................................... 72

PLAYER INDEX

McCullum, Brendon 95
Marshall, James 103
Martin, Chris 105
Mason, Michael 108
Mills, Kyle 111
O'Brien, Iain 126
Oram, Jacob 129
Patel, Jeetan 131
Ryder, Jesse 152
Southee, Tim 177
Styris, Scott 181
Taylor, Ross 188
Vettori, Daniel 198

PAKISTAN
Abdur Rauf 10
Abdur Rehman 12
Danish Kaneria 37
Fawad Alam 49
Iftikhar Anjum 75
Kamran Akmal 85
Mansoor Amjad 101
Misbah-ul-Haq 112
Mohammad Yousuf 114
Nasir Jamshed 121
Salman Butt 153
Sarfraz Ahmed 157
Shahid Afridi 162
Shoaib Akhtar 167
Shoaib Malik 168
Sohail Khan 175
Sohail Tanvir 176
Umar Gul 193
Wahab Riaz 200
Yasir Arafat 205
Yasir Hameed 206
Younis Khan 207

SOUTH AFRICA
Amla, Hashim 15
Bodi, Gulam 19
Botha, Johan 22
Boucher, Mark 23
de Villiers, AB 38
Duminy, J-P 45
Gibbs, Herschelle 58
Harris, Paul 65
Kallis, Jacques 84
McKenzie, Neil 97
Morkel, Albie 115
Morkel, Morne 116
Nel, Andre 123
Ntini, Makhaya 125
Ontong, Justin 128
Peterson, Robin 137
Philander, Vernon 138

Prince, Ashwell 144
Smith, Graeme 174
Steyn, Dale 179
Zondeki, Monde 209

SRI LANKA
Dilshan, Tillakaratne 42
Fernando, Dilhara 50
Jayasuriya, Sanath 79
Jayawardene, Mahela 80
Jayawardene, Prasanna 81
Kapugedera, Chamara 86
Kulasekara, Nuwan 90
Maharoof, Farveez 98
Malinga, Lasith 100
Mendis, Ajantha 109
Muralitharan, Muttiah 118
Prasad, Dammika 143
Samaraweera, Thilan 154
Sangakkara, Kumar 156
Silva, Chamara 171
Tharanga, Upul 190
Udawatte, Mahela 192
Vaas, Chaminda 195
Vandort, Michael 196
Warnapura, Malinda 201

WEST INDIES
Benn, Sulieman 18
Bravo, Dwayne 25
Browne, Patrick 28
Chanderpaul, Shivnarine 30
Chattergoon, Sewnarine 31
Edwards, Fidel 46
Gayle, Chris 57
Jaggernauth, Amit 77
Marshall, Xavier 104
Miller, Nikita 110
Morton, Runako 117
Nash, Brendan 120
Pollard, Kieron 140
Powell, Daren 142
Ramdin, Denesh 147
Rampaul, Ravi 148
Roach, Kemar 150
Sammy, Darren 155
Sarwan, Ramnaresh 158
Smith, Devon 173
Taylor, Jerome 187

OTHER COUNTRIES
Ireland 210
Kenya 212
The Netherlands 214
Scotland 216
Zimbabwe 218

ABDUR RAUF

Full name	**Abdur Rauf Khan**
Born	**December 9, 1978, Renala Khurd, Punjab**
Teams	**Lahore, Sui Northern Gas**
Style	**Right-hand bat, right-arm fast-medium bowler**
Test debut	**No Tests yet**
ODI debut	**Pakistan v Zimbabwe at Sheikhupura 2007-08**

THE PROFILE Tall and well-built in the tradition of Punjabi fast bowlers, Abdur Rauf comes with the seal of approval from Rashid Latif, the former Test wicketkeeper and captain who now heads the national academy. Rauf has been among the top wicket-takers in domestic cricket for some seasons now, and a few judges feel that the selectors missed his best years. He is capable of generating a fair amount of pace with a natural action that brings the ball back in to the right-hander, but it is his ability to extract awkward bounce – and movement on helpful tracks – that has been the key to his successes so far. Rauf was on the fringe of the national team as long ago as 2002-03, when he was chosen in the squads for the series against South Africa and Bangladesh, without getting a game. He toured India with the A team in December 2003, and although he had a generally poor series – along with most of his team-mates – he did contribute a couple of hostile spells. More consistent performances in the domestic circuit finally earned him a call-up to Pakistan's one-day side for the final one-dayer against Zimbabwe in January 2008. He took three wickets – two of them with successive balls to wrap up the innings – and cemented a place for the Asia Cup later in the year. He continued his good start there with two wickets against India, then three more (and the Man of the Match award) as Bangladesh were rolled over for 115.

THE FACTS Abdur Rauf took 8 for 40 (and 6 for 58 in the second innings) for Sui Gas against ADBP at Faisalabad in October 2001 ... That season he took 84 wickets in Pakistan domestic cricket, at 22.08 ... When North West Frontier Province scored 664 for 6 against Baluchistan at Peshawar in March 2008, Rauf took all six wickets to fall, for 193 ... He has never made a first-class century, but has been out twice in the nineties: his highest score is 98 for Multan against Customs at Okara in November 2007 ...

THE FIGURES *to 12.9.08*   www.cricinfo.com

Batting & Fielding	M	Inns	NO	Runs	HS	Avge	S/R	100	50	4s	6s	Ct	St
Tests	0	0	–	–	–	–	–	–	–	–	–	–	–
ODIs	3	0	–	–	–	–	–	–	–	–	–	2	0
T20 Ints	0	0	–	–	–	–	–	–	–	–	–	–	–
First-class	83	131	26	1828	98	17.40	–	0	8	–	–	32	0

Bowling	M	Balls	Runs	Wkts	BB	Avge	RpO	S/R	5i	10m
Tests	0	0	–	–	–	–	–	–	–	–
ODIs	3	160	135	8	3–24	16.87	5.06	20.00	0	0
T20 Ints	0	0	–	–	–	–	–	–	–	–
First-class	83	16568	9902	375	8–40	26.40	3.58	44.18	28	3

ABDUR RAZZAK

Full name	**Khan Abdur Razzak**
Born	**June 15, 1982, Khulna**
Teams	**Khulna, Bangalore Royal Challengers**
Style	**Left-hand bat, slow left-arm orthodox spinner**
Test debut	**Bangladesh v Australia at Chittagong 2005-06**
ODI debut	**Bangladesh v Hong Kong at Colombo 2004**

THE PROFILE The latest in Bangladesh's seemingly never-ending supply of left-arm spinners, Abdur Razzak (no relation to the similarly named Pakistan allrounder) made his mark when he helped unheralded Khulna to their first-ever National Cricket League title in 2001-02. Tall, with a high action, he was given his A-team debut during a five-match one-day series against Zimbabwe early in 2004, and took the opportunity well with 15 wickets, including a matchwinning 7 for 17 in the third encounter on the batting paradise of Dhaka's old Bangabandhu National Stadium. He has an uncanny ability to pin batsmen down, although his action has been questioned in the past (Bangladesh's coaching staff used video technology to help iron out anything suspicious). He took 3 for 17 on his one-day debut against Hong Kong in the Asia Cup in Colombo in 2004, but was reported for a suspect action after the next match, against Pakistan. Left out of the Champions Trophy in England later that year, "Raj" played just one ODI before he was recalled for the home series against Sri Lanka in February 2006. He made his Test debut two months later, called up for the second Test against Australia on a turning track at Chittagong (even the Aussies played three spinners), but failed to take a wicket, and has continued to struggle to take wickets in Tests. But he has become an automatic one-day selection, playing in all Bangladesh's 30 matches in 2006-07 – including throughout the World Cup – taking 50 wickets and maintaining a mean economy rate. He was the only Bangladeshi signed up for the first year of the Indian Premier League in 2008.

THE FACTS Abdur Razzak's best bowling in ODIs is 5 for 33 against Zimbabwe at Bogra in December 2006 ... His best first-class figures of 7 for 11 (10 for 62 in the match) came for Khulna at Sylhet in 2003-04 ... During 2008 Razzak became the third Bangladeshi, after Mohammad Rafique and Mashrafe Mortaza, to take 100 ODI wickets ...

THE FIGURES *to 12.9.08*   www.cricinfo.com

Batting & Fielding	M	Inns	NO	Runs	HS	Avge	S/R	100	50	4s	6s	Ct	St
Tests	3	6	2	84	33	21.00	62.22	0	0	15	0	1	0
ODIs	76	49	21	417	33	14.89	69.50	0	0	29	11	18	0
T20 Ints	9	6	3	8	5	2.66	33.33	0	0	0	0	0	0
First-class	41	66	10	1157	83	20.66	58.08	0	6	–	–	14	0

Bowling	M	Balls	Runs	Wkts	BB	Avge	RpO	S/R	5i	10m
Tests	3	546	337	2	1–109	168.50	3.70	273.00	0	0
ODIs	76	3941	2803	106	5–33	26.44	4.26	37.17	1	0
T20 Ints	9	210	224	14	3–17	16.00	6.40	15.00	0	0
First-class	41	9015	3958	132	7–11	29.98	2.63	68.20	5	1

ABDUR REHMAN

Full name	**Abdur Rehman**
Born	**March 1, 1980, Sialkot, Punjab**
Teams	**Sialkot, Habib Bank**
Style	**Left-hand bat, slow left-arm orthodox spinner**
Test debut	**Pakistan v South Africa at Karachi 2007-08**
ODI debut	**Pakistan v West Indies at Faisalabad 2006-07**

THE PROFILE Abdur Rehman made his international debut late in 2006 at the ripe old age of 26 (elderly considering the usual subcontinental trait of ruthlessly exposing youth to the world's best), and immediately impressed, with two wickets in each of his first three one-dayers against West Indies. He is not a huge turner of the ball, but he is accurate and consistent, and can exploit the rough well. He first gave notice of his ability back in 1999, with five and six wickets in successive matches for Pakistan's Under-19s against South Africa, a home series for which he was chosen after only a couple of first-class matches. His senior opportunities have been limited by the side's several spinners, most of them better batsmen, but Rehman kept himself in contention with good domestic performances: in 2006-07 he was the leading bowler as Habib Bank won the Pentangular Cup, with 11 wickets in an important victory over Sind. He missed the World Cup – a blessing in disguise, perhaps – but was recalled for the one-day series against Sri Lanka in Abu Dhabi, although he played in only one of the three matches. Rehman probably lacks the artillery to cause major concern to batsmen in Tests. However, with Pakistan looking for variety and an ally for Danish Kaneria, he got a chance against South Africa at home at the end of 2007, and took eight wickets in his debut Test – he took 4 for 105 in each innings – and finished the short series with 11 victims, one more than Kaneria managed.

THE FACTS Abdur Rehman took 26 wickets for Habib Bank in the 2006-07 Pentangular Cup in Pakistan, including 11 in the match against Sind ... He had identical figures of 4 for 105 in each innings of his Test debut, the first instance of this since England's Willie Bates took 2 for 43 in both innings against Australia at Melbourne in 1881-82 ... Rehman took 8 for 53 for Habib Bank v Sui Gas in December 2005, a week after claiming 5 for 120 and 6 for 28 against Khan Research Labs ... He made 96 for Habib Bank v National Bank at Multan in January 2006 ...

THE FIGURES *to 12.9.08*   www.cricinfo.com

Batting & Fielding	M	Inns	NO	Runs	HS	Avge	S/R	100	50	4s	6s	Ct	St
Tests	2	3	1	34	25*	17.00	33.66	0	0	5	0	1	0
ODIs	11	8	1	59	31	8.42	45.38	0	0	5	0	2	0
T20 Ints	2	1	1	4	4*	–	80.00	0	0	0	0	1	0
First-class	77	101	11	1593	96	17.70	–	0	7	–	–	31	0

Bowling	M	Balls	Runs	Wkts	BB	Avge	RpO	S/R	5i	10m
Tests	2	750	352	11	4–105	32.00	2.81	68.18	0	0
ODIs	11	594	473	12	2–20	36.41	4.41	49.50	0	0
T20 Ints	2	36	43	2	2–7	21.50	7.16	18.00	0	0
First-class	77	15494	6731	243	8–53	27.69	2.60	63.76	12	3

AFTAB AHMED

Full name	**Aftab Ahmed Chowdhury**
Born	**November 10, 1985, Chittagong**
Teams	**Chittagong**
Style	**Right-hand bat, right-arm medium-pacer**
Test debut	**Bangladesh v New Zealand at Chittagong 2004-05**
ODI debut	**Bangladesh v South Africa at Birmingham 2004**

BANGLADESH

THE PROFILE Aftab Ahmed first came to notice by scoring 79 against South Africa in the Under-19 World Cup in 2002, and the following year he was pitched into the Test squad to face England, despite having done little in two earlier warm-up matches. His selection was initially viewed with suspicion by the local media, who regarded Aftab as something of a one-day cowboy, and indeed his desire to belt the cover off the ball has resulted in some all-too-brief performances, and he has still not done himself justice in Tests, although he did brighten up Chester-le-Street in 2005 with a defiant, carefree 82 not out, the highest score for Bangladesh in the Test series against England. He also finished off the historic one-day win over Australia at Cardiff that year, smashing Jason Gillespie for four and six to seal victory, and before that he had spirited Bangladesh to a 3-2 series triumph with an unbeaten 81 in the final match against Zimbabwe in January 2005. He has been a one-day regular since making his debut late in 2004, playing throughout Bangladesh's ups and downs in the 2007 World Cup, during which his form fell away after he had made six half-centuries in 13 innings from midway in the Champions Trophy the previous October. He struggled with injuries in 2008: after top-edging a ball from Jacques Kallis into his face during a Test against South Africa, he had not long recovered when he fractured a finger in the nets and missed the Asia Cup.

THE FACTS Aftab Ahmed's first five ODI wickets came in one spell, 5 for 31 against New Zealand at Dhaka in November 2004 ... His best bowling analysis in first-class cricket is 7 for 39, for a Bangladesh Cricket Board XI v Central Zone in India's Duleep Trophy in 2004-05 ... Aftab's solitary first-class century was 129 for Chittagong v Dhaka in Dhaka in 2002-03 ... He made 91 for Bangladesh Under-19s in a youth Test against England, captained by Alastair Cook, at Taunton in August 2004 ...

THE FIGURES *to 12.9.08* www.cricinfo.com

Batting & Fielding	M	Inns	NO	Runs	HS	Avge	S/R	100	50	4s	6s	Ct	St
Tests	14	27	3	514	82*	21.41	50.39	0	1	69	3	6	0
ODIs	80	80	6	1874	92	25.32	83.54	0	14	192	49	27	0
T20 Ints	9	9	1	215	62*	26.87	133.54	0	1	25	5	2	0
First-class	35	66	7	1593	129	27.00	59.44	1	6	–	–	21	0

Bowling	M	Balls	Runs	Wkts	BB	Avge	RpO	S/R	5i	10m
Tests	14	314	225	5	2–31	45.00	4.29	62.80	0	0
ODIs	80	739	656	12	5–31	54.66	5.32	61.50	1	0
T20 Ints	9	0	–	–	–	–	–	–	–	–
First-class	35	1610	733	23	7–39	31.86	2.73	70.00	1	0

TIM **AMBROSE**

Full name	**Timothy Raymond Ambrose**
Born	**December 1, 1982, Newcastle, NSW, Australia**
Teams	**Warwickshire**
Style	**Right-hand bat, wicketkeeper**
Test debut	**England v New Zealand at Hamilton 2007-08**
ODI debut	**England v New Zealand at Chester-le-Street 2008**

THE PROFILE   Tim Ambrose arrived in England at 17, and started by playing club cricket for Eastbourne. Sussex soon came calling, encouraged by the fact that he has an English mother. Small and slight, he was soon enlivening many an innings with his punchy strokeplay, particularly a savage square cut almost indistinguishable from that of his Sussex team-mate Murray Goodwin, a long-established master of the stroke. Ambrose scored well as Sussex took their first County Championship title in 2003, finishing with 931 runs at 40. But there was a big cloud on the horizon – the form of Matt Prior, another wicketkeeper/batsman, who did even better that year (1006 runs at 48). For a while they swapped the keeping gloves, but Prior won that particular battle and his mate departed to Edgbaston in 2006. Ambrose was injured early on, but returned with a century in his second match for Warwickshire, and pushed on in 2007, clouting a ferocious 251 not out – with 34 fours – at Worcester in May. Meanwhile Prior's form was falling off after his poor Test debut, and after he had a poor Sri Lankan tour it was, ironically, Ambrose who replaced him. He started well, making 55 in his first Test and a century in his second in New Zealand in 2008, rescuing England after a poor start at Wellington, but at home later in the year he struggled with the bat, and latterly with the gloves. Eventually he lost his place ... to Prior.

THE FACTS   Ambrose made 102 in only his second Test, against New Zealand at Wellington in March 2008 ... He scored 251 not out for Warwickshire at Worcester in May 2007: the only higher score by a Warwickshire wicketkeeper was Geoff Humpage's 254 v Lancashire at Southport in 1982 ... Ambrose hit 52 on his debut for Sussex, against Warwickshire at Edgbaston in September 2001, when he was 18 ... He played for New South Wales in the Australian under-17 finals in January 2000 ...

THE FIGURES *to 12.9.08*   www.cricinfo.com

Batting & Fielding	M	Inns	NO	Runs	HS	Avge	S/R	100	50	4s	6s	Ct	St
Tests	10	15	0	371	102	24.73	42.74	1	2	47	2	30	0
ODIs	5	5	1	10	6	2.50	29.41	0	0	0	0	3	0
T20 Ints	1	0	–	–	–	–	–	–	–	–	–	1	1
First-class	88	136	11	4283	251*	34.26	50.31	6	24	–	–	192	14

Bowling	M	Balls	Runs	Wkts	BB	Avge	RpO	S/R	5i	10m
Tests	10	0	–	–	–	–	–	–	–	–
ODIs	5	0	–	–	–	–	–	–	–	–
T20 Ints	1	0	–	–	–	–	–	–	–	–
First-class	88	6	1	0	–	–	1.00	–	0	0

HASHIM **AMLA**

Full name	**Hashim Mahomed Amla**
Born	**March 31, 1983, Durban, Natal**
Teams	**Dolphins**
Style	**Right-hand bat, occasional right-arm medium-pacer**
Test debut	**South Africa v India at Kolkata 2004-05**
ODI debut	**South Africa v Bangladesh at Chittagong 2007-08**

THE PROFILE An elegant, stroke-filled right-hander blessed with the temperament to make the most of his talent, Hashim Amla was the first South African of Indian descent to reach the Test team. His elevation was hardly a surprise after he reeled off four centuries in his first eight innings in 2004-05, after being appointed captain of the Dolphins (formerly Natal) at the tender age of 21. He toured New Zealand with the Under-19s in 2000-01, captained South Africa at the 2002 Under-19 World Cup, and, after starring for the A team in 2004-05 – he made two hundreds against New Zealand A – made his Test debut against India. He was not an instant success, with serious questions emerging about his technique as he mustered only 36 runs in four innings against England later that season, struggling with an ungainly crouched stance and a bat coming down from somewhere in the region of gully. But he made his second chance count, with 149 against New Zealand at Cape Town in April 2006, followed by big hundreds against New Zealand (again) and India in 2007-08, before a fine undefeated 104 helped save the 2008 Lord's Test. Amla remains a candidate to become South Africa's captain eventually, although currently he is not seen as a one-day player, while he vies with Pakistan's Mohammad Yousuf for the most impressive beard in the game. He is a devout Muslim, and his requests to have logos promoting alcohol removed from his playing gear have been successful.

THE FACTS Amla's highest score is 249, made in nearly 11 hours, for the Dolphins against the Eagles at Bloemfontein in March 2005 ... He averages 104.80 in Tests against New Zealand, but 17.25 v Sri Lanka ... Amla made his first-class debut for KwaZulu-Natal at 16, against Nasser Hussain's 1999-2000 England tourists (and scored 1): in his next match, in February 2002, Amla made his maiden first-class hundred ... His older brother Ahmed also plays for the Dolphins ...

THE FIGURES *to 12.9.08*   www.cricinfo.com

Batting & Fielding	M	Inns	NO	Runs	HS	Avge	S/R	100	50	4s	6s	Ct	St
Tests	29	52	3	1871	176*	38.18	48.35	5	9	248	2	27	0
ODIs	6	5	2	108	46	36.00	76.05	0	0	17	0	2	0
T20 Ints	0	0	–	–	–	–	–	–	–	–	–	–	–
First-class	101	168	15	7074	249	46.23	–	21	34	–	–	80	0

Bowling	M	Balls	Runs	Wkts	BB	Avge	RpO	S/R	5i	10m
Tests	29	42	28	0	–	–	4.00	–	0	0
ODIs	6	0	–	–	–	–	–	–	–	–
T20 Ints	0	0	–	–	–	–	–	–	–	–
First-class	101	309	221	1	1–10	221.00	4.29	309.00	0	0

JAMES **ANDERSON**

Full name	**James Michael Anderson**
Born	**July 30, 1982, Burnley, Lancashire**
Teams	**Lancashire**
Style	**Left-hand bat, right-arm fast-medium bowler**
Test debut	**England v Zimbabwe at Lord's 2003**
ODI debut	**England v Australia at Melbourne 2002-03**

THE PROFILE   A strapping fast bowler, and a superb fielder, James Anderson had played only three one-day games for Lancashire in 2002 when he was hurried into England's one-day squad in Australia that winter as cover for Andy Caddick. He didn't have a number – or even a name – on his shirt, but a remarkable ten-over stint, costing just 12, in century heat at Adelaide earned him a World Cup spot. There, he produced a matchwinning spell against Pakistan before a sobering last-over disaster against Australia. Nonetheless his star was very much in the ascendant, and five wickets followed in the first innings of his debut Test, against Zimbabwe at home in 2003, almost to order. A one-day hat-trick followed against Pakistan ... but then his fortunes waned. For a couple of years he was a peripheral net bowler – and a shadow of his former self when he did get on the field. Previously silent critics noted that his head pointed downwards at delivery, supposedly leading to a lack of control. A lower-back stress fracture kept him out for most of 2006, but he still made the Australian tour and the World Cup. Then, in the absence of the entire Ashes-winning attack in the second half of 2007, Anderson suddenly looked the part of pack leader again. He took 5 for 73 to help square the winter series in New Zealand, and was back among the wickets three months later against the Kiwis at Trent Bridge, when his hostile full-pitched late swing brought him 7 for 43, including a perfect outswinger to castle the dangerous Brendon McCullum.

THE FACTS   Anderson was the first man to take an ODI hat-trick for England, against Pakistan at The Oval in 2003: Steve Harmison followed suit in 2004 ... He took the first six wickets to fall on his way to career-best figures of 7 for 43 for England v New Zealand at Nottingham in 2008 ... Anderson was the Cricket Writers' Club's Young Cricketer of the Year in 2003, the only unanimous choice since the award began in 1950: all 175 members who voted went for him ...

THE FIGURES *to 12.9.08*   www.cricinfo.com

Batting & Fielding	M	Inns	NO	Runs	HS	Avge	S/R	100	50	4s	6s	Ct	St
Tests	29	41	23	246	34	13.66	35.44	0	0	27	0	13	0
ODIs	97	39	19	124	15	6.20	39.36	0	0	8	0	26	0
T20 Ints	10	2	2	1	1*	–	100.00	0	0	0	0	2	0
First-class	81	95	43	491	37*	9.44	–	0	0	–	–	35	0

Bowling	M	Balls	Runs	Wkts	BB	Avge	RpO	S/R	5i	10m
Tests	29	5906	3590	104	7–43	34.51	3.64	56.78	5	0
ODIs	97	4725	3859	127	4–23	30.38	4.90	37.20	0	0
T20 Ints	10	234	322	11	2–24	29.27	8.25	21.27	0	0
First-class	81	14498	8376	291	7–43	28.78	3.46	49.82	13	1

IAN **BELL**

Full name	**Ian Ronald Bell**
Born	**April 11, 1982, Walsgrave, Coventry**
Teams	**Warwickshire**
Style	**Right-hand bat, right-arm medium-pace bowler**
Test debut	**England v West Indies at The Oval 2004**
ODI debut	**England v Zimbabwe at Harare 2004-05**

THE PROFILE Ian Bell was earmarked for greatness long before he was drafted into the England squad in New Zealand in 2001-02, aged 19, as cover for the injured Mark Butcher. Tenacious and technically sound, Bell is in the mould of Michael Atherton, who was burdened with similar expectations on his debut a generation earlier and was similarly adept at leaving the ball outside off. Bell had played only 13 first-class matches when called into that England squad, and his form dipped while he was under the spotlight, but by 2004 he was on the up again. He finally made his Test debut against West Indies that August, stroking 70 at The Oval, before returning the following summer to lift his average to an obscene 297 against Bangladesh. Such rich pickings soon ceased: found out by McGrath and Warne, like so many before him, Bell mustered just 171 runs in the 2005 Ashes series. But, like a true class act, he bounced back better for the experience, collecting 313 runs in three Tests in Pakistan, including a classy century at Faisalabad. And when Pakistan toured in 2006, Bell repeated the dose, with elegant hundreds in each of the first three Tests. He improved his record against the Aussies in 2006-07 without going on to the big score, but solved that problem with some bravura performances, including a long-overdue century, against India late in 2007 in England. He continued to look good the following year, hitting 199 against South Africa at Lord's, while his opening partnership with Matt Prior started to look the part in one-dayers too.

THE FACTS After three Tests, and innings of 70, 65 not out and 162 not out, Bell's average was 297.00: he raised that to 303.00 before Australia started getting him out – only Lawrence Rowe (336), David Lloyd (308) and "Tip" Foster (306) have ever had better averages in Test history ... Bell was the first Englishman to be out for 199 in a Test, against South Africa at Lord's in 2008 ... None of his eight Test centuries has been the only one of the innings ... Bell made 262 not out for Warwickshire v Sussex at Horsham in May 2004 ...

THE FIGURES to 12.9.08 www.cricinfo.com

Batting & Fielding	M	Inns	NO	Runs	HS	Avge	S/R	100	50	4s	6s	Ct	St
Tests	43	77	8	2923	199	42.36	50.68	8	19	343	12	41	0
ODIs	75	72	6	2399	126*	36.34	72.02	1	15	240	11	21	0
T20 Ints	5	5	1	109	60*	27.25	110.10	0	1	14	1	4	0
First-class	134	230	21	9157	262*	43.81	–	23	49	–	–	92	0

Bowling	M	Balls	Runs	Wkts	BB	Avge	RpO	S/R	5i	10m
Tests	43	108	76	1	1–33	76.00	4.22	108.00	0	0
ODIs	75	88	88	6	3–9	14.66	6.00	14.66	0	0
T20 Ints	5	0	–	–	–	–	–	–	–	–
First-class	134	2719	1490	47	4–4	31.70	3.28	57.85	0	0

SULIEMAN **BENN**

Full name	**Sulieman Jamaal Benn**
Born	**July 22, 1981, Haynesville, St James, Barbados**
Teams	**Barbados**
Style	**Left-hand bat, slow left-arm orthodox spinner**
Test debut	**West Indies v Sri Lanka at Providence 2007-08**
ODI debut	**West Indies v Sri Lanka at Port-of-Spain 2007-08**

THE PROFILE A very tall (6ft 7ins) left-arm spinner and a handy lower-order batsman, Sulieman Benn was part of the West Indies B team before becoming a regular for Barbados. Cementing a place in the island side was a long slog, especially for a slow bowler in a land where pace is usually king – and he had to contend with four Test fast bowlers for a berth in the attack. But persistence paid off, and he consolidated his position by taking 32 wickets in 2000-01, his second season, then 24 more in his third. In 2007-08 he took 22 wickets in the Carib Series – more than any other Barbadian – and was rewarded with a call-up to the West Indian squad for the home series against Sri Lanka. He played in the first Test, at Providence in Guyana, and kept the batsmen quiet without threatening to run through a side well schooled against spin. He was recalled for the Barbados Test against Australia, and took 3 for 154 in the second innings as the Aussies romped to 439. His one-day appearances told a similar story – usually thrifty, but seldom dangerous. However, Benn is hard-working and humble – after his original selection he said: "Every Caribbean boy dreams of representing the West Indies and words can't express how I feel. I have been bowling well, the hard work, patience and dedication have paid off with my selection" – and despite stiff competition in the spin department, he is likely to remain near the head of the queue.

THE FACTS Benn's best bowling figures in first-class cricket are 5 for 51 (9 for 87 in the match) for West Indies B against Windward Islands at Kingstown in January 2001 ... He took 5 for 18 for Barbados against the Leeward Islands in a Red Stripe Bowl one-day game in August 2002 ... His highest score is 78 for Barbados against Windward Islands at Bridgetown in February 2002, when he shared an eighth-wicket partnership of 182 with Courtney Browne ...

THE FIGURES *to 12.9.08*   www.cricinfo.com

Batting & Fielding	M	Inns	NO	Runs	HS	Avge	S/R	100	50	4s	6s	Ct	St
Tests	2	4	0	51	28	12.75	50.00	0	0	5	1	1	0
ODIs	4	4	1	31	23*	10.33	73.80	0	0	3	0	0	0
T20 Ints	1	0	–	–	–	–	–	–	–	–	–	0	0
First-class	40	63	10	1077	78	20.32	–	0	5	–	–	32	0

Bowling	M	Balls	Runs	Wkts	BB	Avge	RpO	S/R	5i	10m
Tests	2	636	366	7	3–59	52.28	3.45	90.85	0	0
ODIs	4	234	199	2	1–39	99.50	5.10	117.00	0	0
T20 Ints	1	12	19	0	–	–	9.50	–	0	0
First-class	40	8935	4060	140	5–51	29.00	2.72	63.82	5	0

GULAM **BODI**

Full name	**Gulam Hussain Bodi**
Born	**January 4, 1979, Hathuran, India**
Teams	**Titans**
Style	**Left-hand bat, slow left-arm unorthodox spinner**
Test debut	**No Tests yet**
ODI debut	**South Africa v Zimbabwe at Bulawayo 2007-08**

THE PROFILE Gulam Bodi started out as a left-arm chinaman bowler, and did so well in his first full season for KwaZulu/Natal – 29 wickets at 25.86 in 2000-01 – that he was called up for the one-day leg of South Africa's tour of the West Indies early in 2001, although he didn't get there in the end as he broke a finger in his last game before setting off. Bodi was born in India, but his family moved to Johannesburg when he was 12. He went on to represent SA Schools and played in the Under-19 World Cup. He was also the unwitting cause of Kevin Pietersen's decision to seek his fortune in England: Pietersen blamed the quota system, which insisted on a number of non-white players in provincial sides, when KwaZulu/Natal left him out in favour of Bodi. After moving to Easterns (later renamed the Titans), Bodi improved his batting, although his bowling took more of a back seat. The introduction of Twenty20 cricket to South Africa reinvigorated his game, and following a successful run at the top of the Titans' order he was given a chance in the one-dayers in Zimbabwe in August 2007, after a number of senior players were rested. He started with 51 and 32 in a couple of easy wins, and sealed a place in the squad for the inaugural World Twenty20 championship, although he didn't actually play. It's hard to see him getting a game when everyone is fit, but he remains a handy wild card to have in reserve.

THE FACTS Bodi scored 160 not out for Titans v Eagles at Bloemfontein in February 2007 ... He made 51 in his first ODI, against Zimbabwe at Bulawayo in August 2007, only the second half-century for South Africa on debut after Shaun Pollock's 66 not out against England at Cape Town in 1995-96 ... Bodi took 6 for 63 for KwaZulu/Natal against Gauteng at Durban in March 2001 ...

THE FIGURES *to 12.9.08*   www.cricinfo.com

Batting & Fielding	M	Inns	NO	Runs	HS	Avge	S/R	100	50	4s	6s	Ct	St
Tests	0	0	–	–	–	–	–	–	–	–	–	–	–
ODIs	2	2	0	83	51	41.50	62.87	0	1	9	1	1	0
T20 Ints	1	1	0	8	8	8.00	32.00	0	0	0	0	0	0
First-class	66	103	13	2982	160*	33.13	–	6	13	–	–	29	0

Bowling	M	Balls	Runs	Wkts	BB	Avge	RpO	S/R	5i	10m
Tests	0	0	–	–	–	–	–	–	–	–
ODIs	2	6	8	0	–	–	8.00	–	0	0
T20 Ints	1	0	–	–	–	–	–	–	–	–
First-class	66	3851	2441	61	6–63	40.01	3.80	63.13	2	0

DOUG **BOLLINGER**

Full name	**Douglas Erwin Bollinger**
Born	**July 24, 1981, Baulkham Hills, Sydney**
Teams	**New South Wales**
Style	**Left-hand bat, left-arm fast-medium bowler**
Test debut	**No Tests yet**
ODI debut	**No ODIs yet**

THE PROFILE The 2007-08 summer was one of change for Doug Bollinger. He finished it with his first national contract, his first spot in an Australian touring party, a new wife, and a fresh head of hair, courtesy of the same company that rethatched Shane Warne and Graham Gooch. Just as he was preparing to depart on his honeymoon, Bollinger heard that he was a late addition to the Test squad to tour the West Indies in May 2008. He was unlucky not to have been named in the first place after topping the Pura Cup wicket-takers with 45 at 15.44, an especially good return considering he missed the last three games of New South Wales's successful campaign with a broken foot. He had been instrumental in getting the Blues to the decider, grabbing 12 wickets in an innings victory over Tasmania and ten in a win against Western Australia. Bollinger made his big breakthrough the previous summer, with 37 wickets for NSW at 28.37, culminating in 5 for 73 in the first innings of the final against Tasmania, and his success helped him earn a contract with Worcestershire (where he was not particularly successful) in 2007. A left-arm fast bowler who mixes sharp pace with a consistent line and length, Bollinger has progressed from steady workhorse to dangerous new-ball option. He spent the 2006 Australian winter at the Academy, and the previous summer had made his name in the one-day Ford Ranger Cup with 15 wickets at 20.33. Bollinger has played for Australia A, but his most famous day came for NSW against South Australia in 2004-05 when he became only the fourth man in Australia's domestic history to claim a one-day hat-trick.

THE FACTS Bollinger took a one-day hat-trick for NSW against South Australia at Canberra in December 2004, dismissing Nos 3, 4 and 5 in the order for ducks ... He took 5 for 15 for Australia A against Pakistan A at Lahore in September 2007 ... Bollinger took 6 for 68 and 6 for 63 for NSW against Tasmania at Sydney in December 2007 ... For Worcestershire in 2007 he took only 16 wickets at 44.56 in seven first-class matches ...

THE FIGURES *to 12.9.08* www.cricinfo.com

Batting & Fielding	M	Inns	NO	Runs	HS	Avge	S/R	100	50	4s	6s	Ct	St
Tests	0	0	–	–	–	–	–	–	–	–	–	–	–
ODIs	0	0	–	–	–	–	–	–	–	–	–	–	–
T20 Ints	0	0	–	–	–	–	–	–	–	–	–	–	–
First-class	45	51	24	204	31*	7.55	–	0	0	–	–	14	0

Bowling	M	Balls	Runs	Wkts	BB	Avge	RpO	S/R	5i	10m
Tests	0	0	–	–	–	–	–	–	–	–
ODIs	0	0	–	–	–	–	–	–	–	–
T00 Ints	0	0	–	–	–	–	–	–	–	–
First-class	45	7709	4284	137	6–63	31.27	3.33	56.27	7	2

RAVI **BOPARA**

Full name	**Ravinder Singh Bopara**
Born	**May 4, 1985, Forest Gate, London**
Teams	**Essex**
Style	**Right-hand bat, right-arm medium-pace bowler**
Test debut	**England v Sri Lanka at Kandy 2007-08**
ODI debut	**England v Australia at Sydney 2006-07**

THE PROFILE   Ravi Bopara has packed a lot in since he signed for Essex at 17 in 2002. He's a busy allrounder – a batsman with two double-centuries under his belt, and a handy medium-pacer. Kevin Mitchell observed in the *Wisden Cricketer:* "He bats with combativeness around No. 6, bowls skiddy cutters and fields loudly. He is impossible to ignore." A good county season in 2006 won him a place in the Academy squad which was based in Perth during the Ashes series. When Kevin Pietersen broke a rib in the first match of the one-day triangular, Bopara was summoned: not worried about having such big boots to fill, he made his debut in front of the Sydney Hill, and bowled Australia's "finisher", Michael Hussey, as England began the amazing turnaround that eventually won them that series. Bopara didn't appear again, but he had done enough to make the World Cup, where he showed impressive resolve in making 52, which almost conjured an unlikely victory against eventual finalists Sri Lanka. A thigh injury kept him out of the early-season ODIs which followed at home, but he was back in September against India, combining with Stuart Broad in the fine rearguard which stole the Old Trafford match, before a broken thumb forced him to miss the inaugural World Twenty20 championship. Bopara played in all three Tests in Sri Lanka in December 2007, but finished with three successive ducks, capped by an embarrassing first-ball run-out, and lost his place. A stunning start to the 2008 English season got him back in the Test squad, but he didn't actually play, and also lost his one-day spot before the summer was out.

THE FACTS   Bopara made 229, his first double-century, for Essex v Northamptonshire at Chelmsford in June 2007, putting on 320 for the third wicket with Grant Flower ... He made 52 for England v Sri Lanka in the World Cup in April 2007, being bowled by the last ball of the match with three runs needed to win; England were 133 for 6, chasing 236, before he faced a ball ... Bopara took 5 for 75 for Essex v Surrey at Colchester in August 2006 ...

THE FIGURES *to 12.9.08*   www.cricinfo.com

Batting & Fielding	M	Inns	NO	Runs	HS	Avge	S/R	100	50	4s	6s	Ct	St
Tests	3	5	0	42	34	8.40	37.53	0	0	7	0	1	0
ODIs	28	24	7	459	58	27.00	66.81	0	2	46	0	10	0
T20 Ints	1	0	–	–	–	–	–	–	–	–	–	0	0
First-class	77	127	18	4381	229	40.19	52.22	9	19	–	–	52	0

Bowling	M	Balls	Runs	Wkts	BB	Avge	RpO	S/R	5i	10m
Tests	3	156	81	1	1–39	81.00	3.11	156.00	0	0
ODIs	28	235	198	4	2–43	49.50	5.05	58.75	0	0
T20 Ints	1	0	–	–	–	–	–	–	–	–
First-class	77	5637	3731	88	5–75	42.39	3.97	64.05	1	0

SOUTH AFRICA

JOHAN **BOTHA**

Full name	**Johan Botha**
Born	**May 2, 1982, Johannesburg**
Teams	**Warriors**
Style	**Right-hand bat, offspinner**
Test debut	**South Africa v Australia at Sydney 2005-06**
ODI debut	**South Africa v India at Hyderabad 2005-06**

THE PROFILE A determined, fiercely competitive individual, Johan Botha started life as a rather ordinary medium-pacer, but one day Mickey Arthur – now South Africa's coach – spotted something else, and Botha dropped his ambitions for speed. He became an offspinner, and started studying the *doosra* (the ball that turns away from the right-hander) in the hope of emulating the likes of Muttiah Muralitharan and Harbhajan Singh. A year later he was touring Sri Lanka with South Africa A, scoring a few runs as well as taking key wickets, which put him under consideration as a potential future Test spinner who could bat – and, when Nicky Boje skipped a one-day series in India late in 2005, Botha got the call. He made a promising debut, gating Irfan Pathan during six tidy overs at Hyderabad, and when the selectors later suspected that the Sydney Test pitch would turn, Botha was sent for (he was already due to go to Australia for the one-dayers) and actually played ahead of Boje. He managed a couple of wickets, but delight turned to dismay when his jerky action was reported, and he was banned by the ICC on suspicion of throwing. Tests in August 2006 showed the right elbow was still flexing more than the permitted 15 degrees, but after further remedial action he was given the green light later that year. Botha made a low-key international return in the Afro-Asia Cup in India in June 2007, but remains in the frame – especially in one-dayers – as South Africa continue their long search for a matchwinning spinner.

THE FACTS Botha's bowling action was declared illegal by the ICC in February 2006, and again that August; he was finally cleared in November 2006 ... His best bowling is 6 for 42, for Eastern Province v Northerns at Port Elizabeth in March 2004, when still a medium-pacer ... He scored 98 for Warriors v Dolphins at Durban late in 2006 ... Botha made 101 for South Africa in an Under-19 Test v New Zealand (for whom Brendon McCullum made 186) in February 2001 ... His record includes two ODIs for the Africa XI ...

THE FIGURES *to 12.9.08* www.cricinfo.com

Batting & Fielding	M	Inns	NO	Runs	HS	Avge	S/R	100	50	4s	6s	Ct	St
Tests	2	2	1	45	25	45.00	32.84	0	0	4	0	1	0
ODIs	32	18	6	208	46	17.33	77.32	0	0	17	1	14	0
T20 Ints	4	3	2	36	28*	36.00	128.57	0	0	3	2	2	0
First-class	50	85	13	2368	98	32.88	–	0	17	–	–	35	0

Bowling	M	Balls	Runs	Wkts	BB	Avge	RpO	S/R	5i	10m
Tests	2	225	178	4	2–57	44.50	4.74	56.25	0	0
ODIs	32	1392	1097	23	3–34	47.69	4.72	60.52	0	0
T20 Ints	4	66	70	3	1–8	23.33	6.36	22.00	0	0
First-class	50	6876	3444	116	6–42	29.68	3.00	59.27	4	1

MARK **BOUCHER**

Full name	**Mark Verdon Boucher**
Born	**December 3, 1976, East London, Cape Province**
Teams	**Warriors, Bangalore Royal Challengers**
Style	**Right-hand bat, wicketkeeper**
Test debut	**South Africa v Pakistan at Sheikhupura 1997-98**
ODI debut	**South Africa v New Zealand at Perth 1997-98**

THE PROFILE It is a measure of the rapidity of Mark Boucher's rise that no-one is quite sure exactly how many records he has held. Fastest to 100 dismissals, highest score by a nightwatchman, most innings without a bye ... they tumbled out so quickly that it was difficult to keep up. Now he is Test cricket's leading wicketkeeper, and second in ODIs. But probably his most significant achievement came in only his second Test, against Pakistan at Johannesburg in February 1998, when he and Pat Symcox added 195, a Test ninth-wicket record, from a desperate 166 for 8. Boucher had made his debut a few months previously when still not 21, rushing to Sheikhupura to replace the injured Dave Richardson, who retired after the Australian tour that followed. Boucher was not everyone's first choice – Nic Pothas had also been waiting patiently – but once he got his hands into the gloves he refused to let them go. He found conditions in England difficult, in the 1998 Tests and the 1999 World Cup, but demonstrated courage and determination in what became a run of 75 consecutive Tests. Those qualities brought him three hundreds in his first 25 matches, and he was also named vice-captain when Shaun Pollock took over from Hansie Cronje, recognition of his willingness to get down and scrap when needed. And Boucher scrapped successfully to regain his spot when a form dip eventually did cost him his place – to Thami Tsolekile, and then AB de Villiers – late in 2004.

THE FACTS Boucher has more dismissals than anyone else in Tests, and only Adam Gilchrist (472) heads him in ODIs ... His 125 v Zimbabwe at Harare in 1999-2000 was a Test record for a nightwatchman until Jason Gillespie surpassed it in 2006 ... Boucher reached his century against Zimbabwe at Potchefstroom in September 2006 in only 44 balls, the second-fastest in all ODIs ... His 75 consecutive Tests between 1997-98 and 2004-05 is a South African record ... His figures include one Test for the World XI and five ODIs for the Africa XI ...

THE FIGURES to 12.9.08   www.cricinfo.com

Batting & Fielding	M	Inns	NO	Runs	HS	Avge	S/R	100	50	4s	6s	Ct	St
Tests	118	167	21	4372	125	29.94	49.88	4	28	532	15	429	20
ODIs	268	197	49	4258	147*	28.77	83.93	1	25	325	73	371	18
T20 Ints	9	7	0	134	36	19.14	89.93	0	0	14	0	9	0
First-class	178	259	38	7395	134	33.46	–	8	45	–	–	600	34

Bowling	M	Balls	Runs	Wkts	BB	Avge	RpO	S/R	5i	10m
Tests	118	8	6	1	1–6	6.00	4.50	8.00	0	0
ODIs	268	0	–	–	–	–	–	–	–	–
T20 Ints	9	0	–	–	–	–	–	–	–	–
First-class	178	26	26	1	1–6	26.00	6.00	26.00	0	0

NATHAN **BRACKEN**

AUSTRALIA

Full name	**Nathan Wade Bracken**
Born	**September 12, 1977, Penrith, New South Wales**
Teams	**New South Wales, Bangalore Royal Challengers**
Style	**Right-hand bat, left-arm fast-medium bowler**
Test debut	**Australia v India at Brisbane 2003-04**
ODI debut	**Australia v West Indies at Melbourne 2000-01**

THE PROFILE The search for a Test-class left-armer, a universal pursuit, first led Australia to Nathan Bracken. Tall and slim like Bruce Reid, Bracken bowls a full length, moves the ball both ways in the air and off the seam, and fitted easily into Australia's rampant one-day squad in 2000-01. He has also been instrumental in resuscitating New South Wales's fortunes, including 6 for 27 in their 2004-05 final win over Queensland and an amazing 7 for 4 earlier that season when South Australia fell for just 29 at the SCG. A shoulder injury cut short his maiden Ashes tour in 2001 after only two matches, but after a spell on the sidelines he returned to the side during the 2003 World Cup, when Jason Gillespie dropped out with a heel injury. Bracken's Test debut finally came in 2003-04, but in three matches against the powerful Indian batting line-up he failed to make real inroads. In the spring of 2004 he was omitted from Australia's list of contracted players, but returned to the one-day scene for the Super Series late the following year. He elbowed his way past Mitchell Johnson to cement a one-day place in 2006-07, and contributed several telling performances in the defence of the World Cup, finishing with 16 wickets at 16.12 – but had to watch as Johnson nailed down a Test spot the following season. Bracken, though, remained a limited-overs regular, and in mid-2008 went top of the ICC's ranking list for one-day bowlers.

THE FACTS Bracken's figures of 7-5-4-7 for New South Wales v South Australia at Sydney in December 2004 were described as "more like a PIN number than a bowling analysis" in the *Sydney Morning Herald*, which also called his yorker-heavy bowling to the South Africans "foot theory" ... He is 6ft 5ins (195cm) tall ... Seven of his 12 Test wickets have come at Brisbane ... Bracken has played 17 ODIs against both India and New Zealand, but has never played against Pakistan ... He averages 12.20 with the ball in ODIs against Sri Lanka – but 94 against Zimbabwe ...

THE FIGURES to 12.9.08   www.cricinfo.com

Batting & Fielding	M	Inns	NO	Runs	HS	Avge	S/R	100	50	4s	6s	Ct	St
Tests	5	6	2	70	37	17.50	62.50	0	0	7	0	2	0
ODIs	92	25	12	164	21*	12.61	70.68	0	0	8	5	17	0
T20 Ints	12	2	1	7	4	7.00	116.66	0	0	0	0	3	0
First-class	63	83	30	898	38*	16.94	–	0	0	–	–	17	0

Bowling	M	Balls	Runs	Wkts	BB	Avge	RpO	S/R	5i	10m
Tests	5	1110	505	12	4-48	42.08	2.72	92.50	0	0
ODIs	92	4481	3238	148	5-47	21.87	4.33	30.27	2	0
T20 Ints	12	233	253	15	3-11	16.86	6.51	15.53	0	0
First-class	63	12620	5302	203	7-4	26.11	2.52	62.16	8	0

DWAYNE **BRAVO**

Full name	**Dwayne John Bravo**
Born	**October 7, 1983, Santa Cruz, Trinidad**
Teams	**Trinidad & Tobago, Mumbai Indians**
Style	**Right-hand bat, right-arm fast-medium bowler**
Test debut	**West Indies v England at Lord's 2004**
ODI debut	**West Indies v England at Georgetown 2003-04**

THE PROFILE Dwayne Bravo is that creature long needed by West Indies, an allrounder. Born in Santa Cruz, like Brian Lara, Bravo made his one-day debut in April 2004, on the tenth anniversary of Lara's 375. He won his first Test cap at Lord's three months later, and took three wickets in the first innings with his medium-paced swingers. He also showed a cool enough temperament to forge a confident start at the crease, displaying a straight bat even though his team was facing a big England total. By the end of the series, West Indies were down and out, but at least they knew they had unearthed a special talent. Bravo scored plenty of runs and claimed a bunch of wickets, but nowhere was his ability more evident than at Old Trafford, where he top-scored and then restricted England with a six-wicket haul. He hit 107 against South Africa in Antigua in April 2005 as his maiden century, and played an even better innings the following November, a magnificent 113 at Hobart which forced the rampant Australians to wait till the fifth day to complete victory. He continued to chip in with useful runs, while a selection of slower balls makes him a handful in one-dayers, if less so in Tests. He's also assured in the field, and was one of the few plusses of the miserable 2007 tour of England, although even he was not immune to throwing his wicket away when well set. He stood in as captain for one Test in South Africa early in 2008 when Chris Gayle was injured, and is a good long-term bet as a future regular skipper.

THE FACTS Bravo's second Test century – 113 at Hobart late in 2005 – came during a stand of 182 with his fellow-Trinidadian Denesh Ramdin, the day after Trinidad & Tobago qualified for the football World Cup for the first time ... Bravo's best Test batting (40.40) and bowling (31.77) averages are both against Australia ... He played 27 Tests before finally finishing on the winning side, against Sri Lanka at Port-of-Spain in April 2008 ... Bravo's brother Darren has also played for Trinidad & Tobago ...

THE FIGURES *to 12.9.08*   www.cricinfo.com

Batting & Fielding	M	Inns	NO	Runs	HS	Avge	S/R	100	50	4s	6s	Ct	St
Tests	31	57	1	1833	113	32.73	48.84	2	11	233	15	30	0
ODIs	88	71	16	1291	112*	23.47	80.68	1	2	109	17	37	0
T20 Ints	8	8	4	74	28*	18.50	137.03	0	0	3	5	2	0
First-class	87	160	7	4786	197	31.28	–	7	27	–	–	71	0

Bowling	M	Balls	Runs	Wkts	BB	Avge	RpO	S/R	5i	10m
Tests	31	5139	2771	70	6–55	39.58	3.23	73.41	2	0
ODIs	88	3415	3013	98	4–32	30.74	5.29	34.84	0	0
T20 Ints	8	74	123	3	2–16	41.00	9.97	24.66	0	0
First-class	87	9268	5036	154	6–11	32.70	3.26	60.18	7	0

TIM **BRESNAN**

ENGLAND

Full name	**Timothy Thomas Bresnan**
Born	**February 28, 1985, Pontefract, Yorkshire**
Teams	**Yorkshire**
Style	**Right-hand bat, right-arm fast-medium bowler**
Test debut	**No Tests yet**
ODI debut	**England v Sri Lanka at Lord's 2006**

THE PROFILE The powerfully built Tim Bresnan was tipped for higher honours in 2001 after becoming, at 16, the youngest player to play for Yorkshire for 20 years. He quickly progressed to England's youth team, and played in two Under-19 World Cups.
The potential took a few years to ripen, but in 2005 Bresnan was given more responsibility in a transitional Yorkshire team, and responded with 47 wickets with swinging deliveries which, if a shade short of being truly fast, travel at a fair rate. He can also bat, making three first-class centuries in 2007, the highest an undefeated 126 for England A against the Indian tourists at Chelmsford, where he and Stuart Broad put on 129 for the eighth wicket. A good start to the previous season had resulted in his call-up for the new-look one-day squad against Sri Lanka in June 2006, but Bresnan fell victim to the flashing blades of Sanath Jayasuriya and friends, and took only two wickets in four appearances in what became a clean sweep for the tourists. He then suffered a back injury, and was not in serious consideration for a World Cup spot. He responded well with the bat in 2007, although his form with the ball dipped a little (34 wickets at 34), before a return to bowling form the following year eventually led to a one-day recall, as a replacement for Ryan Sidebottom, although the surprise return of Steve Harmison meant there was no place for Bresnan as South Africa were swept aside.

THE FACTS Bresnan made all three of his first-class centuries during 2007, including 126 not out for England A against the Indian tourists at Chelmsford ... Bresnan's best bowling figures are 5 for 42 for Yorkshire at Worcester in July 2005 ... He made his Yorkshire first-team debut in a National League match in 2001, when he was just 16 ...

THE FIGURES to 12.9.08   www.cricinfo.com

Batting & Fielding	M	Inns	NO	Runs	HS	Avge	S/R	100	50	4s	6s	Ct	St
Tests	0	0	–	–	–	–	–	–	–	–	–	–	–
ODIs	5	4	1	51	20	17.00	110.86	0	0	4	1	1	0
T20 Ints	1	1	1	6	6*	–	100.00	0	0	0	0	0	0
First-class	71	97	19	2132	126*	27.33	48.12	3	10	–	–	30	0

Bowling	M	Balls	Runs	Wkts	BB	Avge	RpO	S/R	5i	10m
Tests	0	0	–	–	–	–	–	–	–	–
ODIs	5	198	203	4	2–34	50.75	6.15	49.50	0	0
T20 Ints	1	12	20	0	–	–	10.00	–	0	0
First-class	71	10711	5787	185	5–42	31.28	3.24	57.89	3	0

STUART **BROAD**

Full name	**Stuart Christopher John Broad**
Born	**June 24, 1986, Nottingham**
Teams	**Nottinghamshire**
Style	**Left-hand bat, right-arm fast-medium bowler**
Test debut	**England v Sri Lanka at Colombo 2007-08**
ODI debut	**England v Pakistan at Cardiff 2006**

THE PROFILE Stuart Broad was shaping up to be an opening bat just like his dad, Chris, until he suddenly shot up. Already well over six feet, he grew three inches over the winter of 2005. He had already transformed himself into a fast-medium bowler good enough to play for England Under-19s. In 2005 he had taken 30 first-class wickets at 27.69 for Leicestershire, his first county. And it got even better in 2006, as he collected four five-fors before an increasingly inevitable summons to England's full one-day side. He made an impressive start to his international career, keeping a cool head in the mayhem of a Twenty20 match, then claiming the early wicket of Shoaib Malik on his ODI debut at Cardiff. He just missed out on initial selection for the World Cup, but stepped in when Jon Lewis returned home, and nervelessly hit the winning runs in England's last game, against West Indies. Nerves were also notably absent later in 2007 when Broad and Ravi Bopara spirited England to an unlikely one-day win over India at Old Trafford, and he even kept reasonably cool shortly afterwards when being swatted for six sixes in an over by Yuvraj Singh in the World Twenty20. But Broad junior has aspirations to be an allrounder, and showed good form with the bat – especially when driving off the back foot – once he cracked the full Test side, and looks like a genuine No. 8. He flagged a little under a heavy bowling workload in 2008, but he has a smooth action, and as long as his not-so-broad back stands up to the punishment he has a glittering future.

THE FACTS Broad took 5 for 23 as South Africa were bowled out for 83 in an ODI at Trent Bridge in August 2008 ... He scored 91 not out for Leicestershire v Derbyshire at Grace Road in 2007 ... Broad's father, Chris, played 25 Tests for England in the 1980s, scoring 1661 runs with six centuries – he's now a match referee (see page 224) ...

THE FIGURES to 12.9.08   www.cricinfo.com

Batting & Fielding	M	Inns	NO	Runs	HS	Avge	S/R	100	50	4s	6s	Ct	St
Tests	9	12	2	372	76	37.20	55.52	0	3	50	2	4	0
ODIs	37	23	12	236	45*	21.45	66.29	0	0	14	3	10	0
T20 Ints	11	6	2	12	6	3.00	92.30	0	0	1	0	3	0
First-class	46	56	13	1092	91*	25.39	48.19	0	8	–	–	14	0

Bowling	M	Balls	Runs	Wkts	BB	Avge	RpO	S/R	5i	10m
Tests	9	1928	1042	24	3–44	43.41	3.24	88.33	0	0
ODIs	37	1813	1442	55	5–23	26.21	4.77	32.96	1	0
T20 Ints	11	252	355	13	3–37	27.30	8.45	19.38	0	0
First-class	46	7897	4617	153	5–67	30.17	3.50	51.61	6	0

PATRICK **BROWNE**

Full name	**Patrick Anderson Browne**
Born	**January 26, 1982, Bayfield, St Philip, Barbados**
Teams	**Barbados**
Style	**Right-hand bat, wicketkeeper**
Test debut	**No Tests yet**
ODI debut	**West Indies v India at Faridabad 1994-95**

THE PROFILE Patrick Browne is a useful wicketkeeper-batsman who toured England with the West Indian Under-19s in 2001 and slowly became a regular in the Barbados side. In 2006 he returned to England with the A team, and did well enough to be part of the training squad ahead of the South African tour late in 2007. When injuries struck Browne was sent for, supposedly as Denesh Ramdin's understudy, but in the event he made his ODI debut at Port Elizabeth as a specialist batsman, despite still not having a first-class century to his name. He had been batting in a trial match in Barbados when he got the news, and immediately left the crease to pack. "I was a bit in shock because I was playing a game, and suddenly the guys called me off and told me I was called up for the West Indies team to go to South Africa," he said afterwards. "But I was very excited. I have been training hard and I think everything is now coming together with my game. I've brushed up a bit on my keeping and my batting is coming along. I've been doing a lot of wicketkeeping drills and working on my batting, concentration-wise." Browne, who is predominantly a leg-side player, made a good start with the bat in ODIs, with scores of 34, 35 and 49 not out in his three outings in South Africa, although West Indies were whitewashed in the series. But he was dropped after a single failure at home against Australia, and will have to fight with Ramdin for a regular place.

THE FACTS Browne's highest first-class score is 83, for West Indies B against Leeward Islands at Charlestown in the Carib Beer Cup in January 2004 ... He made his ODI debut in South Africa in January 2008, and batted at No. 3 despite having only one one-day fifty to his name: he scored 35, with two sixes ... Browne played for West Indies A against England A in 2005-06, and toured England with the A team in 2006 ...

THE FIGURES to 12.9.08 www.cricinfo.com

Batting & Fielding	M	Inns	NO	Runs	HS	Avge	S/R	100	50	4s	6s	Ct	St
Tests	0	0	–	–	–	–	–	–	–	–	–	–	–
ODIs	5	5	1	134	49*	33.50	74.86	0	0	7	6	2	0
T20 Ints	0	0	–	–	–	–	–	–	–	–	–	–	–
First-class	47	82	4	1672	83	21.43	–	0	9	–	–	101	5

Bowling	M	Balls	Runs	Wkts	BB	Avge	RpO	S/R	5i	10m
Tests	0	0	–	–	–	–	–	–	–	–
ODIs	5	0	–	–	–	–	–	–	–	–
T20 Ints	0	0	–	–	–	–	–	–	–	–
First-class	47	6	0	0	–	–	0.00	–	0	0

BEAU **CASSON**

Full name	**Beau Casson**
Born	**December 7, 1982, Subiaco, Perth**
Teams	**New South Wales**
Style	**Right-hand bat, slow left-arm unorthodox spinner**
Test debut	**Australia v West Indies at Bridgetown 2007-08**
ODI debut	**No ODIs yet**

THE PROFILE   After he had battled injuries, poor form and switching states in the previous few years, the planets finally aligned for Beau Casson in 2007-08. He became NSW's first-choice spinner while Stuart MacGill was absent (first in the Test team and then recovering from surgery). Casson relished the extra responsibility, and used the helpful SCG conditions to collect 29 wickets at 35.13. He also made valuable lower-order runs (485 at 60.62). He scored 89 and grabbed four wickets as NSW won the Pura Cup final, and his late run of form earned him a national contract and a place on the 2008 Caribbean tour. Not even the most optimistic Casson fan could have predicted all this after a miserable 2006-07 season, when he managed only seven wickets at 72 and was light-years behind MacGill and Brad Hogg in the national slow-bowling pecking order. However, Hogg's retirement and the failure of Cullen Bailey and Dan Cullen to impress left a vacancy for a back-up for MacGill. So Casson was the man on the spot when MacGill suddenly retired mid-tour, and Casson made his Test debut at Bridgetown, taking three wickets as Australia slowly worked their way through West Indies' batting to win a high-scoring game. A left-arm wrist-spinner capable of big turn and with a hard-to-pick wrong'un, Casson moved from Perth to Sydney in 2006, searching for a way to halt his inflating bowling average. But a shoulder injury hampered him, and he needed surgery at the end of the season. Casson was also born with a heart defect, but it is regularly monitored and has not caused him any problems so far.

THE FACTS   Casson's highest score is 99, for New South Wales against South Australia at Sydney in March 2008 ... He took 6 for 64 (10 for 176 in the match) in only his second first-class game, for Western Australia against South Australia at Adelaide in December 2002 ... Casson was part of the Australian team (captained by Cameron White) that won the Under-19 World Cup in New Zealand in 2002 ...

THE FIGURES *to 12.9.08*   www.cricinfo.com

Batting & Fielding	M	Inns	NO	Runs	HS	Avge	S/R	100	50	4s	6s	Ct	St
Tests	1	1	0	10	10	10.00	22.72	0	0	1	0	2	0
ODIs	0	0	–	–	–	–	–	–	–	–	–	–	–
T20 Ints	0	0	–	–	–	–	–	–	–	–	–	–	–
First-class	42	66	12	1274	99	23.59	35.84	0	6	–	–	21	0

Bowling	M	Balls	Runs	Wkts	BB	Avge	RpO	S/R	5i	10m
Tests	1	192	129	3	3–86	43.00	4.03	64.00	0	0
ODIs	0	0	–	–	–	–	–	–	–	–
T20 Ints	0	0	–	–	–	–	–	–	–	–
First-class	42	7514	4455	110	6–64	40.50	3.55	68.30	4	1

SHIVNARINE **CHANDERPAUL**

Full name	**Shivnarine Chanderpaul**
Born	**August 16, 1974, Unity Village, Demerara, Guyana**
Teams	**Guyana, Durham, Bangalore Royal Challengers**
Style	**Left-hand bat, occasional legspinner**
Test debut	**West Indies v England at Georgetown 1993-94**
ODI debut	**West Indies v India at Faridabad 1994-95**

THE PROFILE Crouched and crabby at the crease, Shivnarine Chanderpaul proves there is life beyond the coaching handbook. He never seems to play in the V, or off the front foot, but uses soft hands, canny deflections and a whiplash pull to maintain an average nudging 50 over more than 100 Tests. Early on he had a problem converting fifties into hundreds, and also missed a lot of matches, to the point that some thought him a hypochondriac. That was rectified when a large piece of floating bone was removed from his foot in 2000: suitably liberated, he set about rectifying his hundreds problem too, collecting three in four Tests against India early in 2002, and two more against Australia the following year, including 104 in the successful chase for a world-record 418 in Antigua. A good run in South Africa in 2003-04 preceded a tough one at home against England – only his second lean trot in a decade – but he rediscovered his form in England, narrowly missing twin tons in the 2004 Lord's Test. The following year he was appointed captain during an acrimonious contracts dispute, and celebrated with 203 at home in Guyana, although he was too passive in the field to prevent South Africa taking the series. In April 2006 he stood down, after an Australian tour in which he struggled with the bat and the microphone. In England in 2007 he was back to his limpet best, top-scoring in each of his five innings, and going more than 1000 minutes without being out in Tests, for the third time in his career (he did it again in 2008). It's not all defence, though: he can blast with the best in one-dayers.

THE FACTS Chanderpaul averages 71.86 in Tests against India, but only 28.77 v Zimbabwe ... He scored 303 not out for Guyana v Jamaica at Kingston in January 1996 ... At Georgetown in April 2003 Chanderpaul reached his century against Australia in only 69 balls – the third-fastest in Test history by balls faced ... He averages 57.46 in Tests at home, and 42.28 away ... He once managed to shoot a policeman in the hand in his native Guyana, mistaking him for a mugger ...

THE FIGURES *to 12.9.08*   www.cricinfo.com

Batting & Fielding	M	Inns	NO	Runs	HS	Avge	S/R	100	50	4s	6s	Ct	St
Tests	112	193	30	8001	203*	49.08	43.26	19	49	970	20	47	0
ODIs	235	221	34	7573	150	40.49	70.65	8	52	647	74	65	0
T20 Ints	6	6	1	133	41	26.60	102.30	0	0	12	2	4	0
First-class	225	368	63	16087	303*	52.74	–	45	82	–	–	132	0

Bowling	M	Balls	Runs	Wkts	BB	Avge	RpO	S/R	5i	10m
Tests	112	1680	845	8	1–2	105.62	3.01	210.00	0	0
ODIs	235	740	636	14	3–18	45.42	5.15	52.85	0	0
T20 Ints	6	0	–	–	–	–	–	–	–	–
First-class	225	4610	2434	56	4–48	43.46	3.16	82.32	0	0

SEWNARINE **CHATTERGOON**

Full name	**Sewnarine Chattergoon**
Born	**April 3, 1981, Fyrish, West Bank, Berbice, Guyana**
Teams	**Guyana**
Style	**Left-hand bat, occasional legspinner**
Test debut	**West Indies v Sri Lanka at Port-of-Spain 2007-08**
ODI debut	**West Indies v Zimbabwe at Georgetown 2005-06**

THE PROFILE Sewnarine Chattergoon is a solid and stylish left-hand opening batsman who was called into the West Indies squad after showing good form for the A team in the home series against England A in early in 2006, when he scored 107 in the second four-day match and 81 in the first one-dayer before he was sidelined by injury. Also that season he hit 119 against Barbados in the one-day KFC Cup final, which Guyana went on to win. All of this led to a place in the one-day side against Zimbabwe, and he made 54 not out in his second match, sharing an unbroken opening stand of 156 with Chris Gayle as West Indies romped to a ten-wicket win in St Lucia. He slipped out of the reckoning after a modest 2006-07 season, but was back to his best early in 2008, and a patient 130 against Trinidad & Tobago paved the way for a recall. He did well in his three ODIs in South Africa, scoring 34, 52 and 48, and back home earned a first Test cap against Sri Lanka, in a match which started on his 27th birthday. He scored 46 in his first innings, but his second Test ended painfully when he injured his ankle sliding to stop a boundary against Australia. But Chattergoon, who is also an exceptional slip fielder, could be the ideal foil for the aggressive Gayle at the top of the West Indian batting order.

THE FACTS Chattergoon made 143 for Guyana against Bangladesh A at Georgetown in February 2002, when he shared an opening stand of 340 with Azeemul Haniff (235) ... He made 107 for West Indies A v England A at Gros Islet in March 2006 ... Chattergoon was the 11th player to make his Test debut on his birthday, and the first since Ricardo Powell (also of West Indies) in 1999-2000 ... His brother Hemnarine Chattergoon has played for Canada ...

THE FIGURES *to 12.9.08*   www.cricinfo.com

Batting & Fielding	M	Inns	NO	Runs	HS	Avge	S/R	100	50	4s	6s	Ct	St
Tests	2	4	0	76	46	19.00	59.37	0	0	9	0	3	0
ODIs	11	10	1	293	54*	32.55	65.11	0	2	45	3	3	0
T20 Ints	0	0	–	–	–	–	–	–	–	–	–	–	–
First-class	52	90	3	2838	143	32.62	–	4	16	–	–	38	0

Bowling	M	Balls	Runs	Wkts	BB	Avge	RpO	S/R	5i	10m
Tests	2	0	–	–	–	–	–	–	–	–
ODIs	11	80	48	1	1–1	48.00	3.60	80.00	0	0
T20 Ints	0	0	–	–	–	–	–	–	–	–
First-class	52	318	131	7	4–9	18.71	2.47	45.42	0	0

PIYUSH **CHAWLA**

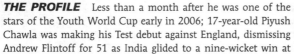

Full name	**Piyush Pramod Chawla**
Born	**December 24, 1988, Aligarh, Uttar Pradesh**
Teams	**Uttar Pradesh, Kings XI Punjab**
Style	**Left-hand bat, legspinner**
Test debut	**India v England at Mohali 2005-06**
ODI debut	**India v Bangladesh at Dhaka 2006-07**

THE PROFILE Less than a month after he was one of the stars of the Youth World Cup early in 2006; 17-year-old Piyush Chawla was making his Test debut against England, dismissing Andrew Flintoff for 51 as India glided to a nine-wicket win at Mohali. He had always been a young achiever: Chawla first hit the headlines for Uttar Pradesh's Under-14s, scoring 121 then taking 15 wickets for 69 in the demolition of Rajasthan's juniors. In October 2005 he bamboozled Sachin Tendulkar with a googly in the final of the Challenger Trophy (a trial tournament for India's one-day team), and dismissed Mahendra Singh Dhoni and Yuvraj Singh as well: then he led the wicket-takers at the Youth World Cup in Sri Lanka. He took 4 for 8 as the holders Pakistan were shot out for 109 in the final, then surveyed the wreckage with 25 not out as India were demolished for 79 themselves. Although he is no slouch with the bat, it is as a legspinner that Chawla has made his mark – he already has wonderful control of his variations, with a well-disguised googly and a flipper, and is not afraid to give the ball air. In 2007, he was given an extended run in the one-day team, replacing Anil Kumble who retired from ODIs after the World Cup, and impressed with his cool bowling against England. He also did well with India's A team, then was among the leading wicket-takers in the inaugural IPL season early in 2008 with 17, which helped him regain his one-day place for the Asia Cup.

THE FACTS Piyush Chawla was 17 years 75 days old when he made his Test debut in March 2006: the only younger Indian debutant was Sachin Tendulkar ... He took 4 for 12 and 6 for 46 as India A hammered a Zimbabwe Select XI at Bulawayo in July 2007... Chawla scored 146 while captaining India in an Under-19 Test in Pakistan in September 2006: he added 119 (and then took 5 for 19) v New Zealand U19s at Lincoln in January 2007 ...

THE FIGURES *to 12.9.08*   www.cricinfo.com

Batting & Fielding	M	Inns	NO	Runs	HS	Avge	S/R	100	50	4s	6s	Ct	St
Tests	2	2	0	5	4	2.50	23.80	0	0	1	0	0	0
ODIs	21	10	5	28	13*	5.60	65.11	0	0	2	0	9	0
T20 Ints	0	0	–	–	–	–	–	–	–	–	–	–	–
First-class	35	48	2	1211	82	26.32	–	0	11	–	–	15	0

Bowling	M	Balls	Runs	Wkts	BB	Avge	RpO	S/R	5i	10m
Tests	2	205	137	3	2–66	45.66	4.00	68.33	0	0
ODIs	21	1102	911	28	4–23	32.53	4.96	39.35	0	0
T20 Ints	0	0	–	–	–	–	–	–	–	–
First-class	35	7120	3558	142	6–46	25.05	2.99	50.14	8	1

AUSTRALIA

STUART **CLARK**

Full name	**Stuart Rupert Clark**
Born	**September 28, 1975, Sutherland, Sydney, NSW**
Teams	**New South Wales**
Style	**Right-hand bat, right-arm fast-medium bowler**
Test debut	**Australia v South Africa at Cape Town 2005-06**
ODI debut	**Australia v World XI at Melbourne 2005-06**

THE PROFILE Stuart Clark is a tall and lanky opening bowler often described as "in the Glenn McGrath mould". Appropriately, in his opening Test series in South Africa early in 2006, 30-year-old Clark replaced the temporarily absent McGrath and experienced a dream entry: 20 wickets at 15.75 made him Player of the Series. A borderline selection for the first Test, he earned victory with 5 for 55 and 4 for 34, the third-best match figures by an Australian debutant after Bob Massie and Clarrie Grimmett. A former real-estate agent in Sydney, Clark was a late cricket developer, finally emerging at 27 after a battle with body as much as talent. He earned a central contract with 45 wickets in 2001-02, but lost it the following summer after ankle and rib injuries. Hernia surgery was next, quickly followed by a leg problem, but he took 40 wickets in NSW's 2004-05 Pura Cup triumph. Clark, who troubles–batsmen with his height (6ft 5½ins or 197cm) and seam movement, showed there was room for him and McGrath in the same side by topping the averages (26 wickets at 17.03) in the 2006-07 Ashes whitewash, although after that he was a back number in the World Cup. The following season, with McGrath finally retired, Clark took 21 wickets in six home Tests and 13 more in three in the Caribbean. The child of English-born parents who met in India, he became a father in 2006, and his life after cricket is already mapped out: once he finishes his current masters degree in commerce Clark wants to study law and plans to work in finance.

THE FACTS During the memorable 2005 Ashes tour, Clark was twice called into the Australian squad from county cricket with Middlesex as cover for injured bowlers, but did not play in a Test ... His nickname is "Sarfraz", after a vague resemblance – in appearance and run-up – to the former Pakistan fast bowler ... Clark's international debut was against the World XI in October 2005, and his first wicket was Kevin Pietersen ... He took 8 for 58 for NSW against Western Australia – a hat-trick reducing them to 2 for 4 – at Perth in Feb 2007 ...

THE FIGURES *to 12.9.08*   www.cricinfo.com

Batting & Fielding	M	Inns	NO	Runs	HS	Avge	S/R	100	50	4s	6s	Ct	St
Tests	18	18	3	177	39	11.80	67.04	0	0	14	3	3	0
ODIs	36	11	7	67	16*	16.75	85.89	0	0	6	1	10	0
T20 Ints	9	0	–	–	–	–	–	–	–	–	–	0	0
First-class	93	120	32	1189	62	13.51	–	0	1	–	–	27	0

Bowling	M	Balls	Runs	Wkts	BB	Avge	RpO	S/R	5i	10m
Tests	18	4054	1739	81	5–32	21.46	2.57	50.04	2	0
ODIs	36	1702	1391	50	4–54	27.82	4.90	34.04	0	0
T20 Ints	9	216	237	13	4–20	18.23	6.58	16.61	0	0
First-class	93	19346	9318	344	8–58	27.08	2.88	56.23	13	1

MICHAEL **CLARKE**

Full name	**Michael John Clarke**
Born	**April 2, 1981, Liverpool, New South Wales**
Teams	**New South Wales**
Style	**Right-hand bat, slow left-arm orthodox spinner**
Test debut	**Australia v India at Bangalore 2003-04**
ODI debut	**Australia v England at Adelaide 2002-03**

THE PROFILE   Michael Clarke was being touted as Australia's next captain before he'd even played a Test. And when he marked his eventual debut with 151 against India in October 2004, his future looked even brighter than the yellow motorbike he received as Man of the Match. Another thrilling century followed on his home debut, and his first Test season ended with the Allan Border Medal. Then came the fall. Barely a year later he received the fateful phone-call: dropped after 15 century-less Tests. He was told to tighten his technique, especially early on against swing. Clarke remained a one-day fixture, but had to wait until the low-key Bangladesh series early in 2006 to reclaim that Test spot. He cemented his place with two tons in the 2006-07 Ashes whitewash, did well in the World Cup, averaging 87.20, and scored a century in each of Australia's three Test series in 2007-08: he also took charge in a few one-day games when Ricky Ponting was injured. He started as a ravishing shotmaker who did not so much take guard as take off: he radiated a pointy-elbowed elegance reminiscent of the young Greg Chappell or Mark Waugh, who both also waited uncomplainingly for a Test opening then started with a ton. Unlike them, Clarke cut his teeth in Australia's one-day side. His impact in pyjamas was startling: 208 runs before being dismissed. His bouncy fielding and searing run-outs, usually from square on, add to his value, while his left-arm tweakers can surprise (they once shocked six Indians in a Test at Mumbai). A cricket nut since he was in nappies, "Pup" honed his technique against the bowling machine at his dad's indoor centre.

THE FACTS   Clarke scored a century on his Test debut, 151 v India at Bangalore in 2004-05, and the following month added another in his first home Test, 141 v New Zealand at Brisbane: only two other batsmen (Harry Graham and Kepler Wessels) have done this for Australia ... Clarke averages 51.71 in Tests against England (and 216 v Sri Lanka), but only 20.75 v Pakistan ... A skin-cancer scare late in 2005 persuaded Clarke to swap a traditional cap for a wide-brimmed sunhat ...

THE FIGURES to 12.9.08   www.cricinfo.com

Batting & Fielding	M	Inns	NO	Runs	HS	Avge	S/R	100	50	4s	6s	Ct	St
Tests	35	54	7	2212	151	47.06	55.87	7	8	244	14	31	0
ODIs	140	124	28	4077	130	42.46	79.62	3	30	349	27	54	0
T20 Ints	14	10	3	147	37*	21.00	126.72	0	0	6	6	6	0
First-class	90	151	14	5911	201*	43.14	–		20	22	–	–	87	0

Bowling	M	Balls	Runs	Wkts	BB	Avge	RpO	S/R	5i	10m
Tests	35	769	341	16	6–9	21.31	2.66	48.06	1	0
ODIs	140	1772	1515	45	5–35	33.66	5.12	39.37	1	0
T20 Ints	14	84	122	4	1–13	30.50	8.71	21.00	0	0
First-class	90	1823	930	27	6–9	34.44	3.06	67.51	1	0

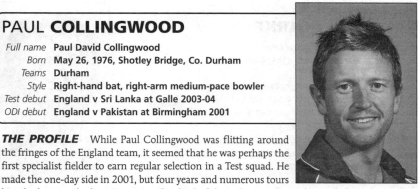

ENGLAND

PAUL **COLLINGWOOD**

Full name	**Paul David Collingwood**
Born	**May 26, 1976, Shotley Bridge, Co. Durham**
Teams	**Durham**
Style	**Right-hand bat, right-arm medium-pace bowler**
Test debut	**England v Sri Lanka at Galle 2003-04**
ODI debut	**England v Pakistan at Birmingham 2001**

THE PROFILE While Paul Collingwood was flitting around the fringes of the England team, it seemed that he was perhaps the first specialist fielder to earn regular selection in a Test squad. He made the one-day side in 2001, but four years and numerous tours later had won only three Test caps. The third of those, however, was the single biggest match of his generation: the 2005 Ashes decider against Australia at The Oval. He still seemed destined to be the uncomplaining stand-in – but that winter struck 96 and 80 at Lahore, and added a brilliant century against India, as England struggled with injuries. Then a coruscating Lord's 186 against Pakistan booked a middle-order place at last, and Collingwood later joined rarefied company with an Ashes double-century at Adelaide. He remained a superb fielder, capable of breathtaking moments at backward point or in the slips. With the bat he stands still, plays straight, and has all the shots. In Australia in 2002-03 he started the one-dayers as 12th man, but was soon spanking a memorable maiden century against Sri Lanka, which clinched his spot for the 2003 World Cup; after England's travails in the 2007 tournament, he took over as one-day captain, although he gave it up late the following year. Just before that he probably saved his Test career when, after a season-long horror trot, he hit 135 against South Africa at Edgbaston. His bowling, which verges on the dibbly-dobbly, is negligible in Tests, but given the right conditions he can be irresistible in one-dayers – as at Trent Bridge in 2005, when he followed a rapid century against Bangladesh with 6 for 31.

THE FACTS Collingwood's century and six wickets in the same match – against Bangladesh at Nottingham in 2005 – is unmatched in ODI history: his 6 for 31 that day are also England's best one-day bowling figures ... He made 206 at Adelaide in December 2006, England's first double-century in a Test in Australia since Wally Hammond in 1936-37 ... In September 2006 he became the 11th man to play 100 ODIs for England ...

THE FIGURES *to 12.9.08*   www.cricinfo.com

Batting & Fielding	M	Inns	NO	Runs	HS	Avge	S/R	100	50	4s	6s	Ct	St
Tests	39	72	8	2689	209	42.01	45.48	6	11	313	15	52	0
ODIs	149	134	29	3689	120*	35.18	76.37	4	20	270	48	86	0
T20 Ints	14	13	0	330	79	25.38	140.42	0	2	22	15	2	0
First-class	161	284	23	9301	206	35.63	–		20	45	–	–	178	0

Bowling	M	Balls	Runs	Wkts	BB	Avge	RpO	S/R	5i	10m
Tests	39	1287	687	14	3–23	49.07	3.20	91.92	0	0
ODIs	149	3854	3214	83	6–31	38.72	5.00	46.43	1	0
T20 Ints	14	150	237	13	4–22	18.23	9.48	11.53	0	0
First-class	161	9071	4584	119	5–52	38.52	3.03	76.22	1	0

ALASTAIR **COOK**

Full name	**Alastair Nathan Cook**
Born	**December 25, 1984, Gloucester**
Teams	**Essex**
Style	**Left-hand bat, occasional offspinner**
Test debut	**England v India at Nagpur 2005-06**
ODI debut	**England v Sri Lanka at Manchester 2006**

THE PROFILE Those in the know were saying that the tall, dark and handsome Alastair Cook was destined for great things very early on. A correct and stylish left-hander strong on the pull, Cook was thrown straight in at the deep end by Essex only a year after he left Bedford School. He captained England in the Under-19 World Cup early in 2004, making two centuries in leading them to the semi-final, then scored his maiden first-class hundred later that year. After a fine 2005, which included a double-century against the touring Australians, he was called up by England when injuries struck the following spring. He had been touring the Caribbean with England A when the SOS came but, unfazed, he cracked 60 against India at Nagpur then added a magnificent 104 to become the 16th England batsman to make a century on debut. He succumbed to illness himself before that tour was done, but bounced back with 89 against Sri Lanka at Lord's in May 2006, then made sure his name was on MCC's honours board by scoring 105 against Pakistan two months later. He made another upright century in the next Test, at Manchester, and survived a tough Ashes baptism, scoring 276 runs (with 116 at Perth) in the 2006-07 whitewash. Bowlers began to notice a tendency to play around the front pad, but Cook still did well at home in 2007 – with two hundreds against West Indies – and 2008, when he reached 50 five times in Tests without going on to three figures. There was one downer, though: he lost his one-day place after a moderate run.

THE FACTS Cook was the 16th England batsman to make a century on Test debut: the previous two (Andrew Strauss and Graham Thorpe) were also left-handers ... Cook's stand of 127 with Marcus Trescothick v Sri Lanka at Lord's in 2005 was the second-highest in Tests by unrelated players who share a birthday (they were both born on Christmas Day), behind the 163 of Vic Stollmeyer and Kenneth Weekes (both born January 24) for West Indies at The Oval in 1939 ...

THE FIGURES *to 12.9.08*   www.cricinfo.com

Batting & Fielding	M	Inns	NO	Runs	HS	Avge	S/R	100	50	4s	6s	Ct	St
Tests	34	62	2	2573	127	42.88	46.29	7	14	307	1	33	0
ODIs	22	22	0	691	102	31.40	68.07	1	3	76	0	7	0
T20 Ints	2	2	0	24	15	12.00	96.00	0	0	4	0	1	0
First-class	88	158	11	6625	195	45.06	53.34	18	36	–	–	89	0

Bowling	M	Balls	Runs	Wkts	BB	Avge	RpO	S/R	5i	10m
Tests	34	6	1	0	–	–	1.00	–	0	0
ODIs	22	0	–	–	–	–	–	–	–	–
T20 Ints	2	0	–	–	–	–	–	–	–	–
First-class	88	162	118	3	3–13	39.33	4.37	54.00	0	0

DANISH KANERIA

Full name **Danish Parabha Shanker Kaneria**
Born **December 16, 1980, Karachi, Sind**
Teams **Karachi, Habib Bank, Essex**
Style **Right-hand bat, legspinner**
Test debut **Pakistan v England at Faisalabad 2000-01**
ODI debut **Pakistan v Zimbabwe at Sharjah 2001-02**

THE PROFILE A tall, wiry legspinner, and only the second Hindu to play Test cricket for Pakistan, Danish Kaneria mastered the dark arts of wrist-spin at an early age. His stock ball drifts in to the right-hander, and he has a googly as cloaked as any in recent history. His whirling approach is reminiscent of Abdul Qadir's, and he picked up the baton from Mushtaq Ahmed as Pakistan's premier legspinner. Kaneria was hyped as a secret weapon when England toured Pakistan in 2000-01, and although his impact in that series was minimal, he has since made his mark. Initially he did so against Bangladesh, but then turned it on against South Africa too, in October 2003, when his five-for decided the Lahore Test. Since then, Kaneria has confirmed himself as a matchwinner, and has quietly moved past 200 Test wickets. Two tours in 2004-05 – to Australia and the graveyard of legspin, India – were arduous but satisfying stepping stones to the big league. In each series he outscalped the opposition's leading legspinner – Shane Warne, then Anil Kumble – and although Pakistan still lost to Australia, Kaneria's 19 wickets were crucial in securing a morale-boosting draw in India. He ended 2005 with two more matchwinning last-day turns against England at home, but proved expensive when the teams reconvened the following summer in England, where he has had a lot of success with Essex. A back number in one-dayers, he had played only one of Pakistan's previous 27 ODIs before being a surprise inclusion for the 2007 World Cup. He did well enough, but lost his place again in the fallout from that disastrous campaign.

THE FACTS Danish Kaneria was only the second Hindu to play for Pakistan – the first, 1980s wicketkeeper Anil Dalpat, is his cousin ... He took 12 for 92 in his third Test, against Bangladesh in August 2001 ... Kaneria averages 16.41 v Bangladesh – but 45.14 v England ... He has conceded more than 100 runs in an innings 32 times in 51 Tests ... He took 0 for 208 for Essex v Lancashire at Manchester in 2005, equalling the most expensive wicketless spell in the County Championship, set by Peter Smith, another Essex legspinner, in 1934 ...

THE FIGURES to 12.9.08   www.cricinfo.com

Batting & Fielding	M	Inns	NO	Runs	HS	Avge	S/R	100	50	4s	6s	Ct	St
Tests	51	69	31	260	29	6.84	47.70	0	0	35	2	16	0
ODIs	18	10	8	12	6*	6.00	54.54	0	0	1	0	2	0
T20 Ints	0	0	–	–	–	–	–	–	–	–	–	–	–
First-class	142	178	71	1090	65	10.18	–	0	1	–	–	48	0

Bowling	M	Balls	Runs	Wkts	BB	Avge	RpO	S/R	5i	10m
Tests	51	14994	7458	220	7-77	33.90	2.98	68.15	12	2
ODIs	18	854	683	15	3-31	45.53	4.79	56.93	0	0
T20 Ints	0	0	–	–	–	–	–	–	–	–
First-class	142	37853	18144	681	7-39	26.64	2.87	55.58	47	6

JOE **DENLY**

Full name	**Joseph Liam Denly**
Born	**March 16, 1986, Canterbury, Kent**
Teams	**Kent**
Style	**Right-hand bat, occasional legspinner**
Test debut	**No Tests yet**
ODI debut	**No ODIs yet**

THE PROFILE Joe Denly has been associated with Kent since he was 13, and made his first-class debut for them against Oxford University in 2004, having the misfortune to be out for a duck in the only two overs that rain allowed during the whole match. He did rather better against Cambridge two years later, hitting twin centuries. For some time he found first-team opportunities elusive with Kent, but when the former captain David Fulton was released (the fear that Denly might go elsewhere may have contributed to that decision) a place became available at the start of 2007. Denly grabbed it eagerly, finishing with 1003 runs at 41.79. A good puller and hooker, he carried on in 2008, playing pace with ease, although he was a little less assured against spin – Paul Coupar wrote in the *Wisden Cricketer* that "in excellent touch otherwise, he handled Danish Kaneria's leg-spin like soap in the bath". But it was Denly's one-day form that really caught the eye. Kent steamed to the Twenty20 Cup in 2007, with Denly making 279 runs, and he was even more prolific the following year with 451, although this time Kent lost in the final. And in 2008 he carried that form over to the longer limited-overs game, making more than 400 runs, including 102 against Durham in the Friends Provident semi-final (again Kent lost the final), and also played for England Lions against South Africa. Denly's opening partnership with Rob Key proved a major success in all forms of the one-day game, putting both of them in the frame for England calls.

THE FACTS Denly scored 115 and 107 not out for Kent against Cambridge UCCE at Fenner's in May 2006 – then did not play another first-class game for four months ... His highest score of 149 came against Somerset at Tunbridge Wells in May 2008 ... Denly scored five half-centuries in the Twenty20 Cup in 2008, including 91 (from 57 balls) against Essex at Beckenham ...

THE FIGURES to 12.9.08   www.cricinfo.com

Batting & Fielding	M	Inns	NO	Runs	HS	Avge	S/R	100	50	4s	6s	Ct	St
Tests	0	0	–	–	–	–	–	–	–	–	–	–	–
ODIs	0	0	–	–	–	–	–	–	–	–	–	–	–
T20 Ints	0	0	–	–	–	–	–	–	–	–	–	–	–
First-class	38	65	4	2350	149	38.52	62.18	6	12	–	–	15	0

Bowling	M	Balls	Runs	Wkts	BB	Avge	RpO	S/R	5i	10m
Tests	0	0	–	–	–	–	–	–	–	–
ODIs	0	0	–	–	–	–	–	–	–	–
T20 Ints	0	0	–	–	–	–	–	–	–	–
First-class	38	691	344	10	2–13	34.40	2.98	69.10	0	0

AB **de VILLIERS**

Full name	**Abraham Benjamin de Villiers**
Born	**February 17, 1984, Pretoria**
Teams	**Titans, Delhi Daredevils**
Style	**Right-hand bat, occ. medium-pacer, wicketkeeper**
Test debut	**South Africa v England at Port Elizabeth 2004-05**
ODI debut	**South Africa v England at Bloemfontein 2004-05**

THE PROFILE Few Test newcomers have been asked to play so many roles so quickly as AB de Villiers, and fewer still have risen to the challenge with such alacrity that, at just 21, he was already being regarded as the future of South African cricket. He is a natural sportsman, gifted at tennis, golf, cricket and rugby. Cricket won out, however, and after starring for the Under-19s he made his Titans debut in 2003-04, racking up five half-centuries in 438 runs. He won his first Test cap against England the following season, and, after a composed debut as an opener, was handed the wicketkeeping gloves for the second Test, which he helped save with a maiden half-century down at No. 7. By the end of the series, however, he was opening again, and after falling eight short of a deserved century in the first innings at Centurion, made instant amends second time around. His development continued apace in the Caribbean, where he helped seal the series with a wonderful 178 at Bridgetown. Then came the almost inevitable dip in fortunes. In Australia in 2005-06 de Villiers managed just 152 runs at 25.33 – despite playing Shane Warne well – and missed the one-dayers. But he re-established himself in 2006-07, especially impressive in the shorter game, although he had a curious World Cup, collecting four ducks as well as a rousing 92 against Australia and a stroke-filled 146 – despite suffering with terrible cramp – against West Indies. He came good in Tests in 2007-08 with centuries against West Indies and India (his first double), before a memorable 174 at Headingley put his side one up on England.

THE FACTS AB de Villiers made 217 not out at Ahmedabad in April 2008, after India had been bowled out for 76 ... He averages 52.62 in five Tests at Centurion – but only 11.22 from five at Johannesburg ... He scored 151, his maiden first-class century, for Titans v Western Province Boland in October 2004, sharing a stand of 317 with Martin van Jaarsveld ... de Villiers has not yet been dismissed for 0 in Tests, but collected four ducks during the 2007 World Cup ... His record includes five ODIs for the Africa XI ...

THE FIGURES *to 12.9.08*   www.cricinfo.com

Batting & Fielding	M	Inns	NO	Runs	HS	Avge	S/R	100	50	4s	6s	Ct	St
Tests	44	77	6	2955	217*	41.61	53.41	6	14	379	9	59	1
ODIs	72	68	7	2202	146	36.09	83.56	3	13	244	39	44	0
T20 Ints	11	10	3	133	52*	19.00	109.01	0	1	14	3	12	1
First-class	66	117	11	4667	217*	44.02	57.37	9	26	–	–	103	2

Bowling	M	Balls	Runs	Wkts	BB	Avge	RpO	S/R	5i	10m
Tests	44	198	99	2	2–49	49.50	3.00	99.00	0	0
ODIs	72	12	22	0	–	–	11.00	–	0	0
T20 Ints	11	0	–	–	–	–	–	–	–	–
First-class	66	204	99	2	2–49	49.50	3.00	102.00	0	0

DHIMAN GHOSH

Full name	**Dhiman Ghosh**
Born	**November 23, 1987, Dinajpur**
Teams	**Chittagong**
Style	**Right-hand bat, wicketkeeper**
Test debut	**No Tests yet**
ODI debut	**Bangladesh v Pakistan at Karachi 2007-08**

THE PROFILE For a time Chittagong's Dhiman Ghosh was seen as the natural successor to the long-serving national wicketkeeper Khaled Mashud. Ghosh played for Bangladesh A and the national Under-19 team in 2003-04, being part of the side which beat Australia in the Youth World Cup, and the following season emphasised his batting potential too with 115 against Khulna, whose attack that day included four Test bowlers. But Ghosh was pushed back by the sudden emergence of the even younger Mushfiqur Rahim, who muscled his way on to the 2005 England tour at 16, and two years later displaced Mashud for the World Cup. But then Mushfiqur had troubles of his own, losing batting form so completely that he made only four runs in five ODIs early in 2008 – including three successive ducks – and Ghosh was one of four new players called up, after two consistent domestic seasons in which he had averaged around 30 with the bat and kept consistently tidily. He played through three successive series, against South Africa, Ireland and Pakistan, without exactly setting the world alight, although he did take four catches at Lahore, in a match where Pakistan lost only five wickets. But as Bangladesh continued to struggle – losing all eight games against Test sides, most by large margins – Ghosh found batting success elusive. His highest score in nine attempts was 29, and Mushfiqur returned for the Asia Cup, also played in Pakistan, in July 2008. But he still failed to reach 50, so the position of wicketkeeper/batsman is still up for grabs.

THE FACTS Dhiman Ghosh cracked a 65-ball century on his way to 147 in a one-day game for Chittagong against Rajshahi at Fatullah in April 2007 ... He has also scored two first-class centuries for Chittagong, 115 against Khulna in March 2005, and 100 not out v Rajshahi in March 2007 ... Ghosh is also a part-time offspinner, removing his pads to take 3 for 7 for Chittagong against Barisal in March 2006 ... He made 151 for the Bangladesh Academy in a four-day match against Australia's Northern Territory in Darwin in September 2007 ...

THE FIGURES *to 12.9.08*   www.cricinfo.com

Batting & Fielding	M	Inns	NO	Runs	HS	Avge	S/R	100	50	4s	6s	Ct	St
Tests	0	0	–	–	–	–	–	–	–	–	–	–	–
ODIs	14	12	3	126	30	14.00	62.68	0	0	9	1	9	4
T20 Ints	1	1	0	1	1	1.00	50.00	0	0	0	0	0	1
First-class	40	70	7	1820	115	28.88	63.88	2	8	–	–	98	11

Bowling	M	Balls	Runs	Wkts	BB	Avge	RpO	S/R	5i	10m
Tests	0	0	–	–	–	–	–	–	–	–
ODIs	14	0	–	–	–	–	–	–	–	–
T20 Ints	1	0	–	–	–	–	–	–	–	–
First-class	40	289	178	9	3–7	19.77	3.69	32.11	0	0

MAHENDRA SINGH **DHONI**

INDIA

Full name	**Mahendra Singh Dhoni**
Born	**July 7, 1981, Ranchi, Bihar**
Teams	**Jharkhand, Chennai Super Kings**
Style	**Right-hand bat, wicketkeeper**
Test debut	**India v Sri Lanka at Chennai 2005-06**
ODI debut	**India v Bangladesh at Chittagong 2004-05**

THE PROFILE The spectacular arrival of Virender Sehwag was bound to inspire others to bat with the same approach. But the odds of a clone emerging from the backwaters of Jharkhand (formerly Bihar) were highly remote. That was until Mahendra Singh Dhoni arrived (a one-time railway ticket collector, his first love was football). He can be muscularly swashbuckling with the bat, and secure with the wicketkeeping gloves. It wasn't until 2004 that he became a serious contender for national selection, after some stirring performances – a rapid hundred as East Zone clinched the Deodhar Trophy, and an audacious 60 in the Duleep Trophy final. But it was two centuries against Pakistan A that established him as a clinical destroyer of bowling attacks and earned him a senior chance. In just his fifth ODI – against Pakistan in April 2005 – Dhoni cracked a dazzling 148, putting even Sehwag in the shade, and followed that with a colossal 183 not out against Sri Lanka in November, breaking Adam Gilchrist's record for the highest ODI score by a wicketkeeper. He made an instant impact at Test level, too, pounding 148 at Faisalabad in only his fifth match, when India were struggling to avoid the follow-on. His keeping has improved, and he quickly established himself as a key member of a revitalised side. He stepped up to captain India in the World Twenty20 championship in September 2007, then made headlines as the most expensive signing ($1.5million) for the inaugural Indian Premier League season, in which he skippered Chennai to the final before angering some by pulling out of a Test series in Sri Lanka.

THE FACTS Dhoni's unbeaten 183 against Sri Lanka at Jaipur in November 2005 is the highest score in ODIs by a wicketkeeper, and included 120 in boundaries – 10 sixes and 15 fours – a record at the time but later beaten by Herschelle Gibbs ... The only other Indian to score a century in an ODI in which he kept wicket is Rahul Dravid ... Dhoni's record includes three ODIs for the Asia XI ...

THE FIGURES *to 12.9.08*   www.cricinfo.com

Batting & Fielding	M	Inns	NO	Runs	HS	Avge	S/R	100	50	4s	6s	Ct	St
Tests	29	47	5	1418	148	33.76	63.02	1	9	177	26	68	14
ODIs	120	107	27	3793	183*	47.41	91.30	4	24	298	90	121	36
T20 Ints	10	9	2	172	45	24.57	111.68	0	0	13	4	2	0
First-class	68	110	8	3481	148	34.12	–	4	22	–	–	172	30

Bowling	M	Balls	Runs	Wkts	BB	Avge	RpO	S/R	5i	10m
Tests	29	6	13	0	–	–	13.00	–	0	0
ODIs	120	0	–	–	–	–	–	–	–	–
T20 Ints	10	0	–	–	–	–	–	–	–	–
First-class	68	36	33	0	–	–	5.50	–	0	0

TILLAKARATNE **DILSHAN**

SRI LANKA

Full name	**Tillakaratne Mudiyanselage Dilshan**
Born	**October 14, 1976, Kalutara**
Teams	**Bloomfield, Basnahira South, Delhi Daredevils**
Style	**Right-hand bat, offspinner**
Test debut	**Sri Lanka v Zimbabwe at Bulawayo 1999-2000**
ODI debut	**Sri Lanka v Zimbabwe at Bulawayo 1999-2000**

THE PROFILE Tillakaratne Mudiyanselage Dilshan, who started life as Tuwan Mohamad Dilshan before converting to Buddhism, is a light-footed right-hander who burst onto the international scene with an unbeaten 163 against Zimbabwe in only his second Test in November 1999. Technically sound, comfortable against fast bowling, possessed of quick feet, strong wrists and natural timing, Dilshan has talent in abundance. But that bright start was followed by a frustrating 15 months when he was shovelled up and down the order, and in and out of the side. After a lean series against England in 2001 – 51 runs in four innings – he didn't play another Test until England toured again at the end of 2003. He came back mentally stronger, and determined to play his own natural aggressive game. This approach was immediately successful, with several good scores against England and Australia, and then – rather more surprisingly for someone who started as a wicketkeeper – came some impressive bowling performances with his offspin. He has continued to be a steady influence in the middle order, and was one of four centurions in the innings victory over India in July 2008. He put a lean trot in ODIs in 2006-07 behind him just in time for the World Cup, where he made some useful runs, without going on to a big score, in Sri Lanka's march to the final. He brings an added dimension to the team, especially in one-day cricket, with his brilliant fielding – he effected four run-outs in the first tri-series final at Adelaide in February 2006.

THE FACTS Dilshan's 23 first-class centuries include 200 not out while captaining North Central Province against Central in Colombo in February 2005 ... His highest Test score of 168 came against Bangladesh in Colombo in September 2005: he put on 280 with Thilan Samaraweera, a Sri Lankan fifth-wicket record in Tests ... Dilshan made his first ODI century in the record total of 443 for 9 against the Netherlands at Amstelveen in July 2006 ... He started as a wicketkeeper and has 23 first-class stumpings to his name ...

THE FIGURES *to 12.9.08* www.cricinfo.com

Batting & Fielding	M	Inns	NO	Runs	HS	Avge	S/R	100	50	4s	6s	Ct	St
Tests	48	75	9	2533	168	38.37	58.62	5	12	323	7	52	0
ODIs	152	129	26	2994	117*	29.06	80.26	1	14	242	15	67	1
T20 Ints	7	6	1	70	38	14.00	102.94	0	0	2	4	4	0
First-class	178	288	20	10000	200*	37.31	–	23	44	–	–	311	23

Bowling	M	Balls	Runs	Wkts	BB	Avge	RpO	S/R	5i	10m
Tests	48	654	308	7	2–4	44.00	2.82	93.42	0	0
ODIs	152	2538	1980	46	4–29	43.04	4.68	55.17	0	0
T20 Ints	7	66	62	3	2–4	20.66	5.63	22.00	0	0
First-class	178	3170	1501	49	5–49	30.63	2.84	64.69	1	0

DOLAR MAHMUD

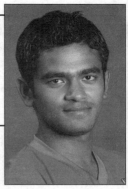

Full name	**Mohammad Dolar Mahmud**
Born	**December 30, 1988, Narail, Khulna**
Teams	**Khulna**
Style	**Right-hand bat, right-arm fast-medium bowler**
Test debut	**No Tests yet**
ODI debut	**Bangladesh v Pakistan at Mirpur 2008**

THE PROFILE Dolar Mahmud is a handy fast-medium bowler who was part of Bangladesh's squad for the Under-19 World Cups of 2006 and 2008. He was only 17 at the first one, but failed to shine in either, although his 36 against England in 2008 helped Bangladesh to a narrow 13-run victory in a low-scoring game. Despite these uninspiring returns, the selectors liked the look of his easy action, and kept faith, giving him plenty of representative experience at the lower levels. Shortly after taking a hat-trick for Khulna against Rajshahi in a domestic match – and hitting the winning boundary to end the game – he toured South Africa with the Under-19s at the end of 2007, and took five wickets in the second Test at Potchefstroom. Generally Mahmud did enough to earn promotion to the full squad, and fulfilled his dream of playing for the national side when he made his full ODI debut in the Kitply Cup at home in Bangladesh in June 2008. Again the returns were modest – he failed to score in either of his innings, but did take a wicket (Kamran Akmal and Virender Sehwag) in each of his two matches. This was enough for him to retain his place for the Asia Cup, where he finally got off the mark with the bat (he hit his second ball for six, after a first-ball single), although this was only against the lowly United Arab Emirates – when they played Sri Lanka he failed to take a wicket. Mahmud doesn't turn 20 until the very end of 2008, but the jury is out on his international future, as he has to contend for a place with several bowlers of similar style.

THE FACTS Dolar Mahmud took a hat-trick for Khulna against Rajshahi at Khulna in November 2007: his victims included Test players Junaid Siddique and Mushfiqur Rahim ... Mahmud finished that innings with 7 for 52, his best first-class figures cricket ... He also took 5 for 44 against Barisal in November 2006 ... Mahmud played in the Under-19 World Cups of 2006 and 2008 ... He took 5 for 75 in an Under-19 Test against South Africa in December 2007 ...

THE FIGURES to 12.9.08   www.cricinfo.com

Batting & Fielding	M	Inns	NO	Runs	HS	Avge	S/R	100	50	4s	6s	Ct	St
Tests	0	0	–	–	–	–	–	–	–	–	–	–	–
ODIs	4	3	0	20	20	6.66	142.85	0	0	1	1	0	0
T20 Ints	0	0	–	–	–	–	–	–	–	–	–	–	–
First-class	15	28	4	312	63	13.00	53.51	0	1	–	–	6	0

Bowling	M	Balls	Runs	Wkts	BB	Avge	RpO	S/R	5i	10m
Tests	0	0	–	–	–	–	–	–	–	–
ODIs	4	103	165	3	1–27	55.00	9.61	34.33	0	0
T20 Ints	0	0	–	–	–	–	–	–	–	–
First-class	15	2162	1147	43	7–52	26.67	3.18	50.27	2	0

RAHUL **DRAVID**

INDIA

Full name	**Rahul Sharad Dravid**
Born	**January 11, 1973, Indore, Madhya Pradesh**
Teams	**Karnataka, Bangalore Royal Challengers**
Style	**Right-hand bat, occasional wicketkeeper**
Test debut	**India v England at Lord's 1996**
ODI debut	**India v Sri Lanka at Singapore 1995-96**

THE PROFILE   Rahul Dravid is the best No. 3 batsman to play for India. He averages more than 55 from there – but impressive as his stats are, they don't show his importance, or the beauty of his batting. When he started, he was pigeonholed as a blocker: his early nickname was "The Wall". But as the years passed, Dravid grew in stature, finally reaching maturity under Sourav Ganguly's captaincy. As a New India emerged, so did a new Dravid: first, he transformed himself into an astute middle-order one-day finisher, then strung together a series of awe-inspiring Test performances. His golden phase really began with a supporting act, at Kolkata early in 2001, when his 180 helped VVS Laxman create history against Australia. But from then on, Dravid became India's most valuable player, saving Tests at Port Elizabeth, Georgetown and Nottingham, and winning them at Leeds, Adelaide, Kandy and Rawalpindi. At one point he hit four double-centuries in 15 Tests. As India finished off their 2004 Pakistan tour with a win, thanks to Dravid's epic 270, his average crept past Tendulkar's – and stayed ahead until late in 2008. In October 2005 he was appointed as one-day captain, began with a 6-1 hammering of Sri Lanka at home, and soon succeeded Ganguly as Test skipper too. He continued to score well, and bounced back from the crushing disappointment of an early exit from the 2007 World Cup by leading India to a rare series victory in England, although his own batting lacked sparkle. He relinquished the captaincy after that, and there have been signs of fallibility since – he made only one Test century in the year from September 2007, and lost his one-day place.

THE FACTS   Dravid hit centuries in four successive Test innings in 2002, three in England and one against West Indies ... He kept wicket in 73 ODIs ... Unusually, Dravid averages more in away Tests (56.62) than at home in India (50.36) ... He averages 97.90 in Tests against Zimbabwe, but only 36.51 v South Africa ...   Dravid's record includes one Test and three ODIs for the World XI, and one ODI for the Asia XI ...

THE FIGURES to 12.9.08   www.cricinfo.com

Batting & Fielding	M	Inns	NO	Runs	HS	Avge	S/R	100	50	4s	6s	Ct	St
Tests	125	216	26	10240	270	53.92	41.93	25	52	1285	14	176	0
ODIs	333	308	40	10585	153	39.49	71.22	12	81	930	40	193	14
T20 Ints	0	0	–	–	–	–	–	–	–	–	–	–	–
First-class	244	403	58	19407	270	56.25	–	52	99	–	–	294	1

Bowling	M	Balls	Runs	Wkts	BB	Avge	RpO	S/R	5i	10m
Tests	125	120	39	1	1–18	39.00	1.95	120.00	0	0
ODIs	333	186	170	4	2–43	42.50	5.48	46.50	0	0
T20 Ints	0	0	–	–	–	–	–	–	–	–
First-class	244	617	273	5	2–16	54.40	2.65	123.40	0	0

J-P **DUMINY**

Full name	**Jean-Paul Duminy**
Born	**April 14, 1984, Strandfontein, Cape Town**
Teams	**Cape Cobras**
Style	**Left-hand bat, occasional offspinner**
Test debut	**No Tests yet**
ODI debut	**South Africa v Sri Lanka at Colombo 2004-05**

THE PROFILE A slightly built but stylish top-order left-hand batsman, Jean-Paul (better known as "J-P") Duminy was rewarded for some consistent domestic performances with a place on South Africa's tour of Sri Lanka in 2004. He struggled in the one-dayers there, scoring only 29 runs in five attempts (22 of them in one innings), and dropped off the national radar for a couple of years. But he continued to make runs in South Africa, and was recalled for the home series against Zimbabwe in September 2006, although his 115 runs for once out counted for little against such weak opposition. He was given an extended run after the 2007 World Cup, and showed signs of developing into a late-innings "finisher" in the style of another left-hander, Michael Bevan, with some composed displays at home against West Indies, when he batted into the final over in three successive matches, all of which were eventually won. He finished that series with 227 runs at 113.50, although he was less of a hit in England later in 2008. Duminy is also a superb fielder, while his part-time offbreaks occasionally come in handy. He broke into the strong Western Province side early in 2002, when he was just 17, and made two centuries in the 2003-04 season, which he finished with an average of 72.57. He still averages more than 50 in first-class cricket, but hasn't had a chance in Tests yet because of South Africa's imposing top order.

THE FACTS Duminy scored 169 as Cape Cobras followed on against the Eagles at Stellenbosch in February 2007 ... He scored 265 not out for the South African Academy against Pakistan's one at Lahore in August 2005 ... Duminy made 116 in an Under-19 Test at Worcester in August 2003, before being caught and bowled by Alastair Cook ... He is not related to the JP Duminy who played three Tests for South Africa in the 1920s ...

THE FIGURES *to 12.9.08*   www.cricinfo.com

Batting & Fielding	M	Inns	NO	Runs	HS	Avge	S/R	100	50	4s	6s	Ct	St
Tests	0	0	–	–	–	–	–	–	–	–	–	4	0
ODIs	33	28	7	682	79*	32.47	73.33	0	3	52	6	8	0
T20 Ints	5	5	0	82	36	16.40	126.15	0	0	9	3	5	0
First-class	45	75	14	3236	169	53.04	49.34	9	18	–	–	31	0

Bowling	M	Balls	Runs	Wkts	BB	Avge	RpO	S/R	5i	10m
Tests	0	0	–	–	–	–	–	–	–	–
ODIs	33	222	200	3	1–6	66.66	5.40	74.00	0	0
T20 Ints	5	0	–	–	–	–	–	–	–	–
First-class	45	1233	739	16	4–89	46.18	3.59	77.06	0	0

FIDEL **EDWARDS**

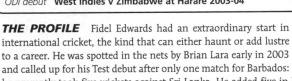

Full name	**Fidel Henderson Edwards**
Born	**February 6, 1982, Gays, St Peter, Barbados**
Teams	**Barbados**
Style	**Right-hand bat, right-arm fast bowler**
Test debut	**West Indies v Sri Lanka at Kingston 2002-03**
ODI debut	**West Indies v Zimbabwe at Harare 2003-04**

THE PROFILE Fidel Edwards had an extraordinary start in international cricket, the kind that can either haunt or add lustre to a career. He was spotted in the nets by Brian Lara early in 2003 and called up for his Test debut after only one match for Barbados: he promptly took five wickets against Sri Lanka. He added five in his first overseas Test, and six in his first ODI. Edwards has a slingy round-arm action not unlike Jeff Thomson's – or Lasith Malinga's – which leaves him vulnerable to back strains. It doesn't often seem to result in him straying down leg, though, which seems probable when you first see him, and his unusual action has troubled many distinguished batsmen. He is more of a protégé of his neighbour Corey Collymore than of his half-brother Pedro Collins, a left-armer – who replaced him when another injury (a hamstring this time) forced him out of the series against India in mid-2006. Edwards bowls fast, can swing the ball and reverse it too, but insists that he doesn't go for out-and-out pace – which is just as well, because he has learned that pace without control leads straight to the boundary at international level. He showed his increased maturity with a testing spell in Antigua in June 2006 that had India's Virender Sehwag in all kinds of trouble before a hamstring twanged. And he hurried England's batsmen up in 2007, taking nine wickets in two Tests and ten – including 5 for 45 at Lord's – as West Indies won the one-day series 2-1, then took eight wickets, including both openers in both innings, in the first Test against Australia at Kingston in May 2008.

THE FACTS Edwards had played only one first-class match – taking one wicket – before his Test debut against Sri Lanka at Kingston in June 2003, when he took 5 for 36 ... He also took 6 for 22 on his ODI debut, against Zimbabwe at Harare in November 2003 ... Edwards opened the bowling against England at Bridgetown in April 2004 (and several times subsequently) with his half-brother, Pedro Collins ... Edwards averages 28.37 with the ball in home Tests, but 53.02 overseas ... Unoriginally, his nickname is "Castro" ...

THE FIGURES *to 12.9.08*   www.cricinfo.com

Batting & Fielding	M	Inns	NO	Runs	HS	Avge	S/R	100	50	4s	6s	Ct	St
Tests	34	57	16	176	21	4.29	24.14	0	0	22	2	4	0
ODIs	39	16	11	50	12*	10.00	46.72	0	0	4	0	3	0
T20 Ints	5	0	–	–	–	–	–	–	–	–	–	0	0
First-class	53	84	28	304	40	5.42	–	0	0	–	–	7	0

Bowling	M	Balls	Runs	Wkts	BB	Avge	RpO	S/R	5i	10m
Tests	34	5767	3854	95	5–36	40.56	4.06	60.70	6	0
ODIs	39	1787	1456	52	6–22	28.00	4.88	34.36	2	0
T20 Ints	5	86	102	2	1–14	51.00	7.11	43.00	0	0
First-class	53	8326	5552	157	5–22	35.36	4.00	53.03	8	1

GRANT **ELLIOTT**

NEW ZEALAND

Full name	**Grant David Elliott**
Born	**March 21, 1979, Johannesburg, South Africa**
Teams	**Wellington**
Style	**Right-hand bat, right-arm medium-pacer**
Test debut	**New Zealand v England at Napier 2007-08**
ODI debut	**New Zealand v England at Edgbaston 2008**

THE PROFILE   Grant Elliott left his native South Africa for New Zealand in 2001 looking for new horizons, and found them in March 2008 when he was named in NZ's 13-man squad for the first Test against England less than a year after completing his residency qualification. He missed out then, but won his first cap in the final Test after Jacob Oram was injured. However, Elliott was not a success, with two batting failures and a solitary wicket, although he was included in the squad for the one-dayers in England later in the year. A compact and correct batsman, and a swing bowler with a measured run-up and a nice high action, he enjoyed a productive season for Wellington in 2006-07, with 361 runs at 45.12, and backed that up with 565 at 37.66 the following year. In England, he took three wickets in the second ODI, and made 56 in the third, but it was his controversial run-out in the fourth one at The Oval which made all the headlines – after he collided with the bowler while trying a quick single Elliott was lying on the ground clutching his thigh when the bails were removed, and Paul Collingwood (in what turned out to be his last match as England's one-day captain) declined to withdraw the appeal. Elliott stomped off, and later the New Zealand dressing-room door was firmly shut in Collingwood's face. It remains to be seen whether Elliott will make a more conventional mark on international cricket: his batting could be useful, but his bowling might just not be quick enough to make an impression.

THE FACTS   Elliott scored 196 not out for Wellington against Auckland in April 2008 ... He represented South Africa in the Under-19 World Cup in 1997-98, and also played a one-day game for South Africa A against India A in 2001-02 ... Elliott's maiden first-class century came for Griqualand West against the Bangladesh tourists at Kimberley in October 2000 ...

THE FIGURES *to 12.9.08*   www.cricinfo.com

Batting & Fielding	M	Inns	NO	Runs	HS	Avge	S/R	100	50	4s	6s	Ct	St
Tests	1	2	0	10	6	5.00	19.23	0	0	0	0	2	0
ODIs	6	3	1	103	56	51.50	70.06	0	1	6	1	1	0
T20 Ints	0	0	–	–	–	–	–	–	–	–	–	–	–
First-class	42	66	3	1907	196*	30.26	–	5	9	–	–	29	0

Bowling	M	Balls	Runs	Wkts	BB	Avge	RpO	S/R	5i	10m
Tests	1	144	85	1	1–27	85.00	3.54	144.00	0	0
ODIs	6	146	80	9	3–14	8.88	3.28	16.22	0	0
T20 Ints	0	0	–	–	–	–	–	–	–	–
First-class	42	4653	2148	60	4–56	35.80	2.76	77.55	0	0

FARHAD REZA

Full name	**Farhad Reza**
Born	**June 16, 1986, Rajshahi**
Teams	**Rajshahi**
Style	**Right-hand bat, right-arm medium-pacer**
Test debut	**No Tests yet**
ODI debut	**Bangladesh v Zimbabwe at Harare 2006**

THE PROFILE Farhad Reza is a busy player: a middle-order batsman who loves to pull, a skiddy medium-pacer, and a fine fielder. He was called up to the national squad for the tour of Zimbabwe in July 2006 after scoring the most runs in the previous season's domestic club league. He had made an even more eye-catching start in first-class cricket the year before, when he was only 18, starting with 99 on debut and finishing up with 769 runs at 42 in 2004-05. Reza made his international debut at Harare, and made 50 – off 57 balls – to become the first Bangladeshi to score a half-century in his first match. He continued this good start when the team moved on to Kenya, with unbeaten knocks of 34 and 41 steering his side home in two of the games. He also opened the bowling in a couple of those Kenyan matches, but proved a little expensive: batting is definitely his stronger suit, although he did take 5 for 42 against Ireland early in 2008. He has found it tougher against stronger opposition, and lost his place for a while after the Champions Trophy in India in 2006-07, when he made only 41 runs and failed to take a wicket in three games. He missed out on initial selection for the 2007 World Cup, although Habibul Bashar, the captain at the time, hinted that he might have been useful. He was called up to the squad when Tapash Baisya was injured, but didn't actually get a game in the Caribbean.

THE FACTS Farhad Reza made 50 in his first ODI, the first man to make a half-century on debut for Bangladesh ... His highest score (and only first-class century) is 177 for Rajshahi against Khulna at Rajshahi in April 2005 ... On his first-class debut, earlier in that 2004-05 season, Reza was out for 99 for Rajshahi against Chittagong at Bogra ... He took 6 for 54 for Rajshahi against Sylhet at Rajshahi in February 2007, and a week later took 5 for 70 (his only other five-for) against Dhaka at Fatullah ...

THE FIGURES *to 12.9.08*   www.cricinfo.com

Batting & Fielding	M	Inns	NO	Runs	HS	Avge	S/R	100	50	4s	6s	Ct	St
Tests	0	0	–	–	–	–	–	–	–	–	–	–	–
ODIs	32	29	6	390	50	16.95	64.89	0	1	37	8	12	0
T20 Ints	7	5	0	50	19	10.00	87.71	0	0	3	2	3	0
First-class	30	54	8	1671	177	36.32	58.06	1	12	–	–	17	0

Bowling	M	Balls	Runs	Wkts	BB	Avge	RpO	S/R	5i	10m
Tests	0	0	–	–	–	–	–	–	–	–
ODIs	32	1127	1015	22	5–42	46.13	5.46	51.22	1	0
T20 Ints	7	90	165	4	2–34	41.25	11.00	22.50	0	0
First-class	30	3154	1424	57	6–54	24.98	2.70	55.33	2	0

FAWAD ALAM

Full name	**Fawad Alam**
Born	**October 8, 1985, Karachi, Sind**
Teams	**Karachi, Sind, National Bank**
Style	**Left-hand bat, slow left-arm orthodox spinner**
Test debut	**No Tests yet**
ODI debut	**Pakistan v Sri Lanka at Abu Dhabi 2006-07**

THE PROFILE Fawad Alam was one of Pakistan's young achievers: he made his first-class debut at 17, and was part of the side that won the Under-19 World Cup in Dhaka early in 2004. He didn't sparkle in the final, but his unbeaten 43 against India in the semi had done much to get Pakistan there in the first place. A talented left-hander, Fawad scored 1027 runs at 53.60 in 2005-06, his first full season, and averaged around 50 over the following two seasons as well, just to show that was no fluke. He has another string to his bow as a handy slow left-armer. In December 2006 he guided Karachi to the final of the Twenty20 Cup, where they lost to the defending champions Sialkot despite Fawad's valiant 54, which followed five wickets: he left without a winner's medal but with a clutch of other awards – Man of the Final, Man of the Series, Best Batsman and Best Bowler. Shortly afterwards he led Pakistan's Academy on their tour of Bangladesh. All this led to a call to the full national team in the wake of the disastrous 2007 World Cup campaign. He made a low-key start, falling to the only ball he faced on his ODI debut, against Sri Lanka in the heat of Abu Dhabi: surprisingly, he wasn't given a bowl. The selectors kept faith, however, and he played in the World Twenty20 championship and most of Pakistan's ODIs at the start of 2008, although he failed to shine with bat or ball, beyond a 63 not out against the minnows of Hong Kong. The talent is obvious, but he needs a big performance against one of the major sides to move him out of the "promising" category.

THE FACTS Fawad Alam took 5 for 27 and then hit 54 for Karachi against Sialkot in the final of the ABN-AMRO Cup, Pakistan's domestic Twenty20 Cup competition, in December 2006: they still lost ... He was part of the Pakistan side that won the Under-19 World Cup in Bangladesh in March 2004 ... Fawad scored 151 for National Bank at Hyderabad in December 2007 ... His father, Tariq Alam, had a long first-class career in Pakistan ...

THE FIGURES to 12.9.08   www.cricinfo.com

Batting & Fielding	M	Inns	NO	Runs	HS	Avge	S/R	100	50	4s	6s	Ct	St
Tests	0	0	–	–	–	–	–	–	–	–	–	–	–
ODIs	10	8	6	130	63*	65.00	89.65	0	1	9	1	3	0
T20 Ints	3	2	2	19	16*	–	172.72	0	0	1	1	1	0
First-class	39	66	12	2655	151	49.16	–	4	18	–	–	21	0

Bowling	M	Balls	Runs	Wkts	BB	Avge	RpO	S/R	5i	10m
Tests	0	0	–	–	–	–	–	–	–	–
ODIs	10	356	317	4	1–8	79.25	5.34	89.00	0	0
T20 Ints	3	42	44	3	2–29	14.66	6.28	14.00	0	0
First-class	39	1313	621	19	4–27	32.68	2.83	69.10	0	0

DILHARA **FERNANDO**

Full name	**Congenige Randhi Dilhara Fernando**
Born	**July 19, 1979, Colombo**
Teams	**Sinhalese SC, Worcestershire, Mumbai Indians**
Style	**Right-hand bat, right-arm fast-medium bowler**
Test debut	**Sri Lanka v Pakistan at Colombo 2000**
ODI debut	**Sri Lanka v South Africa at Paarl 2000-01**

THE PROFILE When Dilhara Fernando burst onto the international scene, young and raw, he soon inspired hope that he would be the long-term replacement for Chaminda Vaas as the cutting edge of Sri Lanka's attack. He has natural pace – six months after his debut he was clocked at 91.9mph in Durban – hits the pitch hard, and moves the ball off the seam. He rattled India at Galle in 2001, taking five wickets and sending Javagal Srinath to hospital. At first he paid for an inconsistent line and length, but worked hard with the former Test opening bowler Rumesh Ratnayake and became more reliable. He also learnt the art of reverse swing, and developed a well-disguised slower one. But injuries intervened. Fernando was quick during the 2003 World Cup, but bowled a lot of no-balls, a problem he later blamed on a spinal stress fracture. He returned after six months, only for another one to be detected in January 2004. He reclaimed his place in the national squad later that year, and has been thereabouts ever since, often going for a few in ODIs but always threatening wickets. Between injuries, he has been a Test regular too, although the no-ball problem resurfaced, and he was omitted after the first Test against Pakistan in March 2006 before returning later that year for the one-day series in England, which Sri Lanka swept 5-0, with Fernando grabbing three quick wickets in the first match at Lord's. He beat off the challenge of Nuwan Zoysa for a place in the 2007 World Cup, where he did well against England but managed only two other wickets – one in the final, when he brought down the curtain on Adam Gilchrist's epic 149.

THE FACTS Fernando averages 17.69 with the ball in Tests against Bangladesh – but 43.63 v India, even though his best figures of 5 for 42 came against them ... He took 6 for 27 against England in Colombo in September 2007: overall he averages 20.05 against England in ODIs, but 70.42 in 14 matches v South Africa ... Fernando's record includes one ODI for the Asia XI ...

THE FIGURES to 12.9.08   www.cricinfo.com

Batting & Fielding	M	Inns	NO	Runs	HS	Avge	S/R	100	50	4s	6s	Ct	St
Tests	30	38	12	184	36*	7.07	30.46	0	0	20	1	10	0
ODIs	128	50	30	201	20	10.05	60.00	0	0	16	1	23	0
T20 Ints	8	4	1	24	21	8.00	120.00	0	0	4	0	0	0
First-class	87	93	27	480	42	7.27	–	0	0	–	–	35	0

Bowling	M	Balls	Runs	Wkts	BB	Avge	RpO	S/R	5i	10m
Tests	30	4700	2848	84	5–42	33.90	3.63	55.95	3	0
ODIs	128	5520	4766	163	6–27	29.23	5.18	33.86	1	0
T20 Ints	8	168	181	10	3–19	18.10	6.46	16.80	0	0
First-class	87	11947	7108	252	6–29	28.20	3.56	47.40	6	0

ANDREW **FLINTOFF**

ENGLAND

Full name	**Andrew Flintoff**
Born	**December 6, 1977, Preston, Lancashire**
Teams	**Lancashire**
Style	**Right-hand bat, right-arm fast bowler**
Test debut	**England v South Africa at Nottingham 1998**
ODI debut	**England v Pakistan at Sharjah 1998-99**

THE PROFILE In 2005, "Freddie" Flintoff established himself as England's best allrounder since Ian Botham, reaping 402 runs and 24 wickets in the Ashes series. It propelled him to the superstar status his admirers had long believed was within his grasp. Big, northern and proud of it, he hammers the ball, then uses his colossal frame to reach 90mph – which, with his accuracy and mastery of reverse-swing, make him among the most intimidating bowlers around. Flintoff's precocious skills led to a Test debut at 20, but then he struggled with weight, motivation and back trouble. By 2001-02 he was a reformed character, and tonked a maiden Test ton in New Zealand, then did well at home. But when England flew to Australia in October 2002, Flintoff could hardly walk after a hernia operation. He returned as the most economical bowler at the 2003 World Cup, then starred against South Africa, thumping a therapeutic 95 in the remarkable Oval comeback after a defiant Lord's century. In the Caribbean early in 2004 he finally learned to slip the handbrake and become a genuine attacking option with the ball, something he continued in that amazing Ashes series. Then, when Michael Vaughan was injured, he stepped into the breach as captain in India, setting him up for the fall: Australia's revenge. Flintoff occasionally looked powerless during the Ashes whitewash, struggling for runs and wickets, and things got worse during the World Cup, when he lost the vice-captaincy after being found drunk in charge of a pedalo at 3am. A third ankle operation ruined his 2007 summer, but he finally returned in mid-2008 looking strong and lean, and anxious for another tilt at the Ashes.

THE FACTS Flintoff won 47 Test caps before he played against Australia ... In 2005 he was the fourth cricketer to be voted BBC Sports Personality of the Year, following Jim Laker (1956), David Steele (1975) and Ian Botham (1981) ... He took 68 Test wickets in 2005, a record for an England bowler ... Flintoff averages 51.25 with the bat and 24.69 with the ball in Tests v West Indies ... His record includes one Test and three ODIs for the World XI ...

THE FIGURES to 12.9.08 — www.cricinfo.com

Batting & Fielding	M	Inns	NO	Runs	HS	Avge	S/R	100	50	4s	6s	Ct	St
Tests	70	116	8	3494	167	32.35	63.52	5	24	470	80	47	–
ODIs	133	115	16	3277	123	33.10	88.75	3	18	298	89	43	0
T20 Ints	7	7	1	76	31	12.66	126.66	0	0	7	2	5	0
First-class	171	271	22	8588	167	34.48	–	15	50	–	–	176	0

Bowling	M	Balls	Runs	Wkts	BB	Avge	RpO	S/R	5i	10m
Tests	70	13300	6636	206	5–58	32.21	2.99	64.56	2	0
ODIs	133	5258	3815	159	5–56	23.99	4.35	33.06	1	0
T20 Ints	7	150	161	5	2–23	32.20	6.44	30.00	0	0
First-class	171	20761	10116	319	5–24	31.71	2.92	65.08	3	0

DANIEL **FLYNN**

Full name	**Daniel Raymond Flynn**
Born	**April 16, 1985, Rotorua**
Teams	**Northern Districts**
Style	**Left-hand bat, occasional slow left-arm spinner**
Test debut	**England v New Zealand at Lord's 2008**
ODI debut	**New Zealand v England at Christchurch 2007-08**

THE PROFILE The early days of Daniel Flynn's international career will be remembered for him walking off Old Trafford in May 2008 with a mouthful of blood and two fewer teeth than he started with, after being hit by a ball from James Anderson. Such an injury could have severely dented the confidence (as well as the gums) of a young batsman, but Flynn is made of sterner stuff. He made his first-class debut for Northern Districts soon after the 2003-04 Under-19 World Cup, in which he captained New Zealand. A stocky, powerful left-hander, he struck his maiden century in December 2005, but two mixed seasons followed, and it wasn't until 2007-08 that he showed his true colours – particularly in one-dayers – which earned him a call-up to the national Twenty20 squad. He didn't get many opportunities in his early games, but was named for the tour of England that followed, and also earned a national contract for 2008-09. He made his Test debut at Lord's, playing a cool defensive knock of 29 not out from 118 balls in the second innings that led his captain Daniel Vettori to declare that "He's got the No. 6 spot basically for as long as he wants it". Flynn then suffered that sickening blow in the mouth in the next game. However, he was fit enough to play in the final Test at Trent Bridge, where to general disappointment he was out one short of a maiden fifty, and can expect a decent run in the middle order now Stephen Fleming – an altogether different type of left-hander – has retired.

THE FACTS Flynn made his maiden first-class hundred (107) for Northern Districts against Otago at Gisborne in December 2005, then didn't make another one for almost two years ... In 2007-08 he hit 143 (from 117 balls) against Wellington and 149 (from 141 balls, with six sixes) against Canterbury in one-day games for ND ...

THE FIGURES *to 12.9.08*   www.cricinfo.com

Batting & Fielding	M	Inns	NO	Runs	HS	Avge	S/R	100	50	4s	6s	Ct	St
Tests	3	5	2	91	49	30.33	33.57	0	0	11	0	1	0
ODIs	8	6	1	83	35	16.60	60.58	0	0	7	0	4	0
T20 Ints	2	2	0	24	23	12.00	114.28	0	0	1	1	0	0
First-class	30	51	7	1379	110	31.34	41.23	4	4	–	–	10	0

Bowling	M	Balls	Runs	Wkts	BB	Avge	RpO	S/R	5i	10m
Tests	3	0	–	–	–	–	–	–	–	–
ODIs	8	0	–	–	–	–	–	–	–	–
T20 Ints	2	6	7	0	–	–	7.00	–	0	0
First-class	30	198	87	0	–	–	2.63	–	0	0

JAMES **FRANKLIN**

Full name	**James Edward Charles Franklin**
Born	**November 7, 1980, Wellington**
Teams	**Wellington**
Style	**Left-hand bat, left-arm fast-medium bowler**
Test debut	**New Zealand v Pakistan at Auckland 2000-01**
ODI debut	**New Zealand v Zimbabwe at Taupo 2000-01**

THE PROFILE A left-armer who can swing the ball, James Franklin was introduced to international cricket when barely out of his teens after New Zealand suffered a run of injuries. He made his one-day debut in 2000-01, and played two home Tests against Pakistan the same season, but struggled to make an impact and soon lost his place. Back in domestic cricket he worked on his batting, which he had neglected, and filled out generally. He returned to the side in England in 2004. He was playing league cricket in Lancashire, but was called up when Shane Bond went home with a back injury. Franklin was included for the third Test at Trent Bridge, and although New Zealand lost he did his cause no harm with six wickets, five of them Test century-makers. He stayed on for the one-dayers that followed, and picked up the match award at Chester-le-Street for his 5 for 42 as England were skittled for 101. Then, in Bangladesh, he grabbed a Test hat-trick at Dhaka. Back home he took 6 for 119 against Australia in March 2005, and bowled superbly – getting the ball to reverse-swing – against Sri Lanka a month later, although his figures didn't reflect his excellence. More wickets followed against West Indies, then in April 2006 Franklin did his allrounder claims no harm with an unbeaten 122 – and a stand of 256 with Stephen Fleming – against South Africa at Cape Town. He bowled capably during the 2007 World Cup, although he was occasionally expensive – as when he took 3 for 74 in eight overs as Australia cut loose in Grenada. A stubborn knee injury, which eventually required surgery, kept him out for most of the 2007-08 home season and the England tour that followed.

THE FACTS Franklin was the fourth man to take a hat-trick and score a century in Tests – the first three were Johnny Briggs of England and Pakistan's Abdul Razzaq and Wasim Akram; Irfan Pathan has since joined them ... The only other New Zealander to take a Test hat-trick was Peter Petherick in 1976-77 ... Franklin made 208, for Wellington v Auckland in 2005-06: in the previous match, against Central Districts, he had taken a career-best 7 for 30 ...

THE FIGURES *to 12.9.08* www.cricinfo.com

Batting & Fielding	M	Inns	NO	Runs	HS	Avge	S/R	100	50	4s	6s	Ct	St
Tests	21	28	5	505	122*	21.95	40.46	1	1	50	4	9	0
ODIs	65	44	15	508	45*	17.51	74.81	0	0	35	6	19	0
T20 Ints	3	3	2	34	18	34.00	113.33	0	0	2	2	2	0
First-class	89	131	19	3106	208	27.73	–	3	14	–	–	31	0

Bowling	M	Balls	Runs	Wkts	BB	Avge	RpO	S/R	5i	10m
Tests	21	3577	2143	76	6–119	28.19	3.59	47.06	3	0
ODIs	65	2804	2392	64	5–42	37.37	5.11	43.81	1	0
T20 Ints	3	60	63	3	3–23	21.00	6.30	20.00	0	0
First-class	89	14655	7689	310	7–30	24.80	3.14	47.27	11	1

PETER **FULTON**

Full name	**Peter Gordon Fulton**
Born	**February 1, 1979, Christchurch, Canterbury**
Teams	**Canterbury**
Style	**Right-hand bat, occasional right-arm medium-pacer**
Test debut	**New Zealand v West Indies at Auckland 2005-06**
ODI debut	**New Zealand v Bangladesh at Chittagong 2004-05**

THE PROFILE Peter Fulton, a tall middle-order batsman nicknamed "Two-Metre Peter", initially made his mark on first-class cricket by extending his maiden century to 301 not out for Canterbury against Auckland in March 2003, in only his second full season. His 9½-hour innings contained 45 fours and three sixes. Fulton is a product of Canterbury Country, an area rich in cricket history but which had never previously produced an international player. His 301 also broke the monopoly of Otago, where the five previous New Zealand triple-centuries all came from. The following season he made 728 runs at 42.82, including two more centuries, and – after a consistent A-team tour of South Africa – was called up to the senior one-day squad for the trip to Bangladesh in November 2004. He played one match there, but it was another 12 months before he featured again. This time he made the most of his chance, with 70 not out, 32, 50 and 112 against Sri Lanka, which led to a Test baptism: he added 75 in his second match, as New Zealand took an unbeatable lead over West Indies. John Bracewell, NZ's outgoing coach, believed Fulton has the tools to open, although he had problems there against South Africa early in 2006. He did well in the World Cup, but struggled against England at home in 2008, not reaching double figures in five international innings, then had a quiet tour of England, collecting a duck in his only international outing, a Twenty20 game. With the openers failing in the Tests in England, perhaps it's time for Fulton to show Bracewell whether he was right or not.

THE FACTS Fulton's 301 not out was the fifth-highest maiden century in all first-class cricket: the highest is 337 not out by Pervez Akhtar for Pakistan Railways in 1964-65 ... Fulton also scored 221 not out for Canterbury v Otago in Dunedin in 2004-05, when he shared an unbroken national sixth-wicket record stand of 293 with Neil Broom ... Fulton averages 52 in ODIs against Sri Lanka, but 13.83 v England (and 4.00 v Scotland) ... His uncle, Roddy Fulton, played for Canterbury and Northern Districts in the 1970s ...

THE FIGURES to 12.9.08   www.cricinfo.com

Batting & Fielding	M	Inns	NO	Runs	HS	Avge	S/R	100	50	4s	6s	Ct	St
Tests	7	10	1	236	75	26.22	51.86	0	1	35	5	6	0
ODIs	44	41	5	1239	112	34.41	73.79	1	8	102	17	15	0
T20 Ints	10	10	1	117	25	13.00	98.31	0	0	5	6	3	0
First-class	65	106	11	4275	301*	45.00	–	7	23	–	–	47	0

Bowling	M	Balls	Runs	Wkts	BB	Avge	RpO	S/R	5i	10m
Tests	7	0	–	–	–	–	–	–	–	–
ODIs	44	0	–	–	–	–	–	–	–	–
T20 Ints	10	0	–	–	–	–	–	–	–	–
First-class	65	673	399	11	4-49	36.27	3.55	61.18	0	0

GAUTAM **GAMBHIR**

INDIA

Full name	**Gautam Gambhir**
Born	**October 14, 1981, Delhi**
Teams	**Delhi, Delhi Daredevils**
Style	**Left-hand bat, occasional legspinner**
Test debut	**India v Australia at Mumbai 2004-05**
ODI debut	**India v Bangladesh at Dhaka 2002-03**

THE PROFILE As a 17-year-old stripling in 2000, left-hander Gautam Gambhir's attacking strokeplay set tongues wagging. Compact footwork and high bat-speed befuddled the bowlers, who paid the price for mistaking his slight build and shy demeanour for signs of meekness, as cautious defence was replaced by the aerial route over point. His success took him close to the Test side when Zimbabwe toured early in 2002. He pasted successive double-centuries, for Delhi and for the Board President's XI against the tourists, and seemed to be a certainty for an opening spot – but surprisingly he missed out. Gambhir soldiered on, pressing his case in the Caribbean with India A early in 2003, and joined the one-day squad when several senior players asked to be rested following that year's World Cup. He finally made the Test side late the following year, hitting 96 against South Africa in his second match and 139 against Bangladesh in his fifth. Leaner times followed, punctuated by cheap runs in Zimbabwe, and although he celebrated his one-day return after 30 months on the sidelines with 103 against Sri Lanka in April 2005, he struggled for big scores and found himself on the outer again, missing the following year's tour of the West Indies. After the disasters of the 2007 World Cup Gambhir was tried again, collecting another one-day hundred against Bangladesh, which earned him a trip to England. He sat out the Tests, but made a mark in the one-dayers with 51 at Headingley. He made two centuries in the Australian one-day tri-series early in 2008, and carried his good form into the inaugural IPL season.

THE FACTS Gambhir has scored three first-class double-centuries, the highest 233 not out for Delhi v Railways in November 2002 ... He averages 87.00 in Tests against Bangladesh – but 2.00 v Australia ... Gambhir was the leading Indian runscorer of the inaugural IPL season, with 534 at a strike rate of 140.89 for Delhi Daredevils ... In January 2001 he scored 212 in an Under-19 Test against England (captained by Ian Bell), sharing an opening stand of 391 with Vinayak Mane ...

THE FIGURES *to 12.9.08*   www.cricinfo.com

Batting & Fielding	M	Inns	NO	Runs	HS	Avge	S/R	100	50	4s	6s	Ct	St
Tests	17	29	2	1002	139	37.11	57.58	1	6	138	1	17	0
ODIs	60	60	6	1987	113	36.79	81.73	5	11	231	9	17	0
T20 Ints	9	8	0	299	75	37.37	128.32	0	4	34	6	3	0
First-class	97	162	17	7814	233*	53.88	–		24	33	–	–	63	0

Bowling	M	Balls	Runs	Wkts	BB	Avge	RpO	S/R	5i	10m
Tests	17	0	–	–	–	–	–	–	–	–
ODIs	60	6	13	0	–	–	13.00	–	0	0
T20 Ints	9	0	–	–	–	–	–	–	–	–
First-class	97	385	277	7	3–12	39.57	4.31	55.00	0	0

SOURAV **GANGULY**

Full name	**Sourav Chandidas Ganguly**
Born	**July 8, 1972, Calcutta (now Kolkata), Bengal**
Teams	**Bengal, Kolkata Knight Riders**
Style	**Left-hand bat, right-arm medium-pace bowler**
Test debut	**India v England at Lord's 1996**
ODI debut	**India v West Indies at Brisbane 1991-92**

THE PROFILE Some felt he couldn't play the bouncer, others swore he was divine on the off side; some laughed at his lack of athleticism, others admired his ability to galvanise a side. Sourav Ganguly's ability to polarise opinion has long been an ongoing Indian soap opera. He remains India's most successful captain, and has been among the best one-day batsmen, combining grace with surgical precision in his strokeplay. After he toured Australia at 19 his career stalled before a scintillating debut century at Lord's in 1996: soon he was forming a destructive opening partnership in one-dayers with Sachin Tendulkar. He took over the captaincy in 2000, and quickly proved to be tough and intuitive. India started winning overseas, and began a streak that took them all the way to the 2003 World Cup final. Later that year, Ganguly's incandescent hundred at Brisbane set the tone for an epic series in which India fought the Aussies to a standstill. Victory in Pakistan turned him into a cult figure, but that turned out to be a watershed: things went pear-shaped when his loss of form coincided with some insipid Indian one-day performances. Ganguly was dropped, and looked to be finished – but fought back for another World Cup in 2007, and another England tour, when his 57 at The Oval steadied India's nerves as the series was won. Then he stroked a magnificent career-best 239 against Pakistan at Bangalore, which followed a long-overdue first Test century in front of his adoring Kolkata fans. However, it wasn't long before his place was in question again, after the collective failure of India's big-name batsmen in Sri Lanka in mid-2008.

THE FACTS Ganguly made 131 on his Test debut, at Lord's in 1996, and scored 136 in his next innings, at Nottingham ... He is one of only seven batsmen to score 10,000 runs in ODIs, three of them Indians ... Ganguly averages 59.50 in ODIs against South Africa, but only 22.31 v Australia ... He captained in 49 Tests, winning 21, both Indian records ... Ganguly's record includes three ODIs for the Asia XI ...

THE FIGURES *to 12.9.08*   www.cricinfo.com

Batting & Fielding	M	Inns	NO	Runs	HS	Avge	S/R	100	50	4s	6s	Ct	St
Tests	109	180	15	6888	239	41.74	51.36	15	34	873	55	71	0
ODIs	311	300	23	11363	183	41.02	73.70	22	72	1122	190	100	0
T20 Ints	0	0	–	–	–	–	–	–	–	–	–	–	–
First-class	236	372	41	14520	239	43.86	–	30	83	–	–	165	0

Bowling	M	Balls	Runs	Wkts	BB	Avge	RpO	S/R	5i	10m
Tests	109	3117	1681	32	3–28	52.53	3.23	97.40	0	0
ODIs	311	4561	3849	100	5–16	38.49	5.06	45.61	2	0
T20 Ints	0	0	–	–	–	–	–	–	–	–
First-class	236	10908	6004	164	6–46	36.60	3.30	66.51	4	0

CHRIS **GAYLE**

Full name **Christopher Henry Gayle**
Born **September 21, 1979, Kingston, Jamaica**
Teams **Jamaica, Kolkata Knight Riders**
Style **Right-hand bat, offspinner**
Test debut **West Indies v Zimbabwe at Port-of-Spain 1999-2000**
ODI debut **West Indies v India at Toronto 1999-2000**

THE PROFILE A thrusting left-hander, Chris Gayle earned himself a black mark on his first senior tour – to England in 2000 – when the new boys were felt to be insufficiently respectful of their elders. But a lack of respect, for opposition bowlers at least, has served him well since then. Tall and imposing at the crease, he loves to carve through the covers off either foot, and has the ability to decimate the figures of even the thriftiest of opening bowlers. In a lean era for West Indian cricket in general – and fast bowling in particular – Gayle's pugnacious approach has become an attacking weapon in its own right, in Tests as well as one-dayers. His 79-ball century at Cape Town in January 2004, after South Africa had made 532, was typical of his no-holds-barred approach. Gayle's good run ended when England came calling early in 2004, and he averaged only 26 against a potent pace attack which exposed a lack of positive footwork. But men with little footwork often baffle experts, and after an uncharacteristic century against Bangladesh, he exacted his revenge on England's bowlers with a battering not seen since Lara's 400, before coming within a whisker of emulating Lara himself with 317 against South Africa in Antigua. Gayle also bowls brisk non-turning offspin, which make him a genuine one-day allrounder. In England in 2007 he took over the one-day captaincy after a miserable Test series, and electrified the side with unexpected flair. Gayle – whose initial appointment was vetoed by an out-of-touch board – was suddenly a realistic option as Test captain. He led his side to a stunning Test victory in South Africa late in 2007, although the series was eventually lost.

THE FACTS Gayle's 317 against New Zealand in Antigua in May 2005 has been exceeded for West Indies only by Brian Lara (twice) and Garry Sobers ... Gayle hit the first century in Twenty20 internationals, 117 v South Africa at Johannesburg in September 2007 ... He made 208 for Jamaica v West Indies B in February 2001, sharing an unbroken opening stand of 425 with Leon Garrick ... His record includes three ODIs for the World XI ...

THE FIGURES *to 12.9.08*   www.cricinfo.com

Batting & Fielding	M	Inns	NO	Runs	HS	Avge	S/R	100	50	4s	6s	Ct	St
Tests	73	131	5	4804	317	38.12	57.22	7	29	755	39	75	0
ODIs	186	181	13	6616	153*	39.38	80.81	16	37	798	112	85	0
T20 Ints	5	5	0	193	117	38.60	164.95	1	1	18	11	2	0
First-class	147	264	20	10558	317	43.27	–	23	55	–	–	133	0

Bowling	M	Balls	Runs	Wkts	BB	Avge	RpO	S/R	5i	10m
Tests	73	5741	2537	63	5–34	40.26	2.65	91.12	2	0
ODIs	186	6188	4839	149	5–46	32.47	4.69	41.53	1	0
T20 Ints	5	51	53	2	2–22	26.50	6.23	25.50	0	0
First-class	147	11107	4557	120	5–34	37.97	2.48	91.80	2	0

HERSCHELLE **GIBBS**

Full name **Herschelle Herman Gibbs**
Born **February 23, 1974, Green Point, Cape Town**
Teams **Cape Cobras, Glamorgan, Deccan Chargers**
Style **Right-hand bat, occasional legspinner**
Test debut **South Africa v India at Calcutta 1996-97**
ODI debut **South Africa v Kenya at Nairobi 1996-97**

THE PROFILE Herschelle Gibbs was summoned from the classroom at 16 to make his first-class debut in 1990: his feet moved beautifully at the crease, but struggled to find the ground in real life. Admitting that a Test debut in front of 70,000 at Eden Gardens wasn't as nerve-wracking as his final exams, as well as the fact that he reads little other than magazines and comics, contributed to a reputation for simplicity: his passion for one-liners and verbal jousting hampered his advancement, and his brush with career death in the match-fixing scandal added to the impression of one who had failed to grasp the magnitude of his impact on South Africa's youth. But Gibbs can be a warm and generous person, and at the crease no shot is beyond him, while opening did not temper his desire for explosive entertainment. The speed of his hands is hypnotic, frequently allowing him to hook off the front foot and keep out surprise lifters. His trademark is the lofted extra-cover drive, hit inside-out with the certainty of a square cut. At backward point he is almost the equal of Jonty Rhodes. Gibbs has two double-centuries among his 14 Test tons, and 20 one-day hundreds too – the best of them in March 2006, when his 111-ball 175 powered South Africa past Australia's 434 with a ball to spare in arguably the greatest one-day cracker of them all. He had a subdued 2006-07, not managing an international century and being briefly banned after an injudicious remark was picked up by the stump mikes. He started and finished the World Cup well, but lost his Test place to the steadier Neil McKenzie, although he continues as a one-day force.

THE FACTS Gibbs and Graeme Smith are the only opening pair to share three stands of 300 or more in Tests ... He hit six sixes in an over from Holland's Daan van Bunge during the 2007 World Cup, winning a million dollars for charity ... He averages 56.42 in Tests against New Zealand, but only 23.30 v Sri Lanka ... He has been bowled in 33 (23%) of his Test innings ...

THE FIGURES *to 12.9.08*   www.cricinfo.com

Batting & Fielding	M	Inns	NO	Runs	HS	Avge	S/R	100	50	4s	6s	Ct	St
Tests	90	154	7	6167	228	41.95	50.26	14	26	887	47	94	0
ODIs	232	225	16	7589	175	36.31	83.14	20	35	866	122	100	0
T20 Ints	9	9	1	182	90*	22.75	135.82	0	2	24	6	2	0
First-class	185	319	13	13076	228	42.73	–	31	58	–	–	164	0

Bowling	M	Balls	Runs	Wkts	BB	Avge	RpO	S/R	5i	10m
Tests	90	6	4	0	–	–	4.00	–	0	0
ODIs	232	0	–	–	–	–	–	–	–	–
T20 Ints	9	0	–	–	–	–	–	–	–	–
First-class	185	138	78	3	2–14	26.00	3.39	46.00	0	0

MARK **GILLESPIE**

Full name **Mark Raymond Gillespie**
Born **October 17, 1979, Wanganui**
Teams **Wellington**
Style **Right-hand bat, right-arm fast-medium bowler**
Test debut **New Zealand v South Africa at Centurion 2007-08**
ODI debut **New Zealand v Sri Lanka at Napier 2006-07**

THE PROFILE   With a run-up reminiscent of Bob Willis or even Dennis Lillee – although he lacks the pace of either – Mark Gillespie came to prominence as a specialist one-day "death" bowler for Wellington. He backed that up in first-class cricket with 43 wickets at 23.16 in 2005-06, although that season ended badly when he was struck below the eye, suffering multiple fractures and a smashed eye socket, while batting against Canterbury. Three months later he was back, taking three quick wickets as New Zealand A beat their Australian counterparts at Darwin: he followed that up with 5 for 35 against India A at Cairns. Gillespie was rewarded with a place in the Champions Trophy squad in October 2006, although he did not actually get a game. When he was finally given an opportunity, at home against Sri Lanka, he showed signs that his domestic form could translate to the international arena, his 3 for 39 in a heavy defeat at Auckland being particularly impressive. He followed that with a decent showing in the tri-series in Australia, where he deceived some with his pace but leaked too many runs on occasions. His best moment was probably a stunning tumbling outfield catch to dismiss top-scorer Ed Joyce as England slid to a heavy defeat at Adelaide. He made a bittersweet Test debut against South Africa late in 2007 – sweet because he took five wickets, but bitter because he bagged a pair and New Zealand lost heavily. He added six more wickets in his next Test, against England, including Paul Collingwood (twice) and Kevin Pietersen, but missed out on the Test portion of the England tour that followed, although he was back for the one-dayers.

THE FACTS   Gillespie was only the fifth New Zealander to take five wickets in an innings on Test debut (Tim Southee soon became the sixth) ... Gillespie also took 5 for 58 on his first-class debut, for Wellington v Otago at Alexandra in March 2000 ... The following season he made 81 not out, still his highest score, against the same opponents ... Gillespie has made a century for Tawa, his Wellington club, and is nicknamed the "Tawa Terror" ...

THE FIGURES *to 12.9.08*   www.cricinfo.com

Batting & Fielding	M	Inns	NO	Runs	HS	Avge	S/R	100	50	4s	6s	Ct	St
Tests	2	4	0	9	9	2.25	17.64	0	0	1	0	0	0
ODIs	28	13	7	91	28	15.16	78.44	0	0	8	1	6	0
T20 Ints	11	6	4	21	7	10.50	72.41	0	0	0	0	1	0
First-class	50	65	10	899	81*	16.34	–	0	3	–	–	8	0

Bowling	M	Balls	Runs	Wkts	BB	Avge	RpO	S/R	5i	10m
Tests	2	390	278	11	5–136	25.27	4.27	35.45	1	0
ODIs	28	1338	1220	31	3–27	39.35	5.47	43.16	0	0
T20 Ints	11	210	225	10	4–7	25.50	7.28	21.00	0	0
First-class	50	9373	4944	204	6–42	24.23	3.16	45.94	10	0

MANPREET **GONY**

Full name	**Manpreet Singh Gony**
Born	**January 4, 1984, Roopnagar, Punjab**
Teams	**Punjab, Chennai Super Kings**
Style	**Right-hand bat, right-arm fast-medium bowler**
Test debut	**No Tests yet**
ODI debut	**India v Hong Kong at Karachi 2008**

INDIA

THE PROFILE Manpreet Gony, a tall, well-built seamer, was almost unknown in India before he made a splash for the Chennai Super Kings in the inaugural Indian Premier League tournament early in 2008. Gony only made his first-class debut for Punjab in November 2007, his selection helped by defections to the breakaway Indian Cricket League, but he hardly set the world alight during his five matches in the Ranji Trophy – 13 wickets at 47, with a best of 3 for 86 against Hyderabad. He made more of a mark in limited-overs cricket, taking four wickets for North Zone in successive matches in the Deodhar Trophy. It was his one-day form that caught the eye of the IPL's chequebook-wavers, and he was an important cog in the later stages as MS Dhoni's Chennai side reached the final. Gony took 2 for 11 in his four overs against Bangalore, dismissing Jacques Kallis early on, but his most important spell came in the semi-final against Kings XI Punjab, when he ripped out the danger men Kumar Sangakkara and Yuvraj Singh for single-figure scores, and then bowled a maiden to Irfan Pathan. He finished with 2 for 14 as Chennai surged to the final, where they lost to Shane Warne's Rajasthan Royals, who won even though Gony again grabbed an early wicket. All this attracted the attention of the national selectors, and Gony was tried in the Asia Cup, where he took two wickets in a comfortable victory over Bangladesh. But it wasn't all good news for Gony during 2008: sadly, his infant son died 15 days after he was born.

THE FACTS Manpreet Gony took 17 wickets in the inaugural IPL season of 2007-08 – the only bowlers to take more were Sohail Tanvir (22), Sreesanth and Shane Warne (both 19) ... Gony's wickets included Rahul Dravid, Herschelle Gibbs, Adam Gilchrist, Sanath Jayasuriya, Jacques Kallis, Kumar Sangakkara, Virender Sehwag and Yuvraj Singh ... Both his ODI wickets were caught in the outfield by Pragyan Ojha ...

THE FIGURES to 12.9.08   www.cricinfo.com

Batting & Fielding	M	Inns	NO	Runs	HS	Avge	S/R	100	50	4s	6s	Ct	St
Tests	0	0	–	–	–	–	–	–	–	–	–	–	–
ODIs	2	0	–	–	–	–	–	–	–	–	–	0	0
T20 Ints	0	0	–	–	–	–	–	–	–	–	–	–	–
First-class	5	7	1	122	48	20.33	55.96	0	0	19	3	0	0

Bowling	M	Balls	Runs	Wkts	BB	Avge	RpO	S/R	5i	10m
Tests	0	0	–	–	–	–	–	–	–	–
ODIs	2	78	76	2	2–65	38.00	5.84	39.00	0	0
T20 Ints	0	0	–	–	–	–	–	–	–	–
First-class	5	1056	618	13	3–86	47.53	3.51	81.23	0	0

HABIBUL BASHAR

Full name	**Qazi Habibul Bashar**
Born	**August 17, 1972, Nagakanda, Kushtia**
Teams	**Khulna**
Style	**Right-hand bat, occasional offspinner**
Test debut	**Bangladesh v India at Dhaka 2000-01**
ODI debut	**Bangladesh v Sri Lanka at Sharjah 1994-95**

THE PROFILE Impish and impulsive, Habibul Bashar has the style and strokes of a genuine Test player. Most of his runs come from cultured drives through midwicket, and most of his dismissals from a fatal addiction to the hook. Before Bangladesh's inaugural Test, "Sumon" promised he would kick the habit, but although he made 71 and 30 he was still out hooking ... twice. After that he carried his country's flimsy middle-order hopes, and inherited the captaincy from Khaled Mahmud in January 2004. After a shaky start in Zimbabwe, he came into his own with a century in St Lucia, as Bangladesh took a first-innings lead in their first Test in the Caribbean. He missed the 2004 Champions Trophy in England with an injured thumb – overall he has underperformed in ODIs for such an attacking player – but returned to captain in England in 2005 when, lo and behold, the hook habit cut him down twice at Lord's. But he restored pride with a hard-hitting 61 to conclude a disappointing series. Habibul's greatest moment as captain came a few weeks later at Cardiff, with a convincing five-wicket win over Australia in the one-day series. The strain of leading a side which kept collapsing started to show, and he hasn't managed a Test century since that one in St Lucia in May 2004. He resigned the one-day captaincy after the 2007 World Cup, and was relieved of the Test job too. Shortly after reaching 3000 runs in his 50th Test early in 2008, he was dropped for the first time, but promised he'd be back: "I am not finished yet. I have had a difficult period over the last year. I have a lot of cricket left in me and I will fight to get my place back in the national team."

THE FACTS Habibul Bashar passed 2000 Test runs for Bangladesh before anyone else had reached 1000: he reached 3000 early in 2008 ... He scored 94 and 55 in their first Test victory, v Zimbabwe at Chittagong in January 2005 ... Habibul only missed two of his country's first 52 Tests, when he had a broken thumb ... He averages 50.36 against Pakistan in Tests, but 20.00 v New Zealand ... Habibul made 224 for Biman Bangladesh v Khulna at Jessore in 2000-01 ....

THE FIGURES *to 12.9.08*   www.cricinfo.com

Batting & Fielding	M	Inns	NO	Runs	HS	Avge	S/R	100	50	4s	6s	Ct	St
Tests	50	99	1	3026	113	30.87	60.27	3	24	401	4	22	0
ODIs	111	105	5	2168	78	21.68	60.45	0	14	–	10	26	0
T20 Ints	0	0	–	–	–	–	–	–	–	–	–	–	–
First-class	87	163	5	5175	224	32.75	–	6	37	–	–	39	0

Bowling	M	Balls	Runs	Wkts	BB	Avge	RpO	S/R	5i	10m
Tests	50	282	217	0	–	–	4.61	–	0	0
ODIs	111	175	142	1	1–31	142.00	4.86	175.00	0	0
T20 Ints	0	0	–	–	–	–	–	–	–	–
First-class	87	814	527	8	2–28	65.87	3.88	101.75	0	0

BRAD **HADDIN**

Full name	**Bradley James Haddin**
Born	**October 23, 1977, Cowra, New South Wales**
Teams	**New South Wales**
Style	**Right-hand bat, wicketkeeper**
Test debut	**Australia v West Indies at Kingston 2007-08**
ODI debut	**Australia v Zimbabwe at Hobart 2000-01**

THE PROFILE For years Brad Haddin held the most nerve-fraying position in Australian cricket – the wicketkeeper-in-waiting, entrusted with warming the seat whenever Adam Gilchrist needed a rest. And now, following Gilchrist's retirement, Haddin is up there to be shot at. He became Australia's 400th Test cricketer in the West Indies early in 2008, and did well enough, playing through the series despite breaking a finger in the first Test, which might explain his comparative (next to Gilchrist) lack of runs. But the injury let in WA's Luke Ronchi for the one-dayers, and at 31 Haddin still faces a battle. The pressures have rarely hindered his batting, and his keeping to a New South Wales attack swinging from Brett Lee to Stuart MacGill has remained sharp. In 2004-05 he scored 916 runs at 57.25, leading the Blues to a one-wicket Pura Cup victory over Queensland, and also posted an impressive limited-overs century for Australia A against Pakistan. Haddin passed 600 runs in each of the following seasons, and although his output dipped to 489 in 2007-08, that still included three centuries. He also played a few ODIs when Gilchrist was rested, and shadowed him on the 2005 Ashes tour and in the 2007 World Cup. A former Australia Under-19 captain who grew up in Gundagai, Haddin began his senior domestic career in 1997-98 with the Australian Capital Territory in their debut Mercantile Mutual Cup season: two years later he was playing for NSW.

THE FACTS Haddin took up a novel batting position behind the stumps when facing a Shoaib Akhtar "free ball" (after a no-ball) in a Twenty20 game for Australia A early in 2005: he reasoned that he had more time to sight the ball, and if it hit the stumps it would confuse the fielders (it did hit the stumps, and he managed a bye) ... Haddin was the unwitting "villain" of the 2005 Ashes Test at Edgbaston: he was the man who threw a ball to Glenn McGrath, who badly sprained his ankle in catching it and missed the match, which England eventually won by just two runs ... Haddin scored 154 for NSW v Victoria in Nov 2004 ...

THE FIGURES to 12.9.08   www.cricinfo.com

Batting & Fielding	M	Inns	NO	Runs	HS	Avge	S/R	100	50	4s	6s	Ct	St
Tests	3	6	1	151	45*	30.20	46.17	0	0	21	1	16	0
ODIs	33	29	2	774	87*	28.66	78.57	0	4	63	21	37	4
T20 Ints	4	3	2	16	6	16.00	66.66	0	0	0	0	2	0
First-class	93	154	17	5637	154	41.14	–	10	32	–	–	279	25

Bowling	M	Balls	Runs	Wkts	BB	Avge	RpO	S/R	5i	10m
Tests	3	0	–	–	–	–	–	–	–	–
ODIs	33	0	–	–	–	–	–	–	–	–
T20 Ints	4	0	–	–	–	–	–	–	–	–
First-class	93	0	–	–	–	–	–	–	–	–

HARBHAJAN SINGH

Full name **Harbhajan Singh**
Born **July 3, 1980, Jullundur, Punjab**
Teams **Punjab, Surrey**
Style **Right-hand bat, offspinner**
Test debut **India v Australia at Bangalore 1997-98**
ODI debut **India v New Zealand at Sharjah 1997-98**

THE PROFILE Harbhajan Singh represents the spirit of the new Indian cricketer. His arrogance and cockiness translate into self-belief and passion on the field, and he has the talent to match. An offspinner with a windmilling, whiplash action, remodelled after he was reported for throwing, he exercises great command over the ball, has the ability to vary his length and pace, and can turn it the other way too. His main wicket-taking ball, however, is the one that climbs wickedly on the unsuspecting batsman from a good length, forcing him to alter his stroke at the last second. In March 2001, it proved too much for the all-conquering Australians, as Harbhajan collected 32 wickets while none of his team-mates managed more than three. He has since been bothered by injury, while in Pakistan early in 2006 he finished with 0 for 355 in two Tests before bouncing back with five-fors in St Kitts and Jamaica (5 for 13 in only 4.3 overs). He had 50 Test caps and more than 200 wickets before he turned 26, and although a slump in 2006-07 cost him his place he was not out of favour for long. Harbhajan's rivalry with the Aussies boiled over in Sydney in January 2008 when he was charged with racially abusing Andrew Symonds. He was given a three-Test ban but the charge was reduced, on appeal, to abuse and insult not amounting to racism. Then in April Harbhajan was involved in another controversy when video evidence showed him slapping his Indian team-mate Sreesanth without any provocation after an IPL game, which cost him an 11-match ban.

THE FACTS Harbhajan's match figures of 15 for 217 against Australia at Chennai in 2000-01 have been bettered for India only by Narendra Hirwani (16 for 136 in 1987-88, also at Chennai) ... Harbhajan took 32 wickets at 17.03 in that three-match series: his haul at Kolkata included India's first-ever Test hat-trick, when he dismissed Ricky Ponting, Adam Gilchrist and Shane Warne ... He has taken 45 wickets at 21.93 in Tests against West Indies, but 25 at 52.04 against Pakistan ... His record includes two ODIs for the Asia XI ...

THE FIGURES to 12.9.08   www.cricinfo.com

Batting & Fielding	M	Inns	NO	Runs	HS	Avge	S/R	100	50	4s	6s	Ct	St
Tests	69	97	18	1209	66	15.30	65.06	0	4	168	16	37	0
ODIs	175	95	26	903	46	13.08	80.33	0	0	75	21	48	0
T20 Ints	10	3	0	9	7	3.00	69.23	0	0	1	0	3	0
First-class	132	176	34	2591	84	18.24	–	0	8	–	–	70	0

Bowling	M	Balls	Runs	Wkts	BB	Avge	RpO	S/R	5i	10m
Tests	69	18952	8985	291	8–84	30.87	2.84	65.12	22	5
ODIs	175	9264	6448	195	5–31	33.06	4.17	47.50	2	0
T20 Ints	10	192	228	9	2–24	25.33	7.12	21.33	0	0
First-class	132	32724	15443	562	8–84	27.47	2.83	58.22	36	7

STEVE **HARMISON**

Full name **Stephen James Harmison**
Born **October 23, 1978, Ashington, Northumberland**
Teams **Durham**
Style **Right-hand bat, right-arm fast bowler**
Test debut **England v India at Nottingham 2002**
ODI debut **England v Sri Lanka at Brisbane 2002-03**

4THE PROFILE With his lofty, loose-limbed action and his painful knack of jamming fingers against bat-handles, Steve Harmison had long been likened, tongue-in-cheek, to the great Curtly Ambrose, when suddenly he loped in and produced a spell that Ambrose himself could hardly have bettered. West Indies were humbled for 47 at Kingston in March 2004, and Harmison took a remarkable 7 for 12. He was initially held back by niggling injuries (including somehow dislocating his shoulder after catching his hand in his trouser pocket while bowling) and a tendency to homesickness on overseas tours, and mixed magical spells with moments when the radar went on the blink. But in the Caribbean he seemed finally to come of age. A dip followed in South Africa, but after a cathartic five-wicket haul against Bangladesh at home in Durham, he tore into Australia's top order at Lord's on the first morning of the 2005 Ashes series. He couldn't secure victory then, but popped up to seal the thrilling two-run win at Edgbaston. A year later he demolished Pakistan with 6 for 19, but the much-hyped 2006-07 Ashes rematch was the pits, kicked off by Harmison's mega-wide with the first ball of the series. He often looked fed up, retired from one-day cricket, and then picked up a hernia during a hit-and-miss series against West Indies. He lost his Test place after a lacklustre performance in New Zealand early in 2008, but plenty of bowling for Durham relocated the magic, and he returned for the Oval Test against South Africa. He seemed to enjoy Kevin Pietersen's captaincy so much that he returned to the one-day side too.

THE FACTS Harmison's 7 for 12 in March 2004, as West Indies were shot out for 47, are the best figures in Tests at Kingston ... Harmison took 67 Test wickets in 2004, a record for an England bowler at the time (Andrew Flintoff beat it by one in 2005) ... His brother Ben also plays for Durham: they were born in Ashington, the same Northumberland village as football's Charlton brothers ... His record includes one Test for the World XI ...

THE FIGURES *to 12.9.08*   www.cricinfo.com

Batting & Fielding	M	Inns	NO	Runs	HS	Avge	S/R	100	50	4s	6s	Ct	St
Tests	58	78	20	691	49*	11.91	59.36	0	0	190	9	7	0
ODIs	51	22	13	67	13*	7.44	57.75	0	0	2	0	8	0
T20 Ints	2	0	–	–	–	–	–	–	–	–	–	1	0
First-class	166	224	62	1656	49*	10.22	–	0	0	–	–	25	0

Bowling	M	Balls	Runs	Wkts	BB	Avge	RpO	S/R	5i	10m
Tests	58	12663	6788	216	7–12	31.42	3.21	58.62	8	1
ODIs	51	2587	2167	72	5–33	30.09	5.02	35.93	1	0
T20 Ints	2	39	42	1	1–13	42.00	6.46	39.00	0	0
First-class	166	32402	16977	597	7–12	28.43	3.14	54.27	22	1

PAUL **HARRIS**

Full name	**Paul Lee Harris**
Born	**Nov 2, 1978, Salisbury (now Harare), Zimbabwe**
Teams	**Titans**
Style	**Right-hand bat, slow left-arm orthodox spinner**
Test debut	**South Africa v India at Cape Town 2006-07**
ODI debut	**South Africa v Bangladesh at Chittagong 2007-08**

THE PROFILE   Slow left-armer Paul Harris is the latest man tasked with curing South African cricket's chief ailment – their continued failure to develop matchwinning spinners for the national team. Tall and not unlike the former England bowler Phil Tufnell in appearance and style, Harris eventually made it into the squad for the 2006-07 series against India, making his debut in the New Year Test at Cape Town, and took four wickets in the first innings, including Sachin Tendulkar and Virender Sehwag. He added the scalp of Rahul Dravid in the second innings: his nagging over-the-wicket line kept the Indians quiet, and helped his side reclaim the initiative. Until then the selectors had ignored Harris, even though he led the the 2005-06 SuperSport Series wicket-takers with 49, and it seemed possible that he might be lost to South African cricket altogether after a successful stint for Warwickshire in 2006 as a Kolpak player. But then Nicky Boje retired, finally disenchanted with his country's treatment of spinners, and the call went out to Harris – a departure from South Africa's usual policy of choosing slow bowlers who can also contribute in the field and with the bat (although he can be a useful blocker). Harris was born in Zimbabwe but grew up in Cape Town, where his rise was originally blocked by Paul Adams and Claude Henderson. More of a roller than a big spinner, he is accurate and can get surprising bounce, from an unprepossessing approach described by one local journalist as "shuffling up like a right-hand bowler trying to bowl left-arm for a laugh".

THE FACTS   Harris took 8 for 58 for Western Province B v Northerns B in the final of the UCB Bowl at Cape Town in December 2002 ... He took 5 for 73 against Pakistan at Karachi in October 2007 ... For Warwickshire v Durham at Chester-le-Street in July 2007 Harris reached his maiden fifty in 34 balls, scoring 45 of his first 51 runs off Mark Davies, with five sixes ... He took 6 for 54 for Titans v Cape Cobras at Benoni in March 2006 ...

THE FIGURES *to 12.9.08*   www.cricinfo.com

Batting & Fielding	M	Inns	NO	Runs	HS	Avge	S/R	100	50	4s	6s	Ct	St
Tests	17	24	4	212	46	10.60	30.63	0	0	22	1	9	0
ODIs	3	0	–	–	–	–	–	–	–	–	–	2	0
T20 Ints	0	0	–	–	–	–	–	–	–	–	–	–	–
First-class	77	94	15	1123	55	14.21	–	0	2	–	–	31	0

Bowling	M	Balls	Runs	Wkts	BB	Avge	RpO	S/R	5i	10m
Tests	17	3378	1507	46	5–73	32.76	2.67	73.43	1	0
ODIs	3	180	83	3	2–30	27.66	2.76	60.00	0	0
T20 Ints	0	0	–	–	–	–	–	–	–	–
First-class	77	16775	7609	252	6–54	30.19	2.72	66.56	12	0

MATTHEW **HAYDEN**

Full name **Matthew Lawrence Hayden**
Born **October 29, 1971, Kingaroy, Queensland**
Teams **Queensland, Chennai Super Kings**
Style **Left-hand bat, occasional right-arm medium-pacer**
Test debut **Australia v South Africa at Johannesburg 1993-94**
ODI debut **Australia v England at Manchester 1993**

THE PROFILE Strength is Matthew Hayden's strength –
both mental and physical. It enabled him to shrug off carping
that he was too limited for Test cricket because of the way he
plays around his front pad. Before his maiden first-class innings,
he asked if anyone had made 200 on debut, then went out and smacked 149. The runs have
rarely abated since. Tall and powerful, he batters the ball at and through the off side. He
has also made himself a fine catcher in the cordon. In 2000-01 he slog-swept his way to
549 runs in India, an Australian record for a three-Test series, and by the end of 2001 had
formed a prolific opening partnership with Justin Langer. Late in 2003 he hammered 380
against Zimbabwe, briefly borrowing the Test record from Brian Lara. A lack of form and
footwork restricted him in 2005, but a disastrous Ashes series was salvaged with 138 at The
Oval. It was the awkward beginning of a resurgence that saved his career. Usually playing
more patiently, he collected hundreds in the next three Tests. He remained determined to
win back his one-day place, too: after 18 months out he roared back in 2006-07, and
finished the World Cup as the leading runscorer, with 659 at more than a run a ball. He
later revealed he was carrying a fractured toe and a broken bone in his other foot. An
Achilles injury sent him home early from Australia's tour of the West Indies in 2008, but
he pooh-poohed retirement talk, saying "I'll be back bigger and better than ever" ... bad
news for bowlers everywhere.

THE FACTS Hayden held the record for the highest Test innings for six months, hitting
380 against Zimbabwe at Perth in October 2003: Brian Lara reclaimed the record with 400
not out, but Hayden's remains the highest in a Test in Australia ... He has scored 21 of his
30 Test centuries in Australia, where his overall average is 62.48 ... Hayden's 181 not out v
New Zealand at Hamilton in 2006-07 is Australia's highest score in ODIs (and the highest
for the losing side in an ODI) ... His record includes one ODI for the World XI ...

THE FIGURES to 12.9.08   www.cricinfo.com

Batting & Fielding	M	Inns	NO	Runs	HS	Avge	S/R	100	50	4s	6s	Ct	St
Tests	94	167	13	8242	380	53.51	60.12	30	27	990	80	121	0
ODIs	161	155	15	6133	181*	43.80	78.96	10	36	636	87	68	0
T20 Ints	9	9	3	308	73*	51.33	143.92	0	4	37	13	1	0
First-class	285	496	46	24186	380	53.74	–	79	98	–	–	289	0

Bowling	M	Balls	Runs	Wkts	BB	Avge	RpO	S/R	5i	10m
Tests	94	54	40	0	–	–	4.44	–	0	0
ODIs	161	6	18	0	–	–	18.00	–	0	0
T20 Ints	9	0	–	–	–	–	–	–	–	–
First-class	285	1097	671	17	3–10	39.47	3.67	64.52	0	0

BEN **HILFENHAUS**

Full name	**Benjamin William Hilfenhaus**
Born	**March 15, 1983, Ulverstone, Tasmania**
Teams	**Tasmania**
Style	**Right-hand bat, right-arm fast-medium bowler**
Test debut	**No Tests yet**
ODI debut	**Australia v New Zealand at Hobart 2006-07**

THE PROFILE A few years ago Ben Hilfenhaus was working on a building site, but now he can safely lay down his trowel after a series of dramatic performances in his first two seasons catapulted him to a national contract. He established himself quickly in 2005-06 – Man of the Match against Victoria in only his second game, ten wickets against NSW, then called up for Australia A after 39 wickets at 30.82 in his first season. "It has been a fast ride," he admitted after picking up the Bradman Young Cricketer of the Year prize in February 2007. A month earlier he played a Twenty20 international and then his first ODI, on his home ground at Hobart, trapping Brendon McCullum in front in his second over. Now he waits for another chance in the wake of Glenn McGrath's retirement. Strong and fit, Hilfenhaus is only the second quick bowler from Tasmania to play for Australia, after Ricky Ponting's uncle Greg Campbell. Shaping the ball away is his speciality, but he can also angle it in: his repertoire was crucial to the Tigers' maiden Pura Cup victory in 2006-07. Hilfenhaus took 60 wickets at 25.38, the third-most in the competition's history, but he and the selectors will have to watch a back-breaking workload – in 2006-07 he delivered 509.1 first-class overs, nearly 200 more than any of his domestic fast-bowling counterparts. This may have come home to roost in 2007-08 when, after a disappointing summer (28 wickets at 43.82), Hilfenhaus went down with a stress fracture of the back that forced him to withdraw for the side selected to go to the West Indies.

THE FACTS Hilfenhaus made his debut for Australia in a Twenty20 international against England at Sydney in January 2007, taking 2 for 16 in his four overs: he had "Hilfy" on his back, as the Aussies had their nicknames on their shirts ... He took 7 for 58 (and 10 for 87 in the match) for Tasmania against New South Wales at Hobart in March 2006 ... Hilfenhaus was named Australia's Bradman Young Cricketer of the Year for 2006-07 by a landslide, polling 97 votes to 11 for the next man (Cullen Bailey) ...

THE FIGURES to 12.9.08   www.cricinfo.com

Batting & Fielding	M	Inns	NO	Runs	HS	Avge	S/R	100	50	4s	6s	Ct	St
Tests	0	0	–	–	–	–	–	–	–	–	–	–	–
ODIs	1	0	–	–	–	–	–	–	–	–	–	1	0
T20 Ints	2	0	–	–	–	–	–	–	–	–	–	0	0
First-class	30	40	15	208	34	8.32	–	0	0	–	–	8	0

Bowling	M	Balls	Runs	Wkts	BB	Avge	RpO	S/R	5i	10m
Tests	0	0	–	–	–	–	–	–	–	–
ODIs	1	42	26	1	1–26	26.00	3.71	42.00	0	0
T20 Ints	2	48	44	3	2–16	14.66	5.50	16.00	0	0
First-class	30	7340	3952	127	7–58	31.11	3.23	57.79	4	1

BRAD **HODGE**

AUSTRALIA

Full name	**Bradley John Hodge**
Born	**December 29, 1974, Sandringham, Victoria**
Teams	**Victoria, Kolkata Knight Riders**
Style	**Right-hand bat, occasional offspinner**
Test debut	**Australia v West Indies at Hobart 2005-06**
ODI debut	**Australia v New Zealand at Auckland 2005-06**

THE PROFILE Brad Hodge is still pushing hard to avoid becoming an Australian cricket nearly man. When he was dropped only five matches into his Test career despite an average of 58.42 it would have been easy for him to disappear into the first-class ranks he has dominated for most of his career. But "don't worry, I'll be back," was his response. He was right, even if it took more than two years. In 2006-07 he smashed 765 Pura Cup runs at 85.00 and made the one-day side when Ricky Ponting rested. He was stranded on 99 when he hit the winning runs at Melbourne and was then one hefty shot short after an unbeaten 97 a fortnight later, also against New Zealand. This earned him a World Cup spot: he made 123 off 89 balls against Holland, but watched the final from the dressing-room, an all-too-familiar viewing platform. Hodge had been picked for his first Test against South Africa in November 2005 after being the reserve batsman on tours to India, New Zealand and England. He started with a fluent 60 and added a sumptuous 203 at Perth. But two Tests later he was dropped, amid whispers of a technical flaw against fast bowling, not helped by a brief drought in the Pura Cup. Hodge picked himself up with a century in the Pura final, and signed for Lancashire, his third English county. He was summoned to the West Indies early in 2008 when Michael Clarke was a late arrival. Expected to stay just a week, Hodge – a smallish right-hander with a classical technique and the ability to direct shots to all parts of the ground – won a Test recall when Matthew Hayden was injured.

THE FACTS Hodge was the fifth Australian to turn his maiden Test century into a double, following Bob Simpson, Sid Barnes, Syd Gregory and Hodge's boyhood idol Dean Jones: Jason Gillespie later joined their ranks ... In 2003 Hodge made 302 not out against Nottinghamshire, the highest score in Leicestershire's history at the time; the following year he was the Man of the Match as Leicestershire won the Twenty20 Cup final ...

THE FIGURES *to 12.9.08*   www.cricinfo.com

Batting & Fielding	M	Inns	NO	Runs	HS	Avge	S/R	100	50	4s	6s	Ct	St
Tests	6	11	2	503	203*	55.88	52.12	1	2	60	1	9	0
ODIs	25	21	2	535	123	30.26	87.51	1	3	51	12	16	0
T20 Ints	8	5	2	94	36	31.33	122.07	0	0	5	3	3	0
First-class	211	370	37	16005	302*	48.06	–	48	59	–	–	123	0

Bowling	M	Balls	Runs	Wkts	BB	Avge	RpO	S/R	5i	10m
Tests	6	12	8	0	–	–	4.00	–	0	0
ODIs	25	66	51	1	1–17	51.00	4.63	66.00	0	0
T20 Ints	8	12	20	0	–	–	10.00	–	0	0
First-class	211	5175	2881	72	4–17	40.01	3.34	71.87	0	0

MATTHEW **HOGGARD**

Full name	**Matthew James Hoggard**
Born	**December 31, 1976, Leeds, Yorkshire**
Teams	**Yorkshire**
Style	**Right-hand bat, right-arm fast-medium bowler**
Test debut	**England v West Indies at Lord's 2000**
ODI debut	**England v Zimbabwe at Harare 2001-02**

THE PROFILE Big and bustling, with the sort of energy coaches kill for, Matthew Hoggard shapes the ball away and is surprisingly slippery off the pitch, although he can look innocuous when the ball refuses to move. Hoggard was one of Yorkshire's bright young things in the late '90s, but it was under Duncan Fletcher and Nasser Hussain that he grew into a senior bowler in the England quartet that swept all before them in 2004. He had taken 7 for 63 at Christchurch in 2001-02, but suffered next winter where his arcing inswing was meat and drink to Australia's left-handers, especially Matthew Hayden. To his credit, Hoggard returned with a snappier run-up to contribute to the fifth-Test win at Sydney. Flashier colleagues still stole the limelight, but Hoggy's moments in the sun were worth waiting for: a hat-trick in Barbados in April 2004, then 12 wickets at Johannesburg the following winter, setting up a series-clinching 2–1 lead. In 2005 he did well as the Ashes were recaptured: satisfyingly, he nailed his old nemesis Hayden three times, including a first-baller at Edgbaston. Unlike some, he never flagged when the Aussies hit back, hard, in 2006-07: the perspiring Hoggard claimed 7 for 109 at Adelaide before the body finally protested; he missed the Sydney finale after playing in England's previous 40 Tests. Back trouble restricted him in 2007, and he slid out of the side after a disappointing performance in New Zealand early in 2008. Then, amid whispers that he had lost a yard of pace, Hoggard was pointedly ignored when England needed a swing bowler for the Headingley Test: the unknown Nottinghamshire paceman Darren Pattinson was chosen instead.

THE FACTS At Bridgetown in March 2004 Hoggard became the third Englishman to take a Test hat-trick against West Indies, following Peter Loader (1957) and Dominic Cork (1995) ... Hoggard took 7 for 61 against South Africa at Johannesburg in 2003-04, and 12 for 205 in the match ... 91 (36.7%) of his Test wickets have been left-handers ... Hoggard took 5 for 49 in an ODI against Zimbabwe at Harare in October 2001 ...

THE FIGURES to 12.9.08   www.cricinfo.com

Batting & Fielding	M	Inns	NO	Runs	HS	Avge	S/R	100	50	4s	6s	Ct	St
Tests	67	92	27	473	38	7.27	22.63	0	0	42	0	24	0
ODIs	26	6	2	17	7	4.25	56.66	0	0	0	0	5	0
T20 Ints	0	0	–	–	–	–	–	–	–	–	–	–	–
First-class	177	227	66	1415	89*	8.78	–	0	3	–	–	49	0

Bowling	M	Balls	Runs	Wkts	BB	Avge	RpO	S/R	5i	10m
Tests	67	13909	7564	248	7–61	30.50	3.26	56.08	7	1
ODIs	26	1306	1152	32	5–49	36.00	5.29	40.81	1	0
T20 Ints	0	0	–	–	–	–	–	–	–	–
First-class	177	32392	16656	616	7–49	27.03	3.08	52.58	20	1

JAMES **HOPES**

AUSTRALIA

Full name **James Redfern Hopes**
Born **October 24, 1978, Townsville, Queensland**
Teams **Queensland, Kings XI Punjab**
Style **Right-hand bat, right-arm medium-pacer**
Test debut **No Tests yet**
ODI debut **Australia v New Zealand at Wellington 2004-05**

THE PROFILE James Hopes was earmarked for higher honours in Australia's youth teams, but took a few years to settle once he made it to the first-class scene. A brisk medium-pacer whose aggressive, exciting batting has been shuffled around the Queensland order, Hopes has scored three Pura Cup centuries (and two for Australia A), and in 2004-05 his average was in the mid-forties. Bowling was his main weapon in 2005-06 – he had 16 wickets in the Pura Cup and 15 more in the one-day competition – but he was unable to transfer his regular success into the international arena. In nine ODI appearances, he did not manage more than one wicket in a match, although his batting showed some promise, with a top score of 43 against Sri Lanka. He was dropped at the end of the VB Series, but when Shane Watson suffered a calf problem in Bangladesh he was replaced by his Queensland team-mate. Despite that, Hopes was briefly cut from the national-contract list and returned to the domestic fray, although he was put on standby when Watson suffered another injury scare during the 2007 World Cup. A regular sweater in the gym, Hopes would love to be a professional golfer, but instead drives powerfully through the covers. He remained a one-day regular in 2007-08, without doing anything outstanding. Evenly balanced as an allrounder – both disciplines still need polish if he is to survive in the international game – his bowling has variety, and tight final overs have regularly picked up wickets and saved runs.

THE FACTS Hopes made his highest score of 146 when opening (with Michael Hussey) for Australia A against Pakistan A at Rawalpindi in September 2005 ... He scored 105 (against West Indies), 51 (v India) and 71 (v Pakistan) in successive innings during the 1997-98 Youth World Cup in South Africa ... Hopes took 6 for 70, his only first-class five-for, for Queensland against Tasmania at Hobart in March 2006 ... Only Michael Kasprowicz (117) has taken more one-day wickets for Queensland than Hopes, who has 110 since his debut in January 2001 ...

THE FIGURES *to 12.9.08*   www.cricinfo.com

Batting & Fielding	M	Inns	NO	Runs	HS	Avge	S/R	100	50	4s	6s	Ct	St
Tests	0	0	–	–	–	–	–	–	–	–	–	–	–
ODIs	36	24	2	499	63	22.68	93.09	0	1	43	1	11	0
T20 Ints	4	1	0	17	17	17.00	85.00	0	0	2	0	1	0
First-class	49	82	1	2648	146	32.69	–	5	13	–	–	22	0

Bowling	M	Balls	Runs	Wkts	BB	Avge	RpO	S/R	5i	10m
Tests	0	0	–	–	–	–	–	–	–	–
ODIs	36	1259	884	27	3–30	32.74	4.21	46.62	0	0
T20 Ints	4	72	73	4	2–26	18.25	6.08	18.00	0	0
First-class	49	6546	3081	85	6–70	36.24	2.82	77.01	1	0

GARETH **HOPKINS**

Full name	**Gareth James Hopkins**
Born	**November 24, 1976, Lower Hutt, Wellington**
Teams	**Auckland**
Style	**Right-hand bat, wicketkeeper**
Test debut	**New Zealand v England at Nottingham 2008**
ODI debut	**New Zealand v England at Chester-le-Street 2004**

THE PROFILE Gareth Hopkins started as a specialist wicketkeeper, but over time his uncompromising batting improved to the point where he was called up for the one-day series in England in 2004 after Brendon McCullum went home to be with his pregnant wife. Hopkins didn't get much chance with the bat – in fact he was run out without facing the only time he made it out to the middle – but performed well enough behind the stumps. McCullum's continued excellence with bat and gloves has meant few chances since then, but Hopkins hung in there, and scored 514 runs at 85.66 for Otago during 2006-07, with three hundreds, which earned him a central contract for 2007-08. McCullum has loomed like an unwanted wedding guest almost throughout Hopkins's career: he was playing for Canterbury when McCullum moved to Christchurch from Otago, which persuaded Hopkins to make the reverse move. Then McCullum decided to return to Otago, so Hopkins upped sticks again and moved to Auckland, where his wife works, even though the Otago think-tank promised that he would still be their preferred keeper. He has also turned out for Northern Districts, and played and coached in Holland. Hopkins was selected for the England tour of 2008, and finally got a Test chance when McCullum felt a twinge in his back and couldn't keep wicket in the third Test at Trent Bridge. In a generally disappointing match for New Zealand, Hopkins batted as soundly as anyone, and kept wicket well.

THE FACTS Hopkins was run out in international cricket before he'd actually faced a ball, against West Indies at Lord's in 2004 ... He scored 113 and 175 not out (still his highest score) for Canterbury against Auckland in February 2003 ... Hopkins has twice made ten dismissals in a match, equalling the New Zealand record – in an unofficial Test against Sri Lanka A at Kandy in October 2005 (including seven in an innings, which also equalled the NZ record), and for Otago against Canterbury at Dunedin in January 2005 ...

THE FIGURES to 12.9.08   www.cricinfo.com

Batting & Fielding	M	Inns	NO	Runs	HS	Avge	S/R	100	50	4s	6s	Ct	St
Tests	1	2	0	27	15	13.50	23.27	0	0	3	0	3	0
ODIs	12	5	0	41	25	8.20	56.94	0	0	3	0	16	0
T20 Ints	1	1	0	6	6	6.00	60.00	0	0	0	0	0	0
First-class	102	162	24	4319	175*	31.29	–	7	19	–	–	267	18

Bowling	M	Balls	Runs	Wkts	BB	Avge	RpO	S/R	5i	10m
Tests	1	0	–	–	–	–	–	–	–	–
ODIs	12	0	–	–	–	–	–	–	–	–
T20 Ints	1	0	–	–	–	–	–	–	–	–
First-class	102	6	13	0	–	–	13.00	–	0	0

NEW ZEALAND

JAMIE **HOW**

Full name **Jamie Michael How**
Born **May 19, 1981, New Plymouth, Taranaki**
Teams **Central Districts**
Style **Right-hand bat, right-arm medium-pacer/offspinner**
Test debut **New Zealand v West Indies at Auckland 2005-06**
ODI debut **New Zealand v Sri Lanka at Queenstown 2005-06**

THE PROFILE Jamie How stepped up to the full New Zealand side in 2005 after some solid performances for Central Districts – 704, 682 and 592 runs in the three seasons from 2002-03. A well-organised opener, more of an accumulator than a dasher, he has a penchant for big scores: after taking a while to find his first-class feet, he scored 163 not out and 158 in consecutive innings in March 2003, against Northern Districts and Canterbury, and started the following season with 169 against Otago. Picked for his one-day debut against Sri Lanka at Queenstown on New Year's Eve 2005, How ensured his celebrations would go well with a sparky 58, including eight fours and a six, in an easy victory. His first encounter with West Indies resulted in 66 in an opening stand of 136 with Nathan Astle, but his other four one-day innings brought him only 17 runs. He played all three Tests against West Indies, and one in South Africa in May 2006 as a late replacement for the injured Peter Fulton. After a moderate domestic season in 2006-07 he fell off the one-day radar and missed the World Cup, but in 2007-08, buoyed by a fine 139 in a high-scoring tied ODI with England and a career-best 92 in the first Test against them, he finally looked the part, and was one of the few batsmen to show anything like Test class on the England tour that followed. He started that trip as NZ's captain, keeping the seat warm while Daniel Vettori was away with the Indian Premier League.

THE FACTS How's 58 against Sri Lanka at Queenstown in December 2005 was the highest score by a New Zealand opener on ODI debut, beating Jock Edwards's 41 against India at Christchurch in February 1976 ... How played in the 1999-2000 Under-19 World Cup in Sri Lanka, when his captain was James Franklin and the wicketkeeper was Brendon McCullum ... How's six highest Test scores have come against England ... He also played soccer for New Zealand's youth sides, but eventually chose cricket ...

THE FIGURES *to 12.9.08*   www.cricinfo.com

Batting & Fielding	M	Inns	NO	Runs	HS	Avge	S/R	100	50	4s	6s	Ct	St
Tests	12	22	1	559	92	26.61	51.14	0	3	73	1	12	0
ODIs	25	23	1	823	139	37.40	70.52	1	6	92	6	9	0
T20 Ints	5	5	0	56	31	11.20	83.58	0	0	5	1	1	0
First-class	70	120	9	3777	169	34.02	–	8	22	–	–	74	0

Bowling	M	Balls	Runs	Wkts	BB	Avge	RpO	S/R	5i	10m
Tests	12	6	4	0	–	–	4.00	–	0	0
ODIs	25	0	–	–	–	–	–	–	–	–
T20 Ints	5	0	–	–	–	–	–	–	–	–
First-class	70	1794	1016	19	3–55	53.47	3.39	94.42	0	0

DAVID **HUSSEY**

AUSTRALIA

Full name	**David John Hussey**
Born	**July 15, 1977, Morley, Western Australia**
Teams	**Victoria, Kolkata Knight Riders**
Style	**Right-hand bat, occasional offspinner**
Test debut	**No Tests yet**
ODI debut	**Australia v West Indies at Basseterre 2007-08**

THE PROFILE The younger brother of Michael, David Hussey copied his sibling's talent for ridiculous scoring in the English county competition. And, like Michael, David was forced to pile up mountains of runs in Australia before gaining the confidence of the national selectors. It took his first thousand-run home season in 2007-08 before he was finally chosen for a tour, the one-day series in the West Indies, and earned his first national contract. Earlier that season he made his Twenty20 international debut against India at the MCG and was not required to bat. Hussey was one of the big surprises in the inaugural Indian Premier League auction when Kolkata paid $625,000 for him – far more than his brother fetched. Despite his crash-and-bash style, David is desperate not to be pigeonholed as a Twenty20 player. His Pura Cup record suggests it is a fair request: only Simon Katich made more runs in 2007-08. Equally impressive was Hussey's one-day form, which included a 60-ball century – the second-fastest in Australia's domestic history, and he was named Victoria's Player of the Year in all three formats. All this followed another prolific season with Nottinghamshire, for whom he amassed 5010 runs at 65.06 over four consistent years. An aggressive batsman with a strong bottom-hand technique, Hussey hit a breathtaking breakthrough 212 not out at nearly a run a ball in 2003-04, his first full season, as Victoria chased a record-breaking 455 for victory at Newcastle: Steve Waugh, the opposing captain, was impressed.

THE FACTS David Hussey hit 275 (with 27 fours and 14 sixes) for Nottinghamshire against Essex at Nottingham in May 2007 ... He reached 50 in only 19 balls – Australia's second-fastest ODI half-century – against West Indies in St Kitts in July 2008 ... Hussey fetched $625,000 at the inaugural Indian Premier League auction in February 2008, much more than his brother Michael ($350,000) and Australia's captain Ricky Ponting ($400,000) ...

THE FIGURES to 12.9.08

www.cricinfo.com

Batting & Fielding	M	Inns	NO	Runs	HS	Avge	S/R	100	50	4s	6s	Ct	St
Tests	0	0	–	–	–	–	–	–	–	–	–	–	–
ODIs	5	4	0	137	52	34.25	113.22	0	2	5	7	4	0
T20 Ints	2	1	0	0	0	0.00	0.00	0	0	0	0	1	0
First-class	120	184	20	9119	275	55.60	70.75	32	39	–	–	143	0

Bowling	M	Balls	Runs	Wkts	BB	Avge	RpO	S/R	5i	10m
Tests	0	0	–	–	–	–	–	–	–	–
ODIs	5	41	36	1	1–16	36.00	5.26	41.00	0	0
T20 Ints	2	18	12	1	1–12	12.00	4.00	18.00	0	0
First-class	120	1791	1188	20	4–105	59.40	3.97	89.55	0	0

MICHAEL **HUSSEY**

Full name	**Michael Edward Killeen Hussey**
Born	**May 27, 1975, Morley, Western Australia**
Teams	**Western Australia, Chennai Super Kings**
Style	**Left-hand bat, occasional right-arm medium-pacer**
Test debut	**Australia v West Indies at Brisbane 2005-06**
ODI debut	**Australia v India at Perth 2003-04**

THE PROFILE English fans couldn't understand why Australia took so long to recognise Michael Hussey's claims. Bradmanesque in county cricket, he was less prolific in Australia, and seemed destined to remain unfulfilled unless the Langer-Hayden-Ponting top-order triumvirate cracked. Finally, late in 2005 Langer's fractured rib gave Hussey a break after 15,313 first-class runs, a record for an Australian before wearing baggy green. His first Test was a disappointment, but he relaxed for his second and made an attractive century. More hundreds followed, including a memorable 122 against South Africa at the MCG, when he and Glenn McGrath added 107 for the last wicket. The fairytale continued in the 2006-07 Ashes, when he topped the batting averages with 91.60, although his one-day form did finally drop off a little. Like Langer and Graeme Wood, predecessors as left-hand WA openers, Hussey has a tidy, compact style. Skilled off front foot and back, he is attractive to watch once set, which he was regularly at Northants, Gloucestershire and Durham. Reinventing himself in one-day cricket as an agile fielder and innovative batsman with cool head and loose wrists, once he made the national side Hussey underlined his credentials with some more Bradman-like scoring. He supplanted Michael Bevan as the Aussies' one-day "finisher", although he was hardly needed as Australia steamrollered the 2007 World Cup. His sky-high standards dipped a little in 2008, with a modest Test series in the West Indies.

THE FACTS Hussey scored 229 runs in ODIs before he was dismissed, and had an average of 100.22 after 32 matches ... He took only 166 days to reach 1000 runs in Tests, beating the 228-day record established by England's Andrew Strauss in 2005 ... Hussey's 331 not out against Somerset at Taunton in 2003 is the highest individual score for Northamptonshire, and he was only the third man to make three triple-centuries in the County Championship ... He has captained Australia in four ODIs, and lost the lot ... Hussey averages 80.42 in Tests in Australia ...

THE FIGURES to 12.9.08   www.cricinfo.com

Batting & Fielding	M	Inns	NO	Runs	HS	Avge	S/R	100	50	4s	6s	Ct	St
Tests	25	42	8	2325	182	68.38	51.39	8	9	251	16	25	0
ODIs	93	71	28	2457	109*	57.13	85.52	2	16	181	41	55	0
T20 Ints	13	7	1	137	37	22.83	129.24	0	0	11	6	8	0
First-class	205	366	36	17828	331*	54.02	–	47	78	–	–	227	0

Bowling	M	Balls	Runs	Wkts	BB	Avge	RpO	S/R	5i	10m
Tests	25	66	37	0	–	–	3.36	–	0	0
ODIs	93	192	167	2	1–22	83.50	5.21	96.00	0	0
T20 Ints	13	0	–	–	–	–	–	–	–	–
First-class	205	1506	809	20	3–34	40.45	3.22	75.30	0	0

RAO **IFTIKHAR ANJUM**

Full name	**Rao Iftikhar Anjum**
Born	**December 1, 1980, Khanewal, Punjab**
Teams	**Islamabad, Zarai Taraqiati Bank**
Style	**Right-hand bat, right-arm fast-medium bowler**
Test debut	**Pakistan v Sri Lanka at Kandy 2005-06**
ODI debut	**Pakistan v Zimbabwe at Multan 2004-05**

THE PROFILE With a high arm action modelled on Glenn McGrath's, Iftikhar Anjum is another addition to Pakistan's seemingly endless production line of pace bowlers. Iftikhar, however, is more Aqib Javed than Waqar Younis, and his outswinger is considered by many to be just as lethal as Aqib's. He can bowl reverse-swing, when the ball gets a bit rougher, and has good control over his yorkers. Iftikhar has performed consistently well on the domestic circuit, taking 336 of his 344 first-class wickets on Pakistan's generally lifeless pitches, including 73 in 2000-01, his first full season. Two years later, some stellar performances propelled him towards the national side: Iftikhar captained the Zarai Taraqiati Bank to victory in the Patron's Trophy final at Karachi, taking 7 for 85 in the first innings and ending with ten in the match. Not surprisingly, he was included in Pakistan's one-day squad for the series against India early in 2004, before making his debut that September. He has since been a handy back-up bowler in one-dayers, although he rarely plays when everyone is fit. A long injury list meant he won his first Test cap in Sri Lanka in April 2006: he was expensive and didn't take a wicket as Pakistan won inside three days. That probably led to his initial exclusion from the England tour in 2006, although he was called up later as injuries struck the squad again, only to go home himself after his father died. He was one of the few to emerge with much credit from the 2007 World Cup, taking five wickets in the first two games. He wasn't needed with the ball in the final match, against Zimbabwe, but earlier made 32 – from just 16 balls – to boost the total to a massive 349.

THE FACTS Iftikhar Anjum's best bowling figures are 7 for 59, for Zarai Taraqiati Bank against WAPDA at Hyderabad in February 2005 ... Two years previously he took 7 for 85 (10 for 116 in the match) against the same opposition in the Patron's Trophy final at Karachi ... Iftikhar took 7 for 94 – after a career-best innings of 78 – for Zarai Taraqiati Bank against Karachi Port Trust at Peshawar in December 2003 ...

THE FIGURES *to 12.9.08*   www.cricinfo.com

Batting & Fielding	M	Inns	NO	Runs	HS	Avge	S/R	100	50	4s	6s	Ct	St
Tests	1	1	1	9	9*	–	23.07	0	0	2	0	0	0
ODIs	51	27	18	200	32	22.22	63.29	0	0	12	2	10	0
T20 Ints	1	0	–	–	–	–	–	–	–	–	–	0	0
First-class	83	127	27	1660	78	16.60	–	0	5	–	–	49	0

Bowling	M	Balls	Runs	Wkts	BB	Avge	RpO	S/R	5i	10m
Tests	1	84	62	0	–	–	4.42	–	0	0
ODIs	51	2439	1982	61	3–33	32.49	4.87	39.98	0	0
T20 Ints	1	24	33	0	–	–	8.25	–	0	0
First-class	83	15103	8047	344	7–59	23.39	3.19	43.90	21	3

WASIM **JAFFER**

Full name	**Wasim Jaffer**
Born	**Feb 16, 1978, Bombay (now Mumbai), Maharashtra**
Teams	**Mumbai, Bangalore Royal Challengers**
Style	**Right-hand batsman, occasional offspinner**
Test debut	**India v South Africa at Mumbai 1999-2000**
ODI debut	**India v South Africa at Durban 2006-07**

THE PROFILE A triple-century in only his second first-class game meant Wasim Jaffer was anointed as the great new hope of Mumbai cricket. He is a tall, slim opener with the style and panache of the young Mohammad Azharuddin, and much was expected of him on his Test debut in February 2000. But Allan Donald and Shaun Pollock proved too hot to handle – even though he showed glimpses of a steely and unflappable temperament – and his international career was put on hold. Jaffer continued to pile up the runs in domestic cricket, and a string of big scores in 2001-02 won him a place on the West Indian tour. There, he stroked two elegant half-centuries, but a worrying tendency to give it away when set resulted in him losing his place. He reminded the selectors of his quality with some superb batting for the A team in England in 2003, but spent three years in the domestic wilderness before being recalled. He made most of his first chance on return, against England at Nagpur in March 2006, following up a forthright 81 with his maiden Test hundred. He added 212 against West Indies in Antigua in June, and continued to score well as Virender Sehwag's opening partner in the Tests in the Caribbean, doing enough to keep Gautam Gambhir on the sidelines – and when Sehwag was dropped for the 2007 England tour Jaffer formed a surprisingly successful alliance with Dinesh Karthik. He cemented his Test place with 202 against Pakistan in November 2007, but remains surplus to requirements in the one-day game.

THE FACTS Jaffer scored 314 not out in only his second first-class match, for Mumbai against Saurashtra at Rajkot in November 1996; he shared an opening stand of 459 with Sulakshan Kulkarni ... Jaffer has made two Test double-centuries, 212 against West Indies at St John's in June 2006, and 202 against Pakistan at Kolkata in November 2007 ... He was the first man to bag a pair in a Test against Bangladesh, at Chittagong in May 2007; in the next match he made 138 not out ...

THE FIGURES *to 12.9.08*   www.cricinfo.com

Batting & Fielding	M	Inns	NO	Runs	HS	Avge	S/R	100	50	4s	6s	Ct	St
Tests	31	58	1	1944	212	34.10	48.05	5	11	272	3	27	0
ODIs	2	2	0	10	10	5.00	43.47	0	0	2	0	0	0
T20 Ints	0	0	–	–	–	–	–	–	–	–	–	–	–
First-class	157	265	25	11518	314*	47.99	–	32	55	–	–	168	0

Bowling	M	Balls	Runs	Wkts	BB	Avge	RpO	S/R	5i	10m
Tests	31	66	18	2	2–18	9.00	1.63	33.00	0	0
ODIs	2	0	–	–	–	–	–	–	–	–
T20 Ints	0	0	–	–	–	–	–	–	–	–
First-class	157	138	74	2	2–18	37.00	3.21	69.00	0	0

AMIT **JAGGERNAUTH**

Full name	**Amit Sheldon Jaggernauth**
Born	**November 16, 1983, Carapichaima, Trinidad**
Teams	**Trinidad & Tobago**
Style	**Left-hand bat, offspinner**
Test debut	**West Indies v Australia at Kingston 2007-08**
ODI debut	**No ODIs yet**

THE PROFILE A slight offspinner of Indian descent, Trinidad's Amit Jaggernauth has become one of the most consistent performers in domestic cricket since his debut in 2002-03. The following year, in his first full season, he took 30 wickets at 22, and followed that up with 36 at 26. In 2006-07 he was the leading wicket-taker in the Carib Beer Series, and then finished up with 41 wickets the following season. The West Indies selectors, long mistrustful of anything but pace, finally called him in to the squad for the first Test against Sri Lanka at Providence in March 2008. Sulieman Benn, the Barbados slow left-armer, was also in the squad, and romantics looked back to 1950, when two unheralded debutant spinners, Sonny Ramadhin and Alf Valentine, destroyed England. But it wasn't to be: Jaggernauth was left out, and more surprisingly also sat out the second Test on his home turf at Queen's Park Oval (Benn was dropped too) despite taking ten wickets in a match against Barbados the week before. Jaggernauth eventually did get a chance in the first Test against Australia at Kingston in May 2008, bowling tidily without threatening to dominate. He emerged with the wicket of Mike Hussey, but was promptly dropped for the rest of the series as the selectors reverted to their favourite weapon – pace. "Being given the ball with Ricky Ponting and Michael Hussey at the crease was a huge challenge," said Jaggernauth. "I thought I was a bit too aggressive and tried too many things. What I learned is that in terms of my game I need to be a little more patient at this level."

THE FACTS Jaggernauth took 7 for 45 (10 for 79 in the match) for Trinidad & Tobago against Barbados at Pointe-à-Pierre in March 2008 ... Earlier that month he took 7 for 60 – and 12 for 133 in the match – for T&T against the Windward Islands at Roseau ... In March 2007 he took 7 for 65 against the Windwards at Pointe-à-Pierre ...

THE FIGURES to 12.9.08   www.cricinfo.com

Batting & Fielding	M	Inns	NO	Runs	HS	Avge	S/R	100	50	4s	6s	Ct	St
Tests	1	2	1	0	0*	0.00	0.00	0	0	0	0	0	0
ODIs	0	0	–	–	–	–	–	–	–	–	–	–	–
T20 Ints	0	0	–	–	–	–	–	–	–	–	–	–	–
First-class	37	56	23	390	47	11.81	–	0	0	–	–	30	0

Bowling	M	Balls	Runs	Wkts	BB	Avge	RpO	S/R	5i	10m
Tests	1	138	96	2	1–74	96.00	4.17	138.00	0	0
ODIs	0	0	–	–	–	–	–	–	–	–
T20 Ints	0	0	–	–	–	–	–	–	–	–
First-class	37	7846	3466	158	7–45	21.93	2.65	49.65	9	2

PHIL **JAQUES**

Full name	**Philip Anthony Jaques**
Born	**May 3, 1979, Wollongong, New South Wales**
Teams	**New South Wales**
Style	**Left-hand bat, occasional left-arm spinner**
Test debut	**Australia v South Africa at Melbourne 2005-06**
ODI debut	**Australia v South Africa at Melbourne 2005-06**

THE PROFILE   Phil Jaques was on holiday when the Test call finally came. It meant an early-career gamble had paid off: a British passport-holder, Jaques had been the subject of a national tug-of-war in 2003. He had scored 1409 runs for Northamptonshire, but refused to commit to England as "My heart says Australia". After that he maintained such a consistent standard that when Justin Langer was ruled out of the Boxing Day Test against South Africa in December 2005 Trevor Hohns admitted that Jaques "virtually demanded selection". his Test debut was quiet – he walked after squirting Shaun Pollock to short leg for 2, and added 28 in the second innings – but he had been earmarked as a long-term prospect. Another opportunity came in Bangladesh, and he produced a capable 66. Another injury – to Simon Katich this time – led to a one-day call-up during the 2005-06 tri-series. He made a stunning impact with 94, but when Katich returned Jaques was harshly dropped, amid suggestions that his fielding was substandard. In 2006-07 he struck 987 Pura Cup runs at 47, and also made two centuries in three days against the England tourists. And it all paid off: when Langer retired Jaques finally got a chance to seal a Test spot, and did so late in 2007 with twin centuries against Sri Lanka that showed his range. His 100 at the Gabba was full of first-day determination, while his Hobart 150 was in the biffing mode that has dominated domestic attacks. Another hundred, in a big opening stand with Katich, followed at Bridgetown in June 2008.

THE FACTS   Jaques's 94 against South Africa in Melbourne in January 2006 was the highest by an Australian ODI debutant (beating Kepler Wessels's 79 in 1982-83) ... His second ODI was less memorable: out fourth ball for 0 as South Africa bowled Australia out for 93 ... Jaques was the first batsman to score double-centuries for and against Yorkshire, following 222 for Northamptonshire in 2003 with 243 for Yorkshire against Hampshire the next year ... He made 244 and 202 in successive matches for Worcestershire in 2006 ...

THE FIGURES *to 12.9.08*   www.cricinfo.com

Batting & Fielding	M	Inns	NO	Runs	HS	Avge	S/R	100	50	4s	6s	Ct	St
Tests	11	19	0	902	150	47.47	54.23	3	6	99	3	7	0
ODIs	6	6	0	125	94	20.83	71.02	0	1	16	1	3	0
T20 Ints	0	0	–	–	–	–	–	–	–	–	–	–	–
First-class	126	223	9	11605	244	54.22	–	35	54	–	–	98	0

Bowling	M	Balls	Runs	Wkts	BB	Avge	RpO	S/R	5i	10m
Tests	11	0	–	–	–	–	–	–	–	–
ODIs	6	0	–	–	–	–	–	–	–	–
T20 Ints	0	0	–	–	–	–	–	–	–	–
First-class	126	68	87	0	–	–	7.67	–	0	0

SANATH **JAYASURIYA**

Full name	**Sanath Teran Jayasuriya**
Born	**June 30, 1969, Matara**
Teams	**Bloomfield, Ruhuna, Mumbai Indians**
Style	**Left-hand bat, slow left-arm orthodox spinner**
Test debut	**Sri Lanka v New Zealand at Hamilton 1990-91**
ODI debut	**Sri Lanka v Australia at Melbourne 1989-90**

THE PROFILE One of the most uncompromising strikers in world cricket, Sanath Jayasuriya found fame as a pinch-hitter at the 1996 World Cup, then showed he was also capable of massive scoring in Tests, making 340 against India and eventually becoming the first Sri Lankan to win 100 caps. He remains dizzily dangerous, especially on the subcontinent's slower surfaces. Short but muscular, he cuts and pulls with great power; his brutal bat-wielding is at odds with his shy, gentle nature. Streetwise opponents set traps in the gully and third man, but when on song Jayasuriya can be virtually unstoppable, scoring freely on both sides of the wicket. He is also a canny left-arm spinner, mixing his leg-stump darts with clever variations of pace. He had a successful stint as captain after Arjuna Ranatunga was dumped in 1999, but the responsibility took its toll. He stepped down after the 2003 World Cup, and a one-day slump immediately prompted calls for his retirement. But Jayasuriya was far from finished: he bounced back in 2004 with a blazing hundred against Australia and a marathon double-century against Pakistan. He added twin centuries in the Asia Cup, and sailed past 10,000 one-day runs the following year. He looked rusty at first in England in 2006 when summoned from a short-lived Test retirement, but soon showed his old form in pyjamas, with 122 at The Oval then 152 and 157 in successive innings against England and Holland. Then he hit two more tons in the 2007 World Cup before briefly giving Sri Lanka hope in the final with 63. He then retired (again) from Test cricket, but remains a force in the shorter games, hitting his 26th ODI century on his 39th birthday in June 2008.

THE FACTS Jayasuriya made 340 against India in Colombo in August 1997, as Sri Lanka made the highest Test total of 952 for 6: he shared a world-record second-wicket partnership of 576 with Roshan Mahanama ... In the next Test Jayasuriya scored 199 ... He made his first-class debut for Sri Lanka B in Pakistan in 1988-89, and hit 203 and 207, both not out, in successive "Tests" there ... Jayasuriya's record includes four ODIs for the Asia XI ...

THE FIGURES *to 12.9.08*   www.cricinfo.com

Batting & Fielding	M	Inns	NO	Runs	HS	Avge	S/R	100	50	4s	6s	Ct	St
Tests	110	188	14	6973	340	40.07	–	14	31	910	59	78	0
ODIs	421	409	18	12785	189	32.69	91.03	27	66	–	265	118	0
T20 Ints	7	7	1	246	88	41.00	165.10	0	3	31	10	0	0
First-class	261	415	33	14742	340	38.59	–	29	70	–	–	162	0

Bowling	M	Balls	Runs	Wkts	BB	Avge	RpO	S/R	5i	10m
Tests	110	8188	3366	98	5–34	34.34	2.46	83.55	2	0
ODIs	421	14280	11333	310	6–29	36.55	4.76	46.06	4	0
T20 Ints	7	125	155	9	3–21	17.22	7.44	13.88	0	0
First-class	261	15113	6719	205	5–34	32.77	2.66	73.72	2	0

MAHELA **JAYAWARDENE**

Full name	**Denagamage Proboth Mahela de Silva Jayawardene**
Born	**May 27, 1977, Colombo**
Teams	**Sinhalese Sports Club, Wayamba, Kings XI Punjab**
Style	**Right-hand bat, occ. right-arm medium-pacer**
Test debut	**Sri Lanka v India at Colombo 1997-98**
ODI debut	**Sri Lanka v Zimbabwe at Colombo 1997-98**

THE PROFILE A fine technician with an excellent temperament, Mahela Jayawardene's exciting arrival in 1997 heralded the start of a new era for Sri Lanka's middle order. He was the best batsman they had produced since Sanath Jayasuriya, and his rich talent fuelled towering expectations. Perhaps mindful of his first Test, when he went in against India at 790 for 4, he soon developed an appetite for big scores. His 66 then, in the world-record 952 for 6, was followed by a masterful 167 on a Galle minefield against New Zealand in only his fourth Test, and a marathon 242 against India in his seventh. However, after a purple patch from 2000, Jayawardene lost form in 2002. His declining one-day productivity was particularly alarming, although that was partly explained by being shuffled up and down the order. He hardly scored a run in the 2003 World Cup, and was dropped. However, he soon regained his confidence, and benefited from a settled spot at No. 4 after Aravinda de Silva retired. A good Test series against England was followed by more runs in 2004. He deputised as captain for the injured Marvan Atapattu in England in 2006, producing a stunning double of 61 and 119 to lead the amazing rearguard which saved the Lord's Test. Later he put South Africa to the sword in Colombo, hitting a colossal 374 and sharing a world-record stand of 624 with Kumar Sangakkara. He cemented his position as captain during 2006-07, inspiring his side to the World Cup final with 548 runs at 60, including a century in the semi-final victory over New Zealand, then became Sri Lanka's leading Test runscorer during 2007-08, a period that included three successive centuries, one of them a double against England.

THE FACTS Jayawardene made 374 against South Africa in Colombo in July 2006 ... He has taken 68 catches off Muttiah Muralitharan in Tests, a record for a fielder-bowler combination, beating c Mark Taylor b Shane Warne (51) ... Jayawardene holds the record for most Test runs on a single ground (2198 at the SSC in Colombo) ... He averages 56.27 in Tests against India, but only 27.33 v Pakistan ... His record includes five ODIs for the Asia XI ...

THE FIGURES to 12.9.08   www.cricinfo.com

Batting & Fielding	M	Inns	NO	Runs	HS	Avge	S/R	100	50	4s	6s	Ct	St
Tests	98	160	12	7757	374	52.41	52.56	23	32	935	38	136	0
ODIs	283	265	29	7830	128	33.17	76.58	10	48	665	45	151	0
T20 Ints	8	8	2	170	65	28.33	149.12	0	1	17	4	3	0
First-class	178	280	21	13406	374	51.76	–	40	59	–	–	223	0

Bowling	M	Balls	Runs	Wkts	BB	Avge	RpO	S/R	5i	10m
Tests	98	470	232	4	2–32	58.00	2.96	117.50	0	0
ODIs	283	582	558	7	2–56	79.71	5.75	83.14	0	0
T20 Ints	8	6	8	0	–	–	8.00	–	0	0
First-class	178	2870	1535	50	5–72	30.70	3.20	57.40	1	0

PRASANNA **JAYAWARDENE**

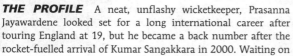

Full name	**Hewasandatchige Asiri Prasanna Wishvanath Jayawardene**
Born	**October 9, 1979, Colombo**
Teams	**Sebastianites, Basnahira South**
Style	**Right-hand bat, wicketkeeper**
Test debut	**Sri Lanka v Pakistan at Kandy 2000**
ODI debut	**Sri Lanka v Pakistan at Sharjah 2002-03**

THE PROFILE A neat, unflashy wicketkeeper, Prasanna Jayawardene looked set for a long international career after touring England at 19, but he became a back number after the rocket-fuelled arrival of Kumar Sangakkara in 2000. Waiting on the sidelines had already been a feature of Jayawardene's career: he made his Test debut against Pakistan in June 2000, but was confined to the dressing-room throughout, as rain washed out play on the last two days before Sri Lanka fielded. The return of Romesh Kaluwitharana briefly pushed him even further down the pecking order, but with the Sri Lankan selectors worried about overburdening Sangakkara in Tests, Jayawardene was recalled in April 2004. Sangakkara soon got the gloves back that time, but there was something of a sea-change two years later after the England tour, during which Jayawardene showed that his batting had improved. He was recalled for South Africa's visit in July 2006, and this time the decision to lighten Sangakkara's load paid off spectacularly – he hammered 287, and shared a world-record stand of 642 with Mahela Jayawardene in the first Test in Colombo. Prasanna Jayawardene (no relation to Mahela) contented himself with a couple of catches and a stumping as the South Africans went down by an innings, but finally seemed to have booked in for a long run behind the stumps – at least in Tests – and clinched his place in June 2007 with a Test ton of his own, against Bangladesh. He continued his batting improvement over the next 12 months, averaging 48 against England and a shade under 40 against India.

THE FACTS Prasanna Jayawardene made 120 not out, his first Test century, against Bangladesh in Colombo in June 2007, sharing a record seventh-wicket stand of 223 with Chaminda Vaas ... He has scored five other first-class centuries, the highest 166 not out for Sebastianites against Panadura at Moratuwa in February 2007 ... All Jayawardene's ODIs have been in the United Arab Emirates (Sharjah and Abu Dhabi) ...

THE FIGURES *to 12.9.08*   www.cricinfo.com

Batting & Fielding	M	Inns	NO	Runs	HS	Avge	S/R	100	50	4s	6s	Ct	St
Tests	21	25	2	616	120*	26.78	43.71	1	2	63	2	41	15
ODIs	6	5	0	27	20	5.40	61.36	0	0	3	0	4	1
T20 Ints	0	0	–	–	–	–	–	–	–	–	–	–	–
First-class	149	230	26	5388	166*	26.41	–	6	25	–	–	359	68

Bowling	M	Balls	Runs	Wkts	BB	Avge	RpO	S/R	5i	10m
Tests	21	0	–	–	–	–	–	–	–	–
ODIs	6	0	–	–	–	–	–	–	–	–
T20 Ints	0	0	–	–	–	–	–	–	–	–
First-class	149	18	9	0	–	–	3.00	–	0	0

MITCHELL **JOHNSON**

AUSTRALIA

Full name **Mitchell Guy Johnson**
Born **November 2, 1981, Townsville, Queensland**
Teams **Queensland**
Style **Left-hand bat, left-hand fast-medium bowler**
Test debut **Australia v Sri Lanka at Brisbane 2007-08**
ODI debut **Australia v New Zealand at Christchurch 2005-06**

THE PROFILE Mitchell Johnson was Australia's most exciting fast-bowling prospect since Brett Lee first dyed his roots. He's quick, he's tall, he's talented – but most of all, he's a left-armer. Only digging up a blond legspinner could create more excitement in Australia, where only two bowlers like him – Alan Davidson and Bruce Reid – have taken 100 Test wickets. Dennis Lillee spotted him at 17, and called him a "once-in-a-generation bowler". Injuries kept intruding, but Johnson played a full season in 2004-05 and was picked for the Australia A tour of Pakistan. Another representative catapult arrived in December 2005, when he was supersubbed into the final match of the one-day series in New Zealand. However, the 2006-07 season was a sobering one. Johnson started by reducing India to 35 for 5 in a one-dayer in Kuala Lumpur, but narrowly missed out to the steadier Stuart Clark in the Ashes series, then had to sit on the sidelines throughout the World Cup as Shaun Tait and Nathan Bracken (another left-armer) bowled consistently well. Test rewards finally came in 2007-08, and he was composed in his opening two matches against Sri Lanka, with eight wickets, and built on that with 16 against India then 10 in the West Indies, although he was less impressive overall in the Caribbean. Johnson, who runs up as if carrying a delivery of milk bottles in his left hand, has the height to worry batsmen and is intent on scaring them as well. Shane Watson, his Queensland team-mate, is impressed: "He has just about the most talent I've ever seen in an allround athlete ... If he can keep improving the sky's the limit."

THE FACTS Johnson was the bowling star of the 2005-06 Pura Cup final, taking 6 for 51 – and ten wickets in the match – as Queensland followed up their mammoth total of 900 for 6 by routing a demoralised Victoria: "What a performance on a flat wicket," said his captain Jimmy Maher ... Johnson took 5 for 26 in an ODI against India at Vadodara in October 2007, and 5 for 29 against West Indies in St Kitts in July 2008 ...

THE FIGURES to 12.9.08   www.cricinfo.com

Batting & Fielding	M	Inns	NO	Runs	HS	Avge	S/R	100	50	4s	6s	Ct	St
Tests	9	9	4	167	50*	33.40	58.18	0	1	21	3	3	0
ODIs	42	18	8	92	24*	9.20	73.01	0	0	5	2	7	0
T20 Ints	8	3	2	14	9	14.00	200.00	0	0	2	0	3	0
First-class	33	42	14	748	54	26.71	–	0	5	–	–	6	0

Bowling	M	Balls	Runs	Wkts	BB	Avge	RpO	S/R	5i	10m
Tests	9	2130	1118	34	4-41	32.88	3.14	62.64	0	0
ODIs	42	1938	1525	65	5-26	23.46	4.72	29.81	2	0
T20 Ints	8	174	202	10	3-22	20.20	6.96	17.40	0	0
First-class	33	6283	3472	111	6-51	31.27	3.31	56.60	2	1

JUNAID SIDDIQUE

Full name	**Mohammad Junaid Siddique**
Born	**October 30, 1987, Rajshahi**
Teams	**Rajshahi**
Style	**Left-hand bat, occasional offspinner**
Test debut	**Bangladesh v New Zealand at Dunedin 2007-08**
ODI debut	**Bangladesh v New Zealand at Auckland 2007-08**

THE PROFILE Junaid Siddique, a solid left-hand opener, made a sensational start in Test cricket at 20 when, along with his fellow debutant Tamim Iqbal, he flayed the New Zealand attack in an opening stand of 161 to light up the inaugural Test at Dunedin's University Oval at the start of 2008. *Wisden* said the pair "started the second innings with an entrancing display of classical strokes, their timing perfect as the ball was distributed around the short boundaries". Sadly, their fine start came to nothing: the other batsmen made only 83 between them, and Bangladesh lost yet again. Junaid also made a stylish 74 against South Africa at Mirpur – no-one else made more than 24 in that innings – to show that his debut performance wasn't a flash in the pan, and cracked 71 on his Twenty20 international debut as well. To set against this, his ODI performances to date have been strangely anaemic, yielding only three double-figure scores and a highest of 21. Junaid worked his way up through Bangladesh's age-group sides, reaching the A team against the England A tourists in 2006-07. That season he recorded a notable double with 88 and 114 not out (in more than five hours) for Rajshahi against Khulna, and was in the 30-man preliminary squad for the World Cup without making the final cut for the Caribbean. He consolidated with more good scores at home – including 120 in a one-day game against Barisal – which got him into the frame for the New Zealand trip, and after his heroics there he also made 103 for the Bangladesh Board XI against the touring South Africans in a match denied first-class status because both sides chose from 12 players.

THE FACTS Junaid Siddique scored 74 on his Test debut at Dunedin in January 2008, putting on 161 for the first wicket – a new national record – with Tamim Iqbal, who was also winning his first cap: it was the highest opening stand between debutants in Tests since Billy Ibadulla and Abdul Kadir put on 249 for Pakistan v Australia at Karachi in 1964-65 ... Junaid hit 71 off 49 balls in his first Twenty20 international, against Pakistan at Cape Town in September 2007... He captained Bangladesh A in England in 2008 ...

THE FIGURES to 12.9.08   www.cricinfo.com

Batting & Fielding	M	Inns	NO	Runs	HS	Avge	S/R	100	50	4s	6s	Ct	St
Tests	4	8	0	183	74	22.87	42.65	0	2	24	0	3	0
ODIs	8	8	0	62	21	7.75	37.57	0	0	6	0	1	0
T20 Ints	1	1	0	71	71	71.00	144.89	0	1	6	3	0	0
First-class	22	41	1	1038	114*	25.95	47.61	1	6	–	–	19	0

Bowling	M	Balls	Runs	Wkts	BB	Avge	RpO	S/R	5i	10m
Tests	4	0	–	–	–	–	–	–	–	–
ODIs	8	6	4	0	–	–	4.00	–	0	0
T20 Ints	1	0	–	–	–	–	–	–	–	–
First-class	22	162	99	1	1–30	99.00	3.66	162.00	0	0

SOUTH AFRICA

JACQUES **KALLIS**

Full name	**Jacques Henry Kallis**
Born	**October 16, 1975, Pinelands, Cape Town**
Teams	**Cape Cobras, Bangalore Royal Challengers**
Style	**Right-hand bat, right-arm fast-medium bowler**
Test debut	**South Africa v England at Durban 1995-96**
ODI debut	**South Africa v England at Cape Town 1995-96**

THE PROFILE In an era of fast scoring and high-octane entertainment, Jacques Kallis is a throwback – an astonishingly effective one – to a more sedate age, when your wicket was to be guarded with your life, and runs were an accidental by-product of crease-occupation. He blossomed after a quiet start into arguably the world's leading batsman, with the adhesive qualities of a Cape Point limpet. In 2005, he was the ICC's first Test Player of the Year, after a run of performances against West Indies and England that marked him out as the modern game's biggest scalp. His batting is not for the romantic: a Kallis century (of which there have now been 30 in Tests) tends to be a soulless affair, with ruthless efficiency taking precedence over derring-do, and he has never quite dispelled the notion that he is a selfish batsman, something the Aussies played on during the 2007 World Cup. He also had a subdued time in England the following year, amid whispers that he was carrying some extra weight. But he has sailed to the top of South Africa's batting charts, and until Andrew Flintoff's emergence was comfortably the world's leading allrounder, capable of swinging the ball sharply at a surprising pace. Strong, with powerful shoulders and a deep chest, Kallis has the capacity (if not always the inclination) to play a wide array of attacking strokes. He won his 100th Test cap in April 2006, and has a batting average in the mid-fifties and nearly 250 wickets in both Tests and ODIs. He's a fine slip fielder too.

THE FACTS Kallis and Shaun Pollock were the first South Africans to play 100 Tests, reaching the mark, appropriately enough, at Centurion in April 2006 ... Kallis averages 169.75 in Tests against Zimbabwe, and scored 388 runs against them in two Tests in 2001-02 without being dismissed ... Including his next innings he batted for a record 1241 minutes in Tests without getting out ... Kallis scored hundreds in five successive Tests in 2003-04 (only Don Bradman, with six, has done better) ... His record includes one Test and three ODIs for the World XI, and two ODIs for the Africa XI ...

THE FIGURES *to 12.9.08*   www.cricinfo.com

Batting & Fielding	M	Inns	NO	Runs	HS	Avge	S/R	100	50	4s	6s	Ct	St
Tests	123	209	33	9761	189*	55.46	43.90	30	48	1094	63	130	0
ODIs	279	265	50	9609	139	44.69	71.21	16	66	754	114	101	0
T20 Ints	3	3	0	39	20	13.00	108.33	0	0	3	2	2	0
First-class	212	347	50	16084	200	54.15	–		47	86	–	–	190	0

Bowling	M	Balls	Runs	Wkts	BB	Avge	RpO	S/R	5i	10m
Tests	123	15989	7495	240	6–54	31.22	2.81	66.62	5	0
ODIs	279	9472	7627	243	5–30	31.38	4.83	40.62	2	0
T20 Ints	3	6	17	0	–	–	17.00	–	0	0
First-class	212	24646	11429	375	6–54	30.47	2.78	65.72	8	0

KAMRAN AKMAL

Full name	**Kamran Akmal**
Born	**January 13, 1982, Lahore, Punjab**
Teams	**Lahore, National Bank, Rajasthan Royals**
Style	**Right-hand bat, wicketkeeper**
Test debut	**Pakistan v Zimbabwe at Harare 2002-03**
ODI debut	**Pakistan v Zimbabwe at Bulawayo 2002-03**

THE PROFILE   Kamran Akmal made his first-class debut at the age of 15 as a useful wicketkeeper and a hard-hitting batsman. Several good performances earned him an A-team spot in 2002, and after doing well he was called up for the Zimbabwe tour ahead of the veteran Moin Khan. He was not expected to play in the Tests, but made his debut – and chipped in with a handy 38 – when Rashid Latif suffered a recurrence of a back injury. Akmal stood in when Latif was suspended against Bangladesh, and then played against India when Moin was injured. However, from October 2004 Akmal became Pakistan's first-choice keeper. He responded with a magnificent showing with the gloves in Australia, then, in 2005, hit five international centuries. Three of them came while opening in one-dayers, and two in Tests, the first saving the match against India at Mohali, while the second, a blistering knock, came in the emphatic series-sealing win over England at Lahore. However, a nightmare series in England in 2006 set him back again. He retained his place throughout 2006-07, without quite regaining his best touch with bat or gloves. He battled back with an important 119 against India in the Kolkata Test, but continued fumbles behind the stumps eventually led to Sarfraz Ahmed being given a run. Akmal was back, though, to cane Bangladesh for an 80-ball ODI century at the start of 2008, although that was not enough to earn him a place in the Asia Cup which followed.

THE FACTS   Five of Kamran Akmal's nine first-class centuries have come in Tests: he scored five international hundreds in December 2005 and January 2006, including 154 in the Lahore Test against England, when he shared a sixth-wicket stand of 269 with Mohammad Yousuf ... Akmal has scored more Test hundreds than any other Pakistan wicketkeeper: Moin Khan made four and Imtiaz Ahmed three ... Akmal scored 102 and 109 in successive ODIs against England in December 2005 ... His brother Adnan has also played first-class cricket in Pakistan ...

THE FIGURES *to 12.9.08*   www.cricinfo.com

Batting & Fielding	M	Inns	NO	Runs	HS	Avge	S/R	100	50	4s	6s	Ct	St
Tests	38	65	4	1944	154	31.86	60.84	5	8	290	2	123	19
ODIs	88	74	10	1621	124	25.32	83.55	4	2	194	14	86	14
T20 Ints	12	8	2	76	21	12.66	108.57	0	0	6	3	6	5
First-class	129	199	24	5563	174	31.78	–	9	26	–	–	407	39

Bowling	M	Balls	Runs	Wkts	BB	Avge	RpO	S/R	5i	10m
Tests	38	0	–	–	–	–	–	–	–	–
ODIs	88	0	–	–	–	–	–	–	–	–
T20 Ints	12	0	–	–	–	–	–	–	–	–
First-class	129	0	–	–	–	–	–	–	–	–

CHAMARA **KAPUGEDERA**

Full name	**Chamara Kantha Kapugedera**
Born	**February 24, 1987, Kandy**
Teams	**Colombo Cricket Club, Kandurata, Chennai Super Kings**
Style	**Right-hand bat, occasional right-arm medium-pacer**
Test debut	**Sri Lanka v England at Lord's 2006**
ODI debut	**Sri Lanka v Australia at Perth 2005-06**

THE PROFILE A naturally aggressive right-hander and a fine fielder, Chamara Kapugedera is one of the few genuinely exciting batsmen the Sri Lankan selectors have unearthed recently from the Under-19s. From his first appearances for Dharmaraja College in Kandy when he was 11, "Kapu" has rarely wasted an opportunity. After a prolific 2003-04 season, when he scored over 1000 runs at schoolboy level, he was picked for the following year's Under-19 tour of Pakistan. He made 112 in the first Test, and bettered that with a stunning 131 in the third one-dayer against youth cricket's world champions at Karachi. The selectors eventually gambled, and fast-tracked him into the national squad after glowing reports from his youth coaches. Kapugedera was picked to go to India in November 2005, but injured his knee. However, he made his ODI debut, still only 18, against Australia at Perth early in 2006. A maiden fifty followed against Pakistan in March. He won his first Test cap at Lord's in May 2006, but was unlucky enough to receive the perfect inswinging yorker first ball from Sajid Mahmood. But he put that disappointment behind him with a composed 50 in the third Test, which Sri Lanka won to level the series. He had a quiet time in 2006-07, missing the World Cup after going 12 ODIs without reaching 50, then the following season stepped up in one-dayers – he hit 95 against West Indies at Port-of-Spain and 75 against India in the Asia Cup in June 2008 – without cracking the Test side.

THE FACTS Kapugedera scored 70 on his first-class debut, for Sri Lanka A v New Zealand A in Colombo in October 2005 ... He was selected for the 2006 tour of England after playing only three first-class matches, and made his maiden century – 134 not out v Sussex at Hove – the game after collecting a first-ball duck on his Test debut at Lord's ... Kapugedera averages 67.50 in ODIs against West Indies – but 1.00 against England ... He played three Under-19 ODIs and finished them with a batting average of 154 ...

THE FIGURES *to 12.9.08*   www.cricinfo.com

Batting & Fielding	M	Inns	NO	Runs	HS	Avge	S/R	100	50	4s	6s	Ct	St
Tests	6	11	1	221	63	22.10	44.20	0	2	31	2	3	0
ODIs	43	36	2	816	95	24.00	73.44	0	5	68	14	9	0
T20 Ints	3	2	0	34	22	17.00	121.42	0	0	1	2	1	0
First-class	28	50	7	1370	134*	31.86	58.54	2	9	151	17	19	0

Bowling	M	Balls	Runs	Wkts	BB	Avge	RpO	S/R	5i	10m
Tests	6	0	–	–	–	–	–	–	–	–
ODIs	43	228	192	2	1–24	96.00	5.05	114.00	0	0
T20 Ints	3	0	–	–	–	–	–	–	–	–
First-class	28	287	164	3	1–1	54.66	3.42	95.66	0	0

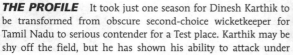

DINESH **KARTHIK**

Full name	**Krishnakumar Dinesh Karthik**
Born	**June 1, 1985, Madras (now Chennai)**
Teams	**Tamil Nadu, Delhi Daredevils**
Style	**Right-hand bat, wicketkeeper**
Test debut	**India v Australia at Mumbai 2004-05**
ODI debut	**India v England at Lord's 2004**

THE PROFILE It took just one season for Dinesh Karthik to be transformed from obscure second-choice wicketkeeper for Tamil Nadu to serious contender for a Test place. Karthik may be shy off the field, but he has shown his ability to attack under pressure and improvise on it. He gave glimpses of batting talent as a 17-year-old, but his keeping wasn't up to scratch and he was dropped for the later stages of the Ranji Trophy. However, in 2004 an impressive display in the Under-19 World Cup in Dhaka (including a whirlwind 70 in a must-win game against Sri Lanka), two vital hundreds in the Ranji Trophy, and an improved showing behind the stumps inevitably resulted in interest from the selectors. He replaced Parthiv Patel in the one-day squad in England in September 2004, and made his debut at Lord's, pulling off a superb stumping to dispose of Michael Vaughan. Then he made his Test debut against Australia, but after managing just one fifty in ten matches, he was dropped in favour of the flamboyant Mahendra Singh Dhoni, whose instant success meant Karthik had to rethink. He reinvented himself as a specialist batsman. After India's forgettable World Cup (for which he was selected but didn't play), Karthik made his first Test century in Bangladesh, forging a successful opening partnership with Wasim Jaffer which continued in England, where he was India's leading scorer in the Tests. But leaner times followed – six single-figure scores in his next ten Test innings – which, allied to some unconvincing keeping when Dhoni missed the Tests in Sri Lanka, meant that Patel was recalled for the deciding Test in August 2008, leaving Karthik needing to re-establish himself.

THE FACTS Karthik's highest score of 134 helped rescue Tamil Nadu from 91 for 6 in a Ranji Trophy match against Mumbai in December 2005 ... He averages 49.33 in Tests against South Africa, but only 1.00 in two Tests against Zimbabwe ... Karthik scored two double-centuries for Tamil Nadu Under-19s in September 2002 ... He prefers his surname to be spelt with two As ("Kaarthik") as it is more astrologically propitious ...

THE FIGURES *to 12.9.08*   www.cricinfo.com

Batting & Fielding	M	Inns	NO	Runs	HS	Avge	S/R	100	50	4s	6s	Ct	St
Tests	21	34	1	967	129	29.30	50.25	1	7	127	4	46	5
ODIs	26	20	5	330	63	22.00	69.76	0	2	30	2	23	2
T20 Ints	6	5	1	67	31*	16.75	115.51	0	0	9	1	3	2
First-class	59	95	5	2825	134	31.38	–	4	19	–	–	157	15

Bowling	M	Balls	Runs	Wkts	BB	Avge	RpO	S/R	5i	10m
Tests	21	0	–	–	–	–	–	–	–	–
ODIs	26	0	–	–	–	–	–	–	–	–
T20 Ints	6	0	–	–	–	–	–	–	–	–
First-class	59	30	28	0	–	–	5.60	–	0	0

SIMON **KATICH**

Full name	**Simon Mathew Katich**
Born	**August 21, 1975, Middle Swan, Western Australia**
Teams	**New South Wales**
Style	**Left-hand bat, slow left-arm unorthodox spinner**
Test debut	**Australia v England at Leeds 2001**
ODI debut	**Australia v Zimbabwe at Melbourne 2000-01**

THE PROFILE Simon Katich had several outstanding achievements in 2007-08. He broke the record for most runs in a Pura Cup season (1506 at 94.12, including 86 and 92 in the final), captained NSW to the title, and regained his Test place. All this must have seemed most unlikely when he lost his national contract the preceding winter (he conceded he was struggling at the highest level and deserved to be dropped). His campaign featured five centuries, including 306 against Queensland, of which 184 came in an extended 150-minute post-lunch session. The Australian selectors, notoriously reluctant to go back to a jettisoned player, just could not ignore his runs, and after 30 months out of the Test side Katich made a hundred in Antigua and added 157 at Bridgetown. Katich had simply been enjoying batting without the expectation heaped on an international player. He had also worked on some technical issues that plagued him during 2005, when he was upset by reverse-swing in the Ashes then bamboozled by Murali in the Super Series. After that Katich was downgraded to a one-day role, but he could not hold down that spot as his top-order wariness was shown up by his fellow opener Adam Gilchrist. Ever since Katich was included in Western Australia's state squad in 1994-95, he looked destined for bigger things. He made his Test debut in England in 2001, then enjoyed surprising success with his chinamen against Zimbabwe at Sydney, later his home ground, at the end of 2003. A maiden Test century followed against India in January 2004.

THE FACTS Katich made 306 for NSW v Queensland in October 2007, the highest score at the SCG since Don Bradman's 452 not out, also against Queensland, in 1929-30 ... Katich made 1506 runs in 2007-08, a record for a Pura Cup/Sheffield Shield season, beating Michael Bevan's 1464 for Tasmania in 2004-05 ... In 2000-01 Katich's 1282 runs for NSW included a century against every other state ... Half of his 12 Test wickets came in one innings, during his 6 for 65 against Zimbabwe at Sydney in 2003-04 ...

THE FIGURES *to 12.9.08*   www.cricinfo.com

Batting & Fielding	M	Inns	NO	Runs	HS	Avge	S/R	100	50	4s	6s	Ct	St
Tests	26	43	3	1579	157	39.47	48.84	4	8	186	3	18	0
ODIs	45	42	5	1324	107*	35.78	68.74	1	9	138	4	13	0
T20 Ints	3	2	0	69	39	34.50	146.80	0	0	8	2	2	0
First-class	185	315	43	14910	306	54.81	–	41	78	–	–	172	0

Bowling	M	Balls	Runs	Wkts	BB	Avge	RpO	S/R	5i	10m
Tests	26	659	406	12	6–65	33.83	3.69	54.91	1	0
ODIs	45	0	–	–	–	–	–	–	–	–
T20 Ints	3	0	–	–	–	–	–	–	–	–
First-class	185	5329	3218	86	7–130	37.41	3.62	61.96	3	0

ZAHEER **KHAN**

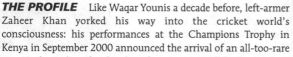

Full name	**Zaheer Khan**
Born	**October 7, 1978, Shrirampur, Maharashtra**
Teams	**Mumbai, Bangalore Royal Challengers**
Style	**Right-hand bat, left-arm fast-medium bowler**
Test debut	**India v Bangladesh at Dhaka 1999-2000**
ODI debut	**India v Kenya at Nairobi 2000-01**

THE PROFILE Like Waqar Younis a decade before, left-armer Zaheer Khan yorked his way into the cricket world's consciousness: his performances at the Champions Trophy in Kenya in September 2000 announced the arrival of an all-too-rare star in the Indian fast-bowling firmament. Well-built, quick and unfazed by reputations, Zaheer can move the ball both ways off the pitch and swing the old ball at a decent pace. After initially struggling to establish himself, he came of age in the West Indies in 2002, when he led the attack with great heart. His subsequent displays in England and New Zealand – not to mention some eye-catching moments at the 2003 World Cup – established him at the forefront of the new pace generation, but a hamstring injury saw him relegated to bit-part performer as India enjoyed some of their finest moments away in Australia and Pakistan. In a bid to jump the queue of left-arm hopefuls, Zaheer put in the hard yards for Worcestershire in 2006, bowling a lot of overs and, against Essex, taking the first nine wickets to fall before Darren Gough's flailing bat – and a dropped catch – spoilt his figures and his chances of a rare all-ten. It worked: Zaheer reclaimed his Test place, survived the fallout from the World Cup, and led the way in England in 2007, where his nine wickets at Trent Bridge gave India the match and the series: *Wisden* named him one of their Cricketers of the Year. An ankle injury restricted him in 2007-08, but he was back for the Sri Lankan tour in July 2008, taking four wickets as India squared the one-day series.

THE FACTS Zaheer Khan's 75 against Bangladesh at Dhaka in December 2004 is the highest score by a No. 11 in Tests: he dominated a last-wicket stand of 133 with Sachin Tendulkar ... He took 9 for 138 for Worcestershire v Essex at Chelmsford in June 2006 – it included a spell of 9 for 28, but a last-wicket stand of 97 cost him the chance of taking all ten wickets ... Khan averages 23.33 with the ball in Tests against New Zealand, but 47.29 v Pakistan ... His record includes six ODIs for the Asia XI ...

THE FIGURES *to 12.9.08*   www.cricinfo.com

Batting & Fielding	M	Inns	NO	Runs	HS	Avge	S/R	100	50	4s	6s	Ct	St
Tests	56	75	18	671	75	11.77	49.44	0	1	69	16	13	0
ODIs	149	85	35	678	34*	13.56	76.43	0	0	58	22	28	0
T20 Ints	1	0	–	–	–	–	–	–	–	–	–	0	0
First-class	115	152	33	1651	75	13.87	–	0	2	–	–	36	0

Bowling	M	Balls	Runs	Wkts	BB	Avge	RpO	S/R	5i	10m
Tests	56	10962	6064	178	5–29	34.06	3.31	61.58	5	0
ODIs	149	7491	6054	210	5–42	28.82	4.84	35.67	1	0
T20 Ints	1	24	15	–	2–15	7.50	3.75	12.00	0	0
First-class	115	23474	13074	472	9–138	27.69	3.34	49.73	26	7

NUWAN **KULASEKARA**

SRI LANKA

|---|---|
Full name	**Kulasekara Mudiyanselage Dinesh Nuwan Kulasekara**
Born	**July 22, 1982, Nittambuwa**
Teams	**Colts**
Style	**Right-hand bat, right-arm fast-medium bowler**
Test debut	**Sri Lanka v New Zealand at Napier 2004-05**
ODI debut	**Sri Lanka v England at Dambulla 2003-04**

THE PROFILE   From a bustling run-up and a whippy open-chested action, Nuwan Kulasekara generates a lively pace, and moves the ball off the seam at around 80mph. He can also maintain a tight line and length, which has seen him develop into something of a one-day specialist: he was part of the 2007 World Cup squad, although he only appeared in two matches and didn't take a wicket. Since then he has been a consistent one-day performer, and took 11 wickets at 14.45 against India at home late in 2008. Oddly, however, his biggest mark on international cricket so far has been with the bat. At Lord's in May 2006 Kulasekara hung on for more than three hours for 64 – his maiden Test fifty – and put on 105 for the ninth wicket with Chaminda Vaas, ensuring that Sri Lanka clung on for a draw after England made them follow on 359 behind. It was his second adhesive performance of the match, following 29 as he and Vaas pushed the first-innings total from 131 for 8 to a more respectable 192. After the next Test, though, he was dropped as his bowling lacked penetration – he tried hard afterwards to add a yard of pace, with some success, although he has managed only one more wicket in two appearances since. Kulasekara had made an instant impression in his first one-dayer, taking 2 for 19 in nine overs as England subsided for 88 at Dambulla in November 2003. That came soon after a fine first season, in which he took 61 wickets at 21.06 for Colts. He started as a softball enthusiast before shifting his focus to cricket, first with Negegoda CC and then with Galle.

THE FACTS   Playing for North Central Province at Dambulla in March 2005, Kulasekara dismissed all of Central Province's top six, finishing with 6 for 71 ... He took 7 for 27 for Colts against Bloomfield in January 2008 ... Kulasekara made 95 for Galle against Nondescripts in Colombo in October 2003: he and Primal Buddika doubled the score from 174 for 6 ... Earlier in 2003 he took 5 for 25 and 5 for 44 in the same fixture as Nondescripts were bowled out for 58 and 73 ...

THE FIGURES *to 12.9.08*   www.cricinfo.com

Batting & Fielding	M	Inns	NO	Runs	HS	Avge	S/R	100	50	4s	6s	Ct	St
Tests	6	9	1	121	64	15.12	43.06	0	1	14	2	2	0
ODIs	37	24	12	189	37	15.75	55.10	0	0	8	1	8	0
T20 Ints	0	0	–	–	–	–	–	–	–	–	–	–	–
First-class	60	82	21	1115	95	18.27	–	0	3	–	–	21	0

Bowling	M	Balls	Runs	Wkts	BB	Avge	RpO	S/R	5i	10m
Tests	6	810	440	5	2–45	88.00	3.25	162.00	0	0
ODIs	37	1630	1208	39	4–40	30.97	4.44	41.79	0	0
T20 Ints	0	0	–	–	–	–	–	–	–	–
First-class	60	8273	4555	197	7–27	23.12	3.30	41.99	8	1

PRAVEEN **KUMAR**

Full name	**Praveenkumar Sakat Singh**
Born	**October 2, 1986, Meerut, Uttar Pradesh**
Teams	**Uttar Pradesh, Bangalore Royal Challengers**
Style	**Right-hand bat, right-arm fast-medium bowler**
Test debut	**No Tests yet**
ODI debut	**India v Pakistan at Jaipur 2007-08**

THE PROFILE   Praveen Kumar is a man of many parts: a fast bowler with the ability to toil away on unresponsive Indian wickets, he can also double up as a carefree hitter down the order and even, sometimes, as a surprise opener. He started in the Uttar Pradesh Under-19 team alongside RP Singh, Piyush Chawla and Suresh Raina, and soon graduated to first-class cricket: he shone on his debut in November 2005, collecting nine wickets against Haryana. Kumar was a key performer – 41 wickets and 368 runs – as his side won the Ranji Trophy in 2005-06, his first season. He followed that with 49 wickets the following term, which earned him a place in the India A squad which contested a one-day tri-series in Kenya in August 2007. He excelled with both bat and ball, winning the Man of the Series award. He continued his fine run in the Challenger Trophy (trial games for the full national team), and was called up for the one-dayers against Pakistan, although he failed to strike in his only outing. But another strong Ranji season – including 8 for 68 in a losing cause in the final against Delhi – earned him a place for the one-day series in Australia early in 2008. He returned with reputation enhanced after claiming ten wickets in his four games, including a matchwinning spell of 4 for 46 in the second (and conclusive) final at Brisbane, and dismissing Adam Gilchrist and Ricky Ponting for single figures in both finals. After that Kumar toiled manfully for Bangalore in the inaugural season of the Indian Premier League, then produced another matchwinning four-wicket effort against Pakistan in a one-dayer in Bangladesh.

THE FACTS   Kumar took 8 for 68 for Uttar Pradesh against Mumbai in the Ranji Trophy final in January 2008 ... He took 5 for 93 (and 4 for 55 in the second innings) on his first-class debut for UP against Haryana at Kanpur in November 2005 ... Kumar scored 78 and 57, and also took 5 for 73 and 5 for 87, for UP against Andhra at Anantapur in January 2006 ...

THE FIGURES *to 12.9.08*   www.cricinfo.com

Batting & Fielding	M	Inns	NO	Runs	HS	Avge	S/R	100	50	4s	6s	Ct	St
Tests	0	0	–	–	–	–	–	–	–	–	–	–	–
ODIs	15	8	3	41	12	8.20	77.35	0	0	2	0	5	0
T20 Ints	1	1	0	6	6	6.00	60.00	0	0	0	0	0	0
First-class	25	42	2	945	78	23.62	74.17	0	5	102	31	4	0

Bowling	M	Balls	Runs	Wkts	BB	Avge	RpO	S/R	5i	10m
Tests	0	0	–	–	–	–	–	–	–	–
ODIs	15	795	642	21	4–31	30.57	4.84	37.85	0	0
T20 Ints	1	12	15	1	1–15	15.00	7.50	12.00	0	0
First-class	25	5649	2709	126	8–68	21.50	2.87	44.83	8	1

ANIL **KUMBLE**

INDIA

Full name	**Anil Kumble**
Born	**October 17, 1970, Bangalore**
Teams	**Karnataka, Bangalore Royal Challengers**
Style	**Right-hand bat, legspinner**
Test debut	**India v England at Manchester 1990**
ODI debut	**India v Sri Lanka at Sharjah 1989-90**

THE PROFILE   No bowler has won more Test matches for India than Anil Kumble. He trades the legspinner's usual yo-yo for a spear, as the ball hacks through the air rather than hanging in it, then comes off the pitch with a kick rather than a kink. He does not beat the bat as much as hit the splice, but has enjoyed stunning success, particularly on Indian soil, where his deliveries burst like water-bombs on the merest crack. Resilient and untiring, for most of his career Kumble struggled to make an impact overseas, but turned that around magnificently in Australia in 2003-04, with 24 wickets in three Tests. Then his 6 for 71 on a flat Multan track helped India win their first Test in Pakistan. He is also a handy batsman, although nervous running hindered him in one-dayers: at The Oval in 2007 he finally reached a century in his 118th Test, a record. He catches well, usually in the gully, despite once being described as moving like "a man on stilts". In December 2001, at home in Bangalore, Kumble became the first Indian spinner to take 300 Test wickets. A year later he passed 300 in one-dayers too, but he retired from the shorter game after the disappointments of the 2007 World Cup. In 2004-05 he pushed his Test tally past 400, then skittled the Aussies at Chennai with 13 wickets. And in January 2008 – by now captain – he was India's first to 600, during a fractious Australian tour which his calmness helped save. Kumble is near the end of a great career now, but his achievements – especially his "Perfect Ten" against Pakistan in February 1999 – speak for themselves.

THE FACTS   Kumble was only the second bowler (after Jim Laker) to take all ten wickets in a Test innings, with 10 for 74 v Pakistan at Delhi in 1998-99 ... He has taken 347 wickets at 24.27 in Tests in India, and 269 at 35.85 overseas: he has taken 288 in Tests that India have won – the next-best is 148, by Harbhajan Singh ... Kumble has taken 108 Test wickets against Australia, and 92 v England... His highest first-class score of 154 not out came for Karnataka v Kerala in November 1991 ... His record includes two ODIs for the Asia XI ...

THE FIGURES *to 12.9.08* — www.cricinfo.com

Batting & Fielding	M	Inns	NO	Runs	HS	Avge	S/R	100	50	4s	6s	Ct	St
Tests	130	171	32	2456	110*	17.66	38.68	1	5	295	9	59	0
ODIs	271	136	47	938	26	10.53	61.06	0	0	57	6	85	0
T20 Ints	0	0	–	–	–	–	–	–	–	–	–	–	–
First-class	241	314	61	5504	154*	21.75	–	7	17	–	–	119	0

Bowling	M	Balls	Runs	Wkts	BB	Avge	RpO	S/R	5i	10m
Tests	130	40259	18069	616	10–74	29.33	2.69	65.35	35	8
ODIs	271	14496	10412	337	6–12	30.89	4.30	43.01	2	0
T20 Ints	0	0	–	–	–	–	–	–	–	–
First-class	241	66208	29008	1128	10–74	25.71	2.62	58.69	72	19

VVS **LAXMAN**

Full name **Vangipurappu Venkata Sai Laxman**
Born **November 1, 1974, Hyderabad, Andhra Pradesh**
Teams **Hyderabad, Deccan Chargers**
Style **Right-hand bat, occasional offspinner**
Test debut **India v South Africa at Ahmedabad 1996-97**
ODI debut **India v Zimbabwe at Cuttack 1997-98**

THE PROFILE At his sublime best, VVS Laxman is a sight for the gods. Wristy, willowy and sinuous, he can match – sometimes even better – Tendulkar for strokeplay. His on-side game is comparable to his idol Azharuddin's, and yet he is decidedly more assured on the off side, and has the rare gift of being able to hit the same ball to either side. The Australians, who have suffered more than most, paid him the highest compliment after India's 2003-04 tour by admitting they did not know where to bowl to him. Laxman, a one-time medical student, finally showed signs of coming to terms with his considerable gifts in March 2001, as he tormented Steve Waugh's thought-to-be-invincible Aussies with a majestic 281 to stand the Kolkata Test on its head. But then he returned to mortality, suffering the frustrations of numerous twenties and thirties, and struggling to hold his one-day place. An uncharacteristic grinding century in Antigua in May 2002 marked his second coming, and he has been a picture of consistency since: often dazzling, but less prone to collaborating in his own dismissal. After the disappointment of being left out of the 2003 World Cup he made an emphatic return with a string of hundreds in Australia, and followed that with a matchwinning 107 in the deciding one-dayer of India's ice-breaking tour of Pakistan in March 2004. Eventually he was confined to Tests, and reached 6000 runs in August 2008, at the end of a series in Sri Lanka in which he scored consistently but was consistently dismissed by the new spin sensation Ajantha Mendis. Earlier in the year Laxman had scored his third Test century at Sydney.

THE FACTS Laxman's 281 against Australia at Kolkata in March 2001 was the highest Test score by an Indian at the time (since passed by Virender Sehwag), and included a Indian-record stand of 376 for the fifth wicket with Rahul Dravid ... He averages 50.63 against Australia, and his highest three scores (281, 178, 167) have all come against them ... Laxman has scored two first-class triple-centuries for Hyderabad – 353 against Karnataka at Bangalore in April 2000, and 301 not out against Bihar at Jamshedpur in February 1998 ...

THE FIGURES to 12.9.08   www.cricinfo.com

Batting & Fielding	M	Inns	NO	Runs	HS	Avge	S/R	100	50	4s	6s	Ct	St
Tests	96	158	21	6000	281	43.79	49.15	12	35	812	4	102	0
ODIs	86	83	7	2338	131	30.76	71.23	6	10	222	4	39	0
T20 Ints	0	0	–	–	–	–	–	–	–	–	–	–	–
First-class	209	340	38	15450	353	51.15	–	44	71	–	–	222	1

Bowling	M	Balls	Runs	Wkts	BB	Avge	RpO	S/R	5i	10m
Tests	96	324	126	2	1–2	63.00	2.33	162.00	0	0
ODIs	86	42	40	0	–	–	5.71	–	0	0
T20 Ints	0	0	–	–	–	–	–	–	–	–
First-class	209	1751	728	21	3–11	34.66	2.49	83.38	0	0

BRETT **LEE**

AUSTRALIA

Full name **Brett Lee**
Born **November 8, 1976, Wollongong, New South Wales**
Teams **New South Wales, Kings XI Punjab**
Style **Right-hand bat, right-arm fast bowler**
Test debut **Australia v India at Melbourne 1999-2000**
ODI debut **Australia v Pakistan at Brisbane 1999-2000**

THE PROFILE If Brett Lee were a Ferrari ... No. There is no
if. He's already the fastest in the world, equal with Shoaib Akhtar
at a flicker above or below 100mph. When Lee releases the
throttle and begins that smooth acceleration, anything can
happen: that leaping, classical delivery might produce a devastating yorker, a slower ball or
a young-Donald outswinger. Lee's career hasn't always been easy. He struggled with injury
and accusations of throwing, and had a strangely barren first Ashes series in 2001 (nine
wickets at 55). Three years later he overcame ankle surgery, but was 12th man for nine
successive Tests. He returned for the 2005 Ashes, and earned plaudits for his never-say-die
attitude with ball and bat, nearly conjuring victory at Edgbaston with a battling 43: Andrew
Flintoff's consoling of Lee at the end was the defining image of that epic series. Lee's 2006
brightened when he partnered Michael Kasprowicz in a nailbiting win at Johannesburg that
eased the pain of that previous near-miss. And when Glenn McGrath first struggled for
impact then withdrew to care for his sick wife, Lee became leader of the attack – a position
he had craved since first crashing onto the Test scene. He claimed 20 wickets in the Ashes
rematch, but picked up another ankle injury in New Zealand which kept him out of the
2007 World Cup. He bounced back in 2007-08, relishing his position as undisputed top
dog in the attack, and followed 40 wickets in six home Tests with 18 in three in the
Caribbean.

THE FACTS Lee took a hat-trick against Kenya in 2002-03, one of only five in the
World Cup ... His older brother Shane played 45 ODIs for Australia between 1995 and
2001 ... Lee averages 20.81 with the ball against New Zealand, but almost double that
(40.61) against England ... He was on the winning side in each of his first ten Tests, a
sequence ended by England's win at Leeds in 2001 ... Lee took 5 for 47 in his first Test
innings, but did not improve on that until his 44th match ...

THE FIGURES *to 12.9.08*   www.cricinfo.com

Batting & Fielding	M	Inns	NO	Runs	HS	Avge	S/R	100	50	4s	6s	Ct	St
Tests	68	77	17	1287	64	21.45	54.81	0	5	156	17	21	0
ODIs	173	85	36	855	57	17.44	80.66	0	2	43	25	41	0
T20 Ints	13	6	3	75	43*	25.00	138.88	0	0	6	3	5	0
First-class	106	124	24	1950	97	19.50	–	0	8	–	–	32	0

Bowling	M	Balls	Runs	Wkts	BB	Avge	RpO	S/R	5i	10m
Tests	68	14764	8550	289	5–30	29.58	3.47	51.08	9	0
ODIs	173	8853	6955	303	5–22	22.95	4.71	29.21	8	0
T20 Ints	13	277	334	12	3–27	27.83	7.23	23.08	0	0
First-class	106	22001	12507	457	7–114	27.36	3.41	48.14	18	2

BRENDON **McCULLUM**

Full name	**Brendon Barrie McCullum**
Born	**September 27, 1981, Dunedin, Otago**
Teams	**Otago, Kolkata Knight Riders**
Style	**Right-hand bat, wicketkeeper**
Test debut	**New Zealand v South Africa at Hamilton 2003-04**
ODI debut	**New Zealand v Australia at Sydney 2001-02**

THE PROFILE Brendon McCullum stepped up to the national side as a wicketkeeper-batsman after an outstanding career in international youth cricket, where he proved capable of dominating opposition attacks. He found it hard to replicate that at the highest level at first, although there were occasional fireworks in domestic cricket. But he finally made his mark in England in 2004, with 200 runs in the Tests, including an entertaining 96 at Lord's. After that near-miss he finally brought up his maiden century in Bangladesh in October, with 143 at Dhaka, and added another hundred in the two-day victory over Zimbabwe in August 2005. He made his ODI debut as a batsman, in the 2001-02 one-day series in Australia, where he made the acquaintance of Brett Lee, who has since let him have more than one beamer, to widespread outrage. Two years later McCullum, by now keeping wicket, forced his way into the Test side for the 2003-04 series against South Africa. With some onlookers murmuring the name "Gilchrist", McCullum hammered 86 from 91 balls as New Zealand overhauled Australia's 346 at Hamilton in February 2007 with one wicket to spare. But he really made his mark in 2007-08, when he enlivened the opening match of the much-hyped Indian Premier League by smacking 158 not out from 73 balls for Kolkata Knight Riders. After that, he was a marked man in England in 2008, and although there were signs that he was having trouble tempering his attacking instincts in the longer game, he lit up Lord's again with 97, and also hit 71 at Trent Bridge. Then he walloped ten sixes in his 166 in a mismatch against Ireland.

THE FACTS McCullum slammed 158 not out from only 73 balls (ten fours and 13 sixes) for Kolkata v Bangalore in the first match of the Indian Premier League ... He is the only man to be out twice in the nineties in Tests at Lord's without ever making a century there ... McCullum hit 166, and shared an opening stand of 266 with James Marshall, in an ODI against Ireland at Aberdeen in July 2008 ... His brother Nathan has played a Twenty20 international for New Zealand ...

THE FIGURES to 12.9.08   www.cricinfo.com

Batting & Fielding	M	Inns	NO	Runs	HS	Avge	S/R	100	50	4s	6s	Ct	St
Tests	35	57	3	1697	143	31.42	64.87	2	10	214	20	101	6
ODIs	135	111	22	2605	166	29.26	90.64	1	13	221	77	150	13
T20 Ints	16	16	2	323	45	23.07	120.07	0	0	31	13	9	3
First-class	74	126	7	3974	160	33.39	–	6	22	–	–	200	13

Bowling	M	Balls	Runs	Wkts	BB	Avge	RpO	S/R	5i	10m
Tests	35	0	–	–	–	–	–	–	–	–
ODIs	135	0	–	–	–	–	–	–	–	–
T20 Ints	16	0	–	–	–	–	–	–	–	–
First-class	74	0	–	–	–	–	–	–	–	–

BRYCE **McGAIN**

AUSTRALIA

Full name	**Bryce Edward McGain**
Born	**March 25, 1972, Mornington, Victoria**
Teams	**Victoria**
Style	**Right-hand bat, legspinner**
Test debut	**No Tests yet**
ODI debut	**No ODIs yet**

THE PROFILE At the age of 35, Bryce McGain went from IT worker to professional cricketer, and did it with such success that within a year he was selected for Australia's four-Test tour of India in October 2008. As the selectors continued the search for the "new Warne", McGain's promising effort during the A-team's rain-affected trip to India in September helped his cause. It followed a domestic season in which he was the leading Pura Cup spinner, with 38 wickets at 34.15, and the joint-highest wicket-taker in the one-day cup, with 15 victims at 24.40. Even more surprising was his Twenty20 contribution: six wickets at 16.16 and an economy rate of 6.46 as Victoria won the title suggested a relaxed legspinner with faith in his skills. That confidence was built over 15 years in Melbourne club cricket. For years it was next to impossible for McGain to break into the state side while Shane Warne, Colin Miller and Cameron White filled the slow-bowling roles. He did play three matches between 2001-02 and 2003-04, but did little, and seemed destined to bowl out his career for Prahran while working in the ANZ Bank's IT section. However, when White was in the Australian one-day side early in 2007, McGain was recalled and grabbed his chance with 6 for 112 against New South Wales at Sydney. He earned his first state contract, quit the day job, and was still hoping for a lengthy career despite his age: "Most first-class cricketers at 35 have had the workload of ten years of cricket, and I haven't." A tall, lean spinner with a quick approach to the crease, McGain's strength is his consistency – his variations are used sparingly but loose balls are even rarer.

THE FACTS McGain took 6 for 112 for Victoria against New South Wales at Sydney in January 2007, and 5 for 112 against them at Melbourne in November 2007 ... He took 3 for 11 in the final of the Ford Ranger Cup (Australia's domestic one-day competition) in February 2008, but Tasmania still won by one wicket ... McGain scored 51 for Denmark against the Leicestershire Cricket Board in the English C&G Trophy in August 2002 ...

THE FIGURES *to 12.9.08*   www.cricinfo.com

Batting & Fielding	M	Inns	NO	Runs	HS	Avge	S/R	100	50	4s	6s	Ct	St
Tests	0	0	–	–	–	–	–	–	–	–	–	–	–
ODIs	0	0	–	–	–	–	–	–	–	–	–	–	–
T20 Ints	0	0	–	–	–	–	–	–	–	–	–	–	–
First-class	19	20	7	158	25	12.15	31.79	0	0	–	–	7	0

Bowling	M	Balls	Runs	Wkts	BB	Avge	RpO	S/R	5i	10m
Tests	0	0	–	–	–	–	–	–	–	–
ODIs	0	0	–	–	–	–	–	–	–	–
T20 Ints	0	0	–	–	–	–	–	–	–	–
First-class	19	20	1928	57	6–112	33.82	3.14	64.63	3	0

NEIL McKENZIE

Full name	**Neil Douglas McKenzie**
Born	**November 24, 1975, Johannesburg, Transvaal**
Teams	**Lions, Durham**
Style	**Right-hand bat, occasional right-arm medium-pacer**
Test debut	**South Africa v Sri Lanka at Galle 2000**
ODI debut	**South Africa v Zimbabwe at Durban 1999-2000**

THE PROFILE Popular and unassuming, if mildly eccentric – one of his more bizarre superstitions was a liking for attaching bats to dressing-room ceilings – Neil McKenzie was a South African middle-order stalwart for four years in the early 2000s, despite a less-than-promising start as an opening batsman in Sri Lanka in 2000. From good cricketing stock (his father Kevin was a carefree middle-order batsman who represented South Africa during the rebel era), Neil captained both the South African Schools and Under-19 sides. He made maiden Test and ODI centuries against New Zealand and Sri Lanka during 2000-01, and seemed to have established himself as a more or less permanent fixture in both teams. Questions were asked about his ability to cope with the very best spinners, which may account for his three-and-a-half year exile from the side from March 2004, at a time when he ought to have been at the height of his career. Marriage and fatherhood calmed his superstitions a little, and McKenzie was eventually recalled to the Test side to face West Indies in January 2008 as an opener in place of Herschelle Gibbs, and cemented his place with 226 in a world-record opening stand with Graeme Smith against Bangladesh shortly afterwards. He did well in England, too, making 138 at Lord's and proving a calming influence in the dressing-room, although Gibbs returned for the one-day series. Neat and economical at the crease, McKenzie is particularly strong on the leg side, although his judgment in leaving off-target balls was a feature of his restrained displays after his comeback.

THE FACTS McKenzie and Graeme Smith broke the 52-year-old Test record with an opening partnership of 415 against Bangladesh at Chittagong in 2007-08 ... McKenzie averages 60.42 in Tests against India, but 22.53 v Sri Lanka (although in ODIs he averages 54.40 v Sri Lanka) ... His father Kevin played for South African representative sides during the 1980s ...

THE FIGURES to 12.9.08   www.cricinfo.com

Batting & Fielding	M	Inns	NO	Runs	HS	Avge	S/R	100	50	4s	6s	Ct	St
Tests	51	82	6	2988	226	39.31	43.24	5	15	375	21	44	0
ODIs	59	51	10	1580	131*	38.53	69.69	2	9	133	8	19	0
T20 Ints	1	0	–	–	–	–	–	–	–	–	–	0	0
First-class	170	287	32	11139	226	43.68	–	28	56	–	–	137	0

Bowling	M	Balls	Runs	Wkts	BB	Avge	RpO	S/R	5i	10m
Tests	51	84	67	0	–	–	4.78	–	0	0
ODIs	59	46	27	0	–	–	3.52	–	0	0
T20 Ints	1	0	–	–	–	–	–	–	–	–
First-class	170	660	364	7	2–13	52.00	3.30	94.28	0	0

FARVEEZ **MAHAROOF**

Full name	**Mohamed Farveez Maharoof**
Born	**September 7, 1984, Colombo**
Teams	**Nondescripts, Wayamba, Delhi Daredevils**
Style	**Right-hand bat, right-arm fast-medium bowler**
Test debut	**Sri Lanka v Zimbabwe at Harare 2003-04**
ODI debut	**Sri Lanka v Zimbabwe at Harare 2003-04**

THE PROFILE Farveez Maharoof is a fast-bowling allrounder of exciting potential, sending down lively seamers from an upright, open-chested action. The selectors fast-tracked him into the national squad early in 2004, as they looked towards the future. Faced with weak opposition in Zimbabwe, the 19-year-old Maharoof picked up a bunch of wickets – including 3 for 3 in his first ODI – but then came up against better players, although his swinging deliveries made an impression when South Africa toured. He had worked his way up through the representative ranks, playing for Sri Lanka's Under-15, U17 and U19 teams, and enjoyed a prolific school career for Wesley College, with a highest score of 243 and best bowling figures of 8 for 20. He has found Test wickets very hard to come by, but his occasionally ferocious hitting has helped him survive in the one-day side. A mean display during the Champions Trophy in England in 2004, when he exploited the end-of-summer conditions expertly, suggested he could be especially useful when Sri Lanka hit seamer-friendly conditions, although his major contribution to the 5-0 one-day clean sweep in England in 2006 was a rapid half-century at Headingley. Most importantly, Maharoof has also shown that he is comfortable under pressure. He was unlucky to miss the 2007 World Cup final after doing well in the lead-up games, although admittedly eight of his nine wickets came against Bermuda and Ireland. But he was back in favour afterwards, grabbing six wickets in three games against Pakistan, before being hampered by side and muscle strains during 2008.

THE FACTS Maharoof had figures of 3-1-3-3 on his ODI debut, as Zimbabwe were bowled out for 35 at Harare in April 2004 ... He took 6 for 14 against West Indies at Mumbai during the 2006-07 Champions Trophy ... Maharoof captained Sri Lanka in the 2004 Under-19 World Cup ... He took 7 for 73 for Bloomfield v Ragama in November 2006, and in March 2008 hit 104, his maiden first-class hundred, for Nondescripts v Chilaw Marians ...

THE FIGURES to 12.9.08   www.cricinfo.com

Batting & Fielding	M	Inns	NO	Runs	HS	Avge	S/R	100	50	4s	6s	Ct	St
Tests	20	31	4	538	72	19.92	40.00	0	3	66	3	6	0
ODIs	79	52	13	761	69	19.51	86.18	0	2	66	18	17	0
T20 Ints	4	2	0	8	8	4.00	80.00	0	0	0	0	0	0
First-class	41	62	6	1162	104	20.75	43.65	1	4	–	–	19	0

Bowling	M	Balls	Runs	Wkts	BB	Avge	RpO	S/R	5i	10m
Tests	20	2628	1458	24	4–52	60.75	3.32	109.50	0	0
ODIs	79	3268	2537	104	6–14	24.39	4.65	31.42	1	0
T20 Ints	4	72	110	2	1–16	55.00	9.16	36.00	0	0
First-class	41	5220	2863	92	7–73	31.11	3.29	56.73	1	0

MAHMUDULLAH

Full name	**Mohammad Mahmudullah**
Born	**February 4, 1986, Mymensingh**
Teams	**Dhaka**
Style	**Right-hand bat, offspinner**
Test debut	**No Tests yet**
ODI debut	**Bangladesh v Sri Lanka at Colombo 2007**

THE PROFILE An offspinning allrounder who is also an assured close-in fielder, Mahmudullah was something of a surprise inclusion in the Bangladesh side for the one-day leg of their chastening tour of Sri Lanka in mid-2007 (all three Tests were lost by an innings, and all three ODIs ended in defeat too). Mahmudullah, who can be a free-flowing batsman, made his international debut in the second one-dayer, scoring 36 and picking up two wickets in his five overs, the first when Tillakaratne Dilshan missed an attempted reverse sweep, and the second when Upul Chandana was brilliantly caught on the long-on boundary. As a bowler he does turn the ball, and can also keep the runs down. Bangladesh have a lot of left-arm spinners, but not many offbreak bowlers have made a mark yet. He had a run in the one-day side in 2008, and although his bowling proved unpenetrative he scored some useful runs down the order, including a maiden fifty against Pakistan at Faisalabad. He spent the 2005 summer on the groundstaff at Lord's: MCC's head coach, the former Middlesex and England batsman Clive Radley, remembers him as "a top cricketer, who struck the ball well with wristy cuts and pulls. He got out too often on the long-leg boundary, but scored some useful runs for us against some good attacks – he made 55 against Surrey Seconds, who included Martin Bicknell. He's an offspin bowler who bowled from quite wide of the crease – he spun it a lot and bowled a good *doosra*."

THE FACTS Mahmudullah sometimes appears on scorecards under his nickname "Riyad" ... He spent some time on the MCC groundstaff in 2005, playing alongside future World Cup players in Daan van Bunge, Kevin O'Brien and William Porterfield ... Mahmudullah's highest first-class score of 81 not out came for Dhaka against Barisal at Mirpur in December 2007 ... He took 5 for 42 for the Bangladesh Academy against their Pakistani counterparts at Savar in April 2007, and a week later took 5 for 68 against the Sri Lanka Academy at Khulna ...

THE FIGURES to 12.9.08   www.cricinfo.com

Batting & Fielding	M	Inns	NO	Runs	HS	Avge	S/R	100	50	4s	6s	Ct	St
Tests	0	0	–	–	–	–	–	–	–	–	–	–	–
ODIs	17	16	5	307	58*	27.90	62.14	0	1	18	0	1	0
T20 Ints	5	5	0	30	16	6.00	66.66	0	0	1	1	3	0
First-class	29	53	7	1427	81*	31.02	–	0	8	–	–	28	0

Bowling	M	Balls	Runs	Wkts	BB	Avge	RpO	S/R	5i	10m
Tests	0	0	–	–	–	–	–	–	–	–
ODIs	17	690	624	8	2–28	78.00	5.42	86.25	0	0
T20 Ints	5	49	48	2	1–19	24.00	5.87	24.50	0	0
First-class	29	1891	989	27	4–64	36.62	3.13	70.03	0	0

LASITH **MALINGA**

Full name **Separamadu Lasith Malinga Swarnajith**
Born **August 28, 1983, Galle**
Teams **Nondescripts, Ruhuna, Mumbai Indians**
Style **Right-hand bat, right-arm fast bowler**
Test debut **Sri Lanka v Australia at Darwin 2004**
ODI debut **Sri Lanka v United Arab Emirates at Dambulla 2004**

THE PROFILE A rare Sri Lankan cricketer from the south whose ever-changing exotic hairstyles make him stand out on and off the park, Lasith Malinga played hardly any proper cricket until he was 17, preferring the softball version in the coconut groves near his home in Rathgama, a village near Galle. But after he was spotted by the former Test fast bowler Champaka Ramanayake, he was hurried into the Galle team, took 4 for 40 and 4 for 37 on his first-class debut, and has hardly looked back since. He bowls with a distinctive and explosive round-arm action – which earned him the nickname "Slinga Malinga" – and generates genuine pace, often disconcerting batsmen who struggle to pick up the ball's trajectory. Malinga was a surprise selection for the 2004 tour of Australia, and soon showed his speed, starting with 6 for 90 against the Northern Territory Chief Minister's XI at Darwin. That paved the way for his inclusion in the Test team, and he acquitted himself well, with six wickets in his first match and four in the second: he added 5 for 80 (nine in the match) against New Zealand at Napier in April 2005. With a propensity for no-balls he was originally seen as too erratic for the one-day side, but buried that reputation with 13 wickets in the 5-0 whitewash of England in 2006. He continued his progress during 2006-07, collecting 18 wickets during the World Cup, including four in four balls against South Africa. However, he struggled against Australia and England in Tests in 2007-08, and was confined to one-day duty afterwards.

THE FACTS Malinga is the only bowler to take four wickets in four balls in international cricket, doing so against South Africa at Providence during the 2007 World Cup ... After he took 5 for 80 (9 for 210 in the match) with his low-slung action against New Zealand at Napier in April 2005, Stephen Fleming unsuccessfully asked the umpires to change their clothing: "There's a period there where the ball gets lost in their trousers" ... Malinga took 6 for 17 as Galle bowled out the Police for 51 in Colombo in November 2003 ...

THE FIGURES to 12.9.08   www.cricinfo.com

Batting & Fielding	M	Inns	NO	Runs	HS	Avge	S/R	100	50	4s	6s	Ct	St
Tests	28	34	13	192	42*	9.14	38.17	0	0	24	4	7	0
ODIs	53	25	11	92	15	6.57	50.27	0	0	5	1	11	0
T20 Ints	7	4	1	53	27	17.66	123.25	0	0	3	3	5	0
First-class	80	97	41	501	42*	8.94	37.86	0	0	–	–	22	0

Bowling	M	Balls	Runs	Wkts	BB	Avge	RpO	S/R	5i	10m
Tests	28	4777	3076	91	5–68	33.80	3.86	52.49	2	0
ODIs	53	2525	2021	79	4–44	25.58	4.80	31.96	0	0
T20 Ints	7	120	140	7	3–43	20.00	7.00	17.14	0	0
First-class	80	11321	7416	242	6–17	30.64	3.93	46.78	6	0

MANSOOR AMJAD

Full name	**Mansoor Amjad**
Born	**December 14, 1987, Sialkot, Punjab**
Teams	**Sialkot, National Bank**
Style	**Right-hand bat, right-arm legspinner**
Test debut	**No Tests yet**
ODI debut	**Pakistan v Sri Lanka at Karachi 2008**

THE PROFILE Mansoor Amjad's leg-spin was at one stage touted as the next big thing in Pakistan cricket. He was an important member of the team that won the Under-19 World Cup in Bangladesh at the start of 2004, taking 16 wickets at 10.56, and seemed set for promotion. Bob Woolmer, the national team's coach at the time, rated him highly, and that faith was justified when he took five wickets for Pakistan A against the England tourists in a warm-up match in Lahore in 2005-06. That same season, a couple of useful performances with the ball against Leicestershire, in Pakistan on a pre-season tour, persuaded the county to sign him up. He had a quiet time with the ball, taking only 12 wickets in 10 first-class county games. Since then, Amjad has improved his batting, almost to the point of it being his stronger suit, although some think his bowling has suffered: he averages nearly 30 with the bat, and has made four first-class hundreds. He finally cracked the national side in April 2008, when he was called up for the Twenty20 international against Bangladesh and wrapped up a disappointing reply with three wickets in his only over. That ensured him a place in the side for the Asia Cup, and he made his ODI debut against Sri Lanka at Karachi, keeping things tight in the face of a fine century from Kumar Sangakkara and emerging with the wicket of Chamara Kapugedera.

THE FACTS Mansoor Amjad took wickets with his second, fifth and sixth balls in international cricket, during the Twenty20 match against Bangladesh at Karachi in April 2008: his figures were 1-0-3-3 ... His highest score is 122 not out, for National Bank against Multan at Sialkot in April 2006 ... Amjad took 6 for 19 (9 for 42 in the match) for Pakistan A against Zimbabwe A at Harare in May 2005 ... He played for Leicestershire in 2006 and 2007, scoring 105 not out against Glamorgan at Leicester in July 2007 ...

THE FIGURES to 12.9.08   www.cricinfo.com

Batting & Fielding	M	Inns	NO	Runs	HS	Avge	S/R	100	50	4s	6s	Ct	St
Tests	0	0	–	–	–	–	–	–	–	–	–	–	–
ODIs	1	1	0	5	5	5.00	50.00	0	0	0	0	0	0
T20 Ints	1	0	–	–	–	–	–	–	–	–	–	2	0
First-class	60	90	13	2290	122*	29.74	–	4	8	–	–	28	0

Bowling	M	Balls	Runs	Wkts	BB	Avge	RpO	S/R	5i	10m
Tests	0	0	–	–	–	–	–	–	–	–
ODIs	1	48	44	1	1–44	44.00	5.50	48.00	0	0
T20 Ints	1	6	3	3	3–33	1.00	3.00	2.00	0	0
First-class	60	8813	5125	154	6–19	33.27	3.48	57.22	6	0

SHAUN **MARSH**

Full name	**Shaun Edward Marsh**
Born	**July 9, 1983, Narrogin, Western Australia**
Teams	**Western Australia, Kings XI Punjab**
Style	**Left-hand bat, occasional slow left-arm spinner**
Test debut	**No Tests yet**
ODI debut	**Australia v West Indies at Kingstown 2007-08**

THE PROFILE As a child Shaun Marsh spent a lot of time in the Australian set-up travelling with his father Geoff, the former Test opener. That international grounding and a backyard net helped develop him into one of the Australia's finest young batsmen. It also gave him a taste of what he could expect on his first trip with the national team when he was picked for the one-dayers in the West Indies in 2008. That came after his most consistent domestic summer, which also earned him his first national contract and WA's Player of the Year award. It was quite a response after he was briefly suspended by the state following a drinking session in November. He fought back to finish the summer as WA's leading one-day runscorer, the top Twenty20 batsman in the country, and a good Pura Cup contributor with 663 runs at 60.27. He was also the surprise hit of the inaugural Indian Premier League, finishing as the top runscorer, which helped press his case for an Australian berth. More gifted than his father ("He's got a few more shots than me," Geoff once said), Shaun is a left-hander who impressed the Waugh twins during his maiden first-class century in 2003. The milestone arrived with two successive sixes over midwicket off Mark's offspin: "It's a pretty good feeling when the Australian captain comes up to you and says well done, mate," said Marsh. The second century had to wait until 2004-05 as he struggled with concentration, the finest trait of his father's batting, and was in and out of the state side for a time, but now the selectors view him as a long-term top-order prospect.

THE FACTS Marsh was the leading scorer in the inaugural Indian Premier League season, with 616 runs for Kings XI Punjab ... He hit 81 on his ODI debut, against West Indies at Kingstown in June 2008 ... Marsh's highest first-class score is 166 not out for Western Australia v Queensland at Perth in November 2007 ... His father, Geoff Marsh, played 50 Tests for Australia from 1985-86 to 1991-92, and his younger brother Mitchell (born October 1991) is a promising batsman too ...

THE FIGURES *to 12.9.08*   www.cricinfo.com

Batting & Fielding	M	Inns	NO	Runs	HS	Avge	S/R	100	50	4s	6s	Ct	St
Tests	0	0	–	–	–	–	–	–	–	–	–	–	–
ODIs	8	8	1	333	81	47.57	76.20	0	3	34	2	0	0
T20 Ints	1	1	0	29	29	29.00	131.81	0	0	1	2	0	0
First-class	47	86	12	2588	166*	34.97	46.99	4	12	–	–	37	0

Bowling	M	Balls	Runs	Wkts	BB	Avge	RpO	S/R	5i	10m
Tests	0	0	–	–	–	–	–	–	–	–
ODIs	8	0	–	–	–	–	–	–	–	–
T20 Ints	1	0	–	–	–	–	–	–	–	–
First-class	47	144	120	2	2–20	60.00	5.00	72.00	0	0

JAMES **MARSHALL**

Full name	**James Andrew Hamilton Marshall**
Born	**February 15, 1979, Warkworth, Auckland**
Teams	**Northern Districts**
Style	**Right-hand bat**
Test debut	**New Zealand v Australia at Auckland 2004-05**
ODI debut	**New Zealand v Australia at Auckland 2004-05**

THE PROFILE James Marshall has been shuttled up and down the batting order for Northern Districts and New Zealand. His initial successes in domestic cricket came as an opener, but he made his ODI debut down the order in February 2005, playing alongside his identical twin Hamish (Australia's captain Ricky Ponting said the only way he could tell them apart was by looking at their bats, which were made by different firms). A few weeks later James was called into the team for the third Test against Australia – but this time as an opener. He was picked on potential: he had a first-class batting average of 28 at the time, and it remains less than 30. He does have a pleasingly solid technique, but lack of runs led to him losing his national contract in 2006, although later that year he did score his first ODI half-century, against Sri Lanka. He concentrated on Northern Districts, and led them to their fifth State Championship title in 2006-07. New Zealand's continued top-order struggles – exacerbated when Hamish disqualified himself by joining the disapproved Indian Cricket League – allowed James to regain his contract and earn a place on the 2008 England tour, following a strong domestic season during which he scored 616 runs at 51. Marshall raised hopes that he might be able to fill the bothersome No. 3 spot after an attractive century against Essex, but as in his previous Tests he struggled against high-class swing. He didn't get a chance in the ODIs against England, but cashed in with 161 against an outclassed Ireland team, which at least boosted an otherwise embarrassing one-day average.

THE FACTS Marshall made his Test debut in the same side as his identical twin Hamish ... Marshall hit 161, and shared an opening stand of 266 with Brendon McCullum, in an ODI against Ireland at Aberdeen in July 2008: in his other ODIs he has scored 89 runs at 9.88 ... He scored 235 for Northern Districts against Canterbury in Christchurch in March 2002 ...

THE FIGURES *to 12.9.08*　　　　　　　　　　　www.cricinfo.com

Batting & Fielding	M	Inns	NO	Runs	HS	Avge	S/R	100	50	4s	6s	Ct	St
Tests	7	11	0	218	52	19.81	39.06	0	1	29	0	5	0
ODIs	10	10	0	250	161	25.00	79.87	1	1	19	4	0	0
T20 Ints	3	2	0	14	13	7.00	93.33	0	0	2	0	0	0
First-class	102	175	8	4996	235	29.91	–	9	26	–	–	104	0

Bowling	M	Balls	Runs	Wkts	BB	Avge	RpO	S/R	5i	10m
Tests	7	0	–	–	–	–	–	–	–	–
ODIs	10	0	–	–	–	–	–	–	–	–
T20 Ints	3	0	–	–	–	–	–	–	–	–
First-class	102	531	299	4	1–5	74.75	3.37	132.75	0	0

XAVIER **MARSHALL**

WEST INDIES

Full name	**Xavier Melbourne Marshall**
Born	**March 27, 1986, St Ann, Jamaica**
Teams	**Jamaica**
Style	**Right-hand bat, occasional offspinner**
Test debut	**West Indies v Sri Lanka at Colombo 2005**
ODI debut	**West Indies v Australia at Melbourne 2004-05**

THE PROFILE   An extreme talent, in the field and with the bat, Xavier Marshall has a fiery temper and equally fiery tongue which, early in 2005, caused him to be reported for bad behaviour three times, but West Indies are desperate for this talented batsman to fulfil his potential. After slapping an unbeaten century in a one-day game against Guyana late in 2004, he was included in the West Indies side for a tour of Australia, and made his ODI debut early in 2005. In June of that year he was named as West Indies' Youth Cricketer of the Year. When a contracts dispute forced the selectors to send a weakened side to Sri Lanka shortly after that Marshall made his Test debut, but four innings as an opener brought him only 17 runs and three dismissals by the canny Chaminda Vaas. Marshall then disappeared off the radar for the best part of three years, before being recalled against Australia in 2008 as the selectors cast around, seemingly in some desperation. His return was a surprise because he had not set the world alight in the domestic season, managing only two half-centuries (indeed he is yet to score a first-class hundred). But Marshall made a classy 53 in Antigua, then bettered that with 38 and – pushed up to open again – 85 in more than three hours as West Indies made a gallant attempt to score 475 to win in Barbados. Then he improved his one-day average no end by hammering 157 not out off the limited Canadian attack in August 2008.

THE FACTS   Marshall, whose middle name is Melbourne, made his international debut at Melbourne in January 2005 ... He made 157 not out against Canada at King City in August 2008, a score exceeded in ODIs for West Indies only by Viv Richards (twice) at Brian Lara: Marshall's 12 sixes broke the ODI record, previously shared by Sanath Jayasuriya and Shahid Afridi ... Marshall's highest first-class score is also his highest Test score – 85 against Australia at Bridgetown in June 2008 ...

THE FIGURES *to 12.9.08*   www.cricinfo.com

Batting & Fielding	M	Inns	NO	Runs	HS	Avge	S/R	100	50	4s	6s	Ct	St
Tests	4	8	0	199	85	24.87	55.58	0	2	30	1	3	0
ODIs	18	18	2	317	157*	19.81	71.71	1	0	32	13	9	0
T20 Ints	1	1	0	36	36	36.00	240.00	0	0	3	3	1	0
First-class	19	35	2	907	85	27.48	–	0	6	–	–	18	0

Bowling	M	Balls	Runs	Wkts	BB	Avge	RpO	S/R	5i	10m
Tests	4	12	0	0	–	–	0.00	–	0	0
ODIs	18	9	6	0	–	–	4.00	–	0	0
T20 Ints	1	0	–	–	–	–	–	–	–	–
First-class	19	12	0	0	–	–	0.00	–	0	0

NEW ZEALAND

CHRIS **MARTIN**

Full name	**Christopher Stewart Martin**
Born	**December 10, 1974, Christchurch, Canterbury**
Teams	**Auckland, Warwickshire**
Style	**Right-hand bat, right-arm fast-medium bowler**
Test debut	**New Zealand v South Africa at Bloemfontein 2000-01**
ODI debut	**New Zealand v Zimbabwe at Taupo 2000-01**

THE PROFILE Chris Martin is an angular fast-medium bowler who receives almost as much attention for his inept batting as for his nagging bowling, which has produced almost 150 Test wickets, including 11 in the match as New Zealand whipped South Africa at Auckland in March 2004. Seven more scalps followed in the next game. It was all the more remarkable as they were his first Tests in almost two years – he had been overlooked since Pakistan piled up 643 at Lahore in May 2002 (Martin 1 for 108). He got his original chance after a crop of injuries, but did not disgrace himself in the first portion of his Test career, taking 34 wickets at 34 in his first 11 Tests, including six as Pakistan were crushed by an innings at Hamilton in 2000-01. Since his return he has lowered that average a little, happy to bowl long spells *à la* Ewen Chatfield – he took 5 for 152 at Brisbane in November 2004, after a surprisingly unproductive England tour. Back in England in 2008, he again failed to make much impression in the Tests (four wickets at 58.75), but he was nonetheless signed up by Warwickshire for a brief spell afterwards. But whatever Martin does with the ball he is likely to be remembered more for his clueless batting: he has had 23 Test ducks, finally reached double figures against Bangladesh in his 36th match (a Test record) in January 2008, and has bagged five pairs (another record). Mind you, he did once manage 25 for his former province, Canterbury, sharing a stand of 75 with Chris Harris.

THE FACTS Very few Test players approach Martin's negative ratio of runs (74) to wickets (140): two that do are England's Bill Bowes (28 runs, 68 wickets) and David Larter (15 runs, 37 wickets) ... Martin is the only man to have been dismissed five times for a pair in Tests ... Between March 2001 and October 2007 he played only two ODIs, but took six wickets in them ... In Tests Martin averages 24.59 with the ball against South Africa, but 102.12 v Australia ...

THE FIGURES to 12.9.08   www.cricinfo.com

Batting & Fielding	M	Inns	NO	Runs	HS	Avge	S/R	100	50	4s	6s	Ct	St
Tests	43	61	30	74	12*	2.38	20.05	0	0	11	0	9	0
ODIs	20	7	2	8	3	1.60	29.62	0	0	0	0	7	0
T20 Ints	6	1	1	5	5*	–	83.33	0	0	0	0	1	0
First-class	129	161	77	345	25	4.10	–	0	0	–	–	25	0

Bowling	M	Balls	Runs	Wkts	BB	Avge	RpO	S/R	5i	10m
Tests	43	8206	4678	140	6–54	33.41	3.42	58.61	8	1
ODIs	20	948	804	18	3–62	44.66	5.08	52.66	0	0
T20 Ints	6	138	193	7	2–14	27.57	8.39	19.71	0	0
First-class	129	24505	12460	404	6–54	30.84	3.05	60.65	18	1

DIMITRI **MASCARENHAS**

Full name	**Adrian Dimitri Mascarenhas**
Born	**October 30, 1977, Chiswick, Middlesex**
Teams	**Hampshire, Rajasthan Royals**
Style	**Right-hand bat, right-arm medium-pacer**
Test debut	**No Tests yet**
ODI debut	**England v West Indies at Lord's 2007**

THE PROFILE Dimitri Mascarenhas is just about the ultimate cosmopolitan cricketer: born in London, to Sri Lankan parents, he was brought up in Western Australia, and still returns there in the English winters (although he turned down a chance to join the WA state squad, to remain available for England). Charging in off a shortish run, large ear-rings jangling, he bends the ball about at just above medium-pace, and is hard to get away: he can also be a fierce striker of the ball. He made an immediate impact on his Hampshire debut in 1996, with 6 for 88 against Glamorgan, but has been more of a hit in one-day cricket. He made the first century at the new Rose Bowl, in 2001, and also took the first Twenty20 hat-trick. In 2004 Shane Warne, then his county captain, expressed surprise that England hadn't tried Mascarenhas in ODIs – and continued to push his case until he finally did get the call, in the middle of 2007, his benefit year. His early matches were unspectacular, although he did keep the runs down. But later that summer against India his rapid 52 nearly conjured an unlikely victory at Edgbaston, then he smacked five successive sixes at The Oval. Mascarenhas was the only Englishman to feature in the inaugural season of the Indian Premier League early in 2008, although in the end he played only once for Warne's title-winning Rajasthan side. After that he seemed to be surplus to England's requirements too, playing only one ODI and one Twenty20 game the following summer.

THE FACTS Mascarenhas took the first hat-trick in a Twenty20 match, for Hampshire v Sussex at Hove in July 2004, on his way to figures of 5 for 14 ... He hit five successive sixes off India's Yuvraj Singh in a one-day international at The Oval in September 2007 ... Mascarenhas was part of the England side that won the Hong Kong Sixes tournament in November 2004 ... His 104 against Worcestershire in May 2001 was the first first-class century scored at the new Rose Bowl ground in Southampton ...

THE FIGURES to 12.9.08   www.cricinfo.com

Batting & Fielding	M	Inns	NO	Runs	HS	Avge	S/R	100	50	4s	6s	Ct	St
Tests	0	0	–	–	–	–	–	–	–	–	–	–	–
ODIs	11	7	2	150	52	30.00	137.61	0	1	5	12	3	0
T20 Ints	10	9	3	81	31	13.50	147.27	0	0	5	5	6	0
First-class	170	259	28	5890	131	25.49	–	7	22	–	–	64	0

Bowling	M	Balls	Runs	Wkts	BB	Avge	RpO	S/R	5i	10m
Tests	0	0	–	–	–	–	–	–	–	–
ODIs	11	426	317	6	3–23	52.83	4.46	71.00	0	0
T20 Ints	10	186	247	10	3–18	24.70	7.96	18.60	0	0
First-class	170	24579	11119	399	6–25	27.86	2.71	61.60	16	0

MASHRAFE MORTAZA

Full name	**Mashrafe bin Mortaza**
Born	**October 5, 1983, Norail, Jessore, Khulna**
Teams	**Khulna**
Style	**Right-hand bat, right-arm fast-medium bowler**
Test debut	**Bangladesh v Zimbabwe at Dhaka 2001-02**
ODI debut	**Bangladesh v Zimbabwe at Chittagong 2001-02**

THE PROFILE Quick and aggressive, Mashrafe Mortaza has emerged as the leader of Bangladesh's pack of young pacemen, although fitness was a problem until an untroubled 2008, when he stayed healthy. At first Mashrafe made great strides under the tutelage of Andy Roberts, working on his stamina, and won his first Test cap against Zimbabwe at Dhaka in 2001-02, in what was his first-class debut – indeed, by mid-2007 he had played only eight first-class matches outside Tests. Though banging it in is his preferred style, "Koushik" proved adept at reining in his attacking instincts to concentrate on line and length. He excelled in the second Test against England in 2003-04, taking 4 for 60 in the first innings to keep Bangladesh in touch, but suffered a twisted knee that kept him out of Tests for over a year. He was recalled towards the end of 2004, and subsequently enhanced his reputation in England, standing head and shoulders above his team-mates in a torrid series. He is not a complete mug with the bat: he has a first-class century to his name, and over 20% of his ODI runs have come in sixes. A persistent back injury caused him to return home early and miss the Test series in Sri Lanka in September 2005 – the sixth time he had failed to finish a tour – but he was soon back again. His 4 for 38 in the 2007 World Cup was key in the defeat of India that propelled Bangladesh into the Super Eights, and the following year he became only the second Bangladeshi – and the first fast bowler – to take 100 wickets in ODIs.

THE FACTS Mashrafe Mortaza was the first Bangladeshi (Nazmul Hossain in 2004-05 was the second) to make his first-class debut in a Test match: only three others have done this since 1899 – Graham Vivian of New Zealand (1964-65), Zimbabwe's Ujesh Ranchod (1992-93) and Yasir Ali of Pakistan (2003-04) ... Mashrafe started the famous ODI victory over Australia at Cardiff in 2005 by dismissing Adam Gilchrist second ball for 0 ... His 6 for 26 v Kenya in Nairobi in August 2006 are Bangladesh's best bowling figures in ODIs ... His record includes two ODIs for the Asia XI ...

THE FIGURES *to 12.9.08*   www.cricinfo.com

Batting & Fielding	M	Inns	NO	Runs	HS	Avge	S/R	100	50	4s	6s	Ct	St
Tests	29	54	4	555	79	11.10	70.07	0	2	65	16	8	0
ODIs	92	74	14	968	51*	16.13	85.66	0	1	71	33	30	0
T20 Ints	9	8	2	90	36	15.00	105.88	0	0	4	5	1	0
First-class	42	75	6	1065	132*	15.43	70.76	1	4	–	–	15	0

Bowling	M	Balls	Runs	Wkts	BB	Avge	RpO	S/R	5i	10m
Tests	29	5015	2748	66	4–60	41.63	3.28	75.98	0	0
ODIs	92	4656	3643	112	6–26	32.52	4.69	41.57	1	0
T20 Ints	9	201	309	6	2–29	51.50	9.22	33.50	0	0
First-class	42	7200	3803	107	4–27	35.54	3.16	67.28	0	0

MICHAEL **MASON**

Full name	**Michael James Mason**
Born	**August 27, 1974, Carterton, Wairarapa**
Teams	**Central Districts**
Style	**Right-hand bat, right-arm fast-medium bowler**
Test debut	**New Zealand v South Africa at Wellington 2003-04**
ODI debut	**New Zealand v Pakistan at Lahore 2003-04**

THE PROFILE Michael Mason earned his place in the New Zealand side the old-fashioned way – by sheer hard work. Mason hails from Mangatainoka, not one of the more prolific development centres of the country's cricket, but he brings a long-valued work ethic associated with many country bowlers before him, including the likes of Ewen Chatfield, Harry Cave, Richard Collinge and Lance Cairns. Like them, Mason is a solid and reliable performer, a workhorse for whom no task is too great. He has been dogged by injuries, but has kept lining up for more. Once described by John Bracewell as "the best line-and-length bowler in the country", Mason was first called up by New Zealand late in 2003, after one of Shane Bond's several injuries and doubts about the availability of Chris Cairns. He toured India without playing a Test, although he did win his first – and so far only – cap at home against South Africa the following March. He has had more chances in ODIs, and after a period out of favour returned to the team in 2006-07, when his 4 for 24 against Sri Lanka won him the match award at Christchurch. He made the cut for the World Cup, where he faded after being on the receiving end of John Davison's opening salvo for Canada, but returned some tidy performances against England at home and away in 2008. At 34, though, Mason does not have time on his side.

THE FACTS At Queenstown on New Year's Eve 2006 Mason started the last over of an ODI, from Sri Lanka's Sanath Jayasuriya, needing one run from six balls to win the match for New Zealand – he didn't manage to score from the first five balls, then, with the tension sky-high, stepped down the pitch and lofted the last one back over the bowler's head for four ... Mason has taken 1 for 179 in three ODIs in Pakistan ... He took 6 for 56 (11 for 115 in the match) for Central Districts v Canterbury at Timaru in January 2003 ...

THE FIGURES *to 12.9.08*   www.cricinfo.com

Batting & Fielding	M	Inns	NO	Runs	HS	Avge	S/R	100	50	4s	6s	Ct	St
Tests	1	2	0	3	3	1.50	9.09	0	0	0	0	0	0
ODIs	25	6	3	22	13*	7.33	50.00	0	0	3	0	4	0
T20 Ints	3	1	0	2	2	2.00	100.00	0	0	0	0	0	0
First-class	68	91	26	1089	64*	16.75	–	0	1	–	–	18	0

Bowling	M	Balls	Runs	Wkts	BB	Avge	RpO	S/R	5i	10m
Tests	1	132	105	0	–	–	4.77	–	0	0
ODIs	25	1119	956	30	4–24	31.86	5.12	37.31	0	0
T20 Ints	3	54	65	2	1–18	32.50	7.22	27.00	0	0
First-class	68	12967	5414	220	6–56	24.60	2.50	58.94	8	1

AJANTHA **MENDIS**

Full name	**Balapuwaduge Ajantha Winslo Mendis**
Born	**March 11, 1985, Moratuwa**
Teams	**Sri Lanka Army, Wayamba, Kolkata Knight Riders**
Style	**Right-hand bat, right-arm off- and legspinner**
Test debut	**Sri Lanka v India at Colombo 2008**
ODI debut	**Sri Lanka v West Indies at Port-of-Spain 2007-08**

THE PROFILE Those batsmen who thought one Sri Lankan mystery spinner was enough found more on their plate during 2008, when the year's bowling sensation Ajantha Mendis stepped up to join Muttiah Muralitharan in the national side. Mendis sends down a mesmerising mixture of offbreaks, legbreaks, top-spinners, googlies and flippers, plus his very own copyright "carrom ball" – one flicked out using a finger under the ball, in the style of the old Australians Jack Iverson and John Gleeson. Mendis was a prolific wicket-taker for the Army in 2007-08, and had taken 46 wickets at 10.56 in six matches when the selectors called him up for the tour of West Indies in April 2008. He was immediately impressive, and ran rings round the Indians – the supposed masters of spin bowling – in the Asia Cup, rather ruining the final by taking 6 for 13 in only his eighth ODI. He was the Man of the Series there after taking 17 wickets all told, and did likewise in his first Test series – against the Indians again – when he took 26 wickets at 18.38 in the three home Tests in July and August, including ten in the second Test at Galle and eight in each of the other two, bamboozling the batsmen with his unpredictability, efficiency and numbing accuracy. Perhaps the most impressive statistic is that he outperformed Murali (21 wickets at 22.23) in that series, the first time since 2001-02 that any Sri Lankan had taken more wickets than Murali in any Test series in which he played more than one match. Mendis's achievements were recognised with not one but two promotions in the Sri Lankan Army following his rise to the international arena.

THE FACTS Mendis took 26 wickets in his first Test series, against India in 2008, the most by anyone in a debut series of three Tests, beating Alec Bedser's 24 for England against India in 1946 ... Mendis took 6 for 13 in the Asia Cup final against India at Karachi in July 2008 ... He took 7 for 27 for Army v Lankan CC at Panagoda in February 2008 ...

THE FIGURES *to 12.9.08*   www.cricinfo.com

Batting & Fielding	M	Inns	NO	Runs	HS	Avge	S/R	100	50	4s	6s	Ct	St
Tests	3	3	0	19	17	6.33	57.57	0	0	2	0	1	0
ODIs	13	7	4	54	15*	18.00	105.88	0	0	6	0	1	0
T20 Ints	0	0	–	–	–	–	–	–	–	–	–	–	–
First-class	22	33	0	406	37	12.30	59.97	0	0	39	3	10	0

Bowling	M	Balls	Runs	Wkts	BB	Avge	RpO	S/R	5i	10m
Tests	3	979	478	26	6–117	18.38	2.92	37.65	2	1
ODIs	13	597	357	33	6–13	10.81	3.58	18.09	2	0
T20 Ints	0	0	–	–	–	–	–	–	–	–
First-class	22	4633	2093	137	7–37	15.27	2.71	33.81	9	2

NIKITA **MILLER**

Full name **Nikita O'Brien Miller**
Born **May 16, 1982, St Elizabeth, Jamaica**
Teams **Jamaica**
Style **Right-hand bat, slow left-arm orthodox spinner**
Test debut **No Tests yet**
ODI debut **West Indies v Australia at Basseterre 2007-08**

THE PROFILE His nickname, "Killer" Miller, suggests a tearaway fast bowler, but in fact Nikita Miller is a tight, nagging slow left-armer who emerged from the 2007-08 West Indian domestic season as the leading wicket-taker with 42 victims. He saved probably his best performance for the final of the Carib Beer Challenge against Trinidad & Tobago at Sabina Park, taking 5 for 29 in the first innings – his maiden first-class five-for – and adding 5 for 92 in the second to set up a nine-wicket win for Jamaica. It was a far cry from the previous season, a disappointing one in which he managed only six wickets and copped some criticism for bowling a negative leg-side line. He changed that in 2008, and varied his flight a little more too. All this earned him a call-up for the one-dayers against Australia which followed the Test series in mid-2008. He played in two of the games and, despite having played little cricket for nearly two months, took a wicket in both his outings in St Kitts. Then he played in the tri-series in Canada, taking 3 for 19 against Bermuda in August. Miller, who has played Lancashire League cricket in England, has a nice loop, and benefited from a tip from the former West Indies coach Bennett King, who suggested he widen his grip on the ball a little to get more purchase: "I now get more rotation on the ball," says Miller, who is also a useful lower-order batsman.

THE FACTS Miller took 42 wickets in the 2007-08 West Indian domestic season, more than anyone else (Amit Jaggernauth took 41) ... Miller took 5 for 29 (10 for 121 in the match) for Jamaica against Trinidad & Tobago at Kingston in April 2008 ... A month earlier he took 4 for 6 at Nain in Jamaica as the Windward Islands were bowled out for 61 ...

THE FIGURES to 12.9.08   www.cricinfo.com

Batting & Fielding	M	Inns	NO	Runs	HS	Avge	S/R	100	50	4s	6s	Ct	St
Tests	0	0	–	–	–	–	–	–	–	–	–	–	–
ODIs	4	1	0	8	8	8.00	72.72	0	0	1	0	1	0
T20 Ints	0	0	–	–	–	–	–	–	–	–	–	–	–
First-class	27	40	9	488	48	15.74	–	0	0	–	–	17	0

Bowling	M	Balls	Runs	Wkts	BB	Avge	RpO	S/R	5i	10m
Tests	0	0	–	–	–	–	–	–	–	–
ODIs	4	240	131	7	3–19	18.71	3.27	34.28	0	0
T20 Ints	0	0	–	–	–	–	–	–	–	–
First-class	27	5942	2102	103	5–29	20.40	2.12	57.68	2	1

NEW ZEALAND

KYLE **MILLS**

Full name **Kyle David Mills**
Born **March 15, 1979, Auckland**
Teams **Auckland**
Style **Right-hand bat, right-arm fast-medium**
Test debut **New Zealand v England at Nottingham 2004**
ODI debut **New Zealand v Pakistan at Sharjah 2000-01**

THE PROFILE Injuries at inopportune times originally affected Kyle Mills's prospects of building a substantial international career. While he was recovering, Shane Bond, Ian Butler and Jacob Oram seized their opportunities, making it harder for Mills, a genuine swing bowler of lively pace, to force his way back. In and out of the team after the 2003 World Cup, he marked another comeback, against Pakistan in 2003-04, by picking up a reprimand for excessive appealing. However, he did enough to earn a call-up for the tour of England in 2004, and made his Test debut in the third match at Trent Bridge. But he suffered a side strain during that game, and was forced to fly home and miss the one-day series. That was a shame, as one-day cricket is really his forte: he played throughout the 2005-06 season, chipping in with wickets in almost every game, even if his once-promising batting had diminished to the point that he managed double figures only once in 16 matches. A feisty temper remains, though: Stephen Fleming had to pull him away from Graeme Smith during a bad-tempered one-day series towards the end of 2005. Mills returned to South Africa for the Tests early in 2006, and picked up eight wickets in the two matches he played, almost doubling his career tally. But injuries impinged again: he had ankle surgery, then broke down with knee trouble – which necessitated another op – in Australia in January 2007. He missed the World Cup, but came back stronger, and finally nailed down a place, following up 5 for 25 in a one-dayer in South Africa with a Test-best 4 for 16 against England at Hamilton.

THE FACTS Mills spanked his only first-class century from No. 9 at Wellington in 2000-01, helping Auckland recover from 109 for 7 to reach 347 ... He averages 20.50 with the ball against West Indies in ODIs, but 39.22 v Australia ... Mills achieved the first ten-wicket haul of his career, and in the process reached 100 first-class wickets, for Auckland against Canterbury in December 2004 ...

THE FIGURES *to 12.9.08* www.cricinfo.com

Batting & Fielding	M	Inns	NO	Runs	HS	Avge	S/R	100	50	4s	6s	Ct	St
Tests	14	23	4	252	57	13.26	41.17	0	1	33	3	3	0
ODIs	84	46	22	382	47	15.91	71.40	0	0	23	12	26	0
T20 Ints	7	6	2	90	33*	22.50	128.57	0	0	6	4	2	0
First-class	57	83	22	1718	117*	28.16	–	1	11	–	–	20	0

Bowling	M	Balls	Runs	Wkts	BB	Avge	RpO	S/R	5i	10m
Tests	14	2210	1078	39	4–16	27.64	2.92	56.66	0	0
ODIs	84	4216	3291	123	5–25	26.75	4.68	34.27	1	0
T20 Ints	7	161	259	7	3–44	37.00	9.65	23.00	0	0
First-class	57	9146	4409	169	5–33	26.08	2.89	54.11	3	1

MISBAH-UL-HAQ

Full name	**Misbah-ul-Haq Khan Niazi**
Born	**May 28, 1974, Mianwali, Punjab**
Teams	**Faisalabad, Sui Gas, Bangalore Royal Challengers**
Style	**Right-hand bat, occasional legspinner**
Test debut	**Pakistan v New Zealand at Auckland 2000-01**
ODI debut	**Pakistan v New Zealand at Lahore 2001-02**

THE PROFILE An orthodox right-hander with a tight technique, Misbah-ul-Haq (no relation to Inzamam-ul-Haq) caught the eye with his unflappable temperament in the triangular one-day tournament in Nairobi in September 2002, making 50 against Kenya and repeating that in the rain-ruined final against Australia. But before Pakistan could hail him as a possible middle-order mainstay, Misbah's form slumped: his highest score in three Tests against Australia was 17, and he was duly dumped. Pakistan's abysmal 2003 World Cup campaign – and the wholesale changes to the team in its aftermath – gave Misbah another chance to redeem himself, but he did little of note in his limited opportunities, and seemed to have been forgotten forever afterwards. He was overlooked for the senior side after another forgettable one-day outing against Zimbabwe in October 2004, although he played quite a bit for the A team, often as captain. He remained a consistent domestic performer, making 951 runs at 50 in 2004-05, 882 the following season, and capping that with 1108 at 61 in 2006-07, but it was nonetheless a shock when Misbah was given a national contract for 2007-08 and called up for the World Twenty20 championship. But he was a surprise hit there, and backed that up with 464 runs in three Tests against India, including two important centuries to ensure there was no danger of following on after India had twice totalled more than 600. Suddenly, rising 34, Misbah was an automatic choice.

THE FACTS Misbah-ul-Haq has made four first-class double-centuries, the highest 208 not out (in a total of 723 for 4) for Punjab v Baluchistan at Sialkot in March 2008 ... He scored 161 and 133, both not out, in successive Tests against India in 2007-08 ... Misbah hit 87 not out, Pakistan's highest score in Twenty20 internationals, against Bangladesh at Karachi in April 2008 ... He averages 44.50 in ODIs against Australia, but only 11.50 in Tests against them ... Misbah scored 218 runs in the inaugural World Twenty20 championship in South Africa late in 2007: only Matthew Hayden and Gautham Gambhir made more ...

THE FIGURES *to 12.9.08*   www.cricinfo.com

Batting & Fielding	M	Inns	NO	Runs	HS	Avge	S/R	100	50	4s	6s	Ct	St
Tests	10	18	2	671	161*	41.93	39.96	2	1	77	4	8	0
ODIs	40	35	7	1085	76	38.75	88.13	0	5	83	22	20	0
T20 Ints	10	10	5	338	87*	67.60	135.20	0	3	23	15	2	0
First-class	130	209	23	9747	208*	52.40	–	30	46	–	–	118	0

Bowling	M	Balls	Runs	Wkts	BB	Avge	RpO	S/R	5i	10m
Tests	10	0	–	–	–	–	–	–	–	–
ODIs	40	24	30	0	–	–	7.50	–	0	0
T20 Ints	10	0	–	–	–	–	–	–	–	–
First-class	130	192	149	3	1–2	49.66	4.65	64.00	0	0

MOHAMMAD ASHRAFUL

Full name	**Mohammad Ashraful**
Born	**July 7, 1984, Dhaka**
Teams	**Dhaka**
Style	**Right-hand bat, legspinner**
Test debut	**Bangladesh v Sri Lanka at Colombo 2001-02**
ODI debut	**Bangladesh v Zimbabwe at Bulawayo 2000-01**

THE PROFILE On September 8, 2001, at the Sinhalese Sports Club in Colombo, Mohammad Ashraful turned a terrible mismatch into a slice of history by becoming the youngest man – or boy – to make a Test century. Bangladesh still crashed to heavy defeat, but "Matin" brought hope and consolation with a sparkling hundred, repeatedly dancing down to hit the Sri Lankan spinners, including Muttiah Muralitharan, back over their heads ... and on his debut, too. It was the day before his 17th birthday according to some sources, and 63 days after it according to most others: either way, he broke the long-standing record set by Mushtaq Mohammad (17 years 82 days) in 1960-61. Inevitably, such a heady early achievement proved hard to live up to, and after a prolonged poor run Ashraful was dropped for England's first visit in October 2003. He returned to the side a better player, but no less flamboyant, as he demonstrated with a glorious unbeaten 158 in defeat against India at Chittagong late in 2004. Still not 21 when Bangladesh made their maiden tour of England the following year, Ashraful confirmed his status as one for the future at Cardiff, when his brilliantly paced century set his side up for their astonishing one-day victory over Australia. He continued to fire spasmodically, a superb 87 bringing victory over South Africa in the 2007 World Cup, but that was surrounded by more low scores. When Habibul Bashar stood down in May 2007 Ashraful took on the captaincy – but the results stayed the same and, still just 24, he looked more careworn by the end of 2008.

THE FACTS Only 12 players have made their Test debuts when younger than Ashraful: four of them are from Bangladesh ... He scored 263, putting on 420 with Marshall Ayub, for Dhaka v Chittagong in November 2006 ... Ashraful averages 58.60 in Tests v India, but only 5.75 v England ... He took the catch that sealed Bangladesh's first Test win, over Zimbabwe at Chittagong in January 2005 ... Ashraful's highest ODI score is 109, against the UAE at Lahore in the 2008 Asia Cup ... His record includes two ODIs for the Asia XI ...

THE FIGURES *to 12.9.08*   www.cricinfo.com

Batting & Fielding	M	Inns	NO	Runs	HS	Avge	S/R	100	50	4s	6s	Ct	St
Tests	42	82	4	1922	158*	24.64	46.53	4	7	234	20	14	0
ODIs	128	121	11	2506	109	22.78	72.53	2	14	258	22	21	0
T20 Ints	8	8	0	143	61	17.87	172.28	0	1	15	5	1	0
First-class	84	158	5	4610	263	30.13	–	12	18	–	–	38	0

Bowling	M	Balls	Runs	Wkts	BB	Avge	RpO	S/R	5i	10m
Tests	42	1183	923	12	2–42	76.91	4.68	98.58	0	0
ODIs	128	384	403	11	3–26	36.63	6.29	34.90	0	0
T20 Ints	8	96	160	5	3–42	32.00	10.00	19.20	0	0
First-class	84	5596	3381	99	7–99	34.15	3.62	56.52	5	0

MOHAMMAD YOUSUF

Full name	**Mohammad Yousuf Youhana**
Born	**August 27, 1974, Lahore, Punjab**
Teams	**Lahore, WAPDA, Lancashire**
Style	**Right-hand bat**
Test debut	**Pakistan v South Africa at Durban 1997-98**
ODI debut	**Pakistan v Zimbabwe at Harare 1997-98**

THE PROFILE Until his conversion to Islam in 2005, Mohammad Yousuf (formerly Yousuf Youhana) was one of the rare Christians to play for Pakistan. After a difficult debut, he quickly established himself as a stylish world-class batsman, and a middle-order pillar alongside Inzamam-ul-Haq and Younis Khan. After becoming a Muslim, he turned into a run machine, shattering Viv Richards's 30-year-old record for Test runs in a calendar year during a stellar 2006. Yousuf gathers his runs through composed, orthodox strokeplay: he is particularly strong driving through the covers and flicking wristily off his legs, and has a backlift as decadent and delicious as any, although a tendency to overbalance when playing across his front leg can get him into trouble. He is quick between the wickets, although not the best judge of a single, and there have recently been signs of increasing sluggishness in the field. Some initially questioned his temperament under pressure, but he began to silence those critics late in 2004. First came a spellbindingly languid century at Melbourne, when he ripped into Shane Warne as few Pakistanis have ever done. A century followed in the Kolkata cauldron, and he ended 2005 with an easy-on-the-eye 223 against England at Lahore, eschewing the waftiness that had previously blighted him. His batting (and his beard) burgeoned in 2006, and it was a surprise when he jeopardised his international future the following year by signing up for the breakaway Indian Cricket League, although he later withdrew.

THE FACTS Since becoming a Muslim Mohammad Yousuf has averaged 78.06 in 20 Tests: in 59 matches beforehand he averaged 47.46 ... He scored 1788 Test runs in 2006, breaking Viv Richards's old calendar-year record of 1710 in 1976 ... Yousuf made double-centuries in successive Tests against England, 223 at Lahore in December 2005 and 202 at Lord's in July 2006 ... In all he has scored four double-centuries in Tests, but had not made another in first-class cricket until he hit 205 not out for Lancashire v Yorkshire at Headingley in 2008 ... His record includes seven ODIs for the Asia XI ...

THE FIGURES to 12.9.08   www.cricinfo.com

Batting & Fielding	M	Inns	NO	Runs	HS	Avge	S/R	100	50	4s	6s	Ct	St
Tests	79	134	12	6770	223	55.49	52.58	23	28	869	47	59	0
ODIs	269	254	40	9242	141*	43.18	75.34	15	62	746	87	53	0
T20 Ints	1	1	0	20	20	20.00	105.26	0	0	2	1	0	0
First-class	122	202	20	9354	223	51.39	–	28	44	–	–	77	0

Bowling	M	Balls	Runs	Wkts	BB	Avge	RpO	S/R	5i	10m
Tests	79	6	3	0	–	–	3.00	–	0	0
ODIs	269	2	1	1	1–0	1.00	3.00	2.00	0	0
T20 Ints	1	0	–	–	–	–	–	–	–	–
First-class	122	18	24	0	–	–	8.00	–	0	0

ALBIE **MORKEL**

Full name	**Johannes Albertus Morkel**
Born	**June 10, 1981, Vereeniging, Transvaal**
Teams	**Titans, Durham, Chennai Super Kings**
Style	**Left-hand bat, right-arm fast-medium bowler**
Test debut	**No Tests yet**
ODI debut	**South Africa v New Zealand at Wellington 2003-04**

THE PROFILE Albie Morkel, a right-arm fast-medium bowler and big-hitting left-handed batsman, was lumbered with the tag of the "new Lance Klusener", and was touted early in his career by Ray Jennings – his provincial coach, and a former national coach too – as someone who could become a world-class allrounder. It hasn't quite happened yet, although he does average over 40 with the bat in first-class cricket, with a double-century to his name, and Twenty20 seems to be tailor-made for his style of play. There have been glimpses of his talent: for his provincial side Easterns (now the Titans) against the touring West Indians at Benoni in 2003-04, he defied food poisoning to score a century – putting on 141 for the ninth wicket with his brother, Morne, with whom he often opens the bowling too – and also took five wickets in the match. Albie was picked for the senior tour of New Zealand shortly after that, and made his one-day international debut there early in 2004: he performed solidly, if unspectacularly, for a while until the selectors looked elsewhere. Morkel was back for the Afro-Asia Cup in June 2007. In the second match, at Chennai, Albie and Morne opened the bowling together for the African XI, the first instance of brothers sharing the new ball in an ODI since Kenya's Martin and Tony Suji did so during the 1999 World Cup. Shortly after that Morkel hit 97 against the outclassed Zimbabweans. His huge sixes were a feature of the inaugural World Twenty20 championship late in 2007, but he was restricted by injury in England the following year.

THE FACTS Albie Morkel made 204 not out, putting on 264 with Justin Kemp, as Titans drew with Western Province Boland in March 2005 after following on ... He took 6 for 36 for Easterns v Griqualand West in December 1999 ... Morkel's brother Morne has also played for South Africa, while another brother, Malan, played for SA Schools ... His record includes two ODIs for the Africa XI, in one of which he opened the bowling with Morne ...

THE FIGURES to 12.9.08

www.cricinfo.com

Batting & Fielding	M	Inns	NO	Runs	HS	Avge	S/R	100	50	4s	6s	Ct	St
Tests	0	0	–	–	–	–	–	–	–	–	–	–	–
ODIs	26	16	1	258	97	17.20	84.03	0	1	24	8	4	0
T20 Ints	11	8	1	196	43	28.00	133.33	0	0	11	14	4	0
First-class	55	79	15	2718	204*	42.46	–	4	17	–	–	22	0

Bowling	M	Balls	Runs	Wkts	BB	Avge	RpO	S/R	5i	10m
Tests	0	0	–	–	–	–	–	–	–	–
ODIs	26	1014	872	30	4–29	29.06	5.15	33.80	0	0
T20 Ints	11	156	163	6	2–12	27.16	6.26	26.00	0	0
First-class	55	8585	4388	144	6–36	30.47	3.06	59.61	3	0

SOUTH AFRICA

MORNE **MORKEL**

Full name **Morne Morkel**
Born **October 6, 1984, Vereeniging, Transvaal**
Teams **Titans, Yorkshire, Rajasthan Royals**
Style **Left-hand bat, right-arm fast bowler**
Test debut **South Africa v India at Durban 2006-07**
ODI debut **Africa XI v Asia XI at Bangalore 2007**

THE PROFILE Morne Morkel, the taller, faster brother of Easterns allrounder Albie, has been a hot property ever since his first-class debut in 2003-04, when he made 44 not out in a ninth-wicket stand of 141 with his brother against the touring West Indians at Benoni. An out-and-out fast bowler, Morne did well in 2004-05, taking 20 wickets at 18.20 apiece, but then sat out most of the following season with injuries, which troubled him again during 2008. But he soon impressed Allan Donald: "He gets serious bounce, and he's got really great pace – genuine pace. He has a great attitude to go with his physical strengths." Morkel shook up the Indians while playing for the Rest of South Africa in December 2006, bowling Virender Sehwag with his first ball and adding the wickets of Laxman, Tendulkar and Dhoni as the tourists lurched to 69 for 5. That got him into the national frame, and he played in the second Test at Durban when Dale Steyn was ruled out, although three wickets and some handy runs in a crushing victory weren't quite enough to keep him in for the final Test, when Steyn was fit again. Morkel played his first ODIs in the Afro-Asia Cup in India in June 2007, and did well again, taking eight wickets in three matches. He played for Kent, the eventual winners, in the qualifying rounds of England's Twenty20 Cup in 2007, and turned out for Yorkshire early the following season, before the start of the South African tour, in which he struggled occasionally with his line but impressed with his pace and bounce.

THE FACTS Morne Morkel took 6 for 66 for a Combined XI v Zimbabwe at Benoni in February 2005 ... He took 5 for 50 against Bangladesh at Dhaka in February 2008 ... His brother Albie has also played for South Africa, while another brother, Malan, played for SA Schools ... Morkel's first three ODIs were for the Africa XI: in one he opened the bowling with Albie, the first instance of brothers sharing the new ball in an ODI since Kenya's Martin and Tony Suji did so during the 1999 World Cup ...

THE FIGURES to 12.9.08   www.cricinfo.com

Batting & Fielding	M	Inns	NO	Runs	HS	Avge	S/R	100	50	4s	6s	Ct	St
Tests	10	12	1	163	35	14.81	54.88	0	0	26	0	0	0
ODIs	13	5	2	58	25	19.33	105.45	0	0	5	2	3	0
T20 Ints	6	1	1	1	1*	–	33.33	0	0	0	0	0	0
First-class	32	40	6	524	57	15.41	48.11	0	1	–	–	15	0

Bowling	M	Balls	Runs	Wkts	BB	Avge	RpO	S/R	5i	10m
Tests	10	1699	1052	32	5–50	32.87	3.71	53.09	1	0
ODIs	13	656	542	21	4–36	25.80	4.95	31.23	0	0
T20 Ints	6	144	142	10	4–17	14.20	5.91	14.40	0	0
First-class	32	5232	3099	103	6–66	30.08	3.55	50.79	3	0

RUNAKO **MORTON**

Full name	**Runako Shakur Morton**
Born	**July 22, 1978, Nevis**
Teams	**Leeward Islands**
Style	**Right-hand bat, occasional offspinner**
Test debut	**West Indies v Sri Lanka at Colombo 2005**
ODI debut	**West Indies v Pakistan at Sharjah 2001-02**

THE PROFILE Runako Morton is fiery on and off the pitch. His career looked to be over before it had properly started when he was expelled from the West Indian Academy in 2001 for a series of disciplinary breaches. He refused to be bowed, and continued to accumulate runs for the Leeward Islands. In February 2002, his penance complete, he was called into an injury-plagued squad. But he threw away his opportunity when he pulled out of the Champions Trophy in September 2002, pretending that his grandmother had died. His career slipped further down the pan when he was arrested in January 2004, in connection with a stabbing incident, but he was given a third chance at redemption in May 2005, being recalled to the one-day squad when South Africa toured, although he didn't actually play. After moving to live in Trinidad – and calming down, he says – he finally made his debut (becoming only the fifth Test player from the tiny island of Nevis) in Sri Lanka in 2005, in a side decimated by a damaging contracts dispute, and also toured New Zealand early in 2006, making two handy scores in the Tests, and adding a defiant one-day century at Napier. He struggled against spin, though, and was pushed up to open in the one-dayers at home against Zimbabwe, helping himself to 79 and 109. But the Indians were an altogether stiffer proposition, and he was dropped after making 23, 1 and 0 against them. He played a few good-looking cameos in England in 2007, although he always gave the impression that a wild swing was never too far away, and was dropped again after two modest Tests against Australia early in 2008. He needs to knuckle down more to become a genuine Test No. 4.

THE FACTS Morton made 201 for the West Indians against MCC at Durham in 2007 ... He withdrew from the 2002 Champions Trophy in Sri Lanka, claiming that his grandmother had died: it later turned out that one of his grandmothers had been dead for 16 years, and the other was still alive ... Morton collected a 31-ball duck against Australia at Kuala Lumpur in September 2006, the longest scoreless innings in ODI history ...

THE FIGURES *to 12.9.08*   www.cricinfo.com

Batting & Fielding	M	Inns	NO	Runs	HS	Avge	S/R	100	50	4s	6s	Ct	St
Tests	15	27	1	573	70*	22.03	48.07	0	4	79	7	20	0
ODIs	49	44	4	1330	110*	33.25	65.93	2	9	110	13	17	0
T20 Ints	5	5	1	56	20	14.00	91.80	0	0	5	2	1	0
First-class	77	129	8	4494	201	37.14	–	10	28	–	–	91	0

Bowling	M	Balls	Runs	Wkts	BB	Avge	RpO	S/R	5i	10m
Tests	15	66	50	0	–	–	4.54	–	0	0
ODIs	49	6	2	0	–	–	2.00	–	0	0
T20 Ints	5	0	–	–	–	–	–	–	–	–
First-class	77	467	289	8	3–17	36.12	3.71	58.37	0	0

MUTTIAH **MURALITHARAN**

Full name	**Muttiah Muralitharan**
Born	**April 17, 1972, Kandy**
Teams	**Tamil Union, Kandurata, Chennai Super Kings**
Style	**Right-hand bat, offspinner**
Test debut	**Sri Lanka v Australia at Colombo 1992-93**
ODI debut	**Sri Lanka v India at Colombo 1993-94**

THE PROFILE Muttiah Muralitharan is one of the most successful bowlers the game has seen, Sri Lanka's greatest player ... and without doubt the most controversial cricketer of the modern age. Murali's rise from humble beginnings – the Tamil son of a hill-country confectioner – to the top of the wicket-taking lists has divided opinion because of his weird bent-armed delivery. From a loose-limbed, open-chested action, his chief weapons are the big-turning offbreak and two top-spinners, one of which goes straight on and the other, the *doosra*, which spins from a rubbery wrist in the opposite direction to his stock ball. However, suspicions about his action surfaced when he was no-balled for throwing in Australia, first on Boxing Day 1995 at Melbourne, then in the subsequent one-day series. He was cleared by ICC after biomechanical analysis concluded that his action, and a deformed elbow which he can't fully straighten, create the "optical illusion of throwing". But the controversy did not die: Murali was called again in Australia in 1998-99, had more tests, and was cleared again. Then his new *doosra* prompted further suspicion, and he underwent yet more high-tech tests in 2004, which ultimately forced ICC to revise their rules on chucking. On the field, Murali continued to pile up the wickets, overtaking Courtney Walsh's Test-record 519 in May 2004: only shoulder trouble, which required surgery, allowed Shane Warne to pass him. Murali returned, potent as ever, flummoxed England with 8 for 70 at Nottingham to square the 2006 series, and sailed past 750 wickets in 2008.

THE FACTS Muralitharan was the second bowler (after Shane Warne) to take 700 Test wickets, and the first to take 1,000 in all international cricket ... His 65 Test five-fors is easily a record (Warne is next with 37) ... Murali has taken nine wickets in a Test innings twice, and his 16 for 220 at The Oval in 1998 is the fifth-best haul in all Tests ... His record includes a Test and three ODIs for the World XI, and four ODIs for the Asia XI ...

THE FIGURES to 12.9.08   www.cricinfo.com

Batting & Fielding	M	Inns	NO	Runs	HS	Avge	S/R	100	50	4s	6s	Ct	St
Tests	123	154	52	1156	67	11.33	69.26	0	1	133	25	69	0
ODIs	314	145	54	542	27	5.95	69.39	0	0	36	7	123	0
T20 Ints	1	0	–	–	–	–	–	–	–	–	–	0	0
First-class	222	266	79	2089	67	11.16	–	0	1	–	–	120	0

Bowling	M	Balls	Runs	Wkts	BB	Avge	RpO	S/R	5i	10m
Tests	123	41000	16604	756	9–51	21.96	2.42	54.23	65	21
ODIs	314	17048	11030	479	7–30	23.02	3.88	35.59	9	0
T20 Ints	1	24	27	2	2–27	13.50	6.75	12.00	0	0
First-class	222	63894	25421	1330	9–51	19.11	2.38	48.04	117	33

MUSHFIQUR RAHIM

Full name	**Mohammad Mushfiqur Rahim**
Born	**September 1, 1988, Bogra**
Teams	**Sylhet**
Style	**Right-hand bat, wicketkeeper**
Test debut	**Bangladesh v England at Lord's 2005**
ODI debut	**Bangladesh v Zimbabwe at Harare 2006**

THE PROFILE   A wild-card inclusion for Bangladesh's maiden tour of England in 2005, Mushfiqur Rahim was just 16 when he was selected for that daunting trip – two Tests in May, followed by six ODIs against England and Australia – even though he hadn't been named in the preliminary squad of 20. Mushfiqur was principally chosen as an understudy to long-serving wicketkeeper Khaled Mashud, but his inclusion was further evidence of Bangladesh's determination to build for a better future. He had done well on an A-team tour of Zimbabwe earlier in 2005, scoring a century in the first Test at Bulawayo, and also enjoyed some success in England the previous year with the Under-19s, making 88 in the second Test at Taunton. He showed more evidence of grit with the full team, with a maiden first-class half-century to soften the pain of defeat against Sussex, followed by a hundred against Northamptonshire. That earned him a call-up – as a batsman – to become the youngest player to appear in a Test at Lord's. He was one of only three players to reach double figures in a disappointing first innings, but a twisted ankle kept him out of the second Test. He also featured in Bogra's inaugural Test, against Sri Lanka the following month, but could make little of the spin of Murali and Malinga Bandara. He supplanted Mashud for the 2007 World Cup, anchoring the win over India with 56 not out, then nicked his Test place too. Rahim started with a defiant 80 in Colombo, but a poor run with the bat early in 2008 – four runs in five ODIs, including three successive ducks – cost him his place.

THE FACTS   Mushfiqur Rahim's hundred for Bangladesh against Northamptonshire in 2005 made him the youngest century-maker in English first-class cricket, beating Sachin Tendulkar's record: Rahim was 16 years 261 days old, 211 days younger than Tendulkar in 1990; the youngest Englishman was 17-year-old Stephen Peters for Essex in 1996 ... Rahim played two Tests – and eight other matches for Bangladesh representative teams – before appearing in a first-class match at home ...

THE FIGURES to 12.9.08   www.cricinfo.com

Batting & Fielding	M	Inns	NO	Runs	HS	Avge	S/R	100	50	4s	6s	Ct	St
Tests	8	16	1	174	80	11.60	33.59	0	1	21	1	8	0
ODIs	35	29	6	476	57	20.69	56.06	0	2	32	3	22	6
T20 Ints	8	6	3	17	6*	5.66	68.00	0	0	0	0	4	7
First-class	27	47	6	1111	115*	27.09	40.84	2	7	–	–	47	4

Bowling	M	Balls	Runs	Wkts	BB	Avge	RpO	S/R	5i	10m
Tests	8	0	–	–	–	–	–	–	–	–
ODIs	35	0	–	–	–	–	–	–	–	–
T20 Ints	8	0	–	–	–	–	–	–	–	–
First-class	27	0	–	–	–	–	–	–	–	–

BRENDAN **NASH**

Full name	**Brendan Paul Nash**
Born	**December 14, 1977, Attadale, Western Australia**
Teams	**Jamaica**
Style	**Left-hand bat, left-arm medium-pacer**
Test debut	**No Tests yet**
ODI debut	**West Indies v Bermuda at King City 2008**

THE PROFILE A smallish (5ft 8ins) but solid strokeplaying left-hander, Brendan Nash played in three Pura Cup finals for Queensland, scoring 96 in one of them, before losing his state contract after a patchy 2006-07 season. After that he decided to try his luck in Jamaica, where his father Paul was born – he swam for Jamaica in the 1968 Mexico Olympics, but the family emigrated to Australia while his wife was pregnant with Brendan. Nash had a fine first season for his new team, proving a consistent scorer. He helped Jamaica win the Carib Beer Cup title: he was left stranded on 91 not out in the match against Guyana, but made no mistake in the next game, against Trinidad & Tobago, with 102. In the Carib Beer Challenge final, also against T&T, he made another century, to finish the season with 422 first-class runs at 46.88 in seven matches. Although he was less prolific in limited-overs games, it was no great surprise when he was called up to the West Indian squad for a triangular one-day series in Canada in August 2008 – although there were murmurs in the Caribbean about an Australian "mercenary" muscling his way in after being jettisoned by his state. However, Nash took any criticism in his stride, made 27 and 39 in the two ODIs in which he batted, and also took five wickets: he now looks set for further honours. He rarely bowled for Queensland, but is a handy containing medium-pacer capable of trundling through his quota in one-dayers. And he remains a fine fielder: earlier in his career he was Australia's substitute fielder in a Test *against* West Indies at the Gabba late in 2005.

THE FACTS Nash was the first white man to play for West Indies since Geoff Greenidge in 1972-73 ... He hit 176 for Queensland against New South Wales at Brisbane in October 2002 ... Nash scored 96 in Australia's Pura Cup final in 2001-02, and 117 in West Indies' Carib Beer Challenge final in April 2008 ...

THE FIGURES to 12.9.08   www.cricinfo.com

Batting & Fielding	M	Inns	NO	Runs	HS	Avge	S/R	100	50	4s	6s	Ct	St
Tests	0	0	–	–	–	–	–	–	–	–	–	–	–
ODIs	3	2	2	66	39*	–	73.33	0	0	9	0	0	0
T20 Ints	0	0	–	–	–	–	–	–	–	–	–	–	–
First-class	36	63	6	1755	176	30.78	–	5	5	–	–	19	0

Bowling	M	Balls	Runs	Wkts	BB	Avge	RpO	S/R	5i	10m
Tests	0	0	–	–	–	–	–	–	–	–
ODIs	3	180	132	5	3–56	26.00	4.40	36.00	0	0
T20 Ints	0	0	–	–	–	–	–	–	–	–
First-class	36	246	88	4	2–7	22.00	2.41	61.50	0	0

NASIR JAMSHED

PAKISTAN

Full name	Nasir Jamshed
Born	December 6, 1989, Lahore, Punjab
Teams	Lahore, National Bank
Style	Left-hand bat
Test debut	No Tests yet
ODI debut	Pakistan v Zimbabwe at Karachi 2007-08

THE PROFILE A hard-hitting left-hand opener prone to ugly hoicks but also capable of some lovely drives and pulls, Nasir Jamshed jumped to national prominence early in 2008, forcing his way into the squad for the one-day series against the touring Zimbabweans after flaying them for 182 from 240 balls in a warm-up game. Jamshed kick-started his international career with a Man of the Match-winning 61 (from 48 balls) in the first game, and 74 (from 64 balls with 14 fours) in the second. Leaner pickings followed, almost inevitably, until he peeled off successive unbeaten scores of 53 and 52 against India and Bangladesh in the Asia Cup in July, to suggest that he had found a permanent place. Jamshed had long been tipped for stardom. He made his first-class debut shortly after turning 15, and made 74: that won him a place in Pakistan's Under-19 team, and he responded with 44 and 204 in his first match, against Sri Lanka. He remained in the Under-19s long enough to ensure they retained their World Cup title early in 2006, with victory in an astonishing final in Colombo (Pakistan were bowled out for 109, but humbled India for 71). He consolidated after that before breaking out in 2007-08, a season in which he topped the runscoring lists with 1353 runs – 800 of them in the Quaid-e-Azam Trophy – including six centuries, which was more than enough to earn him a run in the national team, although there have been murmurs about his weight.

THE FACTS Nasir Jamshed made 74 on his first-class debut for National Bank against Defence Housing Authority at Faisalabad in February 2005, two months after his 15th birthday ... The following month he made 204 for Pakistan Under-19s in the first Test against Sri Lanka in Karachi ... Jamshed scored 61 and 74 in his first two ODIs, against Zimbabwe in January 2008 ...

THE FIGURES to 12.9.08   www.cricinfo.com

Batting & Fielding	M	Inns	NO	Runs	HS	Avge	S/R	100	50	4s	6s	Ct	St
Tests	0	0	–	–	–	–	–	–	–	–	–	–	–
ODIs	9	9	2	343	74	49.00	103.62	0	4	48	6	3	0
T20 Ints	0	0	–	–	–	–	–	–	–	–	–	–	–
First-class	26	43	4	1796	182	46.05	–	6	5	–	–	19	0

Bowling	M	Balls	Runs	Wkts	BB	Avge	RpO	S/R	5i	10m
Tests	0	0	–	–	–	–	–	–	–	–
ODIs	9	0	–	–	–	–	–	–	–	–
T20 Ints	0	0	–	–	–	–	–	–	–	–
First-class	26	6	8	0	–	–	8.00	–	0	0

NAZIMUDDIN

Full name	**Mohammad Nazimuddin**
Born	**October 1, 1985, Chittagong**
Teams	**Chittagong**
Style	**Right-hand bat**
Test debut	**No Tests yet**
ODI debut	**Bangladesh v South Africa at Mirpur 2007-08**

THE PROFILE An attacking right-hander, Nazimuddin started his first-class career for Chittagong at the tender age of 16 in 2001-02, and scored a hundred in his third match. A double-century followed the following season, and the surprise is that he did not receive a call-up to the full national team until early in 2008. He had starred in the last match of the National League in April 2005, following a five-hour 103 with 82 as Chittagong drew with the champions Dhaka. That won him a place in the A team which toured England that summer, and he made 60 against Yorkshire. When England A made the return trip the following season Nazimuddin did his claims no harm, with successive scores of 108, 58 and 42 in the three one-day games he played. Later in the year he was chosen in the squad for the inaugural World Twenty20 championship, and hammered 81 from 50 balls in a warm-up match against Pakistan in Kenya. He didn't fare so well in the tournament proper, managing only 12 runs, with two ducks, in four attempts, and also struggled at first when given a run in the 50-over team, although he did manage 47, cutting and driving well before being run out, against Sri Lanka during the Asia Cup. Nazimuddin has all the shots, but will need to tighten his defence if he is to succeed at international level.

THE FACTS Nazimuddin scored 81 against Pakistan in Nairobi in September 2007, Bangladesh's highest score in a Twenty20 international ... He made his first-class debut in January 2002, three months after his 16th birthday: in his third match he scored 110 ... Aged 17, he scored 204 for Chittagong against Sylhet at Chittagong ... Nazimuddin made 108 in a one-day game against England A at Bogra in March 2007 ...

THE FIGURES to 12.9.08   www.cricinfo.com

Batting & Fielding	M	Inns	NO	Runs	HS	Avge	S/R	100	50	4s	6s	Ct	St
Tests	0	0	–	–	–	–	–	–	–	–	–	–	–
ODIs	7	7	0	90	47	12.85	69.23	0	0	13	1	0	0
T20 Ints	7	7	0	178	81	25.42	112.65	0	1	13	10	0	0
First-class	57	101	8	3358	204	36.10	48.52	7	20	–	–	25	0

Bowling	M	Balls	Runs	Wkts	BB	Avge	RpO	S/R	5i	10m
Tests	0	0	–	–	–	–	–	–	–	–
ODIs	7	0	–	–	–	–	–	–	–	–
T20 Ints	7	0	–	–	–	–	–	–	–	–
First-class	57	156	95	2	1–9	47.50	3.65	78.00	0	0

SOUTH AFRICA

ANDRE **NEL**

Full name	**Andre Nel**
Born	**July 15, 1977, Germiston, Transvaal**
Teams	**Titans, Essex, Mumbai Indians**
Style	**Right-hand bat, right-arm fast bowler**
Test debut	**South Africa v Zimbabwe at Harare 2001-02**
ODI debut	**South Africa v West Indies at Port-of-Spain 2000-01**

THE PROFILE Andre Nel is a muscular fast bowler who has belied his conservative Afrikaans upbringing by amassing a chequered disciplinary record. He was sent home from the A-team tour of Australia in 2003 after being found to be driving under the influence of alcohol. It was only his latest misdemeanour, but he was nonetheless chosen for the one-day portion of the 2003 tour of England, where he was already playing county cricket. Nel was tipped early on as a future international, and first made the headlines early in 2001 when he felled Allan Donald – his hero – with a fierce bouncer. Nel burst into tears as Donald tottered off, and it later emerged that he was following instructions from his coach to target South Africa's premier fast bowler. Further controversy followed when Nel was one of five players caught smoking marijuana during a tour of the Caribbean. However, it was in the home West Indies series of 2003-04, during which he got married, that Nel established himself – and he was only in trouble once, for making facial gestures at Chris Gayle. Back trouble curtailed his progress, but he returned with wickets – and more gurning – against England in 2004-05. He came into his own in Australia in 2005-06, where he was an intimidating presence with 14 wickets and an attacking approach. Four Boxing Day dismissals preceded a strong showing at Sydney, and the Aussie crowds – sensing a kindred spirit to their own Merv Hughes – loved to hate him. Nel, who also performed whole-heartedly in England in 2008, is charming and humorous off the field: he calls his snarling *alter ego* "Gunther the mountain boy".

THE FACTS Nel has taken 52 wickets in ten Tests against West Indies, at an average of 22.01: against Pakistan he averages 55.63 ... He took 10 for 88 in the match in the innings win over West Indies at Bridgetown in April 2005 ... Nel dismissed Brian Lara eight times in Tests (and three more times in ODIs) ... He made his maiden first-class fifty for the South Africans against Bangladesh A at Worcester in July 2008 ...

THE FIGURES *to 12.9.08* www.cricinfo.com

Batting & Fielding	M	Inns	NO	Runs	HS	Avge	S/R	100	50	4s	6s	Ct	St
Tests	36	42	8	337	34	9.91	46.10	0	0	40	5	16	0
ODIs	79	22	12	127	30*	12.70	76.50	0	0	14	3	21	0
T20 Ints	2	1	1	0	0*	–	0.00	0	0	0	0	1	0
First-class	107	120	37	1127	56	13.57	–	0	1	–	–	39	0

Bowling	M	Balls	Runs	Wkts	BB	Avge	RpO	S/R	5i	10m
Tests	36	7630	3919	123	6–32	31.86	3.08	62.03	3	1
ODIs	79	3801	2935	106	5–45	27.68	4.63	35.85	1	0
T20 Ints	2	48	42	2	2–19	21.00	5.25	24.00	0	0
First-class	107	21215	9928	368	6–25	26.97	2.80	57.64	12	1

ASHLEY **NOFFKE**

AUSTRALIA

Full name **Ashley Allan Noffke**
Born **April 30, 1977, Nambour, Queensland**
Teams **Queensland, Bangalore Royal Challengers**
Style **Right-hand bat, right-arm fast-medium bowler**
Test debut **No Tests yet**
ODI debut **Australia v India at Brisbane 2007-08**

THE PROFILE Ashley Noffke bounced into a national contract and on to an Ashes tour in 2001, and has stayed in the selectors' minds ever since despite a series of injuries. In recent seasons he has rediscovered some of the penetration that earned early comparisons with Glenn McGrath, and his 2006-07 contributions earned him a recall to Australia A colours for a trip to Pakistan. His 30 Pura Cup wickets at 24.30 were complemented by two half-centuries, and a strong one-day campaign led to a spot in Australia's preliminary World Twenty20 squad. Further leaps forward followed in 2007-08, when he collected 51 first-class wickets and scored 741 runs, making him only the third Australian after George Giffen and Greg Matthews to complete the 500-run/50-wicket seasonal double. That form earned him his first two Twenty20 international appearances, his initial ODI cap, and a spot on Australia's Test tour of West Indies early in 2008. It was a satisfying set of jumps after he struggled between 2003 and 2005 with back and ankle problems, not helped by a couple of stints in English county cricket that ended in early flights home. His 2001 Ashes experience also finished the same way after he rolled his ankle attempting a soccer-style run-out in a tour game. Noffke hails from the Sunshine Coast, bowls with good rhythm from a high, clean and uncomplicated action, and develops excellent pace through most of his spells. He is also a capable lower-order batsman who can defend stoutly. Off the field he uses the skills learned through a business degree in a sports-shoe enterprise with former team-mate Joe Dawes.

THE FACTS Noffke took 8 for 24 (12 for 108 in the match) for Middlesex at Derby in September 2002 ... His highest score is 114 not out for Queensland against South Australia at Brisbane in December 2003 ... Noffke took a wicket (Daniel Vettori) with his fourth ball in international cricket, in the Twenty20 match against New Zealand at Perth in December 2007 ...

THE FIGURES to 12.9.08   www.cricinfo.com

Batting & Fielding	M	Inns	NO	Runs	HS	Avge	S/R	100	50	4s	6s	Ct	St
Tests	0	0	–	–	–	–	–	–	–	–	–	–	–
ODIs	1	0	–	–	–	–	–	–	–	–	–	0	0
T20 Ints	2	1	0	0	0	0.00	0.00	0	0	0	0	0	0
First-class	100	135	23	3058	114*	27.30	–	2	14	–	–	39	0

Bowling	M	Balls	Runs	Wkts	BB	Avge	RpO	S/R	5i	10m
Tests	0	0	–	–	–	–	–	–	–	–
ODIs	1	54	46	1	1–46	46.00	5.11	54.00	0	0
T20 Ints	2	45	41	4	3–18	10.25	5.46	11.20	0	0
First-class	100	19399	9826	346	8–24	28.39	3.03	56.06	18	1

MAKHAYA **NTINI**

Full name	**Makhaya Ntini**
Born	**July 6, 1977, Mdingi, Cape Province**
Teams	**Warriors, Chennai Super Kings**
Style	**Right-hand bat, right-arm fast bowler**
Test debut	**South Africa v Sri Lanka at Cape Town 1997-98**
ODI debut	**South Africa v New Zealand at Perth 1997-98**

THE PROFILE   Makhaya Ntini has had a fair bit to contend with during his life. A product of the South African Board's development programme, Ntini was discovered as a cattleherd in the Eastern Cape, given a pair of boots and packed off to Dale College, one of the country's best-regarded cricketing nurseries. With an action consciously modelled on Malcolm Marshall's, Ntini found himself touring Australia in 1997-98 when Roger Telemachus failed a fitness test. He made his ODI debut there, bowling well in helpful conditions at Perth, and his first Test – the first black African to play for South Africa – came later the same year. He was then convicted of rape, but cleared on appeal. After that ordeal he returned for the Sharjah tournament in 2000, impressing observers with greater control than before. Although a little short of the pace of a Brett Lee or a Shoaib Akhtar, he steadily improved, getting closer to the stumps but maintaining his high pace and occasional dangerous late inswing, and in 2003 became the first South African to take ten wickets in a Test at Lord's, before devastating West Indies in Trinidad in 2005 with 13 for 132, the best match figures for South Africa. Ntini steamed on, relishing his new role as the pace spearhead, and hurtled past 300 Test wickets during a destructive spell of 6 for 59 against Pakistan at Port Elizabeth in January 2007. Shortly after that, though, he failed to spark at the World Cup, and was dropped for the last two games. He laboured through the following home season, then struggled at first during the 2008 summer in England, before perking up with seven wickets at The Oval, after taking his 350th Test wicket in the previous match.

THE FACTS   Ntini's 13 for 132 (6 for 95 and 7 for 37) at Port-of-Spain in April 2005 are South Africa's best match figures in Tests, surpassing Hugh Tayfield's 13 for 165 at Melbourne in 1952-53 ... He has taken 68 Test wickets against England, and 63 v West Indies ... Ntini has taken 226 (63%) of his Test wickets in 46 matches at home ... Only 23 (6.4%) of his Test wickets have been lbws ... Ntini's record includes one ODI for the World XI ...

THE FIGURES *to 12.9.08*   www.cricinfo.com

Batting & Fielding	M	Inns	NO	Runs	HS	Avge	S/R	100	50	4s	6s	Ct	St
Tests	91	102	35	639	32*	9.53	51.03	0	0	94	8	23	0
ODIs	168	45	22	188	42*	8.17	65.73	0	0	16	5	30	0
T20 Ints	8	2	1	9	5	9.00	112.50	0	0	2	0	0	0
First-class	159	181	60	1128	34*	9.32	–	0	0	–	–	37	0

Bowling	M	Balls	Runs	Wkts	BB	Avge	RpO	S/R	5i	10m
Tests	91	18703	10104	358	7–37	28.22	3.24	52.24	18	4
ODIs	168	8429	6307	257	6–22	24.54	4.48	32.79	4	0
T20 Ints	8	144	212	4	2–22	53.00	8.83	36.00	0	0
First-class	159	29286	16132	555	7–37	29.06	3.30	52.76	23	4

IAIN **O'BRIEN**

NEW ZEALAND

Full name	**Iain Edward O'Brien**
Born	**July 10, 1976, Lower Hutt, Wellington**
Teams	**Wellington**
Style	**Right-hand bat, right-arm fast-medium bowler**
Test debut	**New Zealand v Australia at Christchurch 2004-05**
ODI debut	**New Zealand v England at Napier 2007-08**

THE PROFILE A tenacious seamer from Wellington who doesn't mind bowling into the wind, Iain O'Brien earned his first Test call-up in March 2005 when New Zealand's pace stocks were hit by injuries. He had had a solid State Championship that season, taking 20 wickets at 26.55, but his impact in his two Tests against Australia was limited. O'Brien managed only one wicket in each match, and faded from the selectors' thoughts until 2006-07, when he was included in both the Test and one-day squads when Sri Lanka toured. He wasn't used, however, and had to settle for being the leading wicket-taker in the State Championship with 34 at 20.85. Those figures were enough to keep him in the frame, and he finally added to his Test caps in South Africa in November 2007 after being a late replacement in the touring party because of an injury to Kyle Mills. Still his bowling looked a bit short of the required class, but he made the most of Shane Bond's absence with the disapproved Indian Cricket League: first he took seven wickets in two Tests against Bangladesh, then took over Bond's national contract when it was controversially cancelled owing to his ICL connections. O'Brien missed the home Tests against England, but toured there later in 2008. He was rather surprisingly preferred to the promising youngster Tim Southee in the last two Tests, but justified his selection with four wickets in each game, running in enthusiastically and looking more the part of a genuine Test bowler than before.

THE FACTS O'Brien took 8 for 55 (13 for 117 in the match) for Wellington against Auckland at Wellington in 2006-07 ... He took a hat-trick in a two-day game for Wellington against the New Zealand Academy in November 2004 ... O'Brien has played for the Derbyshire club Matlock, alongside the former England legend Derek Randall ...

THE FIGURES to 12.9.08   www.cricinfo.com

Batting & Fielding	M	Inns	NO	Runs	HS	Avge	S/R	100	50	4s	6s	Ct	St
Tests	8	13	1	48	14*	4.00	41.37	0	0	5	1	1	0
ODIs	1	0	–	–	–	–	–	–	–	–	–	0	0
T20 Ints	0	0	–	–	–	–	–	–	–	–	–	–	–
First-class	59	69	20	401	44	8.18	–	0	0	–	–	8	0

Bowling	M	Balls	Runs	Wkts	BB	Avge	RpO	S/R	5i	10m
Tests	8	1269	690	20	4–74	34.50	3.26	63.45	0	0
ODIs	1	36	59	1	1–59	59.00	9.83	36.00	0	0
T20 Ints	0	0	–	–	–	–	–	–	–	–
First-class	59	10639	5114	209	8–55	24.46	2.88	50.90	9	1

PRAGYAN **OJHA**

Full name	**Pragyan Prayash Ojha**
Born	**September 5, 1986, Bhubaneshwar**
Teams	**Hyderabad, Deccan Chargers**
Style	**Left-hand bat, slow left-arm orthodox spinner**
Test debut	**No Tests yet**
ODI debut	**India v Bangladesh at Karachi 2008**

THE PROFILE   A promising left-arm spinner, Pragyan Ojha seems to have elbowed aside Murali Kartik in the Indian pecking order. After consistent performances at age-group levels, Ojha made a stunning start in first-class cricket for Hyderabad in the Ranji Trophy semi-final at Jaipur in March 2005, when he took the first five wickets to fall in eventual champions Railways' first innings, starting with the sometime Test allrounder Sanjay Bangar. The following season he took 26 wickets, then 33 in 2006-07. These figures were enough to earn him a place in the A team to visit Zimbabwe and Kenya later in 2007 and, when he returned home, he helped spin the A team to an innings victory over South Africa A with 3 for 29 and 5 for 56 in the first Test at Delhi. He showed his control with some decent performances for Deccan Chargers in the inaugural Indian Premier League season early in 2008, finishing with 11 wickets, and was soon called up by the Indian selectors for the Asia Cup in Pakistan. He made an immediate impact in his first match with three outfield catches and an absolute ripper of a delivery which foxed Bangladesh's Raqibul Hasan, his maiden wicket. A couple of tidy performances followed against Sri Lanka, which helped him win a place on the tour of Sri Lanka which came afterwards. With Anil Kumble still partnering Harbhajan Singh, Ojha didn't play in the Tests there, but he did receive another one-day cap.

THE FACTS   Ojha's best bowling figures are 7 for 114, for Hyderabad against Rajasthan at Jaipur in December 2006: the previous week he took 6 for 84 against Maharashtra ... He claimed 6 for 31 (9 for 85 in the match) for India A v Kenya at Mombasa in August 2007 ... On his first-class debut, against Railways at Delhi in March 2005, Ojha took the first five wickets to fall, finishing with 5 for 55 ...

THE FIGURES to 12.9.08   www.cricinfo.com

Batting & Fielding	M	Inns	NO	Runs	HS	Avge	S/R	100	50	4s	6s	Ct	St
Tests	0	0	–	–	–	–	–	–	–	–	–	–	–
ODIs	5	3	2	27	16*	27.00	49.09	0	0	2	0	4	0
T20 Ints	0	0	–	–	–	–	–	–	–	–	–	–	–
First-class	30	42	14	289	35	10.32	34.52	0	0	33	0	12	0

Bowling	M	Balls	Runs	Wkts	BB	Avge	RpO	S/R	5i	10m
Tests	0	0	–	–	–	–	–	–	–	–
ODIs	5	258	173	5	2–28	34.60	4.02	51.60	0	0
T20 Ints	0	0	–	–	–	–	–	–	–	–
First-class	30	6592	3239	121	7–114	26.76	2.94	54.47	8	0

JUSTIN **ONTONG**

Full name	**Justin Lee Ontong**
Born	**January 4, 1980, Paarl, Cape Province**
Teams	**Lions**
Style	**Right-hand bat, offspinner**
Test debut	**South Africa v Australia at Sydney 2001-02**
ODI debut	**South Africa v West Indies at Kingston 2000-01**

THE PROFILE Justin Ontong was the unwitting centre of controversy during his Test debut in January 2002 when it emerged that the South African Board president had overruled the selectors and insisted on his inclusion, as a Cape Colored, ahead of Jacques Rudolph, who is white. The resulting pressure was too much for Ontong, who was "Warned" in both innings, and it was almost three years before he got another chance, in India late in 2004. However, the return was short-lived, as he again failed to establish himself in a strong batting order. After a handful of one-dayers in 2005, it was another two years before he was called up to face West Indies at home. He made 23 in the first ODI at Centurion before a knee injury forced him back on to the bench. His first overseas tour was to the West Indies in 2000-01, when he was so quietly spoken that he earned himself the ironic nickname "Rowdy". Nevertheless, he displayed a resolve and determination in his first games in national colours that underlined the selectors' belief that he was a player to look out for. Ontong is a stylish batsman, and for a while he purveyed an interesting mixture of legbreaks, offies, quicker balls and wrong'uns. That phase didn't last, though, and now his bowling is rarely used. He is also direct evidence of the effect a role model can have on the succeeding generation. Jonty Rhodes was his hero as a young boy, and Ontong is now almost as good in the field.

THE FACTS Ontong scored 166 for Boland against Eastern Province at Port Elizabeth in October 2003 ... He made 61 and 144 not out for the Rest of South Africa against the touring New Zealanders at Benoni in April 2006 ... Ontong is not, as is sometimes claimed, related to the South African-born former Glamorgan allrounder Rodney ...

THE FIGURES to 12.9.08   www.cricinfo.com

Batting & Fielding	M	Inns	NO	Runs	HS	Avge	S/R	100	50	4s	6s	Ct	St
Tests	2	4	1	57	32	19.00	36.77	0	0	8	0	1	0
ODIs	23	13	1	121	32	10.08	64.02	0	0	9	1	11	0
T20 Ints	1	1	0	14	14	14.00	87.50	0	0	0	0	0	0
First-class	103	170	9	6126	166	38.04	–	13	37	–	–	80	0

Bowling	M	Balls	Runs	Wkts	BB	Avge	RpO	S/R	5i	10m
Tests	2	185	133	1	1–79	133.00	4.31	185.00	0	0
ODIs	23	538	396	9	3–30	44.00	4.41	59.77	0	0
T20 Ints	1	12	25	1	1–25	25.00	12.50	12.00	0	0
First-class	103	7982	4269	90	4–66	47.43	3.20	86.68	0	0

JACOB **ORAM**

Full name	**Jacob David Philip Oram**
Born	**July 28, 1978, Palmerston North, Manawatu**
Teams	**Central Districts, Chennai Super Kings**
Style	**Left-hand bat, right-arm fast-medium bowler**
Test debut	**New Zealand v India at Wellington 2002-03**
ODI debut	**New Zealand v Zimbabwe at Wellington 2000-01**

THE PROFILE It's hard to miss Jacob Oram, and not just because of his height of 6ft 6ins (198cm). He is agile in the field, especially at gully, and he complements that with solid fast-medium bowling and aggressive batting. Foot problems cost him a season at a vital stage, but he came back strongly in 2002-03 to seal a regular international place. He narrowly missed a century against Pakistan in the Wellington Boxing Day Test of 2003, but made up for that by carving 119 not out against South Africa, then 90 in the second Test, which earned him an England tour in 2004. By then his bowling was starting to lose its sting, and he went down with back trouble shortly after pounding 126 against Australia at Brisbane in November '04. After nearly 18 months out Oram showed what New Zealand's middle order had been missing, coming in at 38 for 4 at Centurion and making 133, still his highest score. He missed the start of the 2006-07 Australian one-day series with a hamstring injury, but bucked the team up with some stirring performances when he did get there, including a 71-ball century – NZ's fastest, and his first in ODIs – against Australia at Perth. A badly broken finger threatened to keep him out of the 2007 World Cup, but he made it (he said he'd have the finger amputated if that would help: luckily it wasn't necessary) and played his part in the march to the semi-finals. He continued to be a regular member of all New Zealand's sides, although a strange diffidence crept into his batting in England in 2008, when many thought he should have been moved up the order in an inexperienced line-up.

THE FACTS Oram averages 62.00 in Tests against Australia, 52.50 v South Africa – and 10.25 v India ... With the ball he averages 15.50 v Bangladesh, but 79.30 v Australia ... Oram scored his maiden century in only his fourth first-class match, for Central Districts v Canterbury at Christchurch in 1998-99, and his 155 remains his highest score ...

THE FIGURES to 12.9.08   www.cricinfo.com

Batting & Fielding	M	Inns	NO	Runs	HS	Avge	S/R	100	50	4s	6s	Ct	St
Tests	30	53	9	1659	133	37.70	51.66	5	5	197	21	14	0
ODIs	119	87	11	1854	101*	24.39	83.13	1	9	137	58	36	0
T20 Ints	9	8	3	242	66*	48.40	165.75	0	2	20	15	1	0
First-class	76	122	16	3679	155	34.70	–	8	17	–	–	34	0

Bowling	M	Balls	Runs	Wkts	BB	Avge	RpO	S/R	5i	10m
Tests	30	4598	1838	60	4–41	30.63	2.39	76.63	0	0
ODIs	119	5137	3808	124	5–26	30.70	4.44	41.42	2	0
T20 Ints	9	120	202	2	1–14	101.00	10.10	60.00	0	0
First-class	76	9364	3634	143	6–45	25.41	2.32	65.48	3	0

MONTY **PANESAR**

Full name	**Mudhsuden Singh Panesar**
Born	**April 25, 1982, Luton, Bedfordshire**
Teams	**Northamptonshire**
Style	**Left-hand bat, slow left-arm orthodox spinner**
Test debut	**England v India at Nagpur 2005-06**
ODI debut	**England v Australia at Melbourne 2006-07**

THE PROFILE Monty Panesar made his Test debut early in 2006, and by the middle of that year had made himself a cult hero to English crowds enchanted by his enthusiastic wicket celebrations and endearingly erratic fielding. That, and equally amateurish batting, had threatened to hold him back, but when Ashley Giles was ruled out of the 2005-06 Indian tour Panesar received a late summons. He's a throwback to an earlier Northamptonshire slow left-armer, Bishan Bedi, who also twirled away in a *patka*, teasing and tempting with flight and guile, although Panesar, who has huge hands, gives it more of a rip than Bedi did. Panesar took eight wickets on his first-class debut, against Leicestershire in 2001, but he was then held back while he finished university. Finally free from studies, he had a fine season in 2005, taking 46 Championship wickets at 21.54, and was a late addition for the Indian tour. He made his debut at Nagpur, picking up Sachin Tendulkar as his first wicket. He captivated crowds at home in 2006, sending down the ball of the season to bowl Younis Khan to set up victory at Leeds. Despite his burgeoning reputation Panesar missed the first two Ashes Tests in 2006-07 – the returning Giles was surprisingly preferred – then showed what England were missing with 5 for 92 at Perth. Back home he claimed 31 wickets in seven Tests in 2007, and remained the crowd's favourite as Montymania showed no sign of running out of steam. But he struggled in Sri Lanka at the end of the year, his eight Test wickets costing more than 50 each, and laboured a little in England too, while his antics and frequent appealing rubbed some up the wrong way.

THE FACTS Panesar took 7 for 181 for Northamptonshire v Essex at Chelmsford in July 2005 ... He was the first Sikh to play Test cricket for anyone other than India: when Panesar opposed Harbhajan Singh during his debut at Nagpur in 2005-06 it was the first instance of one Sikh bowling to another in a Test ... He was the first Luton-born Test cricketer, and only the seventh to have been born in Bedfordshire, the sixth being Wayne Larkins ...

THE FIGURES *to 12.9.08*   www.cricinfo.com

Batting & Fielding	M	Inns	NO	Runs	HS	Avge	S/R	100	50	4s	6s	Ct	St
Tests	33	45	15	165	26	5.50	30.84	0	0	19	1	6	0
ODIs	26	8	3	26	13	5.20	28.57	0	0	2	0	3	0
T20 Ints	1	1	0	1	1	1.00	50.00	0	0	0	0	0	0
First-class	88	113	40	584	39*	8.00	30.96	0	0	–	–	21	0

Bowling	M	Balls	Runs	Wkts	BB	Avge	RpO	S/R	5i	10m
Tests	33	2699	3643	114	6–37	31.95	2.83	67.53	8	1
ODIs	26	1308	980	24	3–25	40.83	4.49	54.50	0	0
T20 Ints	1	24	40	2	2–40	20.00	10.00	12.00	0	0
First-class	88	20243	9677	312	7–181	31.01	2.86	64.88	18	3

JEETAN **PATEL**

Full name	**Jeetan Shashi Patel**
Born	**May 7, 1980, Wellington**
Teams	**Wellington**
Style	**Right-hand bat, offspinner**
Test debut	**New Zealand v South Africa at Cape Town 2005-06**
ODI debut	**New Zealand v Zimbabwe at Harare 2005-06**

THE PROFILE The son of Indian parents, but born and brought up in Wellington's eastern suburbs, offspinner Jeetan Patel was fast-tracked into the New Zealand one-day side after John Bracewell, the coach, identified him as the sort of slow bowler who could be effective at the death. Patel first played for Wellington in 1999-2000, bowling 59 overs and taking 5 for 145 against Auckland on debut. Three middling seasons followed, and he seemed to be heading nowhere, with an average in the mid-forties. But then he took 6 for 32 against Otago in the last State Championship match of 2004-05, propelling Wellington into the final against Auckland, which they lost. Suddenly good judges were noting his ability to make the ball loop and drift, not unlike a right-handed Daniel Vettori. Bracewell took him to Zimbabwe in August 2005, and he played nine ODIs that season, in eight being either the super-sub or the subbed-out player, as his batting – although better now than when he began – is underwhelming. At home his 2 for 23 from ten overs throttled Sri Lanka at Wellington, then three wickets at Christchurch helped subdue West Indies too. All this put Patel in line for a first Test cap, which came against South Africa at Cape Town in April 2006. And he had a nice long bowl, wheeling away for 42 overs and removing Graeme Smith, Boeta Dippenaar and AB de Villiers at a cost of 117 runs. Since then he has often been used as a foil to Vettori on spinning tracks, usually succeeding in keeping the runs down – not least in most of his six outings in the 2007 World Cup – and has won two more Test caps.

THE FACTS Patel won the Man of the Match award for his tight spell of 2 for 23 against Sri Lanka at Wellington in 2005-06 after being super-subbed into the game ... He also won the match award in his first international Twenty20 match, after taking 3 for 20 v South Africa at Johannesburg in October 2005 ... Patel hit his highest score of 58 not out for Wellington v Otago at Dunedin in 2000-01, after going in as nightwatchman ...

THE FIGURES *to 12.9.08*   www.cricinfo.com

Batting & Fielding	M	Inns	NO	Runs	HS	Avge	S/R	100	50	4s	6s	Ct	St
Tests	3	5	2	67	27*	22.33	49.26	0	0	8	0	1	0
ODIs	30	8	3	57	34	11.40	53.77	0	0	4	1	10	0
T20 Ints	9	4	1	9	5	3.00	64.28	0	0	1	0	3	0
First-class	66	81	32	863	58*	17.61	–	0	2	–	–	22	0

Bowling	M	Balls	Runs	Wkts	BB	Avge	RpO	S/R	5i	10m
Tests	3	869	404	11	3–107	36.72	2.78	79.00	0	0
ODIs	30	1480	1231	37	3–11	33.27	4.99	40.00	0	0
T20 Ints	9	163	223	12	3–20	18.58	8.20	13.58	0	0
First-class	66	11145	5240	126	6–32	41.58	2.82	88.45	3	0

MUNAF **PATEL**

INDIA

Full name	**Munaf Musa Patel**
Born	**July 12, 1983, Ikhar, Gujarat**
Teams	**Maharashtra, Rajasthan Royals**
Style	**Right-hand bat, right-arm fast-medium bowler**
Test debut	**India v England at Mohali 2005-06**
ODI debut	**India v England at Goa 2005-06**

THE PROFILE Few fast men generated as much hype before bowling a ball in first-class – let alone international – cricket as Munaf Patel, from the little town of Ikhar in Gujarat, did early in 2003. Kiran More spotted him and sent him straight to Chennai to train under Dennis Lillee. Soon he was being hailed as the fastest bowler in Indian cricket. But Patel's first-class start was anything but smooth, as he spent more time recovering from injuries than actually playing. He's strongly built, though not overly tall, and bustles up to the crease, gathering momentum before releasing the ball with a windmill-whirl of hands. He has added reverse-swing to his repertoire, and also has a well-directed yorker. In March 2006 he finally received a call from the selectors – now chaired by his old pal More – after taking 10 for 91 in a match against the England tourists for the Board President's XI. He ended the Mohali Test with 7 for 97, the best performance by an Indian fast bowler on debut, and continued to take wickets consistently in the West Indies later in 2006. Things got harder after that. He picked up an ankle niggle in South Africa, and was criticised when it bothered him in the final Test – but he regained full fitness in time for the World Cup, where he did as well as anyone. Then it was a back injury, and Patel returned to the Chennai academy – which he calls his "second home" – to remodel his action. In Australia in 2007-08 he sometimes seemed uninterested, and certainly didn't make the batsmen hop about much. He was left out for six months, but returned for the one-dayers in Sri Lanka in August 2008.

THE FACTS Patel's match figures of 7 for 97 were the best on Test debut by an Indian fast bowler, beating Mohammad Nissar's 6 for 135 against England at Lord's in 1932 (Abid Ali, more of a medium-pacer, took 7 for 116 on debut against Australia in 1967-68) ... Patel's best first-class figures are 6 for 50, for Maharashtra against Railways at Delhi in January 2006 ...

THE FIGURES *to 12.9.08*   www.cricinfo.com

Batting & Fielding	M	Inns	NO	Runs	HS	Avge	S/R	100	50	4s	6s	Ct	St
Tests	9	10	3	32	13	4.57	31.06	0	0	3	1	5	0
ODIs	29	12	5	47	15	6.71	63.51	0	0	4	1	4	0
T20 Ints	0	0	–	–	–	–	–	–	–	–	–	–	–
First-class	37	41	11	434	78	14.46	–	0	1	–	–	10	0

Bowling	M	Balls	Runs	Wkts	BB	Avge	RpO	S/R	5i	10m
Tests	9	1890	940	28	4–25	33.57	2.98	67.50	0	0
ODIs	29	1405	1096	36	4–49	30.44	4.68	39.02	0	0
T20 Ints	0	0	–	–	–	–	–	–	–	–
First-class	37	6746	3165	132	6–50	23.97	2.81	51.10	5	1

SAMIT **PATEL**

Full name	**Samit Rohit Patel**
Born	**November 30, 1984, Leicester**
Teams	**Nottinghamshire**
Style	**Right-hand bat, slow left-arm orthodox spinner**
Test debut	**No Tests yet**
ODI debut	**England v Scotland at Edinburgh 2008**

THE PROFILE Samit Patel was long considered a player of great promise, but struggled to produce the goods consistently at first-team level. A hard-hitting middle-order batsman and a capable slow left-armer seen by the new England captain Kevin Pietersen (a former county team-mate) as capable of bowling leg-stump darts *à la* Sanath Jayasuriya, he represented England at Under-15, U17 and U19 levels, and made his debut for Nottinghamshire's 2nd XI in 1999, when only 14. In 2006, however, Patel slimmed down a little and finally began to show signs of realising his potential, hammering 156 not out, with eight sixes, against Middlesex at Lord's – he hurtled from 100 to 150 in just 17 balls. Some of his most eye-catching performances have come in Twenty20 cricket, including a unique double-wicket maiden against Derbyshire in 2006, but it was in the 50-over game that he first attracted the interest of England's selectors. After making 60 not out for the England Lions against South Africa at Derby in August 2008, Patel was called up for the late-season one-day internationals. Replacing his Nottinghamshire team-mate Graeme Swann in the side, he kept the runs down in his first couple of matches, then struck a brisk 31 at The Oval in his first ODI innings, before ruining South Africa's reply with 5 for 41, his best figures in senior cricket and the best return by an England spinner in one-dayers since Graeme Hick took 5 for 33 against Zimbabwe at Harare in February 2000. Suddenly a left-field pick was looking like an inspired one.

THE FACTS Patel's 5 for 41 for England against South Africa at The Oval in August 2008 are his best bowling figures in senior cricket … He made 176 for Nottinghamshire against Gloucestershire at Bristol in April 2007 … Patel hit 173, his maiden first-class century, in his fifth match, against Durham UCCE at Durham in April 2006 …

THE FIGURES *to 12.9.08*   www.cricinfo.com

Batting & Fielding	M	Inns	NO	Runs	HS	Avge	S/R	100	50	4s	6s	Ct	St
Tests	0	0	–	–	–	–	–	–	–	–	–	–	–
ODIs	6	1	0	31	31	31.00	93.93	0	0	3	0	3	0
T20 Ints	0	0	–	–	–	–	–	–	–	–	–	–	–
First-class	39	58	6	2396	176	46.07	64.40	7	13	–	–	19	0

Bowling	M	Balls	Runs	Wkts	BB	Avge	RpO	S/R	5i	10m
Tests	0	0	–	–	–	–	–	–	–	–
ODIs	6	202	139	8	5–41	17.37	4.12	25.25	1	0
T20 Ints	0	0	–	–	–	–	–	–	–	–
First-class	39	2218	1052	31	4–68	33.93	2.84	71.54	0	0

IRFAN **PATHAN**

INDIA

Full name	**Irfan Khan Pathan**
Born	**October 27, 1984, Baroda, Gujarat**
Teams	**Baroda**
Style	**Left-hand bat, left-arm fast-medium bowler**
Test debut	**India v Australia at Adelaide 2003-04**
ODI debut	**India v Australia at Melbourne 2003-04**

THE PROFILE Irfan Pathan was initially rated the most talented swing and seam bowler to emerge from India since Kapil Dev, and he was soon being thought of as a possible successor for Kapil in the allround department too. He was strikingly composed in his Test debut at 19: his instinct is not just what to bowl to whom and when, but also to keep learning new tricks. Already he possesses perhaps the most potent left-armer's outswinger in world cricket, which helped him to a hat-trick in the first over of the Karachi Test in January 2006, and he's adept at reverse-swing. When batting, he was regularly pushed up the order, sometimes even opening in one-dayers. His first stint at No. 3 produced a spectacular 83 against Sri Lanka – and he has often bailed India out in Tests as well, with 93 and 82 against Sri Lanka late in 2005, and 90 as India piled up 603 against Pakistan at Faisalabad early in 2006. He struggled after that with shoulder trouble. He went to the World Cup but didn't play, then missed the England tour. Pathan returned to the one-day side later in 2007 and, when he proved he had rediscovered his bowling rhythm, was handed a Test recall against Pakistan at Bangalore in December. He celebrated his first Test for 19 months by clubbing his first century, reaching it with his fourth six. He was benched for the first two Tests in Australia, then returned at Perth, where he made 28 and 46 and took five wickets in a famous victory. He remained a one-day fixture, although a side strain kept him out for a while in mid-2008.

THE FACTS Pathan was the first bowler to take a hat-trick in the first over of a Test match, when he dismissed Salman Butt, Younis Khan and Mohammad Yousuf at Karachi in January 2006: from 0 for 3, Pakistan recovered to win by 341 runs ... Pathan took 12 for 126 in the match against Zimbabwe at Harare in September 2005 ... He is one of only five players to have scored a century and taken a hat-trick in Tests ... His brother Yusuf Pathan has also played for India ...

THE FIGURES *to 12.9.08*   www.cricinfo.com

Batting & Fielding	M	Inns	NO	Runs	HS	Avge	S/R	100	50	4s	6s	Ct	St
Tests	29	40	5	1105	102	31.57	53.22	1	6	131	18	8	0
ODIs	104	77	18	1360	83	23.05	78.16	0	5	127	33	18	0
T20 Ints	10	7	4	60	26	20.00	100.00	0	0	2	2	0	0
First-class	75	99	22	2259	111*	29.33	–	2	11	–	–	23	0

Bowling	M	Balls	Runs	Wkts	BB	Avge	RpO	S/R	5i	10m
Tests	29	5884	3226	100	7–59	32.26	3.28	58.84	7	2
ODIs	104	5038	4377	148	5–27	29.57	5.21	34.04	1	0
T20 Ints	10	198	231	12	3–16	19.25	7.00	16.50	0	0
First-class	75	14116	7571	243	7–59	31.15	3.21	58.09	10	3

YUSUF **PATHAN**

Full name **Yusuf Khan Pathan**
Born **November 17, 1982, Baroda, Gujarat**
Teams **Baroda, Rajasthan Royals**
Style **Right-hand bat, offspinner**
Test debut **No Tests yet**
ODI debut **India v Pakistan at Dhaka 2008**

INDIA

THE PROFILE A hard-hitting batsman and handy offspinner, Yusuf Pathan first made his mark for Baroda's age-group teams, and he made his Ranji Trophy debut against Saurashtra in 2001-02. But it wasn't for another three years – by which time his younger brother Irfan was already a Test player – that Yusuf established himself as a regular. Over the next three seasons he scored plenty of runs and took a fair few wickets for Baroda, but didn't do himself justice when called up for two of the Challenger Trophy tournaments which help the selection process for India's one-day side. Eventually, though, his ability to score runs quickly – he had the highest strike rate in the Ranji Trophy in 2006-07 – and some impressive performances in the one-day Deodhar Trophy and Twenty20 domestic tournament were rewarded with a place in India's squad for the inaugural World Twenty20 championship in South Africa, alongside his brother. He didn't play in the qualifying matches, but was drafted in for the final, when he opened and smote his second ball into the stands. He followed that with an impressive showing for the Rajasthan Royals in the inaugural Indian Premier League season early in 2008, finishing with 435 runs at a heady strike rate of 179, boosted by a 21-ball fifty (the IPL's fastest) against the Deccan Chargers. In the final, he helped Shane Warne's team to the title by following up three important wickets with a 39-ball 56. After all that, he was a shoo-in for India's ODI team, although he had little success in his first outings in Bangladesh and Pakistan.

THE FACTS Yusuf Pathan made his international debut in the final of the inaugural World Twenty20 championship in South Africa in September 2007: he hit his second ball, from Mohammad Asif, for six ... Pathan scored 183 for Baroda against Bengal at Baroda in November 2007 ... He took 6 for 47 for Baroda v Tamil Nadu in Chennai in January 2007, and 10 for 119 in the match against Bengal at Baroda in November 2007 ...

THE FIGURES to 12.9.08   www.cricinfo.com

Batting & Fielding	M	Inns	NO	Runs	HS	Avge	S/R	100	50	4s	6s	Ct	St
Tests	0	0	–	–	–	–	–	–	–	–	–	–	–
ODIs	7	3	0	28	25	9.33	68.29	0	0	4	0	4	0
T20 Ints	1	1	0	15	15	15.00	187.50	0	0	1	1	1	0
First-class	31	47	6	1502	183	36.63	87.88	3	7	–	–	28	0

Bowling	M	Balls	Runs	Wkts	BB	Avge	RpO	S/R	5i	10m
Tests	0	0	–	–	–	–	–	–	–	–
ODIs	7	234	193	3	1–9	64.33	4.94	78.00	0	0
T20 Ints	1	6	5	0	–	–	5.00	–	0	0
First-class	31	6042	2599	84	6–47	30.94	2.58	71.92	7	1

DARREN **PATTINSON**

Full name	**Darren John Pattinson**
Born	**August 2, 1978, Grimsby, Lincolnshire**
Teams	**Nottinghamshire**
Style	**Right-hand bat, right-arm fast-medium bowler**
Test debut	**England v South Africa at Leeds 2008**
ODI debut	**No ODIs yet**

THE PROFILE Few people have endured an international baptism as surprising and controversial as Darren Pattinson's. Born in Grimsby but raised in Australia, he had played only 11 first-class matches when he was the shock inclusion in England's side for the Headingley Test against South Africa in July 2008 – and only six of those games had been in England, all in 2008 for Nottinghamshire, for whom Pattinson had impressed as a fastish swing bowler, with 15 wickets in his first two matches for them. Many opponents (and possibly the odd team-mate) thought he was a Kolpak player: his initial matches had been for Victoria, for whom he made his debut at 28 after being plucked out of club cricket for Dandenong – whose captain, on hearing of the England call-up, spluttered: "Surely the Poms have got better bowlers than Patto?" There was even a bizarre conspiracy theory doing the rounds that he had been chosen to stop Australia picking him for the next Ashes series. After all the fuss it was little surprise that Pattinson struggled at first at Leeds, where he replaced the injured Ryan Sidebottom, although he did pick up two wickets later on. Afterwards he was returned post-haste to county cricket, with Michael Vaughan blaming the ructions caused by his selection for England's defeat. Further chances seemed unlikely, although the selectors showed he was still in their thoughts by choosing him for the England Lions, but the man himself was undaunted: "Things have moved on a lot quicker than I expected, and I've set myself new goals which include earning further recognition for England."

THE FACTS Pattinson made his Test debut in 2008 after only 11 first-class matches, five of them for Victoria in Australia ... He took 5 for 22 in his first match for Nottinghamshire, against Kent at Canterbury in April 2008, and 6 for 30 in his second, against Lancashire at Trent Bridge ... His brother James played for Australia in the Under-19 World Cup in 2008 ...

THE FIGURES *to 12.9.08*   www.cricinfo.com

Batting & Fielding	M	Inns	NO	Runs	HS	Avge	S/R	100	50	4s	6s	Ct	St
Tests	1	2	0	21	13	10.50	42.00	0	0	3	0	0	0
ODIs	0	0	–	–	–	–	–	–	–	–	–	–	–
T20 Ints	0	0	–	–	–	–	–	–	–	–	–	–	–
First-class	16	19	2	135	33	7.94	33.75	0	0	17	0	2	0

Bowling	M	Balls	Runs	Wkts	BB	Avge	RpO	S/R	5i	10m
Tests	1	181	96	2	2–95	48.00	3.18	90.50	0	0
ODIs	0	0	–	–	–	–	–	–	–	–
T20 Ints	0	0	–	–	–	–	–	–	–	–
First-class	16	2803	1511	54	6–30	27.98	3.23	51.90	4	0

ROBIN **PETERSON**

Full name	**Robin John Peterson**
Born	**August 4, 1979, Port Elizabeth, Cape Province**
Teams	**Warriors**
Style	**Left-hand bat, slow left-arm orthodox spinner**
Test debut	**South Africa v Bangladesh at Dhaka 2002-03**
ODI debut	**South Africa v India at Colombo 2002-03**

THE PROFILE Spin bowlers of genuine potential are rare in South Africa, more so the jewels who can bat and field well, but Robin Peterson, a left-arm finger-spinner, ticks all three boxes. He has five centuries and over 200 first-class wickets, and is a lurking presence square of the wicket in the field. At first glance his left-arm spin looks a little too plain, but he does turn it given help from the pitch. He also has a *doosra*, which turns in to the right-hander. After a glittering youth career Peterson made his Test debut against Bangladesh in May 2003, taking five wickets and scoring 61, but since then has been seen mainly as a one-day specialist – especially after Brian Lara carted him for a Test-record 28 in an over at the end of 2003 – although he did take 5 for 33 against Bangladesh on a helpful Chittagong track early in 2008, which got him on the plane for the England tour, where Paul Harris was preferred to him in the Tests. Peterson had played some one-dayers in India late in 2005, but had little success, a pattern repeated when the Australians toured early the following year, when he managed only one wicket in three matches. Still, Peterson was the only specialist spinner chosen for the 2006 Champions Trophy and, despite continuing modest returns, for the 2007 World Cup. Again he contributed little with the ball, although his thick-edged four did complete a last-gasp victory over Sri Lanka after Lasith Malinga's four wickets in four balls had derailed what seemed a routine run-chase. The suspicion remains, though, that Peterson doesn't do enough with the ball in international cricket.

THE FACTS Peterson's unlucky 13th over against West Indies at Johannesburg in December 2003 was the most expensive in Test history: Brian Lara hit it for 28 (466444) ... The highest of Peterson's five centuries is 130, for Eastern Province v Gauteng at Johannesburg in October 2002 ... He also made 108 for South Africa A v India A at Bloemfontein in April 2002 ... Peterson took 6 for 67 for Eastern Province v Border at East London in December 1999, and 6 for 16 in a one-day game for EP v Namibia in November 2002 ...

THE FIGURES *to 12.9.08*   www.cricinfo.com

Batting & Fielding	M	Inns	NO	Runs	HS	Avge	S/R	100	50	4s	6s	Ct	St
Tests	6	7	1	163	61	27.16	21.80	0	1	19	1	5	0
ODIs	35	15	4	147	36	13.36	75.77	0	0	14	2	7	0
T20 Ints	3	1	0	8	8	8.00	66.66	0	0	0	0	1	0
First-class	85	133	17	3048	130	26.27	–	5	10	–	–	37	0

Bowling	M	Balls	Runs	Wkts	BB	Avge	RpO	S/R	5i	10m
Tests	6	959	497	14	5–33	35.50	3.10	68.50	1	0
ODIs	35	1252	992	17	2–26	58.35	4.75	73.64	0	0
T20 Ints	3	29	40	3	2–29	13.33	8.27	9.66	0	0
First-class	85	15421	7854	227	6–67	34.59	3.05	67.93	10	1

VERNON **PHILANDER**

Full name	**Vernon Darryl Philander**
Born	**June 24, 1985, Bellville, Cape Province**
Teams	**Cape Cobras, Middlesex**
Style	**Right-hand bat, right-arm fast-medium bowler**
Test debut	**No Tests yet**
ODI debut	**South Africa v Ireland at Belfast 2007**

THE PROFILE The possessor of one of international cricket's more remarkable surnames (Brian Johnston would have loved it, and his initials), Vernon Philander is a powerful allrounder who has done consistently well for the Cape Cobras since breaking into first-class cricket in 2003-04. Before that he toured England with the Under-19s in 2003, and returned there the following year to play for Devon, helping them to a famous C&G Trophy win over Leicestershire, dismissing Brad Hodge in a low-scoring game that eventually finished with the scores level. His nippy, accurate bowling is backed up by some muscular batting, as he demonstrated in only his fourth first-class game when he flogged 168 (out of 283) for Western Province against Griqualand West at Kimberley. In 2006-07 he produced an impressive one-day season for the Cobras, averaging 72 with the bat and 30 with the ball. It was enough to earn him a place in South Africa's squad for their mid-2007 one-day tour of Ireland – a team he'd been lined up to play for before a shin stress fracture ruled him out – and he starred on his ODI debut, which was also his 22nd birthday, taking 4 for 12 to make sure the Irish did not approach South Africa's modest total of 173 from 31 overs in a rain-hit game. Philander then also did well in an Emerging Players tournament in Australia, and was called up for the World Twenty20 championship in September 2007. He played a few matches for Middlesex in 2008 before joining up with the South African one-day squad in England.

THE FACTS In his first ODI, against Ireland on his 22nd birthday in June 2007, Philander took 4 for 12, the second-best figures by a South African on ODI debut after Allan Donald's 5 for 29 in 1991-92 ... Philander scored 168 for Western Province v Griqualand West at Kimberley in November 2004, in only his fourth first-class match ... He took 7 for 64 for Cape Cobras v Lions at Potchefstroom in January 2008 ...

THE FIGURES to 12.9.08   www.cricinfo.com

Batting & Fielding	M	Inns	NO	Runs	HS	Avge	S/R	100	50	4s	6s	Ct	St
Tests	0	0	–	–	–	–	–	–	–	–	–	–	–
ODIs	7	5	2	73	23	24.33	87.95	0	0	7	0	2	0
T20 Ints	7	4	0	14	6	3.50	50.00	0	0	0	0	1	0
First-class	35	55	5	1305	168	26.10	47.52	1	6	–	–	12	0

Bowling	M	Balls	Runs	Wkts	BB	Avge	RpO	S/R	5i	10m
Tests	0	0	–	–	–	–	–	–	–	–
ODIs	7	275	209	6	4–12	34.83	4.56	45.83	0	0
T20 Ints	7	83	114	4	2–23	28.50	8.24	20.75	0	0
First-class	35	5985	2539	114	7–64	22.27	2.54	52.50	3	0

KEVIN **PIETERSEN**

ENGLAND

Full name	**Kevin Peter Pietersen**
Born	**June 27, 1980, Pietermaritzburg, Natal, South Africa**
Teams	**Hampshire**
Style	**Right-hand bat, offspinner**
Test debut	**England v Australia at Lord's 2005**
ODI debut	**England v Zimbabwe at Harare 2004-05**

THE PROFILE Expansive with bat and explosive with bombast, Kevin Pietersen is not one for the quiet life. Bold-minded and big-hitting, he first ruffled feathers by quitting South Africa – he was disenchanted with the race-quota system – in favour of England, his eligibility coming courtesy of an English mother. He never doubted he would play Test cricket: he has self-confidence in spades and, fortunately, sackfuls of talent too. Sure enough, as soon as he was eligible for England, in September 2004, he was chosen for a one-day series in Zimbabwe, where he averaged 104, earning him a late call-up to play ... South Africa. Undeterred by hostile crowds, he announced his arrival with a robust century in the second match at Bloemfontein. Test cricket was next on the to-do list. In 2005 he replaced Graham Thorpe, against Australia, at Lord's ... and coolly blasted a couple of fifties in a losing cause, then, with the Ashes at stake, again showed his eye for the limelight with 158 on the final day at The Oval. "KP" had arrived – and how. The runs kept coming: 158 at Adelaide and 226 against West Indies at Headingley sandwiched two tons in the 2007 World Cup, where he was the star of England's lame campaign. And his star continued to rise. Late in 2008 he succeeded Michael Vaughan as England's captain, and started in fairytale fashion, biffing a hundred as South Africa were beaten in the Oval Test, then inspiring a 4-0 landslide in the one-day series. Ricky Ponting wrote that Pietersen could be "the next superstar of world cricket", and the man himself is unlikely to disagree – or to stop until he is.

THE FACTS Pietersen reached 100 against South Africa at East London in February 2005 from 69 balls, the fastest for England in ODIs ... After 25 Tests he had made 2448 runs, more than anyone else except Don Bradman (3194) ... He averages 98.66 in ODIs v South Africa – and 16.50 v Bangladesh ... Pietersen was out for 158 three times in Tests before going on to 226 against West Indies in May 2007 ... His record includes two ODIs for the World XI ...

THE FIGURES to 12.9.08   www.cricinfo.com

Batting & Fielding	M	Inns	NO	Runs	HS	Avge	S/R	100	50	4s	6s	Ct	St
Tests	43	80	3	3890	226	50.51	63.40	14	11	458	44	29	0
ODIs	82	73	14	2822	116	47.83	87.50	6	19	262	52	31	0
T20 Ints	14	14	1	363	79	27.92	148.77	0	1	39	8	6	0
First-class	127	213	15	10172	254*	51.37	–		36	39	–	–	109	0

Bowling	M	Balls	Runs	Wkts	BB	Avge	RpO	S/R	5i	10m
Tests	43	609	431	4	1–0	107.75	4.24	152.25	0	0
ODIs	82	143	134	4	2–22	33.50	5.62	35.75	0	0
T20 Ints	14	0	–	–	–	–	–	–	–	–
First-class	127	5377	3104	60	4–31	51.73	3.46	89.61	0	0

KIERON **POLLARD**

Full name	**Kieron Adrian Pollard**
Born	**May 12, 1987, Cacariqua, Trinidad**
Teams	**Trinidad & Tobago**
Style	**Right-hand bat, right-arm medium-pacer**
Test debut	**No Tests yet**
ODI debut	**West Indies v South Africa at St George's 2006-07**

THE PROFILE   Kieron Pollard shot to prominence in 2006-07 when still only 19, with his muscular batting doing much to take Trinidad & Tobago to the final of the inaugural Stanford 20/20 competition: in the semi-final, against Nevis, he clobbered 83 in only 38 balls, and then grabbed a couple of wickets with his medium-pacers. That won him a first-class start against Barbados, and it was a memorable one: he got off the mark with a six, and cleared the boundary six more times on his way to 117. Another hundred, and six more sixes, followed in his third match, and in between he hit 87 off 58 balls – seven sixes this time – in a one-dayer against Guyana. That was followed by his inclusion in West Indies' World Cup squad. The cometary rise tailed off a bit after that: he finished his first Carib Beer season with 420 runs at 42, and played only once in the World Cup itself, as a rather surprise selection in the Super Eight match against South Africa (a must-win encounter which West Indies lost, thus putting them out). And he had a modest second season in 2007-08, with eight scores of 28 or fewer sandwiching twin knocks of 85 in the Carib Beer Cup, and two ODIs against Australia only brought scores of 11 and 0. Pollard remains one for the future, and if he can make the final step up to the international arena – one which big hitters like Andrew Symonds took some time to do – he could be a beacon for Caribbean cricket for a long time to come.

THE FACTS   Pollard made 126 on his first-class debut, for Trinidad & Tobago against Barbados at Crab Hill in January 2007: his innings included 11 fours and seven sixes, one of which got him off the mark ... In his second match (against Guyana) he hit 69 in 31 balls, with one four and six sixes, and in his third (against the Leeward Islands) he made 117 from 87 balls with 11 fours and six more sixes ... Pollard was the only player from any country to make his international debut at the 2007 World Cup ...

THE FIGURES *to 12.9.08*   www.cricinfo.com

Batting & Fielding	M	Inns	NO	Runs	HS	Avge	S/R	100	50	4s	6s	Ct	St
Tests	0	0	–	–	–	–	–	–	–	–	–	–	–
ODIs	4	3	0	21	11	7.00	53.84	0	0	1	1	3	0
T20 Ints	1	0	–	–	–	–	–	–	–	–	–	0	0
First-class	13	21	0	721	126	34.33	–	2	3	–	–	17	0

Bowling	M	Balls	Runs	Wkts	BB	Avge	RpO	S/R	5i	10m
Tests	0	0	–	–	–	–	–	–	–	–
ODIs	4	30	31	0	–	–	6.20	–	0	0
T20 Ints	1	0	–	–	–	–	–	–	–	–
First-class	13	211	146	3	2–29	48.66	4.15	70.33	0	0

RICKY **PONTING**

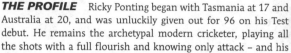

Full name **Ricky Thomas Ponting**
Born **December 19, 1974, Launceston, Tasmania**
Teams **Tasmania, Kolkata Knight Riders**
Style **Right-hand bat, right-arm medium-pace bowler**
Test debut **Australia v Sri Lanka at Perth 1995-96**
ODI debut **Australia v South Africa at Wellington 1994-95**

THE PROFILE Ricky Ponting began with Tasmania at 17 and Australia at 20, and was unluckily given out for 96 on his Test debut. He remains the archetypal modern cricketer, playing all the shots with a full flourish and knowing only attack – and his dead-eye fielding is a force by itself. A gambler and a buccaneer, Ponting is a one-day natural. He has had setbacks, against probing seam and high-class finger-spin, which he plays with hard hands when out of form. In the '90s there were off-field indiscretions that forced him to address an alcohol problem, but his growing maturity was acknowledged when he succeeded Steve Waugh as one-day captain in 2002. It was a seamless transition: Ponting led the 2003 World Cup campaign from the front, clouting a coruscating century in the final, and acceded to the Test crown when Waugh finally stepped down early in 2004. But things changed in 2005. A humiliating one-day defeat by Bangladesh caused the first ripples of dissent against his leadership style, and more followed as the Ashes series progressed. A heroic 156 saved the Manchester Test, but he couldn't save the urn. The result hurt, and the pain lingered. Ponting bounced back by winning 11 of 12 Tests in 2005-06, which was just a warm-up for the Ashes rematch. He led that off with 196 at Brisbane – and was furious to miss his double-century – and remained tight-lipped until the 5-0 whitewash was sealed at Sydney. His batting never wavered, and not long after retaining the World Cup in 2007 he sailed past 20,000 international runs during another successful season.

THE FACTS The only Australians with higher Test batting averages than Ponting's are Don Bradman (99.94) and Michael Hussey (68.38) ... Ponting is the only player to score two hundreds in his 100th Test, v South Africa at Sydney in Jan 2006 ... His 242 v India at Adelaide in 2003-04 is the highest by a player on the losing side in a Test (in the next game he made 257, and they won) ... When he was 8, Ponting's grandmother gave him a T-shirt that read "Under this shirt is a Test player" ... His record includes one ODI for the World XI ...

THE FIGURES *to 12.9.08*　　　　　　　　**www.cricinfo.com**

Batting & Fielding	M	Inns	NO	Runs	HS	Avge	S/R	100	50	4s	6s	Ct	St
Tests	119	199	26	10099	257	58.37	59.04	35	40	1124	62	134	0
ODIs	301	292	35	11113	164	43.24	80.43	26	64	972	136	135	0
T20 Ints	11	10	2	315	98*	39.37	138.15	0	2	32	10	6	0
First-class	216	365	52	18738	257	59.86	–	69	76	–	–	222	0

Bowling	M	Balls	Runs	Wkts	BB	Avge	RpO	S/R	5i	10m
Tests	119	527	231	5	1–0	46.20	2.62	105.40	0	0
ODIs	301	150	104	3	1–12	34.66	4.16	50.00	0	0
T20 Ints	11	0	–	–	–	–	–	–	–	–
First-class	216	1422	757	14	2–10	54.07	3.19	101.57	0	0

DAREN **POWELL**

Full name	**Daren Brent Lyle Powell**
Born	**April 15, 1978, Jamaica**
Teams	**Jamaica**
Style	**Right-hand bat, right-arm fast bowler**
Test debut	**West Indies v New Zealand at Bridgetown 2001-02**
ODI debut	**West Indies v Bangladesh at Dhaka 2002-03**

THE PROFILE Daren Powell began his cricketing life at school in Jamaica as a No. 3 batsman and offspinner, but then came across a concrete pitch that he thought wouldn't suit his spin bowling, so decided to try some medium-pace instead. Seam-up turned out to be the way forward, and Powell has developed into a slippery fast bowler with a rhythmic, high action. But his international career has been less smooth. A solitary Test against New Zealand at home in 2002 was followed by one in India and two in Bangladesh, but pitches in the subcontinent were never going to suit his style of bowling, and he was dropped – without really doing much wrong – and sat on the sidelines for two years. Powell continued to pick up wickets in domestic cricket, and returned for the first Test against South Africa in March 2005, when several players were unavailable owing to a bitter contracts dispute, and did enough to keep his place throughout that season when the others returned. He picked up 5 for 25 on the first day of the second Test against Sri Lanka at Kandy later that year (West Indies still lost heavily), and retained his place for the tour of Australia at the end of 2005. After a spell out of the side, Powell was probably the pick of the faster bowlers in England in 2007 – particularly in the one-dayers, when he seemed to gain a yard of pace. He remained a regular in 2007-08, playing in all West Indies' eight Tests without ever taking more than three wickets in an innings, while his bowling average sneaked worryingly upwards towards the 50 mark

THE FACTS Powell was West Indies' leading wicket-taker at the 2007 World Cup with 14, one more than Dwayne Bravo, and often made early inroads into the opponents' innings ... His best bowling figures of 6 for 49 were for Derbyshire against Durham University at Derby in 2004 ... Powell has also played for Hampshire, and for Gauteng in South Africa ...

THE FIGURES *to 12.9.08*   www.cricinfo.com

Batting & Fielding	M	Inns	NO	Runs	HS	Avge	S/R	100	50	4s	6s	Ct	St
Tests	30	48	3	313	36*	6.95	35.93	0	0	43	3	8	–
ODIs	47	20	3	107	48*	6.29	72.78	0	0	4	5	9	0
T20 Ints	5	1	1	1	1*	–	100.00	0	0	0	0	2	0
First-class	87	125	20	1278	62	12.17	–	0	3	–	–	30	0

Bowling	M	Balls	Runs	Wkts	BB	Avge	RpO	S/R	5i	10m
Tests	30	6045	3452	73	5–25	47.28	3.42	82.80	1	0
ODIs	47	2460	1899	59	4–27	32.18	4.63	41.69	0	0
T20 Ints	5	102	131	2	1–6	65.50	7.70	51.00	0	0
First-class	87	14688	8018	252	6–49	31.81	3.27	58.28	6	0

DAMMIKA **PRASAD**

Full name	**Kariyawasam Tirana Gamage Dammika Prasad**
Born	**May 30, 1983, Ragama**
Teams	**Sinhalese Sports Club, Basnahira North**
Style	**Right-hand bat, right-arm fast-medium bowler**
Test debut	**Sri Lanka v India at Colombo 2008**
ODI debut	**Sri Lanka v Bangladesh at Chittagong 2005-06**

THE PROFILE A prosperous international career looked likely when Dammika Prasad took two wickets in the first over of his one-day international debut, against Bangladesh in Chittagong in February 2006. However, he played only two more games before a back injury kept him on the sidelines for six months. He returned with the A team in India, and also toured England with them in 2007. Then, the following year, he stepped up to the full side again, and made his Test debut against India at the Sara Stadium in Colombo, in a match Sri Lanka won to take the series. Prasad, bustling in and occasionally moving the ball away at a fair pace, ended up with five wickets, including the wicket of Virender Sehwag – India's best batsman in the series – in both innings. He has long had the ability to bowl at the death in ODIs, having worked hard to develop subtle variations including a good yorker. He can also work up a fair pace, and pushed the speedo over 90mph at times during his debut Test. Interestingly, Prasad started his cricket at De Mazenod College in Kandana as a No. 3 batsman (and he has a few first-class fifties under his belt to prove it). He was largely a batsman until he turned 17, and had to try his hand at fast bowling as the school had no-one to take the new ball. Prasad was an instant success, gaining selection for the Under-19 World Cup in 2002 and also winning a six-month scholarship to play in England.

THE FACTS Prasad took the wicket of Shahriar Nafees with his third ball in international cricket, against Bangladesh in Chittagong in February 2006 – and dismissed Aftab Ahmed with his next ball ... Prasad took 6 for 25 (10 for 98 in the match) for Southern Province against Uva at Galle in January 2004 ... He scored 89 for Sri Lanka A against Durham at Chester-le-Street in August 2007 ...

THE FIGURES to 12.9.08   www.cricinfo.com

Batting & Fielding	M	Inns	NO	Runs	HS	Avge	S/R	100	50	4s	6s	Ct	St
Tests	1	1	0	36	36	36.00	64.28	0	0	5	0	0	0
ODIs	3	1	0	8	8	8.00	72.72	0	0	0	0	0	0
T20 Ints	0	0	–	–	–	–	–	–	–	–	–	–	–
First-class	42	46	6	719	89	17.97	60.26	0	5	–	–	11	0

Bowling	M	Balls	Runs	Wkts	BB	Avge	RpO	S/R	5i	10m
Tests	1	168	142	5	3–82	28.40	5.07	33.60	0	0
ODIs	3	126	116	3	2–29	38.66	5.52	42.00	0	0
T20 Ints	0	0	–	–	–	–	–	–	–	–
First-class	42	5434	3342	134	6–25	24.94	3.69	40.55	3	1

ASHWELL **PRINCE**

SOUTH AFRICA

Full name	**Ashwell Gavin Prince**
Born	**May 28, 1977, Port Elizabeth, Cape Province**
Teams	**Cape Cobras, Nottinghamshire, Mumbai Indians**
Style	**Left-hand bat, occasional left-arm spinner**
Test debut	**South Africa v Australia at Johannesburg 2001-02**
ODI debut	**South Africa v Bangladesh at Kimberley 2002-03**

THE PROFILE A crouching left-hander with a high-batted stance and a Gooch-like grimace, Ashwell Prince was helped into the national team by South Africa's controversial race-quota system, although he quickly justified his selection by top-scoring with a gutsy debut 49 against Australia in 2001-02. That, and a matchwinning 48 in the third Test, seemed to have buried his early reputation as a one-day flasher. But then he failed in four successive Tests against Bangladesh and Sri Lanka, and was dropped. Domestic runs won his place back, while valuable runs against West Indies and England made him a one-day regular too. Test hundreds followed early in 2005, against outclassed Zimbabwe and almost-outclassed West Indies, but his 119 at Sydney in January 2006 was an altogether better performance. Prince had struggled against Shane Warne, falling to him in his first four innings of that series, and although he eventually succumbed again it was only after an important stand of 219 with Jacques Kallis. Warne troubled him again in the return series, when Prince's only substantial contribution was a splendid 93 in the third Test at Johannesburg. He smacked a cathartic century against New Zealand in April 2006, then an ankle injury to Graeme Smith meant that Prince was named as South Africa's first black captain, for a tough Test tour of Sri Lanka. He did well in the Tests in England in 2008, with centuries at Lord's and Leeds, but by then he was a back number in ODIs, having been left out following a largely anonymous World Cup. Long rated highly by Ali Bacher, Prince is strong through the off side, and although his throwing has been hampered by a long-term shoulder injury, he remains a fine fielder in the covers.

THE FACTS Prince averages 77.00 in Tests against West Indies – and 10.40 v Bangladesh ... In 18 Test innings against Australia, Prince was dismissed 11 times by Shane Warne ... Prince's highest first-class score is 184, for Western Province Boland against the Lions at Paarl in 2004-05 ... His record includes three ODIs for the Africa XI ...

THE FIGURES *to 12.9.08*   www.cricinfo.com

Batting & Fielding	M	Inns	NO	Runs	HS	Avge	S/R	100	50	4s	6s	Ct	St
Tests	45	74	10	2703	149	42.23	42.53	9	7	295	6	25	0
ODIs	52	41	12	1018	89*	35.10	67.77	0	3	77	4	26	0
T20 Ints	1	1	0	5	5	5.00	83.33	0	0	0	0	0	0
First-class	146	229	30	8405	184	42.23	–	21	39	–	–	88	0

Bowling	M	Balls	Runs	Wkts	BB	Avge	RpO	S/R	5i	10m
Tests	45	96	47	1	1–2	47.00	2.93	96.00	0	0
ODIs	52	12	3	0	–	–	1.50	–	0	0
T20 Ints	1	0	–	–	–	–	–	–	–	–
First-class	146	276	166	4	2–11	41.50	3.60	69.00	0	0

MATT **PRIOR**

Full name	**Matthew James Prior**
Born	**February 26, 1982, Johannesburg, South Africa**
Teams	**Sussex**
Style	**Right-hand bat, wicketkeeper**
Test debut	**England v West Indies at Lord's 2007**
ODI debut	**England v Zimbabwe at Bulawayo 2004-05**

THE PROFILE Sussex wicketkeeper Matt Prior represented England at several junior levels, and completed his set by making his Test debut in May 2007, against West Indies at Lord's. He repaid the faith of Peter Moores, his former county boss turned national coach, with a cracking century – the first by a keeper on debut for England. It was full of solid drives and clumping pulls, and seemed to announce a readymade star, especially when Prior added some acrobatic takes behind the stumps. He finished that series with 324 runs – but there were already rumbles about his keeping technique, which didn't seem to matter while England were winning. But then India arrived, and Prior's fumbles were magnified as the visitors stole the series: he dropped Sachin Tendulkar and VVS Laxman as India made 664 at The Oval. The runs dried up, too, and suddenly Prior's talkativeness behind the stumps, and his footwork, were called into question. Another uninspiring series followed in Sri Lanka and Prior was dropped, in favour of his old Sussex team-mate Tim Ambrose. Prior went back to Hove and sharpened up his technique, and was ready when Ambrose in turn faltered during 2008: Prior returned for the one-dayers against South Africa, looking a more polished performer, and pouched a record-equalling six catches – one of them a one-handed flying stunner – at Trent Bridge. Prior was born in South Africa, but his family moved to England when he was 11 – he says he lost his accent within a week – and he soon joined Sussex, making his debut in 2001.

THE FACTS Prior was the 17th man to score a century on Test debut for England, but the first to keep wicket in the same match: he was the fifth person to score a century on Test debut at Lord's, after Australia's Harry Graham, John Hampshire and Andrew Strauss of England, and India's Sourav Ganguly ... Prior equalled the ODI wicketkeeping record with six catches against South Africa at Nottingham in August 2008 ... He made 201 not out for Sussex v Loughborough UCCE at Hove in May 2004 ...

THE FIGURES to 12.9.08   www.cricinfo.com

Batting & Fielding	M	Inns	NO	Runs	HS	Avge	S/R	100	50	4s	6s	Ct	St
Tests	10	17	3	562	126*	40.14	56.14	1	4	70	4	28	0
ODIs	28	27	2	590	52	23.60	76.03	0	1	74	5	37	3
T20 Ints	5	5	0	116	32	23.20	128.88	0	0	10	5	4	1
First-class	132	209	20	7473	201*	39.53	66.67	18	40	–	–	308	21

Bowling	M	Balls	Runs	Wkts	BB	Avge	RpO	S/R	5i	10m
Tests	10	0	–	–	–	–	–	–	–	–
ODIs	28	0	–	–	–	–	–	–	–	–
T20 Ints	5	0	–	–	–	–	–	–	–	–
First-class	132	0	–	–	–	–	–	–	–	–

SURESH **RAINA**

Full name	**Suresh Kumar Raina**
Born	**November 27, 1986, Ghaziabad, Uttar Pradesh**
Teams	**Uttar Pradesh, Chennai Super Kings**
Style	**Left-hand bat, occasional offspinner**
Test debut	**No Tests yet**
ODI debut	**India v Sri Lanka at Dambulla 2005**

THE PROFILE An aggressive young batsman who has dismantled bowling attacks around India, Suresh Raina puts people in mind of Yuvraj Singh, another powerful left-hander. A string of fine performances at junior level – where he frequently bullied his way to double-hundreds – landed him a place in the Indian Under-19 side. In April 2005, in the final of the Ranji Trophy one-day tournament, Raina strolled in, spanked nine fours and a six in 48 from 33 balls as Uttar Pradesh tied with Tamil Nadu and shared the title, then left to catch the flight home for his school exams. The following season his 620 runs in six matches propelled Uttar Pradesh to the senior Ranji Trophy title. His electric fielding added zing to India's one-day side, and it came as no surprise when, even before he'd managed an ODI fifty, he was fast-tracked into the Test squad against England in March 2006, and the subsequent tour of the West Indies, although he didn't actually play. However, despite three fifties in five one-day knocks against England, the early promise turned out to be a false dawn – he couldn't manage a half-century in 16 more attempts before being dropped early in 2007. It was more than a year before he won his place back. Raina was a non-playing member of the one-day squad in Australia at the start of 2008, but in June he finally played to his true potential, slamming two centuries in the Asia Cup, against Hong Kong and Bangladesh, then made 53 and 76 in Sri Lanka in August as India fought back to win the one-day series there.

THE FACTS Raina scored 203 for Uttar Pradesh against Orissa at Cuttack in November 2007 ... His first ODI century, against Hong Kong at Karachi in June 2008, came from 66 balls (the second-fastest for India after Mohammad Azharuddin's 62-ball effort against New Zealand at Baroda in 1988-89) and included five sixes ... Raina scored 72 in the first Under-19 Test and 63 in the third in England in 2002, when Irfan Pathan was a team-mate ...

THE FIGURES to 12.9.08   www.cricinfo.com

Batting & Fielding	M	Inns	NO	Runs	HS	Avge	S/R	100	50	4s	6s	Ct	St
Tests	0	0	–	–	–	–	–	–	–	–	–	–	–
ODIs	50	42	7	1191	116*	34.02	82.42	2	7	108	19	22	0
T20 Ints	1	1	1	3	3*	–	75.00	0	0	0	0	2	1
First-class	38	66	3	2914	203	46.25	58.61	5	20	–	–	45	0

Bowling	M	Balls	Runs	Wkts	BB	Avge	RpO	S/R	5i	10m
Tests	0	0	–	–	–	–	–	–	–	–
ODIs	50	50	59	1	1–23	59.00	7.08	50.00	0	0
T20 Ints	1	0	–	–	–	–	–	–	–	–
First-class	38	564	246	4	3–40	61.50	2.61	141.00	0	0

DENESH **RAMDIN**

Full name	**Denesh Ramdin**
Born	**March 13, 1985, Couva, Trinidad**
Teams	**Trinidad & Tobago**
Style	**Right-hand bat, wicketkeeper**
Test debut	**West Indies v Sri Lanka at Colombo 2005**
ODI debut	**West Indies v India at Dambulla 2005**

THE PROFILE Denesh Ramdin is a wicketkeeper-batsman of great potential, viewed by many in the Caribbean as the long-term solution to the void which has never really been satisfactorily filled since the retirement of Jeff Dujon in 1991. Originally a fast bowler who kept wicket when he had finished with the ball, Ramdin decided at 13 to concentrate on keeping, honing his reflexes and working on his agility. He led both the Trinidad and West Indies Under-19 sides before being selected, still only 19 and with just 13 first-class games behind him, as the first-choice keeper for the senior tour of Sri Lanka in 2005. He impressed everyone with his work behind and in front of the stumps, and continued to do so in the series in Australia later in 2005. A plucky 71 – he shared a fine partnership of 182 in the second Test with his fellow Trinidadian Dwayne Bravo, just after they'd heard that T&T had qualified for the football World Cup – was his best moment Down Under. Carlton Baugh was preferred for some of the home one-dayers early in 2006, and it was something of a surprise when Ramdin returned for the Tests against India. But he justified his selection with some smooth keeping, and a gritty unbeaten 62 that took West Indies frustratingly close to victory in the series-deciding fourth Test in Jamaica. He started the 2007 series in England with a bright 60 at Lord's, but struggled with the bat after that, while his keeping was patchy, and soon faced a new challenge from Patrick Browne of Barbados, who was preferred for some one-day internationals during 2008.

THE FACTS Ramdin played in the West Indies side that won the Under-15 World Challenge in 2000, beating Pakistan in the final at Lord's; four years later he captained West Indies in the Under-19 World Cup, when they lost the final at Dhaka – to Pakistan ... His highest score is 131 for the West Indians against MCC at Durham in June 2007 ... After averaging 31.00 in Tests in 2005, Ramdin's batting average dipped to 14.22 in 2007 and 18.83 in 2008 ...

THE FIGURES *to 12.9.08*   www.cricinfo.com

Batting & Fielding	M	Inns	NO	Runs	HS	Avge	S/R	100	50	4s	6s	Ct	St
Tests	27	49	6	931	71	21.65	45.83	0	5	122	1	82	2
ODIs	51	39	11	554	74*	19.78	79.25	0	2	49	1	73	4
T20 Ints	8	8	2	90	24*	15.00	118.42	0	0	11	2	3	1
First-class	58	99	11	2274	131	25.84	–	4	10	–	–	159	17

Bowling	M	Balls	Runs	Wkts	BB	Avge	RpO	S/R	5i	10m
Tests	27	0	–	–	–	–	–	–	–	–
ODIs	51	0	–	–	–	–	–	–	–	–
T20 Ints	8	0	–	–	–	–	–	–	–	–
First-class	58	0	–	–	–	–	–	–	–	–

RAVI **RAMPAUL**

Full name	**Ravindranath Rampaul**
Born	**October 15, 1984, Preysal, Trinidad**
Teams	**Trinidad & Tobago**
Style	**Left-hand bat, right-arm fast-medium bowler**
Test debut	**No Tests yet**
ODI debut	**West Indies v Zimbabwe at Bulawayo 2003-04**

THE PROFILE Ravi Rampaul is a tall and well-built fast bowler, but his career has been hamstrung by injuries. Of East Indian descent, he first came to notice as West Indies won the World Under-15 Challenge in England in 2000. Two years later he made his Trinidad debut, and 18 wickets in six matches in 2003 – and some impressive performances for West Indies Under-19s – propelled him to the verge of full international selection. It was his aggressive approach that really caught the eye: in a one-dayer against Antigua & Barbuda he unleashed four successive bouncers at the opener, then finished him off with an unplayable yorker. He was picked to tour southern Africa in 2003-04, and made his ODI debut in Zimbabwe. Rampaul was rarely collared, but hardly ran through sides either – in 14 matches in Africa and the Caribbean that season he took nine wickets, only once managing more than one. Nonetheless he was retained for the 2004 England tour, and played three more one-dayers before he broke down and returned home before the Tests. Shin splints sidelined him for more than a year, and he did not play another first-class match until 2006-07, taking 7 for 51 as T&T beat Barbados in the Carib Beer final. That won him another England tour. Restricted by a groin tear, he again missed the Tests, but helped West Indies turn the one-day series around by demolishing England's middle order with 4 for 41 in the pivotal second match at Edgbaston. He went to South Africa at the end of the year, but took only one wicket in four ODIs and slid out of the side again.

THE FACTS Rampaul took 7 for 51 as Trinidad & Tobago beat Barbados in the final of the Carib Beer Challenge at Pointe-à-Pierre in February 2007 ... His highest score of 64 not out was for West Indies A v Sri Lanka A at Basseterre in December 2006 ... In the World Under-15 Challenge in 2000, Rampaul took 7 for 11 against Holland, and opened both the bowling and the batting in the final at Lord's, as West Indies beat Pakistan ... Rampaul played for Ireland in the Friends Provident Trophy in 2008 ...

THE FIGURES *to 12.9.08*   www.cricinfo.com

Batting & Fielding	M	Inns	NO	Runs	HS	Avge	S/R	100	50	4s	6s	Ct	St
Tests	0	0	–	–	–	–	–	–	–	–	–	–	–
ODIs	30	9	2	88	26*	12.57	68.21	0	0	7	3	3	0
T20 Ints	5	1	1	0	0*	–	0.00	0	0	0	0	0	0
First-class	27	35	3	456	64*	14.25	–	0	2	–	–	10	0

Bowling	M	Balls	Runs	Wkts	BB	Avge	RpO	S/R	5i	10m
Tests	0	0	–	–	–	–	–	–	–	–
ODIs	30	1109	919	25	4–41	36.76	4.97	44.36	0	0
T20 Ints	5	120	177	5	2–35	35.40	8.85	24.00	0	0
First-class	27	3809	2310	76	7–51	30.39	3.63	50.11	3	0

RAQIBUL HASAN

Full name	**Mohammad Raqibul Hasan**
Born	**October 8, 1987, Jamalpur**
Teams	**Barisal**
Style	**Right-hand bat, legspinner**
Test debut	**No Tests yet**
ODI debut	**Bangladesh v South Africa at Chittagong 2007-08**

THE PROFILE Another of Bangladesh's young achievers, Raqibul Hasan toured with Bangladesh A before he had played first-class cricket, made a hundred on his first-class debut, and hit a triple-century – the first in Bangladesh domestic cricket – before he was 20 years old. It was only a matter of time, therefore, until he was given a chance in the full national team, and he duly made his ODI debut in March 2008, scoring 63 in his second match and adding 89 against India in the Kitply Cup and 52 against Sri Lanka in the Asia Cup. Raqibul, who is sometimes known by his nickname "Nirala", is a complete batsman, with a fine cover-drive, although at the moment he is more of an accumulator than a dasher, and may need to up the tempo to claim a regular spot in one-day international cricket. He looks a natural for Tests, though – that triple-century, an innings of 313 not out in a Barisal total of 712 for 7 (another domestic record) against Sylhet, occupied 11 hours. Raqibul has crammed a lot of cricket into his young life: he played in the Under-19 World Cup in Sri Lanka in 2006, travelled to the Top End of Australia with the Academy in August 2007, and joined the Bangladesh A team in England in 2008.

THE FACTS Raqibul Hasan was selected for the Bangladesh A tour of Zimbabwe in 2004-05 before he had played first-class cricket: on his debut, against Zimbabwe A at Bulawayo, he scored 100 ... He scored 313 not out in 11 hours for Barisal against Sylhet at Fatullah in March 2007: he was 19 years 161 days old, the third-youngest triple-centurion in first-class history after Javed Miandad and Wasim Jaffer ...

THE FIGURES *to 12.9.08*   www.cricinfo.com

Batting & Fielding	M	Inns	NO	Runs	HS	Avge	S/R	100	50	4s	6s	Ct	St
Tests	0	0	–	–	–	–	–	–	–	–	–	–	–
ODIs	15	14	0	412	89	29.42	65.18	0	4	32	1	5	0
T20 Ints	0	0	–	–	–	–	–	–	–	–	–	–	–
First-class	22	39	1	1418	313*	37.31	43.68	2	8	–	–	15	0

Bowling	M	Balls	Runs	Wkts	BB	Avge	RpO	S/R	5i	10m
Tests	0	0	–	–	–	–	–	–	–	–
ODIs	15	0	–	–	–	–	–	–	–	–
T20 Ints	0	0	–	–	–	–	–	–	–	–
First-class	22	288	202	4	1–4	50.50	4.20	72.00	0	0

KEMAR **ROACH**

Full name	**Kemar Andre Jamal Roach**
Born	**June 30, 1988, St Lucy, Barbados**
Teams	**Barbados**
Style	**Right-hand bat, right-arm fast-medium bowler**
Test debut	**No Tests yet**
ODI debut	**West Indies v Bermuda at King City 2008**

THE PROFILE A right-arm fast bowler, Kemar Roach was part of the Barbados and West Indies Under-19 teams before, still only 19 and having played only four first-class matches, all of them in 2008, he was called into the squad for the third Test against Australia at Bridgetown in June. He was slightly fortunate still to be around: he had agreed to play for Ombersley in the Birmingham League, but was deemed ineligible as he had played one fewer than the five first-class games required of overseas players by the league's rules. Roach had been spotted by Steve Rhodes, Worcestershire's director of cricket, on a pre-season tour – Rhodes had hoped to include him for a few Second Eleven games. Roach was under no illusions about his international call-up: "I know that when a Test match comes around, they sometimes draft in players in the island where the match is, but I wasn't expecting to be in the squad. I'm quite happy to be there. If selected, I want to put in a good performance." He was right – he didn't play, but he was included for the Twenty20 international shortly afterwards at the Kensington Oval, and took two of the three wickets to fall, disposing of the Australian openers Shaun Marsh and Luke Ronchi after starting with a nervous beamer. He made his one-day debut in the tri-series in Canada later in 2008. Roach has good pace, and a nice flowing action: he suffered a bit with no-balls for a while, but claims to have put that behind him after lots of hard work.

THE FACTS Roach took a hat-trick against Sri Lanka Under-19s in a warm-up match before the 2006 Youth World Cup in Colombo ... He was included in West Indies' squad for the third Test against Australia at Bridgetown in June 2008 after only four first-class games, but did not play in the end ...

THE FIGURES to 12.9.08   www.cricinfo.com

Batting & Fielding	M	Inns	NO	Runs	HS	Avge	S/R	100	50	4s	6s	Ct	St
Tests	0	0	–	–	–	–	–	–	–	–	–	–	–
ODIs	2	0	–	–	–	–	–	–	–	–	–	0	0
T20 Ints	1	0	–	–	–	–	–	–	–	–	–	0	0
First-class	4	4	0	57	16	14.25	–	0	0	–	–	1	0

Bowling	M	Balls	Runs	Wkts	BB	Avge	RpO	S/R	5i	10m
Tests	0	0	–	–	–	–	–	–	–	–
ODIs	2	108	78	3	2–29	26.00	4.33	36.00	0	0
T20 Ints	1	18	29	2	2–29	14.50	9.66	9.00	0	0
First-class	4	334	214	7	3–30	30.57	3.84	47.71	0	0

LUKE **RONCHI**

Full name **Luke Ronchi**
Born **April 23, 1981, Dannevirke, New Zealand**
Teams **Western Australia, Mumbai Indians**
Style **Right-hand bat, wicketkeeper**
Test debut **No Tests yet**
ODI debut **Australia v West Indies at St George's 2007-08**

THE PROFILE New Zealand-born Luke Ronchi quickly confirmed his place as the next in line for Australia's wicketkeeping position in 2008, replacing the injured Brad Haddin for most of the one-dayers in the West Indies and spanking a 22-ball half-century in only his fourth match. An accomplished gloveman, Ronchi (it's pronounced "Ronky") also produces the type of clean hitting that has become a trademark of Western Australia keepers. He took over the role from another rapid-scoring right-hander, Adam Gilchrist's long-serving deputy Ryan Campbell, during 2005-06: two games after Campbell's retirement Ronchi blasted a run-a-ball century against New South Wales. In February 2007 he hammered the fastest hundred in Australian domestic one-day history, his 56-ball century against New South Wales featuring a series of powerful pulls off Stuart Clark. Another highlight was his 89 from 49 balls against an England XI in the Lilac Hill match the previous December. His rewards for a fine season (40 first-class dismissals and 378 Pura Cup runs at 31.50, and 339 one-day runs at 37.66) were a third winter at the Academy and selection for the Australia A tour of Pakistan. Back in 2002-03 Ronchi had marked his first-class debut with 90 and 33 against Tasmania, and then outlined his method: "I just tried to have fun and it went from there." His idea of fun includes a wild 67 from 24 balls in the first Twenty20 game in Australia and 40 off 13 for the Prime Minister's XI against the Pakistanis, both in 2004-05.

THE FACTS Ronchi reached 50 from only 22 balls in his second ODI innings (his fourth match) against West Indies in St Kitts in July 2008, equalling Australia's second-fastest ODI half-century at the time ... He reached his hundred against NSW at Perth in February 2007 in only 56 balls, an Australian domestic one-day record ... Ronchi has also scored three first-class centuries, the highest 107 for Australia A v Pakistan A at Lahore in September 2007 ...

THE FIGURES to 12.9.08   www.cricinfo.com

Batting & Fielding	M	Inns	NO	Runs	HS	Avge	S/R	100	50	4s	6s	Ct	St
Tests	0	0	–	–	–	–	–	–	–	–	–	–	–
ODIs	4	2	0	76	64	38.00	205.40	0	1	6	6	5	2
T20 Ints	1	1	0	36	36	36.00	163.63	0	0	6	1	0	0
First-class	30	47	6	1487	107	36.26	88.04	3	9	–	–	101	6

Bowling	M	Balls	Runs	Wkts	BB	Avge	RpO	S/R	5i	10m
Tests	0	0	–	–	–	–	–	–	–	–
ODIs	4	0	–	–	–	–	–	–	–	–
T20 Ints	1	0	–	–	–	–	–	–	–	–
First-class	30	0	–	–	–	–	–	–	–	–

JESSE **RYDER**

Full name	**Jesse Daniel Ryder**
Born	**August 6, 1984, Masterton, Wellington**
Teams	**Wellington**
Style	**Left-hand bat, right-arm medium-pacer**
Test debut	**No Tests yet**
ODI debut	**New Zealand v England at Wellington 2007-08**

THE PROFILE Jesse Ryder had a troubled childhood, and latterly has battled with his weight and demons of his own: just after establishing himself in the one-day side after a series of promising performances early in 2008, he injured tendons in his hand when he smashed a window in a bar at 5.30 in the morning shortly after celebrating a tight series victory over England. It took some time to clear up, keeping him out of the England tour that followed. But Ryder is talented: New Zealand Cricket had already forgiven him for refusing to play for their A team the year before (he briefly threatened to try to qualify for England, where both his grandfathers come from) and they gave him yet another chance despite concerns about his drinking habits. Ryder gives the ball a good thump, and looks a natural for one-day cricket. He seemed to have found his niche in that series against England: his lowest score in the five ODIs was 23, and he biffed 79 not out in the second game at Hamilton, going run for run with Brendon McCullum in a rollicking opening stand of 165 which won the game with half the overs unused. Ryder can also bowl useful medium-pace, Craig McMillan-style. He returned to action in July 2008 by captaining NZ's Emerging Players to victory in a tournament in Australia and, if he can control himself (he has said that he will stop drinking if that was a condition of his return to the national side) then a bright future awaits.

THE FACTS Ryder scored 236 for Wellington against Central Districts at Palmerston North in March 2005 ... Three of his five first-class centuries have come against Canterbury, against whom he averages 52.88 ... Ryder played two one-day games for Ireland in 2007 before being dumped after missing the plane to the next match ...

THE FIGURES to 12.9.08   www.cricinfo.com

Batting & Fielding	M	Inns	NO	Runs	HS	Avge	S/R	100	50	4s	6s	Ct	St
Tests	0	0	–	–	–	–	–	–	–	–	–	–	–
ODIs	5	5	1	196	79*	49.00	91.16	0	1	23	6	2	0
T20 Ints	2	2	0	34	22	17.00	100.00	0	0	6	0	2	0
First-class	39	61	4	2439	236	42.78	–	5	13	–	–	32	0

Bowling	M	Balls	Runs	Wkts	BB	Avge	RpO	S/R	5i	10m
Tests	0	0	–	–	–	–	–	–	–	–
ODIs	5	48	64	2	2–14	32.00	8.00	24.00	0	0
T20 Ints	2	18	24	1	1–2	24.00	8.00	18.00	0	0
First-class	39	2335	1064	41	4–23	25.95	2.73	56.95	0	0

SALMAN BUTT

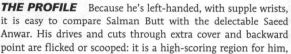

Full name	**Salman Butt**
Born	**October 7, 1984, Lahore, Punjab**
Teams	**Lahore, National Bank, Kolkata Knight Riders**
Style	**Left-hand bat, occasional offspinner**
Test debut	**Pakistan v Bangladesh at Multan 2003-04**
ODI debut	**Pakistan v West Indies at Southampton 2004**

PAKISTAN

THE PROFILE   Because he's left-handed, with supple wrists, it is easy to compare Salman Butt with the delectable Saeed Anwar. His drives and cuts through extra cover and backward point are flicked or scooped: it is a high-scoring region for him, as it was for Anwar. He doesn't mind pulling, and off his toes he's efficient, rather than whippy as Anwar was. But in attitude and temperament he is more like Anwar's long-time opening partner, Aamer Sohail. He has a confident air, a certain spikiness, and is a rare young Pakistan player at ease speaking English. Butt first made headlines by smashing 233 during an Under-19 tour of South Africa, and his breakthrough at the highest level came late in 2004. After a maiden one-day century, at Eden Gardens, he made 70 at Melbourne and 108 in the New Year Test at Sydney. Then came the fall: he failed to build on that during 2005, despite another one-day hundred against India, and was dropped as doubts crept in about his defence and his dash. He responded by unveiling startling restraint against England late in the year, grinding out a hundred and two fifties in the Tests, followed by another ton at India's expense. He was dropped again after an uninspiring England tour, and did not feature in 2006-07, which at least meant he was spared the misery of the World Cup – in the aftermath of which he found himself promoted to vice-captain, responding with 74 in a one-dayer against Sri Lanka in Abu Dhabi. He continued his good form with three one-day hundreds in the first six months of 2008, and now looks like one half of the solution to the opening conundrum that has haunted Pakistan since ... well, since Anwar and Sohail retired.

THE FACTS   Salman Butt's first four ODI hundreds – and his seventh – all came against India: he averages 51.00 against them, but only 14.83 against West Indies (and 1.00 v Scotland) ... His highest score is 290, for Punjab against Federal Areas at Lahore in February 2008 ... Butt captained Pakistan in the Under-19 World Cup in New Zealand early in 2002 ...

THE FIGURES *to 12.9.08*   www.cricinfo.com

Batting & Fielding	M	Inns	NO	Runs	HS	Avge	S/R	100	50	4s	6s	Ct	St
Tests	19	36	0	1047	122	29.08	46.95	2	6	153	1	8	0
ODIs	57	57	3	2154	136	39.88	78.32	7	9	272	7	16	0
T20 Ints	8	7	0	108	33	15.42	81.20	0	0	10	0	1	0
First-class	66	115	6	4540	290	41.65	–		12	20	–	–	25	0

Bowling	M	Balls	Runs	Wkts	BB	Avge	RpO	S/R	5i	10m
Tests	19	131	95	1	1–36	95.00	4.35	131.00	–	–
ODIs	57	69	90	0	–	–	7.82	–	0	0
T20 Ints	8	0	–	–	–	–	–	–	–	–
First-class	66	920	635	11	4–82	57.72	4.14	83.63	0	0

THILAN **SAMARAWEERA**

Full name	**Thilan Thusara Samaraweera**
Born	**September 22, 1976, Colombo**
Teams	**Sinhalese Sports Club, Kandurata**
Style	**Right-hand bat, offspinner**
Test debut	**Sri Lanka v India at Colombo 2001-02**
ODI debut	**Sri Lanka v India at Sharjah 1998-99**

THE PROFILE Originally an offspinner, Thilan Samaraweera lived in the shadow of Muttiah Muralitharan early on in his career, only occasionally getting a one-day outing. But after scoring 103 not out on Test debut against India in August 2001, an innings that helped Sri Lanka to a 2-1 series win, he carved out a reputation as a specialist batsman, and the departure of Aravinda de Silva and Hashan Tillakaratne allowed him to secure a place in the middle order, where his patient approach makes him a very valuable foil for some of his more flamboyant colleagues. An adhesive and well-organised player, Samaraweera took a particular liking to his home ground, the Sinhalese Sports Club in Colombo, where he scored three centuries in his first six Tests. He has been branded a Test specialist by the selectors, and has not featured in a one-day international since November 2005 – although a recent reassessment of his no-risks approach led to him being added to the short list for the cancelled Champions Trophy in 2008. His steady offspin is rarely used now, although he has a developing reputation as a partnership-breaker and clearly has the talent to become a useful support bowler. He did not feature in senior internationals in 2006-07, but kept his name in the frame by leading Sri Lanka's A side, and after a century in Port-of-Spain in April 2008 Samaraweera was the most consistent batsman on show as Sri Lanka beat India at home later in the year.

THE FACTS Samaraweera was the third Sri Lankan, after Brendon Kuruppu and Romesh Kaluwitharana, to score a century on Test debut, against India in August 2001 ... That innings, and three of his other Test centuries, was scored at the Sinhalese Sports Club, his home ground in Colombo, where he averages 82.36 in Tests ... He averages 58.65 in home Tests, but only 29.34 away ... Samaraweera's brother Dulip played seven Tests for Sri Lanka in the early 1990s ...

THE FIGURES *to 12.9.08* www.cricinfo.com

Batting & Fielding	M	Inns	NO	Runs	HS	Avge	S/R	100	50	4s	6s	Ct	St
Tests	45	68	10	2552	142	44.00	43.30	9	15	282	1	33	0
ODIs	17	13	1	199	33	16.58	52.50	0	0	15	0	3	0
T20 Ints	0	0	–	–	–	–	–	–	–	–	–	–	–
First-class	195	263	48	9550	206	44.41	–	22	52	–	–	165	0

Bowling	M	Balls	Runs	Wkts	BB	Avge	RpO	S/R	5i	10m
Tests	45	1291	679	14	4–49	48.50	3.15	92.21	0	0
ODIs	17	672	509	10	3–34	50.90	4.54	67.20	0	0
T20 Ints	0	0	–	–	–	–	–	–	–	–
First-class	195	17458	8132	348	6–55	23.36	2.79	50.16	15	2

DARREN **SAMMY**

Full name	**Darren Julius Garvey Sammy**
Born	**December 20, 1983, Micoud, St Lucia**
Teams	**Windward Islands**
Style	**Right-hand bat, right-arm medium-pacer**
Test debut	**West Indies v England at Manchester 2007**
ODI debut	**West Indies v New Zealand at Southampton 2004**

THE PROFILE Darren Julius Garvey Sammy has names invoking images of great leadership. He was the first Test cricketer to emerge from St Lucia, an island rediscovering its cricket culture as the new Beausejour Stadium has captured imaginations, so it was a major feat that he cracked the regional squad. Sammy, who spent some time at Lord's with the MCC cricket staff, is a handy batsman and a tall, nagging medium-pacer. He won a one-day cap in England in 2004, although the match was abandoned, and was called up late to the Champions Trophy squad that September after Jermaine Lawson pulled out with a stress fracture of the back. In July 2006 he was named as St Lucia's captain for the inaugural Stanford 20/20 tournament, and a decent first-class season – 269 runs at 44 in five matches, plus 16 wickets at less than 20 – earned him a recall for the 2007 England tour. He was drafted into the side for the third Test at Old Trafford, and celebrated with seven wickets in the second innings – three of them in one over. His pace is unthreatening, but he brings the ball down from quite a height and wobbles it around enough to unsettle the batsman. "I want to be the workhorse of the team," he pronounced after his dream debut – but sadly he didn't get the chance again on that tour, as he picked up a groin strain while batting during his debut and missed the final Test and the one-dayers that followed, and he has struggled for penetration in his international appearances since.

THE FACTS Sammy took 7 for 66 in his first Test, against England at Old Trafford in 2007: only Alf Valentine, with 8 for 104 against England at Old Trafford in 1950, has returned better figures on Test debut for West Indies ... No play was possible in his first ODI, against New Zealand at Southampton in July 2004, but because the toss was made it counts as an appearance ... Sammy is believed to be the only Seventh Day Adventist ever to have played Test cricket ...

THE FIGURES *to 12.9.08*   www.cricinfo.com

Batting & Fielding	M	Inns	NO	Runs	HS	Avge	S/R	100	50	4s	6s	Ct	St
Tests	5	9	0	147	38	16.33	47.88	0	0	20	0	3	0
ODIs	17	11	2	154	51	17.11	90.58	0	1	8	4	6	0
T20 Ints	5	3	2	22	14*	44.00	88.00	0	0	1	1	1	0
First-class	45	75	5	1675	87	23.92	–	0	12	–	–	56	0

Bowling	M	Balls	Runs	Wkts	BB	Avge	RpO	S/R	5i	10m
Tests	5	843	441	13	7–66	33.92	3.13	64.84	1	0
ODIs	17	590	488	10	2–2	48.80	4.96	59.00	0	0
T20 Ints	5	84	94	7	3–21	13.42	6.71	12.00	0	0
First-class	45	6014	2671	102	7–66	26.18	2.66	58.96	6	0

KUMAR **SANGAKKARA**

Full name **Kumar Chokshanada Sangakkara**
Born **October 27, 1977, Matale**
Teams **Nondescripts, Kandurata, Kings XI Punjab**
Style **Left-hand bat, wicketkeeper**
Test debut **Sri Lanka v South Africa at Galle 2000**
ODI debut **Sri Lanka v Pakistan at Galle 2000**

THE PROFILE Within months of making the side at 22, Kumar Sangakkara had become one of Sri Lanka's most influential players: a talented left-hand strokemaker, a slick wicketkeeper, and a sharp-eyed strategist with an even sharper tongue, capable of riling even the most unflappable. His success was unexpected, for his domestic performances had been relatively modest, but the selectors were immediately justified when he starred in his first one-day tournament, in July 2000. Early on his keeping could be ragged, but his effortless batting oozed class from the start. He possesses the grace of David Gower, but the attitude of an Aussie. At the outset he was happier on the back foot, but a fierce work ethic and a deep interest in the theory of batsmanship helped him, and he is now as comfortable driving through the covers as cutting behind point. He was briefly relieved of keeping duties after the 2003 World Cup: he made more runs, but got the gloves back when Australia visited early in 2004. The extra burden had no obvious effect on his batting: he made 185 against Pakistan in March 2006, and scored consistently in England too. But there was a change of thinking after that, and Prasanna Jayawardene was given the gloves. Sangakkara responded with seven centuries, among them three doubles, in his next nine Tests, including 287 as he and Mahela Jayawardene put on a world record 624 against South Africa, and a magnificent 192 against Australia at Hobart in November 2007. A charismatic personality and an astute thinker – he is training as a lawyer – Sangakkara is tipped as a future captain.

THE FACTS Sangakkara scored 287, and put on 624 (the highest stand in first-class cricket) with Mahela Jayawardene v South Africa in Colombo in July 2006 ... He also made 270, adding 438 with Marvan Atapattu, v Zimbabwe at Bulawayo in May 2004 ... Sangakkara averages 83.05 in Tests when he was not the designated wicketkeeper, but 40.48 when lumbered with the gloves ... Against Bangladesh in 2007 he became only the fourth man to score back-to-back double-centuries in Tests ... His record includes three ODIs for the World XI and four for the Asia XI ...

THE FIGURES *to 12.9.08*   www.cricinfo.com

Batting & Fielding	M	Inns	NO	Runs	HS	Avge	S/R	100	50	4s	6s	Ct	St
Tests	76	125	9	6356	287	54.79	55.85	17	26	841	19	153	20
ODIs	230	213	23	6777	138*	35.66	74.42	10	42	679	29	209	59
T20 Ints	8	7	0	138	30	19.71	106.15	0	0	18	1	3	3
First-class	160	253	19	10566	287	45.15	–	24	50	–	–	309	33

Bowling	M	Balls	Runs	Wkts	BB	Avge	RpO	S/R	5i	10m
Tests	76	6	4	0	–	–	4.00	–	0	0
ODIs	230	0	–	–	–	–	–	–	–	–
T20 Ints	8	0	–	–	–	–	–	–	–	–
First-class	160	132	74	1	1–13	74.00	3.36	132.00	0	0

SARFRAZ AHMED

Full name	**Sarfraz Ahmed**
Born	**May 22, 1987, Karachi, Sind**
Teams	**Sind, Pakistan International Airlines**
Style	**Right-hand bat, wicketkeeper**
Test debut	**No Tests yet**
ODI debut	**Pakistan v India at Jaipur 2007-08**

THE PROFILE Sarfraz Ahmed is a solid rather than spectacular wicketkeeper, who captained Pakistan to the Under-19 World Cup early in 2006, after warming up with half-centuries on successive days in the junior Afro-Asia Cup which preceded it. He has been the recognised understudy to Kamran Akmal at national level since 2007, and every dropped catch by Akmal in that time has pushed Sarfraz's claims for inclusion. At the end of 2007 Akmal's continued poor form led to Sarfraz being drafted in to the squad in the middle of the tour of India – not an action designed to improve Akmal's state of mind – and Sarfraz was parachuted into the decisive last match of the one-day series, taking two catches and not conceding a bye at Jaipur as Pakistan won to clinch the rubber. He had a run in the side after that, and even though Akmal returned to smash a rapid hundred against Bangladesh in April 2008, Sarfraz was preferred for the Asia Cup in June. Although Sarfraz is not as eye-catching a batsman, he had a decent domestic season in 2007-08, scoring 641 runs at 64.10, including a maiden century against Abbottabad. He started in first-class cricket soon after that Under-19 World Cup triumph – ironically he was caught by Akmal in the second innings of his debut – and caught the eye with 28 dismissals in his first full season and 35 in 2007-08. There were those runs, too, although with the bat he is more guts than class – but after Akmal's deterioration, the keeping is more important.

THE FACTS Sarfraz Ahmed scored 117, his only first-class century, for Pakistan International Airlines at Abbottabad in December 2007 ... He also scored 101 in a one-day match for PIA against Zarai Taraqiati Bank at Karachi in March 2008 ... Sarfraz captained Pakistan to victory in the Under-19 World Cup in Sri Lanka in February 2006 ...

THE FIGURES to 12.9.08   www.cricinfo.com

Batting & Fielding	M	Inns	NO	Runs	HS	Avge	S/R	100	50	4s	6s	Ct	St
Tests	0	0	–	–	–	–	–	–	–	–	–	–	–
ODIs	8	2	0	26	19	13.00	56.52	0	0	1	0	6	3
T20 Ints	0	0	–	–	–	–	–	–	–	–	–	–	–
First-class	23	37	11	1178	117	45.30	–	1	10	–	–	61	9

Bowling	M	Balls	Runs	Wkts	BB	Avge	RpO	S/R	5i	10m
Tests	0	0	–	–	–	–	–	–	–	–
ODIs	8	0	–	–	–	–	–	–	–	–
T20 Ints	0	0	–	–	–	–	–	–	–	–
First-class	23	0	–	–	–	–	–	–	–	–

RAMNARESH **SARWAN**

Full name	**Ramnaresh Ronnie Sarwan**
Born	**June 23, 1980, Wakenaam Island, Essequibo, Guyana**
Teams	**Guyana, Kings XI Punjab**
Style	**Right-hand bat, legspinner**
Test debut	**West Indies v Pakistan at Bridgetown 1999-2000**
ODI debut	**West Indies v England at Nottingham 2000**

THE PROFILE A light-footed right-hander, Ramnaresh Sarwan was brought up in the South American rainforest around the Essequibo River. After his first Test innings – 84 against Pakistan – the former England captain Ted Dexter was moved to predict a Test average of 50. And on his first tour, to England in 2000, Sarwan lived up to the hype by topping the averages: his footwork was strikingly confident and precise, and it was a surprise when a horror run of three runs in five innings followed in Australia, but he did better against India at home in 2002. It still took him 28 matches to post his maiden Test century, 119 against Bangladesh in December 2002. He has scored consistently since: he made 392 runs in four Tests against South Africa in 2003-04 then, after a lean run at home against England, stroked a stunning unbeaten 261 against Bangladesh in June 2004. Then came another England tour: he began and ended it on low notes, but was prolific in between. He also played a big part as West Indies reached the final of the one-day series then won the Champions Trophy, and carried on his good form in Australia. After Brian Lara's retirement, "Reggie" Sarwan took on the captaincy for the 2007 England tour – but that ended in tears with an injured shoulder during the second Test, which seems to have permanently affected his throwing. Then a groin strain restricted him in 2008, as Chris Gayle picked up the reins of captaincy. However, West Indies still need a fully fit Sarwan, as a batsman of delightful fluency.

THE FACTS Sarwan's 261 not out at Kingston in June 2004 is the highest score against Bangladesh, and also the highest Test score by a Guyanese batsman, beating Rohan Kanhai's 256 for West Indies v India at Calcutta in 1958-59 ... In ODIs Sarwan averages 69.69 v India – but only 22.40 v Sri Lanka ... He was out for 199 when Guyana played Kenya at Georgetown in February 2004 ... Sarwan made 100 and 111 for the West Indies Board President's XI against the touring Zimbabweans at Pointe-à-Pierre in March 2000 ...

THE FIGURES to 12.9.08   www.cricinfo.com

Batting & Fielding	M	Inns	NO	Runs	HS	Avge	S/R	100	50	4s	6s	Ct	St
Tests	72	129	8	4889	261*	40.40	45.52	11	30	633	11	46	0
ODIs	133	124	26	4300	115*	43.87	76.55	3	27	365	43	37	0
T20 Ints	2	2	0	17	12*	8.50	113.33	0	0	0	1	1	0
First-class	171	290	21	10408	261*	38.69	–	25	59	–	–	127	0

Bowling	M	Balls	Runs	Wkts	BB	Avge	RpO	S/R	5i	10m
Tests	72	1986	1129	23	4–37	49.08	3.41	86.34	0	0
ODIs	133	569	563	16	3–31	35.18	5.93	35.56	0	0
T20 Ints	2	12	10	2	2–10	5.00	5.00	6.00	0	0
First-class	171	4115	2161	54	6–62	40.01	3.15	76.20	1	0

VIRENDER **SEHWAG**

Full name **Virender Sehwag**
Born **October 20, 1978, Delhi**
Teams **Delhi, Delhi Daredevils**
Style **Right-hand bat, offspinner**
Test debut **India v South Africa at Bloemfontein 2001-02**
ODI debut **India v Pakistan at Mohali 1998-99**

INDIA

THE PROFILE Virender Sehwag is a primal talent whose rough edges make him all the more appealing. Soon after his Test-debut century late in 2001 he was already eliciting comparisons with his idol Sachin Tendulkar. It is half-true: Sehwag is also short and square, and plays the straight drive, back-foot punch and whip off the hips identically – but he leaves Sachin standing when it comes to audacity. Asked to open in England in 2002, Sehwag proved an instant hit, with 84 and 106 in the first two Tests. And he kept conjuring up pivotal innings, none so significant as India's first triple-century (brought up, characteristically, with a six), in Pakistan early in 2004. Surprisingly, he struggled in one-day cricket after an electric start, and endured a run of 60 games from January 2004 in which he averaged below 30. His fitness levels also dropped, but he continued to sparkle in Tests, with a magnificent 254 – and an opening stand of 410 with Rahul Dravid – against Pakistan at Lahore in January 2006. Then, in June, he came excruciatingly close (99 not out) to a century before lunch on the first day in St Lucia, a feat not yet accomplished by an Indian. Despite hammering 114 against Bermuda in the 2007 World Cup, Sehwag got the chop afterwards – from Tests (not surprising after a modest run) and one-dayers too (more of a shock). He missed the England tour, but practised hard, lost a stone, and in March 2008 bounced back with another triple-century, against South Africa at Chennai. Sehwag also bowls effective, loopy offspin, and is a reliable catcher in the slips.

THE FACTS Sehwag's 319 against South Africa at Chennai in March 2008 is India's highest Test score: his 309 v Pakistan at Multan in March 2004 is their only other triple-century ... At Chennai Sehwag reached 300 in 278 balls, the fastest-known Test triple-century (he is third on the list too) ... He made 105 on his Test debut, v South Africa in November 2001 ... Sehwag carried his bat (201 out of 329) against Sri Lanka at Galle in mid-2008 ... His record includes a Test and three ODIs for the World XI, and seven ODIs for the Asia XI ...

THE FIGURES *to 12.9.08*   www.cricinfo.com

Batting & Fielding	M	Inns	NO	Runs	HS	Avge	S/R	100	50	4s	6s	Ct	St
Tests	60	102	4	5157	309	52.62	77.45	15	14	735	58	46	0
ODIs	191	186	7	5810	130	32.45	99.14	9	29	797	88	74	0
T20 Ints	9	8	0	172	68	21.50	130.30	0	1	19	6	0	0
First-class	119	195	8	9502	309	50.81	–	29	32	–	–	104	0

Bowling	M	Balls	Runs	Wkts	BB	Avge	RpO	S/R	5i	10m
Tests	60	1789	902	24	3–12	37.58	3.02	74.54	0	0
ODIs	191	3781	3313	80	3–25	41.41	5.25	47.26	0	0
T20 Ints	9	6	20	0	–	–	20.00	–	0	0
First-class	119	6288	3254	87	4–32	37.40	3.10	72.27	0	0

OWAIS **SHAH**

Full name **Owais Alam Shah**
Born **October 22, 1978, Karachi, Pakistan**
Teams **Middlesex**
Style **Right-hand bat, occasional offspinner**
Test debut **England v India at Mumbai 2005-06**
ODI debut **England v Australia at Bristol 2001**

THE PROFILE Owais Shah was a schoolboy prodigy, making 64 for Middlesex in a one-dayer against Yorkshire when only 16, and captaining England to victory in the Under-19 World Cup in February 1998. A silky strokemaker, strong on the leg side, he seemed set for a stellar career, and after a couple of low-key seasons played for England in 2001, scoring 28 not out against Australia in his first ODI and 62 against Pakistan in his second. So far, so good ... but then he dropped off the radar, amid suggestions that his fielding wasn't up to scratch. He was in and out of the one-day side until the 2002-03 Australian tri-series, when he made only one decent contribution, and was then forgotten for three years. It seemed to be a classic case of wasted talent, but he was revitalised by Twenty20 cricket, and finished 2005 with more first-class runs than anyone else. When England had personnel problems in India that winter Shah was summoned, and lit up his Test debut with two cocky innings of 88 and 38 ... before being forgotten again. He got another chance early in 2007, but struggled, and was dumped as soon as Michael Vaughan regained fitness. However, he kept his name in the frame with a sparkling Twenty20 innings against West Indies, which ensured him another run in the one-day side and a place in the inaugural World Twenty20 championship in September 2007, just after he scored a fine maiden ODI century against India. It's hard to believe that Shah has only just turned 30: his best days may still lie ahead.

THE FACTS Shah scored 203 for Middlesex agaist Derbyshire at Southgate in 2001 ... He captained England Under-19 to victory in the Youth World Cup in February 1998, beating New Zealand in the final at Johannesburg: his team-mates included Robert Key and Chris Schofield ... Shah hit 55 from 35 balls as England won their Twenty20 international against West Indies at The Oval in June 2007 ... He hit hundreds on successive days against Lancashire at Old Trafford in 2006, in different competitions ...

THE FIGURES to 12.9.08   www.cricinfo.com

Batting & Fielding	M	Inns	NO	Runs	HS	Avge	S/R	100	50	4s	6s	Ct	St
Tests	2	4	0	136	88	34.00	44.73	0	1	19	1	1	0
ODIs	47	43	5	1052	107*	27.68	76.18	1	6	76	12	13	0
T20 Ints	10	9	1	235	55*	29.37	135.05	0	1	18	9	3	0
First-class	194	329	30	12756	203	42.66	–	34	65	–	–	150	0

Bowling	M	Balls	Runs	Wkts	BB	Avge	RpO	S/R	5i	10m
Tests	2	0	–	–	–	–	–	–	–	–
ODIs	47	114	126	3	1–18	42.00	6.63	38.00	0	0
T20 Ints	10	0	–	–	–	–	–	–	–	–
First-class	194	1914	1307	22	3–33	59.40	4.09	87.00	0	0

ENGLAND

SHAHADAT HOSSAIN

Full name	**Kazi Shahadat Hossain**
Born	**August 7, 1986, Dhaka**
Teams	**Dhaka**
Style	**Right-hand bat, right-arm fast-medium bowler**
Test debut	**Bangladesh v England at Lord's 2005**
ODI debut	**Bangladesh v Kenya at Bogra 2005-06**

THE PROFILE Shahadat Hossain was discovered during a talent-spotting camp in Narayanganj, and whisked away to the Bangladesh Institute of Sports for refinement. He was picked for the 2004 Under-19 World Cup, where he stood out as a promising fast bowler in a tournament which generally lacked firepower, and was rapidly called up for the A team. Shahadat – who's also known as "Rajib" – has all the necessary attributes for a genuine fast bowler. He is tall, comes in off a smooth run-up, and doesn't put unnecessary pressure on his body with a slightly open-chested delivery position. He has a strong frame, and endurance in abundance. He is naturally aggressive and, above everything, has raw pace. His Test debut at Lord's in 2005 was a chastening experience, as he conceded 101 runs in just 12 overs. But he was just 18: after that he did well against Sri Lanka in 2005-06, taking four wickets in an innings in Colombo and again at Chittagong before going one better in Bogra's inaugural Test with 5 for 86. And he excelled against South Africa early in 2008, when his 6 for 27 gave his side a rare first-innings lead – and an even rarer sniff of victory – at Mirpur. He struggled against the Australians in April 2006, having only the wicket of Ricky Ponting to show for 67 overs of effort, and was in and out of the side in 2006-07, playing only once in the World Cup (and being hit around in the sobering defeat by Ireland). However, he is still only 22, and if he continues to progress he could be a force for Bangladesh in the years to come.

THE FACTS Shahadat Hossain's 6 for 27 against South Africa at Mirpur in February 2008 is Bangladesh's second-best bowling analysis in Tests, and the best by a fast bowler ... He took Bangladesh's first hat-trick in ODIs, against Zimbabwe at Harare in August 2006 ... Shahadat took only two wickets – both against Kenya – in his first six ODIs ... He took 5 for 63 and 5 for 53 in successive A-team Tests in Zimbabwe in February 2005 ...

THE FIGURES to 12.9.08   www.cricinfo.com

Batting & Fielding	M	Inns	NO	Runs	HS	Avge	S/R	100	50	4s	6s	Ct	St
Tests	15	29	8	140	31	6.66	36.84	0	0	18	0	3	0
ODIs	40	20	13	46	9*	6.57	43.39	0	0	3	0	4	0
T20 Ints	2	2	1	3	3*	3.00	60.00	0	0	0	0	0	0
First-class	33	56	20	363	37*	10.08	48.27	0	0	–	–	7	0

Bowling	M	Balls	Runs	Wkts	BB	Avge	RpO	S/R	5i	10m
Tests	15	2184	1541	42	6–27	36.69	4.23	52.00	2	0
ODIs	40	1707	1609	40	3–34	40.22	5.65	42.67	0	0
T20 Ints	2	48	66	3	2–22	22.00	8.25	16.00	0	0
First-class	33	4862	3240	99	6–27	32.72	3.99	49.11	5	0

SHAHID AFRIDI

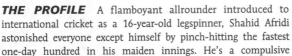

Full name **Sahibzada Mohammad Shahid Khan Afridi**
Born **March 1, 1980, Khyber Agency**
Teams **Karachi, Habib Bank, Deccan Chargers**
Style **Right-hand bat, legspinner**
Test debut **Pakistan v Australia at Karachi 1998-99**
ODI debut **Pakistan v Kenya at Nairobi 1996-97**

THE PROFILE A flamboyant allrounder introduced to international cricket as a 16-year-old legspinner, Shahid Afridi astonished everyone except himself by pinch-hitting the fastest one-day hundred in his maiden innings. He's a compulsive shotmaker, and although until 2004 that was too often his undoing, he eventually blossomed into one of the most dangerous players around. A string of incisive contributions culminated in a violent century against India in April 2005: the only faster ODI hundred was Afridi's own. A few weeks before, he had smashed 58 in 34 balls, and also grabbed three crucial wickets, as Pakistan memorably squared the Test series at Bangalore. And so it continued: a Test ton against West Indies, important runs against England, then, early in 2006, he went berserk on some flat pitches against India. An Afridi assault is laced with lofted drives and short-arm jabs over midwicket. He's at his best when forcing straight, and at his weakest pushing at the ball just outside off. But perhaps the biggest improvement has been in his legspin. When conditions suit, he gets turn as well as lazy drift, but variety is the key: there's a vicious faster ball and an offbreak too. He shocked everyone when, after finally establishing himself, he announced his retirement from Tests early in 2006. To less surprise, he retracted his retirement a fortnight later and toured England, but has not played a five-day game since. Rather oddly, he hasn't yet made much of a mark in Twenty20 cricket with the bat, although he has had some success with the ball.

THE FACTS In his second match (he hadn't batted in the first) Shahid Afridi hit the fastest hundred in ODIs, from only 37 balls, v Sri Lanka in Nairobi in October 1996 ... Afridi has the highest strike rate – 111.12 runs per 100 balls – of anyone with more than 20 innings in ODIs ... In successive Tests against India in 2006 he hit 103 (from 80 balls) at Lahore, and 156 (128 balls, six sixes) at Faisalabad ... Only Sanath Jayasuriya (265) has hit more sixes in ODIs ... Afridi's record includes three ODIs for the Asia XI and two for the World XI ...

THE FIGURES to 12.9.08   www.cricinfo.com

Batting & Fielding	M	Inns	NO	Runs	HS	Avge	S/R	100	50	4s	6s	Ct	St
Tests	26	46	1	1683	156	37.40	86.13	5	8	216	50	10	0
ODIs	265	249	16	5479	109	23.51	111.22	4	29	505	247	92	0
T20 Ints	11	10	0	168	39	16.80	169.69	0	0	15	8	3	0
First-class	104	172	4	5365	164	31.93	–	12	27	–	–	67	0

Bowling	M	Balls	Runs	Wkts	BB	Avge	RpO	S/R	5i	10m
Tests	26	3092	1640	47	5–52	34.89	3.18	65.78	1	0
ODIs	265	10810	8342	239	5–11	34.90	4.63	45.23	2	0
T20 Ints	11	249	280	15	4–19	18.66	6.74	16.60	0	0
First-class	104	12498	6377	240	6–101	26.57	3.06	52.07	8	0

SHAHRIAR NAFEES

Full name	**Shahriar Nafees Ahmed**
Born	**January 25, 1986, Dhaka**
Teams	**Barisal**
Style	**Left-hand bat**
Test debut	**Bangladesh v Sri Lanka at Colombo 2005-06**
ODI debut	**Bangladesh v England at Nottingham 2005**

THE PROFILE As a left-hand opening batsman, Shahriar Nafees is a rarity among Bangladesh cricketers, and at the age of 19 he was thrust into the Test squad for their maiden tour of England with just five first-class matches behind him. He hadn't fared too badly in those, however, with 350 runs at 35, and his Under-19 coach reckoned he had the talent and temperament to become a future Test captain. With Nafees Iqbal and Javed Omar established as Bangladesh's opening pair, the England trip was a case of watching and learning for Shahriar. He did get an opportunity in the one-day series, and cashed in with 75 in the last game against Australia. He made his Test debut in Sri Lanka in September 2005, and made 51 in his second match. He also got starts in all the one-day games, but converted only one into a fifty. Then in April 2006 he exploded in sensational fashion against the might of Australia, stroking his way to a brilliant hundred, his maiden first-class ton as well as his first in Tests, at Fatullah. His stunning 138, with 19 fours, set up a scarcely believable first-day total of 355 for 5 as the Aussies reeled. He added 33 in the second innings, and a brisk 79 in the second Test to show that this was no flash in the pan. He cashed in against the minnows with three one-day hundreds off Zimbabwe and one against Bermuda, but found life harder after that against the big boys – he was dropped after six innings in the World Cup produced only 31 runs and a top score of 12, and did little of note during 2008 beyond a punchy 69 against South Africa in the Chittagong Test.

THE FACTS Shahriar Nafees's 138 against Australia at Fatullah in 2005-06 was his maiden century in first-class cricket: his previous-highest score was 97, for the Board President's XI against the touring Zimbabweans in January 2005 ... Shahriar hit four of Bangladesh's first seven ODI hundreds ... He averages 62.41 in ODIs against Zimbabwe, with three hundreds, but only 10 v England (and 0 v Canada) ... Shahriar captained Bangladesh Under-19 in a one-day game against England, skippered by Alastair Cook, in 2004 ...

THE FIGURES to 12.9.08   www.cricinfo.com

Batting & Fielding	M	Inns	NO	Runs	HS	Avge	S/R	100	50	4s	6s	Ct	St
Tests	15	30	0	810	138	27.00	54.03	1	4	117	1	11	0
ODIs	60	60	5	1859	123*	33.76	69.68	4	10	232	7	11	0
T20 Ints	1	1	0	25	25	25.00	147.05	0	0	3	1	1	0
First-class	39	77	2	2290	138	30.53	56.95	2	17	–	–	24	0

Bowling	M	Balls	Runs	Wkts	BB	Avge	RpO	S/R	5i	10m
Tests	15	0	–	–	–	–	–	–	–	–
ODIs	60	0	–	–	–	–	–	–	–	–
T20 Ints	1	0	–	–	–	–	–	–	–	–
First-class	39	18	20	0	–	–	6.66	–	0	0

SHAKIB AL HASAN

Full name	**Shakib Al Hasan**
Born	**March 24, 1987, Magura, Khulna**
Teams	**Khulna**
Style	**Left-hand bat, slow left-arm orthodox spinner**
Test debut	**Bangladesh v India at Chittagong 2006-07**
ODI debut	**Bangladesh v Zimbabwe at Harare 2006**

THE PROFILE   Shakib Al Hasan first came to prominence in Bangladesh's Under-19 team late in 2005, when he blasted 83 not out from only 62 balls to take his side to victory over England in a one-day tournament in Dhaka. A fortnight later he was at it again, with an 82-ball century against Sri Lanka, after taking three wickets with his slow left-armers. He was reportedly only 15 at the time, although when his birthdate eventually emerged he turned out to be 18. Soon Shakib was in the A team, smashing 55 not out in 32 balls then grabbing four wickets as Zimbabwe A were swept aside at Kwekwe in July 2006. A full debut was not far off, and it duly came against the full Zimbabwe side (such as it is) the following month: he took a wicket and then strolled in at No. 4 to make 30 not out in the matchwinning partnership. A stylish left-hander, Shakib proved remarkably consistent at first, being dismissed in single figures only once in 18 one-dayers leading up to the 2007 World Cup: that run included 134 not out against Canada, Bangladesh's highest score in ODIs. The heady start continued in the Caribbean with a half-century in the famous win over India, and another against England. After the World Cup came his first taste of personal failure – only 17 runs in three innings in Sri Lanka. His flattish bowling has rarely been collared, and he maintains an impressively low one-day economy rate, although he struggles to take wickets in Tests.

THE FACTS   Shakib Al Hasan made 134 not out against Canada at St John's in February 2007, Bangladesh's highest score in ODIs, and added another century against Pakistan in April 2008 ... He averages 38.40 in ODIs against Pakistan – and 0.00 against West Indies ... Shakib made 108, his maiden first-class century, for Khulna v Chittagong at Khulna in October 2007 ... He took 6 for 79 for Khulna at Sylhet in April 2005 ... His name is sometimes spelt "Saqibul Hasan" on scorecards ...

THE FIGURES *to 12.9.08*   www.cricinfo.com

Batting & Fielding	M	Inns	NO	Runs	HS	Avge	S/R	100	50	4s	6s	Ct	St
Tests	6	11	1	217	41*	21.70	42.88	0	0	28	0	3	0
ODIs	51	49	9	1292	134*	32.30	68.25	2	7	120	3	8	0
T20 Ints	7	7	0	93	26	13.28	109.41	0	0	9	1	2	0
First-class	28	51	6	1445	108	32.11	–	2	7	–	–	17	0

Bowling	M	Balls	Runs	Wkts	BB	Avge	RpO	S/R	5i	10m
Tests	6	654	314	3	2–44	104.66	2.88	218.00	0	0
ODIs	51	2423	1719	50	3–18	34.38	4.25	48.46	0	0
T20 Ints	7	150	180	8	4–34	22.50	7.20	18.75	0	0
First-class	28	4345	1846	52	6–79	35.50	2.54	83.55	2	0

ISHANT **SHARMA**

INDIA

Full name	**Ishant Sharma**
Born	**September 2, 1988, Delhi**
Teams	**Delhi, Kolkata Knight Riders**
Style	**Right-hand bat, right-arm fast-medium bowler**
Test debut	**India v Bangladesh at Dhaka 2006-07**
ODI debut	**India v South Africa at Belfast 2007**

THE PROFILE Tall fast bowlers have always been a much-prized rarity in Indian cricket. Their earliest Tests featured Mohammad Nissar, a few years ago Abey Kuruvilla flitted across the international scene ... and now there's Ishant Sharma, 6ft 4ins tall and still growing. He's regularly above 80mph (130kph), and possesses a sharp and deceptive bouncer, delivered from a high-arm action with long hair flying photogenically. He started to play seriously at 14, rose quickly, and played one-dayers for Delhi in 2005-06 when only 17. The following season he took 4 for 65 from 34 overs on his first-class debut and finished his first term with 29 wickets at 20.10. Early in 2007 he was on the verge of reinforcing the national team in South Africa – flights had been booked and visa arrangements made – but in the end he was left to concentrate on domestic cricket and a youth tour. However, when Munaf Patel was injured again in Bangladesh in May, Sharma finally did get on the plane, and took a wicket in a landslide victory at Dhaka. In Australia at the end of 2007 he looked the real deal, especially in the Perth Test, when he dismissed Ricky Ponting during a sensational spell, and again in the one-dayers as India surprised the hosts to snaffle the series. Then, in August 2008, he took three crucial wickets to settle the Galle Test. His relatively frail physique is a worry, so the selectors need to make sure he is not overbowled – but if he can stay fit and healthy he is set for a successful career.

THE FACTS Ishant Sharma took 4 for 34 in his first senior match for Delhi, a one-day game against Jammu & Kashmir in February 2006 ... He took 5 for 35 for Delhi against Baroda in December 2006 ... In 2006-07, his first season of first-class cricket, Sharma took 29 wickets at 20.10 for Delhi, then made his Test debut in only his seventh match ...

THE FIGURES to 12.9.08   www.cricinfo.com

Batting & Fielding	M	Inns	NO	Runs	HS	Avge	S/R	100	50	4s	6s	Ct	St
Tests	9	14	9	92	23	18.40	32.97	0	0	10	0	5	0
ODIs	17	6	4	13	8	6.50	36.11	0	0	1	0	4	0
T20 Ints	1	1	1	3	3*	–	50.00	0	0	0	0	0	0
First-class	24	25	18	1070	23	15.28	31.10	0	0	11	0	8	0

Bowling	M	Balls	Runs	Wkts	BB	Avge	RpO	S/R	5i	10m
Tests	9	1483	833	23	5–118	36.21	3.37	64.47	0	0
ODIs	17	811	695	22	4–38	31.59	5.14	36.86	0	0
T20 Ints	1	8	8	0	–	–	6.00	–	0	0
First-class	24	4477	2251	81	5–35	27.79	3.01	55.27	2	0

ROHIT **SHARMA**

Full name	**Rohit Gurunathan Sharma**
Born	**April 30, 1987, Bansod, Nagpur, Maharashtra**
Teams	**Mumbai, Deccan Chargers**
Style	**Right-hand bat, offspinner**
Test debut	**No Tests yet**
ODI debut	**India v Ireland at Belfast 2007**

THE PROFILE Rohit Sharma made a stellar start to his first-class career, hitting 205 against Gujarat in only his fourth match for Mumbai, in December 2006, after a near-miss of 95 in his previous game. He actually made his first-class debut for India A, in the Top End Series in Australia a few months before, and had also represented West Zone in the Duleep Trophy. He exuded class in the Youth World Cup in Sri Lanka earlier in 2006, cracking three half-centuries in six days in mid-tournament before missing out in the low-scoring final, when India were shot out for 71 in response to Pakistan's unimposing 109. Sharma was at No. 3 then, which may well turn out to be his best position in the long run as he is an adaptable batsman, strong off the back foot, equally happy as accumulator or aggressor. He finished the 2006-07 Indian season with 600 runs at 40, plus 356 in one-dayers and a 49-ball Twenty20 century against Gujarat, which all earned him a national call as the dust settled on India's disastrous 2007 World Cup campaign. He made his ODI debut in Ireland, retained his place for the one-day leg of the tour of England that followed, then had a couple of useful innings in the World Twenty20 championship in South Africa. After that he had a run in the one-day side, with solid if unspectacular results – his best innings to date was an undefeated 70 against Sri Lanka at Canberra in February 2008 during the successful tri-series campaign in Australia.

THE FACTS Rohit Sharma extended his maiden first-class century to 205, for Mumbai against Gujarat in December 2006... He also hit 101 not out, off only 45 balls, against Gujarat in a Twenty20 match in April 2007 ... Sharma made 404 runs at a strike rate of 147.98 in the inaugural IPL season in 2008 ... He hit 142 not out for West Zone against North Zone in a one-day Deodhar Trophy match at Udaipur in March 2006 ...

THE FIGURES to 12.9.08   www.cricinfo.com

Batting & Fielding	M	Inns	NO	Runs	HS	Avge	S/R	100	50	4s	6s	Ct	St
Tests	0	0	–	–	–	–	–	–	–	–	–	–	–
ODIs	28	27	5	543	70*	24.68	73.87	0	4	41	4	11	0
T20 Ints	6	4	3	96	50*	96.00	139.13	0	1	10	4	2	0
First-class	20	29	1	1042	205	37.21	–	1	6	–	–	16	0

Bowling	M	Balls	Runs	Wkts	BB	Avge	RpO	S/R	5i	10m
Tests	0	0	–	–	–	–	–	–	–	–
ODIs	28	95	63	0	–	–	3.97	–	0	0
T20 Ints	6	0	–	–	–	–	–	–	–	–
First-class	20	330	187	1	1–12	187.00	3.40	330.00	0	0

SHOAIB AKHTAR

Full name	**Shoaib Akhtar**
Born	**August 13, 1975, Rawalpindi, Punjab**
Teams	**Islamabad, KRL, Kolkata Knight Riders, Surrey**
Style	**Right-hand bat, right-arm fast bowler**
Test debut	**Pakistan v West Indies at Rawalpindi 1997-98**
ODI debut	**Pakistan v Zimbabwe at Harare 1997-98**

THE PROFILE Shoaib Akhtar electrified the 1999 World Cup with his spectacular run-up and blistering speed. Star status was sealed by a flop of unruly hair, a talent for showboating and a vivid nickname – "The Rawalpindi Express". But it was too much, too young. Breaking the 100mph barrier seemed to matter more than cementing his place. He was twice sidelined after throwing allegations, and although his action was cleared – tests showed a hyper-extensible elbow – injuries often impinged. He was back in 2002, shaking up the Aussies with five-fors in Brisbane and Colombo. He promised much in the 2003 World Cup, but came a cropper, especially in a needle encounter with Sachin Tendulkar. Then Pakistan lost a series to India, and Shoaib felt the heat as his commitment was questioned. He blew hot and cold in Australia in 2004-05, by turns Pakistan's most incisive threat and their most disinterested player. Worries about fitness and attitude kept him out for most of 2005, but he bounced back at the end with 17 England wickets, mixing yorkers and bouncers with lethal slower balls. But just when he seemed to be back there were further whispers about his action, then he missed most of the 2006 England tour with ankle trouble, and next he was banned for two years after a positive drug test. The ban was lifted on appeal, but it and various injuries kept him out of the 2007 World Cup. He was back later that year – briefly, being sent home from the World Twenty20 championship after a dressing-room spat left Mohammad Asif with a bat-bruised thigh – but then copped a five-year ban early in 2008 for criticising the board. The end? No ... it was later reduced to 18 months, then suspended. Shoaib isn't quite finished yet.

THE FACTS Shoaib was clocked at 100.04mph by an unofficial speed-gun during a one-dayer v New Zealand in April 2002: he also recorded 100.23mph (161.3kph) at the 2003 World Cup ... His best figures in Tests and ODIs both came against New Zealand ... Against England in the 2003 World Cup Shoaib was the fifth No. 11 to top-score in an ODI innings, with 43 ... His record includes three ODIs for the Asia XI and two for the World XI ...

THE FIGURES to 12.9.08   www.cricinfo.com

Batting & Fielding	M	Inns	NO	Runs	HS	Avge	S/R	100	50	4s	6s	Ct	St
Tests	46	67	13	544	47	10.07	41.43	0	0	53	22	12	0
ODIs	138	67	31	345	43	9.58	73.24	0	0	22	10	17	0
T20 Ints	3	1	1	1	1*	–	100.00	0	0	0	0	1	0
First-class	128	178	49	1550	59*	12.01	–	0	1	–	–	38	0

Bowling	M	Balls	Runs	Wkts	BB	Avge	RpO	S/R	5i	10m
Tests	46	8143	4574	178	6–11	25.69	3.37	45.74	12	2
ODIs	138	6558	5081	219	6–16	23.20	4.64	29.94	4	0
T20 Ints	3	66	83	5	2–22	16.60	7.54	13.20	0	0
First-class	128	19845	11924	450	6–11	26.49	3.60	44.10	28	2

SHOAIB MALIK

Full name	**Shoaib Malik**
Born	**February 1, 1982, Sialkot, Punjab**
Teams	**Sialkot, PIA, Delhi Daredevils**
Style	**Right-hand bat, offspinner**
Test debut	**Pakistan v Bangladesh at Multan 2001-02**
ODI debut	**Pakistan v West Indies at Sharjah 1999-2000**

THE PROFILE Short of wicketkeeping, there are few roles Shoaib Malik hasn't tried. He has batted everywhere from 1 to 10 in one-dayers, though he has now settled at 3 or 4. He began in Tests in the lower order, but lately has been opening. As an offspinner, everything about his bowling, from the short-stepping run-up to the *doosra*, bears a striking similarity to Saqlain Mushtaq's. His action isn't clean, though: he has been reported twice, first in October 2004, after which he played primarily as a batsman for the next six months before undergoing elbow surgery. He was reported again in November 2005, and had another operation early in 2006, which kept him out of the Tests in England. And then, in the wake of the disasters of the 2007 World Cup, came his biggest challenge ... captaincy. It didn't start well: after losing a short series to South Africa he also lost the first Test in India, then picked up an injury and had to watch as his battered side was labelled by some as Pakistan's worst ever to tour the old enemy. It was a slightly different story in ODIs, although he was flattered to be in charge for a record run of 11 consecutive victories early in 2008, since ten of them came against the undemanding opposition of Zimbabwe and Bangladesh. Shoaib is an uncomplicated batsman, free with checked drives and cuts, or slogging when needed. His finest performance so far in Tests came when he defied Murali with an unbeaten eight-hour 148 to earn a draw in Colombo in March 2006.

THE FACTS Shoaib Malik extended his first Test century, against Sri Lanka in Colombo in March 2006, to 148 not out in 448 minutes as Pakistan forced a draw ... He made 90, 95 and 106 in successive one-day innings against India in February 2006 ... Shoaib has batted in every position except No. 11 in ODIs, averaging 63.75 from No. 2, 59.88 from No. 4, and 41.40 at No. 3 (and 7.50 at No. 10) ... He took 7 for 81 for Pakistan International Airlines against WAPDA at Faisalabad in February 2001 ...

THE FIGURES *to 12.9.08*   www.cricinfo.com

Batting & Fielding	M	Inns	NO	Runs	HS	Avge	S/R	100	50	4s	6s	Ct	St
Tests	21	35	5	1076	148*	35.86	42.86	1	6	143	9	9	0
ODIs	167	148	20	4576	143	35.75	79.32	6	29	380	55	60	0
T20 Ints	12	12	2	313	57	31.30	128.27	0	2	22	12	3	0
First-class	78	119	14	3002	148*	28.59	–	6	14	–	–	37	0

Bowling	M	Balls	Runs	Wkts	BB	Avge	RpO	S/R	5i	10m
Tests	21	1507	871	13	4–42	67.00	3.46	115.92	0	0
ODIs	167	5715	4319	124	4–19	34.83	4.53	46.08	0	0
T20 Ints	12	36	45	3	2–15	15.00	7.50	12.00	0	0
First-class	78	10010	4989	163	7–81	30.60	2.99	61.41	5	1

PETER **SIDDLE**

Full name	**Peter Matthew Siddle**
Born	**November 25, 1984, Traralgon, Victoria**
Teams	**Victoria**
Style	**Right-hand bat, right-arm fast bowler**
Test debut	**No Tests yet**
ODI debut	**No ODIs yet**

THE PROFILE Victoria's Peter Siddle has long been considered one of the most dangerous fast bowlers in Australia – but he has also long been considered one of the most fragile. A shoulder reconstruction sidelined him for most of 2006-07, then he dislocated the joint at the start of the following season, and aggravated it again during an otherwise successful season. Despite this he finished the 2007-08 season with 33 wickets in just five matches, at the fine average of 15.75. He destroyed South Australia early in the campaign with 5 for 27 as they were skittled for 77, rattled the Redbacks again later in the summer with 6 for 57, and collected 5 for 61 in a win over Tasmania. Then he took nine wickets in the Pura Cup final against New South Wales at the SCG, although by then Siddle's shoulder was very sore, and he underwent reconstructive surgery only a week later. He emerged fitter than ever, helped by advice from Australia's fast-bowling coach Troy Cooley, and was a surprise inclusion in the squad for the four-Test tour of India in October 2008. after touring there with the A team the previous month. "The shoulder is coming along well and the body feels terrific," he said. "I've been able to get myself fit and into good shape, and I just can't wait to get going." The burly Siddle grew up in Morwell in rural Victoria, and was a promising competitive wood-chopper when he eventually took up cricket at 14. He has genuine pace and the ability to swing the ball, and attended the Australian Academy in 2004, 2006 and 2007.

THE FACTS Siddle took 6 for 57 for Victoria against South Australia at St Kilda in January 2008 ... He took 9 for 167 in the match in the Pura Cup final against New South Wales at Sydney in March 2008, although Victoria still lost ... Siddle took 5 for 16 and 6 for 31 for Victoria's Under-17s against South Australia in the national U17 championship in January 2002 ...

THE FIGURES to 12.9.08 www.cricinfo.com

Batting & Fielding	M	Inns	NO	Runs	HS	Avge	S/R	100	50	4s	6s	Ct	St
Tests	0	0	–	–	–	–	–	–	–	–	–	–	–
ODIs	0	0	–	–	–	–	–	–	–	–	–	–	–
T20 Ints	0	0	–	–	–	–	–	–	–	–	–	–	–
First-class	11	15	4	126	28	11.45	33.33	0	0	8	1	2	0

Bowling	M	Balls	Runs	Wkts	BB	Avge	RpO	S/R	5i	10m
Tests	0	0	–	–	–	–	–	–	–	–
ODIs	0	0	–	–	–	–	–	–	–	–
T20 Ints	0	0	–	–	–	–	–	–	–	–
First-class	11	1709	888	41	6–57	21.65	3.11	41.68	4	0

RYAN **SIDEBOTTOM**

Full name **Ryan Jay Sidebottom**
Born **January 15, 1978, Huddersfield, Yorkshire**
Teams **Nottinghamshire**
Style **Left-hand bat, left-arm fast-medium bowler**
Test debut **England v Pakistan at Lord's 2001**
ODI debut **England v Zimbabwe at Harare 2001-02**

THE PROFILE Although Ryan Sidebottom's long curly hair made him one of the most recognisable faces on the county circuit, for six years he seemed destined to be a one-cap wonder, just like his father, Arnie. The junior Sidebottom (who like his dad was also a useful footballer, having trials for Sheffield United) did well for England A in the West Indies early in 2001, and made his Test debut against Pakistan at Lord's later that year: he didn't move it much, failed to take a wicket, and was promptly sent back to county cricket. He was playing for Yorkshire then, but a move to Trent Bridge in 2004 revitalised him. He took 50 wickets for the first time in 2005, repeated the dose the following year, and when Matthew Hoggard was injured at the start of 2007 Sidebottom was the surprise packet unveiled by the selectors. He was an instant success back at Headingley, taking eight wickets (five of them lbw) as West Indies were sunk. Crucially for a bowler who rarely nudges the speedo above 80mph, he now swung the ball in, as well as away – the first left-armer to do this regularly for England since John Lever a generation earlier. Sidebottom kept his place, taking 24 wickets in six Tests despite suffering more than most from fallible catching behind the bat. In six Tests against New Zealand in 2008, home and away, he starred with 41 victims, including ten wickets and a hat-trick at Napier, but the workload began to tell: he started snapping at team-mates, and missed some matches towards the end of the home season with strains. Time will tell if he is just a shooting star.

THE FACTS Sidebottom took 7 for 47 against New Zealand at Napier in March 2008: two Tests earlier, at Hamilton, his ten wickets in the match included a hat-trick ... His father, Arnie, played one Test for England against Australia in 1985 ... He took 6 for 16 (and 5 for 27) for Yorkshire against Kent at Leeds in June 2000 ... One of his nicknames is "Sexual Chocolate", after a fictional band in an Eddie Murphy film who all had long flowing hair ...

THE FIGURES *to 12.9.08*   www.cricinfo.com

Batting & Fielding	M	Inns	NO	Runs	HS	Avge	S/R	100	50	4s	6s	Ct	St
Tests	18	27	10	266	31	15.64	34.77	0	0	32	0	5	0
ODIs	16	10	5	51	15	10.20	60.71	0	0	3	0	3	0
T20 Ints	4	1	1	5	5*	–	125.00	0	0	1	0	2	0
First-class	126	163	48	1361	54	11.83	–	0	1	–	–	45	0

Bowling	M	Balls	Runs	Wkts	BB	Avge	RpO	S/R	5i	10m
Tests	18	4272	1952	76	7-47	25.68	2.74	56.21	5	1
ODIs	16	865	661	24	3-19	27.54	4.58	36.04	0	0
T20 Ints	4	92	102	8	3-16	12.75	6.65	11.50	0	0
First-class	126	22236	10371	410	7-47	25.29	2.79	54.23	17	2

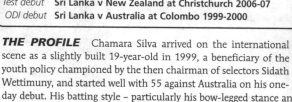

CHAMARA **SILVA**

Full name	**Lindamlilage Prageeth Chamara Silva**
Born	**December 14, 1979, Panadura**
Teams	**Bloomfield, Basnahira South, Deccan Chargers**
Style	**Right-hand bat, occasional legspinner**
Test debut	**Sri Lanka v New Zealand at Christchurch 2006-07**
ODI debut	**Sri Lanka v Australia at Colombo 1999-2000**

THE PROFILE   Chamara Silva arrived on the international scene as a slightly built 19-year-old in 1999, a beneficiary of the youth policy championed by the then chairman of selectors Sidath Wettimuny, and started well with 55 against Australia on his one-day debut. His batting style – particularly his bow-legged stance and flamboyant cover-drives – attracted immediate comparisons with the great Aravinda de Silva. Wristy, and quick on his feet, he is a good sweeper and cutter, and loves to loft the ball over the covers. But Silva failed to nail down a regular place despite his obvious talent, and was quietly dropped after the 2002 England tour. Over the next four years he was a prolific domestic scorer, and eventually caught the eye of Tom Moody, Sri Lanka's coach, who couldn't understand why he was not in the national squad. Silva did well for the A team in India, and won a long-overdue recall for the senior tour of New Zealand at the end of 2006. He won his first Test cap at Christchurch, but bagged a pair in a five-wicket defeat. However, the management kept faith for the second Test at Wellington, and he rewarded them handsomely, scoring 61 and a magnificent unbeaten 152. A maiden one-day century followed in India, just three weeks before the 2007 World Cup, where he was consistently in the runs, reeling off three successive half-centuries at the start and only once failing to reach double figures in Sri Lanka's march to the final. Since then, though, his scores have been modest – only one Test fifty, and a slightly more consistent record in ODIs, during 2007-08.

THE FACTS   Silva made 152 not out in his second Test, against New Zealand at Wellington in December 2006, after bagging a pair in his first: he is only the seventh batsman ever to score a Test century after a debut pair, and the first one to atone immediately in his second match ... Silva's 55 against Australia in August 1999 is the highest by any Sri Lankan on ODI debut: the only other half-century was by Sunil Wettimuny, with 53 not out against Australia at The Oval in the 1975 World Cup ...

THE FIGURES *to 12.9.08*   www.cricinfo.com

Batting & Fielding	M	Inns	NO	Runs	HS	Avge	S/R	100	50	4s	6s	Ct	St
Tests	11	17	1	537	152*	33.56	62.88	1	2	68	1	7	0
ODIs	55	48	4	1324	107*	30.09	70.50	1	11	113	8	17	0
T20 Ints	7	6	1	82	38	16.40	102.50	0	0	8	2	2	0
First-class	112	189	12	6472	152*	36.56	–	13	38	–	–	88	0

Bowling	M	Balls	Runs	Wkts	BB	Avge	RpO	S/R	5i	10m
Tests	11	102	65	1	1–57	65.00	3.82	102.00	0	0
ODIs	55	24	21	1	1–21	21.00	5.25	24.00	0	0
T20 Ints	7	18	15	1	1–4	15.00	5.00	18.00	0	0
First-class	112	1855	1271	35	4–85	36.31	4.11	53.00	0	0

RUDRA PRATAP **SINGH**

Full name	**Rudra Pratap Singh**
Born	**December 6, 1985, Rae Bareli, Uttar Pradesh**
Teams	**Uttar Pradesh, Deccan Chargers**
Style	**Right-hand bat, left-arm fast-medium bowler**
Test debut	**India v Pakistan at Faisalabad 2005-06**
ODI debut	**India v Zimbabwe at Harare 2005-06**

THE PROFILE Rudra Pratap Singh first made the headlines at the Under-19 World Cup in Bangladesh in 2004, taking eight wickets at 24.75 and bowling well at the death. Later that year he joined the conveyor belt of Indian left-arm seamers, after 34 wickets in six Ranji Trophy games for Uttar Pradesh, the joint-highest for the summer. He made the national one-day squad at the end of 2005, and took two wickets in his second over of international cricket, against Zimbabwe at Harare in September. He took four wickets (and the match award) against Sri Lanka in his third game, and three more in his fourth, before four barren games cost him his place during the West Indies tour in May 2006. He also won the match award on his Test debut for some persistent bowling on a shirtfront at Faisalabad, where Pakistan ran up 588. He spent a while on the sidelines, but remained well thought of in the Indian squad, as Virender Sehwag confirmed: "RP is a very talented bowler – his specialty is that he can bring the ball in to the right-handers and swing it both ways." He put an early-season stint with Leicestershire to good use in 2007, forcing his way into the side for the three-Test series in England. He took 5 for 59 in a tidy display of swing bowling at Lord's, knocking over Michael Vaughan in both innings, troubling him from round the wicket. An up-and-down time followed: after four-fors in the Sydney and Perth Tests, he lost his place after three wicketless matches later in 2008, but remained in the one-day shake-up.

THE FACTS RP Singh won the Man of the Match award on his Test debut – even though there were six centuries in the match, at Faisalabad in January 2006: Singh took 4 for 89 in Pakistan's first innings of 588 ... He averages 19.41 with the ball in ODIs against Sri Lanka, but 70.00 v West Indies ... Singh took 2 for 25 in the semi-final of the Under-19 World Cup in February 2004 – but Pakistan won by two wickets ...

THE FIGURES *to 12.9.08*   www.cricinfo.com

Batting & Fielding	M	Inns	NO	Runs	HS	Avge	S/R	100	50	4s	6s	Ct	St
Tests	13	17	3	91	30	6.50	36.40	0	0	11	1	6	0
ODIs	45	16	9	56	12*	8.00	42.74	0	0	2	0	11	0
T20 Ints	8	1	1	1	1*	–	100.00	0	0	0	0	1	0
First-class	39	51	11	334	41*	8.35	–	0	0	–	–	16	0

Bowling	M	Balls	Runs	Wkts	BB	Avge	RpO	S/R	5i	10m
Tests	13	2330	1564	40	5–59	39.10	4.02	58.25	1	0
ODIs	45	2109	1861	59	4–35	31.54	5.29	35.74	0	0
T20 Ints	8	168	191	13	4–13	14.69	6.82	12.92	0	0
First-class	39	6910	3909	140	5–33	27.92	3.39	49.35	7	1

DEVON **SMITH**

Full name	**Devon Sheldon Smith**
Born	**Oct 21, 1981, Hermitage, Sauteurs, St Patrick, Grenada**
Teams	**Windward Islands**
Style	**Left-hand bat, occasional offspinner**
Test debut	**West Indies v Australia at Georgetown 2002-03**
ODI debut	**West Indies v Australia at Kingston 2002-03**

THE PROFILE A belligerent left-handed opener whose eye makes up for a lack of footwork, Grenada's Devon Smith was drafted into the Test squad for the home series against India early in 2002, after making 750 runs in the Busta Cup. He didn't play, though, and made his debut against Australia the following year. Smith blazed 62 in his first Test, but bagged a pair in the next one. Early in 2004 he dragged West Indies out of a hole with a stroke-filled century against England on the first day of the series at Kingston. But just as he began to settle in, he fractured a thumb in the nets: he missed the next two Tests, then was dropped after three failures in the return series in England. He started the 2005-06 Australian tour well, making a hundred against Queensland then 88 in the first Test at Brisbane, but five single-figure scores followed, and the axe fell again. In one-dayers he was originally overshadowed by another Smith, the unrelated Dwayne, but both played in the 2007 World Cup, Devon making 61 in West Indies' last match, the thriller against England, which ensured him another English tour. He made several starts in the Tests there, crunching some classy cover-drives, but got out too often when set, making five scores between 16 and 42 before a double failure at The Oval. Smith kept himself in the reckoning with 91 in a Test at Johannesburg, but then more middling scores found him out of the team before the end of 2008, and he remains another underachiever in a West Indian side rather too full of them.

THE FACTS Smith scored 61 (in 34 balls) in his first Twenty20 international, against England at The Oval in June 2007 ... His highest first-class score is 181, for West Indies A against Lancashire at Liverpool in July 2002: he also made 180 for the Windward Islands against Kenya at Kingstown in February 2004, when he shared an opening stand of 309 with Romel Currency ... Smith has never played an ODI against Pakistan ...

THE FIGURES to 12.9.08   www.cricinfo.com

Batting & Fielding	M	Inns	NO	Runs	HS	Avge	S/R	100	50	4s	6s	Ct	St
Tests	24	45	2	1045	108	24.30	46.52	1	3	150	0	19	0
ODIs	26	24	2	512	91	23.27	67.99	0	2	55	4	10	0
T20 Ints	5	5	0	166	61	33.20	123.88	0	2	19	3	0	0
First-class	105	190	8	6579	181	36.14	–	14	32	–	–	85	0

Bowling	M	Balls	Runs	Wkts	BB	Avge	RpO	S/R	5i	10m
Tests	24	0	–	–	–	–	–	–	–	–
ODIs	26	0	–	–	–	–	–	–	–	–
T20 Ints	5	0	–	–	–	–	–	–	–	–
First-class	105	420	208	2	1–2	104.00	2.97	210.00	0	0

GRAEME **SMITH**

SOUTH AFRICA

Full name	**Graeme Craig Smith**
Born	**February 1, 1981, Johannesburg, Transvaal**
Teams	**Cape Cobras, Rajasthan Royals**
Style	**Left-hand bat, occasional offspinner**
Test debut	**South Africa v Australia at Cape Town 2001-02**
ODI debut	**South Africa v Australia at Bloemfontein 2001-02**

THE PROFILE   In March 2003, Graeme Smith became South Africa's youngest captain at 22, when Shaun Pollock was dumped after a disastrous World Cup. A tall, aggressive left-hand opener, Smith had few leadership credentials – and only a handful of caps – but the selectors' faith was instantly justified: in England in 2003 he collected back-to-back double-centuries. Reality bit back the following year, with Test-series defeats in Sri Lanka and India. There was also a run of 11 losses in 12 ODIs, a mixed time in New Zealand, and the start of an ultimately fruitless series against England. Yet Smith continued to crunch runs aplenty: his 125 to square the New Zealand series was a minor epic. He yields to no-one physically, but can be subdued by more insidious means: by the end of 2004, as Matthew Hoggard's inswinger had him frequently fumbling around his front pad, even the runs started to dry up. But he roared back in the Caribbean in 2005, with hundreds in three successive Tests. Then, early next year, he orchestrated a 3-2 home win over Australia in probably the best one-day series ever played. Smith kick-started the reply to 434 for 4 in the Jo'burg decider with 90 from 55 balls, adding 187 with Herschelle Gibbs in just 20.1 overs, and they eventually won with a ball to spare. Smith did well at the 2007 World Cup, except when it really mattered – a wild stroke gifted Nathan Bracken his wicket as South Africa subsided in the semi. A baton-charge to 85 squared the home Test series against West Indies at the start of 2008, and later that year achieved what he narrowly missed in 2003 – winning a Test series in England.

THE FACTS   In the first Test against England in 2003 Smith scored 277 at Birmingham, the highest score by a South African in Tests: in the second he made 259, the highest Test score by a visiting player at Lord's, beating Don Bradman's 254 in 1930 ... He averages 71.88 in Tests against West Indies, but only 22.25 against Australia ... Smith played four matches for Somerset in 2005, scoring 311 against Leicestershire in one of them ... His record includes one Test for the World XI (as captain) and one ODI for the Africa XI ...

THE FIGURES *to 12.9.08*   www.cricinfo.com

Batting & Fielding	M	Inns	NO	Runs	HS	Avge	S/R	100	50	4s	6s	Ct	St
Tests	70	124	7	5761	277	49.23	60.91	16	22	756	17	92	0
ODIs	135	133	9	5046	134*	40.69	81.82	7	36	589	31	71	0
T20 Ints	12	12	2	364	89*	36.40	127.27	0	3	52	7	8	0
First-class	107	186	12	8712	311	50.06	–	24	32	–	–	147	0

Bowling	M	Balls	Runs	Wkts	BB	Avge	RpO	S/R	5i	10m
Tests	70	1319	801	8	2–145	100.12	3.64	164.87	0	0
ODIs	135	1026	951	18	3–30	52.83	5.56	57.00	0	0
T20 Ints	12	24	57	0	–	14.25	–	0	0	
First-class	107	1687	1048	11	2–145	95.27	3.72	153.36	0	0

SOHAIL KHAN

Full name	**Sohail Khan**
Born	**March 6, 1984, Malakand, North-West Frontier Province**
Teams	**Sind, Sui Southern Gas**
Style	**Right-hand bat, right-arm fast-medium bowler**
Test debut	**No Tests yet**
ODI debut	**Pakistan v Zimbabwe at Faisalabad 2007-08**

THE PROFILE Hailing from Malakand in the North-West Frontier Province, but based in Karachi where he was schooled by Rashid Latif at the national academy, Sohail Khan had a dream debut first-class season in 2007-08. Playing for Sui Southern Gas, he took 65 wickets in his first nine games, starting with five in each innings of his debut against Customs and making it three five-fors in a row in the first innings of his next match. The highlight was an astonishing haul of 16 wickets – 7 for 80 and 9 for 109 – against WAPDA in Karachi in December 2007, to break Fazal Mahmood's 51-year-old mark for the best match figures in Pakistan (Sui Gas still lost the match). Sohail – who's usually known as Sohail Pathan on the circuit – finished the season with 91 wickets at 18.72. Inevitably, all this caught the eyes of the selectors, and he was drafted in to the one-day team towards the end of the series against Zimbabwe early in 2008 – oddly, his first ODI was also his first senior limited-overs game. He took a late wicket, then excised Bangladesh's middle order with 3 for 30 at Multan to confirm his promise before being left out of the Asia Cup. But Sohail could well be the next big thing in Pakistan fast bowling: tall and well-built, he remains raw and has two lengths: very short or very full. But despite a lumbering action, he has that rare commodity – pace. And given that, he could feature very prominently over the next few years.

THE FACTS Sohail Khan took ten wickets on his first-class debut, for Sui Southern Gas against Customs in Karachi in October 2007 ... In his ninth match, he took 7 for 80 and 9 for 109 against WAPDA, the best match figures in first-class cricket in Pakistan (previously Fazal Mahmood's 15 for 76 for Punjab v Combined Services in Lahore in 1956-57 ... Sohail's first ODI, in January 2008, was also his first senior one-day game ... He took 91 wickets at 18.72 in his first season of first-class cricket ...

THE FIGURES *to 12.9.08* www.cricinfo.com

Batting & Fielding	M	Inns	NO	Runs	HS	Avge	S/R	100	50	4s	6s	Ct	St
Tests	0	0	–	–	–	–	–	–	–	–	–	–	–
ODIs	3	0	–	–	–	–	–	–	–	–	–	0	0
T20 Ints	0	0	–	–	–	–	–	–	–	–	–	–	–
First-class	14	16	5	138	29	12.54	42.33	0	0	14	1	3	0

Bowling	M	Balls	Runs	Wkts	BB	Avge	RpO	S/R	5i	10m
Tests	0	0	–	–	–	–	–	–	–	–
ODIs	3	139	111	4	3–30	27.75	4.79	34.75	0	0
T20 Ints	0	0	–	–	–	–	–	–	–	–
First-class	14	3094	1704	91	9–109	18.72	3.30	34.00	10	2

SOHAIL TANVIR

Full name	**Sohail Tanvir**
Born	**December 12, 1984, Rawalpindi, Punjab**
Teams	**Rawalpindi, Khan Research Labs, Rajasthan Royals**
Style	**Left-hand bat, left-arm fast-medium bowler**
Test debut	**Pakistan v India at Delhi 2007-08**
ODI debut	**Pakistan v South Africa at Lahore 2007-08**

THE PROFILE   Sohail Tanvir made an immediate mark in first-class cricket, scoring an unbeaten 97 in only his second match for Rawalpindi in October 2004, when he shared a last-wicket stand of 173 with Yasir Ali that more than doubled the score. And when he was called up to replace Shoaib Akhtar (sent home in disgrace) at the World Twenty20 championship in South Africa in September 2007, Tanvir made an impression again – not with the bat, initially, although he did swipe the first ball he received in international cricket for six, but with his bowling. He bustles in and delivers brisk left-arm off the wrong foot, and is a bit faster than he looks. He developed quickly, adding good changes of pace – helped by the fact that he can also bowl respectable left-arm spin if required – and has an excellent, deceptive yorker. In the space of a year he became, with the minimum of fuss, Pakistan's premier limited-overs bowler. He took four key wickets as Pakistan won the decisive one-dayer of their five-match series in India in November 2007, and grabbed five wickets in vain against Sri Lanka at the Asia Cup in mid-2008. In between he returned the best figures of the inaugural Indian Premier League. Tanvir was tried in Tests, too, but although he kept it tight he struggled to make much impression in two matches on batsmen's pitches in India at the end of 2007.

THE FACTS   Sohail Tanvir hit sixes off the first and third balls he received in international cricket – from Sreesanth of India in the World Twenty20 final at Johannesburg in September 2007 ... Tanvir took 6 for 14 for Rajasthan Royals against Chennai Super Kings at Jaipur in May 2008, the best bowling figures in any Twenty20 match, and the best in the first season of the IPL ...   He has made three first-class hundreds, the highest 132 for Federal Areas v Baluchistan at Karachi in February 2008 ...

THE FIGURES to 12.9.08   www.cricinfo.com

Batting & Fielding	M	Inns	NO	Runs	HS	Avge	S/R	100	50	4s	6s	Ct	St
Tests	2	3	0	17	13	5.66	38.63	0	0	4	0	2	0
ODIs	24	15	5	135	59	15.00	103.05	0	1	11	2	7	0
T20 Ints	7	1	0	12	12	12.00	300.00	0	0	0	2	1	0
First-class	26	42	8	1125	132	33.08	–	3	6	–	–	10	0

Bowling	M	Balls	Runs	Wkts	BB	Avge	RpO	S/R	5i	10m
Tests	2	504	316	5	3–83	63.20	3.76	100.80	0	0
ODIs	24	1233	1012	36	5–48	28.11	4.92	34.25	1	0
T20 Ints	7	156	184	7	3–31	26.28	7.07	22.28	0	0
First-class	26	5343	2999	91	6–41	32.95	3.36	58.71	4	0

TIM **SOUTHEE**

Full name	**Timothy Grant Southee**
Born	**December 11, 1988, Whangarei**
Teams	**Northern Districts**
Style	**Right-hand bat, right-arm fast-medium bowler**
Test debut	**New Zealand v England at Napier 2007-08**
ODI debut	**New Zealand v England at Chester-le-Street 2008**

THE PROFILE Few players have made such a remarkable Test debut as 19-year-old Tim Southee managed at Napier in March 2008. First, swinging the ball at a healthy pace, he took 5 for 55 as England were restricted to 253, his victims including Andrew Strauss for 0 and Kevin Pietersen for 129. Later, with New Zealand in a hopeless position on the final day, he strolled in and smashed 77 not out from just 40 balls, with nine sixes, five of them off an unamused Monty Panesar. His second Test, at Lord's in May 2008, was rather more mundane – one run, no wickets – and he fell ill after that and lost his place to the persevering Iain O'Brien. But Southee is definitely one for the future: he has long been in the thoughts of New Zealand's selectors. He made his first-class debut for Northern Districts at 18 in February 2007, and the following season showed significant promise, claiming 6 for 68 in a particularly impressive effort against Auckland. He was named in the squad for the Under-19 World Cup, but had to interrupt his preparations when he was drafted into the senior set-up for the Twenty20 games against England in early 2008. He ended the Under-19 World Cup as the second-highest wicket-taker, with 17, and was named Player of the Tournament. After that he'd barely had time to unpack when the Test call came his way, and he didn't disappoint.

THE FACTS Southee hit nine sixes in his first Test innings, a number exceeded only by four players, none of whom was making his debut ... He had earlier become the sixth New Zealander to take five wickets in an innings on Test debut, following Fen Cresswell (1949), Alex Moir (1950-51), Bruce Taylor (1964-65), Paul Wiseman (1997-98) and Mark Gillespie (2007-08) ... Southee was named Player of the Tournament at the 2007-08 Under-19 World Cup, after taking 17 wickets ... He took 6 for 68 for Northern Districts in Auckland in December 2007 ...

THE FIGURES to 12.9.08 · www.cricinfo.com

Batting & Fielding	M	Inns	NO	Runs	HS	Avge	S/R	100	50	4s	6s	Ct	St
Tests	2	3	1	83	77*	41.50	120.28	0	1	5	9	0	0
ODIs	7	3	0	12	6	4.00	75.00	0	0	0	1	1	0
T20 Ints	2	2	1	13	12*	13.00	108.33	0	0	2	0	0	0
First-class	17	19	3	278	77*	17.37	78.75	0	2	25	15	1	0

Bowling	M	Balls	Runs	Wkts	BB	Avge	RpO	S/R	5i	10m
Tests	2	379	198	5	5–55	39.60	3.13	75.80	1	0
ODIs	7	324	271	16	4–38	16.93	5.01	20.25	0	0
T20 Ints	2	48	60	3	2–22	20.00	7.50	16.00	0	0
First-class	17	3411	1628	61	6–68	26.68	2.86	55.91	3	0

SREESANTH

Full name	**Shanthakumaran Sreesanth**
Born	**February 6, 1983, Kothamangalam, Kerala**
Teams	**Kerala, Kings XI Punjab**
Style	**Right-hand bat, right-arm fast-medium bowler**
Test debut	**India v England at Nagpur 2005-06**
ODI debut	**India v Sri Lanka at Nagpur 2005-06**

THE PROFILE   For three seasons, Sreesanth was little more than a quiz question, as the only Kerala bowler to take a Ranji Trophy hat-trick. He started as a legspinner, idolising Anil Kumble, then once he turned to pace his rise was rapid but, since he played for a weak side, almost unnoticed. Not too many bowlers play in the Duleep Trophy in their first season, but Sreesanth did, in 2002-03 after taking 22 wickets in his first seven games. His progress was halted by a hamstring injury, but he returned stronger, with a more side-on action and increased pace, and a superb display at the 2005 Challenger Trophy (trial matches for the national squad) propelled him into the side for the Sri Lanka series. Later he snapped up 6 for 55 against England, the best one-day figures by an Indian fast bowler at home. Idiosyncratic, with an aggressive approach – to the stumps and the game – he can be expensive in one-dayers, but is also a wicket-taking bowler. He can do it in Tests, too: in Antigua in June 2006 he fired out Ramnaresh Sarwan and Brian Lara (both for 0) in successive overs. He sometimes rubs opponents up the wrong way: in England in 2007 he sent down a beamer at Kevin Pietersen then overstepped by a yard for a bouncer at Paul Collingwood, while a barge on Michael Vaughan earned him a fine. But there is talent among the tantrums: Sreesanth took nine wickets in the series, which India won, then grabbed 19 for Kings XI Punjab in the inaugural Indian Premier League season early in 2008, although his Test form tailed off a little.

THE FACTS   Sreesanth took a hat-trick for Kerala v Himachal Pradesh in the Ranji Trophy in November 2004 ... He is only the second man from Kerala to play for India, after Tinu Yohannan, another fast-medium bowler ... Sreesanth did not score a run in ODIs until his 16th match, although that was only his fourth innings ... He took 19 wickets in the first IPL season, the same as Shane Warne and exceeded only by Sohail Tanvir (22) ...

THE FIGURES to 12.9.08   www.cricinfo.com

Batting & Fielding	M	Inns	NO	Runs	HS	Avge	S/R	100	50	4s	6s	Ct	St
Tests	14	21	7	217	35	15.50	64.97	0	0	29	4	2	0
ODIs	41	16	8	34	10*	4.25	36.17	0	0	1	0	6	0
T20 Ints	10	3	2	20	19*	20.00	142.85	0	0	4	0	2	0
First-class	42	57	19	388	35	10.21	46.80	0	0	–	–	7	0

Bowling	M	Balls	Runs	Wkts	BB	Avge	RpO	S/R	5i	10m
Tests	14	2873	1573	50	5–40	31.46	3.28	57.46	1	0
ODIs	41	1925	1856	59	6–55	31.45	5.78	32.62	1	0
T20 Ints	10	204	288	7	2–12	41.14	8.47	29.14	0	0
First-class	42	7649	4165	128	5–40	32.53	3.26	59.75	3	0

DALE **STEYN**

Full name	**Dale Willem Steyn**
Born	**June 27, 1983, Phalaborwa, Limpopo Province**
Teams	**Titans, Bangalore Royal Challengers**
Style	**Right-hand bat, right-arm fast bowler**
Test debut	**South Africa v England at Port Elizabeth 2004-05**
ODI debut	**Africa XI v Asia XI at Centurion 2005-06**

THE PROFILE Dale Steyn's rise to the South African side was as rapid as his bowling: he was picked for the first Test against England in December 2004 little more than a year after his first-class debut. A rare first-class cricketer from the far north of South Africa, from the Limpopo province close to the Kruger National Park and the Zimbabwe border, Steyn is genuinely fast, and moves the ball away. He sprints up and hurls the ball down aggressively, often following up with a snarl for the batsman, *à la* Allan Donald. He took eight wickets in three Tests against England before returning to the finishing school of domestic cricket, so missed the massacres that followed against Zimbabwe, before being recalled in April 2006 and responding with 5 for 47 as New Zealand were routed at Centurion. He couldn't quite nail down a regular spot, though, despite six wickets in a win over India at Cape Town the following January. He had half a season of county cricket with Essex in 2005, after being recommended by Darren Gough, and also rattled a few helmets for Warwickshire in 2007. But Steyn really came of age in 2007-08, taking 20 wickets in two home Tests against New Zealand, followed by 20 in three against West Indies, then 14 in two matches on Bangladesh's traditionally slow tracks. Finally he blew India away with 5 for 23 as they subsided to 76 all out and defeat at Ahmedabad in April. Much was expected of him in England later in 2008, but he broke his thumb and missed the last two Tests.

THE FACTS Steyn took 8 for 41 (14 for 110 in the match) for Titans v Eagles at Bloemfontein in December 2007 ... He took 10 for 93 and 10 for 91 in successive home Tests against New Zealand in November 2007 ... Steyn improved his highest first-class score by 745% when he scored 82 for Essex v Durham in July 2005: his previous-highest was 11 ... He made his official ODI debut for the Africa XI, and his record includes two matches for them ...

THE FIGURES to 12.9.08   www.cricinfo.com

Batting & Fielding	M	Inns	NO	Runs	HS	Avge	S/R	100	50	4s	6s	Ct	St
Tests	25	30	8	235	33*	10.68	47.09	0	0	27	5	7	0
ODIs	18	6	3	19	6	6.33	51.35	0	0	1	0	2	0
T20 Ints	2	1	1	1	1*	–	100.00	0	0	0	0	0	0
First-class	65	74	19	712	82	12.94	55.02	0	2	–	–	12	0

Bowling	M	Balls	Runs	Wkts	BB	Avge	RpO	S/R	5i	10m
Tests	25	4790	2882	128	6–49	22.51	3.61	37.42	8	2
ODIs	18	750	718	18	3–65	39.88	5.74	41.66	0	0
T20 Ints	2	42	26	5	4–9	5.20	3.71	8.40	0	0
First-class	65	12095	6798	278	8–41	24.45	3.37	43.50	16	4

ANDREW **STRAUSS**

Full name	**Andrew John Strauss**
Born	**March 2, 1977, Johannesburg, South Africa**
Teams	**Middlesex**
Style	**Left-hand bat**
Test debut	**England v New Zealand at Lord's 2004**
ODI debut	**England v Sri Lanka at Dambulla 2003-04**

THE PROFILE Andrew Strauss, a fluid and attractive left-hand opener, had a rapid rise to prominence. His stock rose after Angus Fraser stood down as Middlesex's captain to write for *The Independent*. Strauss filled the breach admirably: 1400 runs in 2003, his first full season in charge, proved he was unfazed by responsibility. He was born in Johannesburg, but – schooled at Radley College and Durham University – is a very English product. At the crease, there is something of Graham Thorpe about his ability to accumulate runs without recourse to big shots, and it was this that first earned him a one-day place in 2003-04. He confirmed his star quality – and his affinity for Lord's – with a century on Test debut against New Zealand (hastening Nasser Hussain's retirement) in May 2004, and added another in his first ODI there, against West Indies two months later. But that was only a warm-up: in South Africa that winter, Strauss won the first Test almost single-handedly with 126 and 94 not out, and added two further hundreds on his way to 656 runs in the series. In 2005 he overcame initial uncertainties against McGrath and Warne to record two more tons in England's historic Ashes victory. Things have gone less swimmingly since. After seven hundreds in his first 19 Tests, the next 34 produced only five, as bowlers probed outside off and fed a penchant for a rather uppish pull/hook. The one-day runs dried up, too, and he lost his place. He probably saved his Test career with 177 in the final Test at Napier in March 2008, but another moderate series against South Africa later in the year raised further questions.

THE FACTS Strauss was the 15th England player to score a century on Test debut, with 112 v New Zealand at Lord's in May 2004 ... In July 2006 he became only the third man to make a century on debut as England captain, following Archie MacLaren (1897-98) and Allan Lamb (1989-90); Kevin Pietersen followed suit in 2008 ... England have never lost a Test in which Strauss has scored a century ... He opened with Ben Hutton, who was also born in Johannesburg, for school (Radley), university (Durham) and county (Middlesex) ...

THE FIGURES to 12.9.08   www.cricinfo.com

Batting & Fielding	M	Inns	NO	Runs	HS	Avge	S/R	100	50	4s	6s	Ct	St
Tests	53	98	2	3943	177	41.07	48.87	12	14	495	6	66	0
ODIs	78	77	7	2239	152	31.98	75.82	2	14	240	8	28	0
T20 Ints	3	3	0	51	33	17.00	130.76	0	0	7	0	1	0
First-class	160	284	12	10906	177	40.09	–		26	49	–	–	132	0

Bowling	M	Balls	Runs	Wkts	BB	Avge	RpO	S/R	5i	10m
Tests	53	0	–	–	–	–	–	–	–	–
ODIs	78	6	3	0	–	–	3.00	–	0	0
T20 Ints	3	0	–	–	–	–	–	–	–	–
First-class	160	90	79	2	1–16	39.50	5.26	45.00	0	0

SCOTT **STYRIS**

Full name	**Scott Bernard Styris**
Born	**July 10, 1975, Brisbane, Australia**
Teams	**Auckland, Deccan Chargers**
Style	**Right-hand bat, right-arm medium-pacer**
Test debut	**New Zealand v West Indies at St George's 2001-02**
ODI debut	**New Zealand v India at Rajkot 1999-2000**

THE PROFILE Scott Styris, who was born in Australia but moved to New Zealand when he was six, had a long apprenticeship in domestic cricket, playing almost ten years for Northern Districts before finally making the Test side. By the time of his debut, in Grenada in June 2002, he had been a one-day regular for three years, and had done nothing to suggest that he was a Test batsman – he had 418 runs at 16 in 40 ODIs, and was regarded more as a containing medium-pacer. But he thumped an uncomplicated 107 in his first Test innings, added 69 not out in the second, and became a permanent fixture, finally adding solidity at the giddy heights of No. 4 – from where, in March 2004, his 170 set up a winning total against South Africa at Auckland. On that 2002 tour of the Caribbean he took 6 for 25 at Port-of-Spain, New Zealand's best ODI bowling analysis at the time (since beaten by Shane Bond, twice). Styris continued to score consistently – in a county stint for Middlesex, for his new province Auckland, and for New Zealand. A back injury kept him out of the home series against Sri Lanka late in 2006, but he was fit in time for the World Cup, where he never failed to reach double figures in nine visits to the crease, including 87 against England, 80 v West Indies and 111 v Sri Lanka – all not out – and he finished with 499 runs at 83.16. Soon after that he announced his retirement from Tests, in order to concentrate on one-day cricket ... and his lucrative Indian Premier League contract.

THE FACTS Styris was the seventh New Zealander to score a century on Test debut, following Jackie Mills, Bruce Taylor, Rodney Redmond, Mark Greatbatch, Mathew Sinclair and Lou Vincent ... He averages only 19.70 in ODIs against Australia, despite making 101 against them at Christchurch in 2005-06 ... He has made two centuries in the World Cup, but finished on the losing side both times ... Styris was actually awarded his first cap on the eve of the Karachi Test against Pakistan in May 2002, only for it to be taken back when the match was cancelled after a bomb blast ...

THE FIGURES to 12.9.08   www.cricinfo.com

Batting & Fielding	M	Inns	NO	Runs	HS	Avge	S/R	100	50	4s	6s	Ct	St
Tests	29	48	4	1586	170	36.04	51.34	5	6	205	13	23	0
ODIs	153	132	21	3699	141	33.32	79.20	4	23	292	59	59	0
T20 Ints	14	13	0	251	66	19.30	110.08	0	1	18	10	3	0
First-class	118	197	18	5494	212*	30.69	–	9	26	–	–	91	0

Bowling	M	Balls	Runs	Wkts	BB	Avge	RpO	S/R	5i	10m
Tests	29	1960	1015	20	3–28	50.75	3.10	98.00	0	0
ODIs	153	5241	4163	121	6–25	34.40	4.76	43.31	1	0
T20 Ints	14	135	170	5	2–33	34.00	7.55	27.00	0	0
First-class	118	12411	6232	203	6–32	30.69	3.01	61.13	9	1

GRAEME **SWANN**

Full name	**Graeme Peter Swann**
Born	**March 24, 1979, Northampton**
Teams	**Nottinghamshire**
Style	**Right-hand bat, offspinner**
Test debut	**No Tests yet**
ODI debut	**South Africa v England at Bloemfontein 1999-2000**

THE PROFILE Self-confident and gregarious, Graeme Swann is an aggressive offspinner, not afraid to give the ball a real tweak, and a hard-hitting middle-order batsman. He made his maiden century for Northamptonshire in 1998, his first season, and was often promoted in one-dayers to provide oomph. Fast-tracked into the England A team in southern Africa, he took 21 wickets at 25.61, and averaged 22 with the bat. He claimed a place in the revamped England squad which toured South Africa in 1999-2000 under new coach Duncan Fletcher, but Swann found life outside the Test side frustrating, although he did play an ODI, in which he bravely continued to give the ball a rip. However, he was less impressive off the field – what some saw as confidence, others interpreted as arrogance or cheek – and slid out of the international reckoning. After marking time with Northants for a while, not helped by Monty Panesar's arrival, Swann packed his bags for Trent Bridge in 2005 – a decision immediately justified when he helped Nottinghamshire win the Championship that year. Improved returns in 2007 earned him an England recall for the winter tour on what were expected to be spinning tracks in Sri Lanka. He took 4 for 34 in a one-day win at Dambulla, but more modest performances followed against New Zealand, home and away, and by the end of 2008 Swann had been replaced in the one-day side by his county colleague Samit Patel. But Swann wasn't too bothered by the prospect of missing out on the possible riches to be gained from Sir Allen Stanford and the Indian Premier League: "I'd probably only waste the money on helicopters and a Ferrari."

THE FACTS Swann took 7 for 33 (after not bowling in the first innings) for Northamptonshire v Derbyshire in June 2003 ... He took 8 for 118 for England in an Under-19 Test against Pakistan at Taunton in 1998 ... Swann made 183 for Northants v Gloucestershire at Bristol in August 2002, helping Michael Hussey (310 not out) put on 318 for the sixth wicket ... Swann's brother Alec played for Northamptonshire and Lancashire ...

THE FIGURES to 12.9.08   www.cricinfo.com

Batting & Fielding	M	Inns	NO	Runs	HS	Avge	S/R	100	50	4s	6s	Ct	St
Tests	0	0	–	–	–	–	–	–	–	–	–	–	–
ODIs	12	9	0	136	34	15.11	72.34	0	0	12	0	7	0
T20 Ints	3	2	2	18	15*	–	150.00	0	0	2	0	0	0
First-class	169	237	17	5929	183	26.95	–	4	30	–	–	123	0

Bowling	M	Balls	Runs	Wkts	BB	Avge	RpO	S/R	5i	10m
Tests	0	0	–	–	–	–	–	–	–	–
ODIs	12	534	387	14	4–34	27.64	4.34	38.14	0	0
T20 Ints	3	60	67	5	2–21	13.40	6.70	12.00	0	0
First-class	169	27993	14032	427	7–33	32.86	3.00	65.55	15	3

SYED RASEL

Full name	**Syed Rasel**
Born	**July 3, 1984, Jessore, Khulna**
Teams	**Khulna**
Style	**Left-hand bat, left-arm medium-pacer**
Test debut	**Bangladesh v Sri Lanka at Colombo 2005-06**
ODI debut	**Bangladesh v Sri Lanka at Colombo 2005-06**

THE PROFILE A sensational spell of swing bowling for Bangladesh A at Canterbury in August 2005 propelled Syed Rasel into the international reckoning at the age of 21. He had missed the senior tour earlier in the season, but, having steadily developed his trade on a difficult five-week trip, Rasel tore through Kent's defences with 7 for 50 in the first innings, and finished with 10 for 91 in the match. It wasn't enough to win the game, but he was immediately drafted into the senior squad for the tour of Sri Lanka that followed in September, and he made his Test and one-day debuts there. With shades of Chaminda Vaas in his left-arm approach, Rasel took six wickets in his first two matches, including 4 for 129 in the second Test, a match that Bangladesh lost by an innings. Nevertheless, he soon had his revenge on home soil, taking 2 for 28 at Bogra the following February, as Sri Lanka slumped to their first-ever one-day defeat at Bangladesh's hands. He rose through the ranks from divisional cricket in his home province of Khulna, and his ability to swing the ball at a modest pace sets him apart from many of his rivals. He injured his foot in a motorbike accident shortly before the Champions Trophy in India in October 2006, but recovered to play, and did enough over the season to claim a World Cup place. He troubled many batsmen in the Caribbean with his left-arm approach, only once failing to take a wicket in seven starts, but took a step backwards in 2008, not helped when he dislocated his collarbone while fielding in New Zealand.

THE FACTS Fourteen of Syed Rasel's ODI wickets have come against Kenya (at 15.21), and 16 (at 28.25) against Sri Lanka ... He took 7 for 55 (11 for 109 in the match) for Khulna in Dhaka, and 8 for 67 at Barisal, both in 2003-04 ... Rasel took 0 for 97 in three ODIs during 2008 ... His first four Tests – and his sixth – were all against Sri Lanka ...

THE FIGURES to 12.9.08 www.cricinfo.com

Batting & Fielding	M	Inns	NO	Runs	HS	Avge	S/R	100	50	4s	6s	Ct	St
Tests	6	12	4	37	19	4.62	38.94	0	0	6	0	0	0
ODIs	34	18	6	56	15	4.66	40.28	0	0	5	0	4	0
T20 Ints	7	3	1	7	6	3.50	77.77	0	0	1	0	1	0
First-class	42	65	22	445	33	10.34	41.20	0	0	–	–	7	0

Bowling	M	Balls	Runs	Wkts	BB	Avge	RpO	S/R	5i	10m
Tests	6	879	573	12	4–129	47.75	3.91	73.25	0	0
ODIs	34	1773	1236	44	4–22	28.09	4.18	40.29	0	0
T20 Ints	7	150	166	3	1–10	55.33	6.64	50.00	0	0
First-class	42	7083	3463	119	8–67	29.10	2.93	59.52	3	2

ANDREW **SYMONDS**

Full name	**Andrew Symonds**
Born	**June 9, 1975, Birmingham, Warwickshire, England**
Teams	**Queensland, Deccan Chargers**
Style	**Right-hand bat, right-arm medium-pace or offbreaks**
Test debut	**Australia v Sri Lanka at Galle 2004**
ODI debut	**Australia v Pakistan at Lahore 1998-99**

THE PROFILE Andrew Symonds brings gusto to whatever he does, whether firing down offbreaks or medium-pacers, hurling his bulk around the outfield, or ruffling the bowler's hair after a wicket. He saves his loudest grunt for batting. For Gloucestershire, when only 20, he scythed a world-record 16 sixes in an innings against Glamorgan, and 20 in the match (another record). For some time his flaw was to attempt one six too many: during four years in and out of the one-day side he wasted opportunities galore. But one day changed everything: striding out with Australia sinking against Pakistan during the 2003 World Cup, Symonds sculpted a masterly 143 from 125 balls. Until then, he had just 762 one-day runs at 23: ever since he has averaged around 50. He had even more trouble in Tests. He struggled in two matches in Sri Lanka in 2004: almost two years later he received an extended run as Australia tried to find a Flintoff, but couldn't reproduce that one-day consistency. Faced with the axe, he cracked a huge six – the first of five – against South Africa at the MCG to open his account in a pressure-relieving 72, but remained a borderline selection until, recalled after Damien Martyn's sudden retirement, he dug Australia out of a hole against England at Melbourne in December 2006 with a forthright 156, putting on 279 with his Queensland buddy Matthew Hayden. At last he looked at home in the Test side, and has averaged over 75 since. He also played his part as the World Cup was retained in 2007, but a spiky attitude remained a problem. After clashing with Harbhajan Singh early in the year he was sent home from a one-day series against Bangladesh in 2008 after missing a team meeting to go fishing, and was left out for the Test tour of India.

THE FACTS Birmingham-born Symonds was voted *England's* Young Cricketer of the Year in 1995, but turned down an England A tour that winter and pledged his future to Australia, where he grew up ... He played 71 ODIs before winning his first Test cap, a record at the time ... Symonds first came to notice as a 13-year-old, after a partnership of 466 with Matthew Mott, who also went on to play first-class cricket ...

THE FIGURES to 12.9.08   www.cricinfo.com

Batting & Fielding	M	Inns	NO	Runs	HS	Avge	S/R	100	50	4s	6s	Ct	St
Tests	22	34	5	1295	162*	44.65	66.51	2	9	137	27	17	0
ODIs	193	157	33	5006	156	40.37	92.78	6	29	443	102	80	0
T20 Ints	13	10	4	337	85*	56.16	170.20	0	2	33	10	3	0
First-class	215	356	33	14113	254*	43.69	–	40	63	–	–	149	0

Bowling	M	Balls	Runs	Wkts	BB	Avge	RpO	S/R	5i	10m
Tests	22	1908	839	23	3–50	36.47	2.63	82.95	0	0
ODIs	193	5827	4861	129	5–18	37.68	5.00	45.17	1	0
T20 Ints	13	185	277	8	2–14	34.62	8.98	23.12	0	0
First-class	215	16979	8448	231	6–105	36.57	2.98	73.50	2	0

SHAUN **TAIT**

Full name	**Shaun William Tait**
Born	**Feb 22, 1983, Bedford Park, Adelaide, South Australia**
Teams	**South Australia**
Style	**Right-hand bat, right-arm fast bowler**
Test debut	**Australia v England at Nottingham 2005**
ODI debut	**Australia v England at Sydney 2006-07**

THE PROFILE Shaun Tait's shoulder-strong action slung him on to the 2005 Ashes tour, where he played in two of the Tests, but it soon disrupted his quest for further impact. With a muscular but unrefined method that seems to invite pain, Tait returned from England only to hurt himself in a grade match. Shoulder surgery forced him out for the rest of the year, but fortunately there seemed to be no reduction in his frightening pace, which has sometimes been clocked above 99mph (160kph). An abbreviated 2005-06 featured 6 for 41 in the domestic one-day final, an amazing combination of spot-on speed and 14 wides. His old-fashioned approach of yorkers and bumpers, mixed with a modern dose of reverse-swing, had brought him 65 wickets in 2004-05, his first full home season, earning him that Ashes trip and exciting followers to believe that Tait and Brett Lee might be the 21st century's version of Lillee and Thomson. A hamstring twang delayed Tait's one-day entry until February 2007, but despite mixed results (much speed, less accuracy) in his first four games he was bravely included in the World Cup squad and, helped when Lee pulled out injured, was one of the stars in the Caribbean, blowing away 23 batsmen, more than anyone except Glenn McGrath. Again there was a cost: he had to have elbow surgery in mid-2007, and eventually he withdrew from cricket altogether, citing physical and emotional exhaustion. He did not bowl a ball for six months, but is determined to regain his mojo – and his Australian place – in 2008-09.

THE FACTS Tait took 8 for 43 for South Australia v Tasmania at Adelaide in January 2004, the best figures in Australian domestic one-day cricket ... He played for Durham in 2004, bowling 21 no-balls in his first match, against Somerset, in figures of 12-0-113-0: in his second (and last) game the damage was 6-0-63-0 ... Tait took 23 wickets in the 2007 World Cup, equal with Muttiah Muralitharan and behind only Glenn McGrath (26) ... His best first-class figures are 7 for 99, for SA v Queensland at Adelaide in November 2004 ...

THE FIGURES to 12.9.08   www.cricinfo.com

Batting & Fielding	M	Inns	NO	Runs	HS	Avge	S/R	100	50	4s	6s	Ct	St
Tests	3	5	2	20	8	6.66	43.47	0	0	4	0	0	0
ODIs	18	1	0	11	11	11.00	110.00	0	0	1	1	2	0
T20 Ints	1	0	–	–	–	–	–	–	–	–	–	0	0
First-class	46	65	26	455	68	11.66	50.83	0	2	–	–	12	0

Bowling	M	Balls	Runs	Wkts	BB	Avge	RpO	S/R	5i	10m
Tests	3	414	302	5	3–97	60.40	4.37	82.80	0	0
ODIs	18	849	774	33	4–39	23.45	5.46	25.72	0	0
T20 Ints	1	24	22	2	2–22	11.00	5.50	12.00	0	0
First-class	46	8409	5131	185	7–29	27.73	3.66	45.45	7	1

BANGLADESH

TAMIM IQBAL

Full name **Tamim Iqbal Khan**
Born **March 20, 1989, Chittagong**
Teams **Chittagong**
Style **Left-hand bat**
Test debut **Bangladesh v New Zealand at Dunedin 2007-08**
ODI debut **Bangladesh v Zimbabwe at Harare 2006-07**

THE PROFILE The flamboyant left-hander Tamim Iqbal is one of Bangladesh's most assured young batsmen, and one of their hardest hitters. Selected for the 2007 World Cup after just four ODIs – in which he amassed only 57 runs against Zimbabwe, Bermuda and Canada – Tamim proceeded to light up the start of the competition with 51 off only 53 balls to ensure that Bangladesh's pursuit of India's modest 191 got off to a flying start. Shrugging off a blow on the neck when he missed a hook at Zaheer Khan, Tamim jumped down the wicket and smashed him over midwicket for six. Bangladesh duly administered the victory which virtually ensured that they, not India, would progress to the Super Eights. All this came three days before the 18th birthday of a player with cricket in his veins (his brother and uncle played for Bangladesh as well). Tamim, who hates to get bogged down, struggled to reproduce this form afterwards – it wasn't until his 18th ODI, in Sri Lanka in July 2007, that he reached 50 again. But after that he made a flying start to his Test career, too, hitting 53 and 84 against New Zealand in January 2008. Before his World Cup adventures, his most notable innings came for the Under-19s against England at the end of 2005, when he flayed 112 from just 71 balls, with six sixes. He is particularly strong square of the wicket, and has a good flick shot, but his almost premeditated charges down the track – while spectacular – sometimes bring his downfall.

THE FACTS Tamim Iqbal scored 53 and 84 on his Test debut, against New Zealand in Dunedin in January 2008, sharing a national-record opening stand of 161 in the second innings with Junaid Siddique ... Tamim's two first-class centuries came within a week in March 2006, 118 and 113 for Chittagong against Dhaka and Sylhet ... His brother, Nafees Iqbal, has played 11 Tests and 18 ODIs for Bangladesh, while their uncle, Akram Khan, played eight Tests and 44 ODIs, and captained them in pre-Test days ...

THE FIGURES *to 12.9.08*   www.cricinfo.com

Batting & Fielding	M	Inns	NO	Runs	HS	Avge	S/R	100	50	4s	6s	Ct	St
Tests	4	7	0	177	84	25.28	51.90	0	2	27	1	0	0
ODIs	42	42	0	1050	129	27.38	69.73	1	8	133	12	15	0
T20 Ints	8	8	0	91	32	11.37	81.98	0	0	13	0	1	0
First-class	23	40	1	1518	118	38.71	65.68	2	13	–	–	7	0

Bowling	M	Balls	Runs	Wkts	BB	Avge	RpO	S/R	5i	10m
Tests	4	0	–	–	–	–	–	–	–	–
ODIs	42	1	6	0	–	–	36.00	–	0	0
T20 Ints	8	0	–	–	–	–	–	–	–	–
First-class	23	108	67	0	–	–	3.72	–	0	0

JEROME **TAYLOR**

Full name	**Jerome Everton Taylor**
Born	**June 22, 1984, St Elizabeth, Jamaica**
Teams	**Jamaica**
Style	**Right-hand bat, right-arm fast bowler**
Test debut	**West Indies v Sri Lanka at Gros Islet 2002-03**
ODI debut	**West Indies v Sri Lanka at Kingstown 2002-03**

THE PROFILE Jerome Taylor was just 18, with a solitary limited-overs game for Jamaica to his name, when he was called into the squad for the final one-dayer of West Indies' home series against Sri Lanka in June 2003. It was the culmination of an explosive first season for Taylor, who was named the most promising fast bowler in the 2003 Carib Beer Series after picking up 21 wickets at 20.14 in six first-class matches. That haul included a second-innings 8 for 59 in Jamaica's five-wicket victory over Trinidad & Tobago. After a persistent back injury, he bounced back with 26 more wickets at 16.61 in the 2004-05 Carib Beer Cup, which – along with the prolonged contracts dispute which opened up places in the squad – helped him force his way back into international contention. He had a quiet tour of New Zealand early in 2006, bowling tightly in the one-dayers but playing only one Test. However, the inexperienced Zimbabweans found Taylor's pace too hot to handle in the Caribbean shortly afterwards: he took 2 for 19 and 4 for 24 in the first two games, winning the match award in both. He continued his good form when the Indians arrived, taking three wickets as West Indies picked up a consolation victory at the end of the one-day series, then collecting nine – including his first five-wicket haul – in vain in the deciding Test at Kingston in July 2006. He impressed in one-dayers in 2006-07, with 13 wickets in the Champions Trophy, and showed occasional signs of fire in the Tests in England in 2007, without much success: but he looked good in taking 19 wickets in four home Tests in 2008.

THE FACTS Taylor was 18 years 363 days old when he made his Test debut in June 2003: only six men have played for West Indies at a younger age, the most recent of them Garry Sobers in 1953-54 and Alfie Roberts two years later ... Taylor took 8 for 59 (10 for 81 in the match) in only his third first-class game, for Jamaica v Trinidad & Tobago at Port-of-Spain in March 2003 ... He took 5 for 48 in an ODI against Zimbabwe at Bulawayo in December 2007 ...

THE FIGURES *to 12.9.08*   www.cricinfo.com

Batting & Fielding	M	Inns	NO	Runs	HS	Avge	S/R	100	50	4s	6s	Ct	St
Tests	20	33	6	369	31	13.66	52.11	0	0	48	6	3	0
ODIs	50	19	7	133	43*	11.08	98.51	0	0	11	4	14	0
T20 Ints	4	1	1	7	7*	–	140.00	0	0	0	1	1	0
First-class	54	82	17	820	40	12.61	–	0	0	–	–	13	0

Bowling	M	Balls	Runs	Wkts	BB	Avge	RpO	S/R	5i	10m
Tests	20	3643	2186	63	5–50	34.69	3.60	57.82	2	0
ODIs	50	2602	2028	75	5–48	27.04	4.67	34.69	1	0
T20 Ints	4	72	88	7	3–6	12.57	7.33	10.28	0	0
First-class	54	8583	4616	181	8–59	25.50	3.22	47.41	10	2

ROSS **TAYLOR**

Full name	**Luteru Ross Poutoa Lote Taylor**
Born	**March 8, 1984, Lower Hutt, Wellington**
Teams	**Central Districts**
Style	**Right-hand bat, offspinner**
Test debut	**New Zealand v South Africa at Johannesburg 2007-08**
ODI debut	**New Zealand v West Indies at Napier 2005-06**

THE PROFILE Ross Taylor was singled out for attention from an early age – he captained New Zealand in the 2001-02 Under-19 World Cup – but it was only in 2005 that he made the big breakthrough. He started the year by extending his maiden first-class century to 184, then began the following season with such a bang that the selectors were bound to come calling. Fives sixes in 107 in a warm-up game against Otago were followed by an identical score in a State Shield one-dayer, also against Otago, in January 2006. He then cracked 121 against Wellington, 114 against long-suffering Otago in the semi-final, then 50 in the final against Canterbury. Taylor rounded off a fine season with 106 as CD won the State Championship final at Wellington. He finished with 537 first-class runs at 38, and 649 in one-dayers at an average of 59 and a breakneck strike rate. It all led to a call-up for the final two ODIs of West Indies' tour early in 2006, and a regular place the following season. He flogged Sri Lanka – Murali and all – for an unbeaten 128 in only his third ODI, and showed that was no fluke with an equally muscular 117 against Australia at Auckland in February 2007. All of this made him a cert for the World Cup, but he was a disappointment there, his only score above 10 being 85 against Kenya. A belated Test debut followed against South Africa in November, and he hit 120 against England in his third match, before entrancing Old Trafford with an unbeaten 154 in the return series, during which he also showed that he could fill the gap in the slips left by Stephen Fleming's retirement.

THE FACTS Only two batsmen – Martin Donnelly and Bevan Congdon (twice) – have made higher Test scores in England than Taylor's 154 not out at Manchester in 2008 ... He made his highest score of 217 for Central Districts against Otago at Napier in December 2006 ... He hit 66 from 22 balls in a Twenty20 match against Otago in January 2006 ... Taylor won the 2002 New Zealand Young Player to Lord's scholarship, following the likes of Martin Crowe and Ken Rutherford ...

THE FIGURES *to 12.9.08*   www.cricinfo.com

Batting & Fielding	M	Inns	NO	Runs	HS	Avge	S/R	100	50	4s	6s	Ct	St
Tests	8	16	1	597	154*	39.80	61.60	2	3	89	5	12	0
ODIs	45	41	8	1179	128*	35.72	84.75	2	6	118	25	28	0
T20 Ints	13	12	1	196	62	17.81	127.27	0	1	11	12	11	0
First-class	50	83	3	3060	217	38.25	–	7	16	–	–	48	0

Bowling	M	Balls	Runs	Wkts	BB	Avge	RpO	S/R	5i	10m
Tests	8	20	10	0	–	–	3.00	–	0	0
ODIs	45	30	32	0	–	–	6.40	–	0	0
T20 Ints	13	0	–	–	–	–	–	–	–	–
First-class	50	590	326	4	2–34	81.50	3.31	147.50	0	0

SACHIN **TENDULKAR**

Full name	**Sachin Ramesh Tendulkar**
Born	**April 24, 1973, Bombay (now Mumbai)**
Teams	**Mumbai, Mumbai Indians**
Style	**Right-hand bat, occasional medium-pace/legspin**
Test debut	**India v Pakistan at Karachi 1989-90**
ODI debut	**India v Pakistan at Gujranwala 1989-90**

THE PROFILE You only have to attend a one-dayer at the Wankhede Stadium, and watch the lights flicker and the floor tremble as the massive wave of applause echoes around the ground when he comes in, to realise what Sachin Tendulkar means to Mumbai ... and India. Age, and troublesome elbow and shoulder injuries, may have dimmed the light a little – he's now more of an accumulator than an artist – but he's still light-footed with bat in hand, the nearest thing to Bradman, as The Don himself recognised before his death. Sachin seems to have been around for ever: that's because he made his Test debut at 16 in 1989, shrugging off a blow on the head against Pakistan; captivated England in 1990, with a maiden Test century; and similarly enchanted Australia in 1991-92. Two more big hundreds lit up the 2007-08 series Down Under, but he was unusually subdued in Sri Lanka in mid-2008. Still, he leads the list of ODI runscorers by a country mile, and owns the records for most centuries in Tests and one-dayers too. Fitness and desire permitting, he could reach 100 hundreds in international cricket before he's done. Until he throttled back in his thirties, he usually looked to attack, but although Dravid scores just as heavily, and Sehwag is more explosive, Tendulkar's is still the wicket the opposition want most. Small, steady at the crease before a decisive move forward or back, he remains a master, and his whipped flick to fine leg is an object of wonder. He could have starred as a bowler, as he can do offbreaks, legbreaks, or dobbly medium-pacers, and remains a handy option, especially in one-dayers.

THE FACTS Tendulkar passed his childhood idol Sunil Gavaskar's record of 34 Test centuries in December 2005, with 109 v Sri Lanka at Delhi: in seven Tests afterwards his highest score was 34 ... No one is close to his record of 42 ODI centuries – Sanath Jayasuriya is next with 27 ... He has hit nine centuries against Australia in Tests, and eight in ODIs ... Tendulkar's first mark on the record books came when he was 14, in an unbroken stand of 664 with another future Test batsman, Vinod Kambli, in a school game ...

THE FIGURES to 12.9.08   www.cricinfo.com

Batting & Fielding	M	Inns	NO	Runs	HS	Avge	S/R	100	50	4s	6s	Ct	St
Tests	150	244	25	11877	248*	54.23	–	39	49	–	47	98	0
ODIs	417	407	38	16361	186*	44.33	85.49	42	89	1785	166	122	0
T20 Ints	1	1	0	10	10	10.00	83.33	0	0	2	0	1	0
First-class	250	392	40	20640	248*	58.63	–	65	95	–	–	165	0

Bowling	M	Balls	Runs	Wkts	BB	Avge	RpO	S/R	5i	10m
Tests	150	3862	2212	42	3–10	52.66	3.43	91.95	0	0
ODIs	417	8009	6795	154	5–32	44.12	5.07	52.00	2	0
T20 Ints	1	15	12	1	1–12	12.00	4.80	15.00	0	0
First-class	250	7221	4101	67	3–10	61.20	3.40	107.77	0	0

UPUL **THARANGA**

Full name	**Warushavithana Upul Tharanga**
Born	**February 2, 1985, Balapitiya**
Teams	**Nondescripts, Ruhuna**
Style	**Left-hand bat, occasional wicketkeeper**
Test debut	**Sri Lanka v India at Ahmedabad 2005-06**
ODI debut	**Sri Lanka v West Indies at Dambulla 2005-06**

THE PROFILE Upul Tharanga's call-up to Sri Lanka's one-day squad in July 2005 brightened a year marred by the Indian Ocean tsunami, which washed away his family home in Ambalangoda, a fishing town on the west coast. From an early age Tharanga, a wispy left-hander blessed with natural timing, had been tipped for the big time, playing premier-league cricket at 15 and passing seamlessly through the various national age-group squads. He first caught the eye during the Under-19 World Cup in Bangladesh early in 2004, with 117 against South Africa and 61 in 42 balls against India in the next game. Then, after a successful Under-19 tour of Pakistan, the Sri Lankan board sent him to play league cricket in Essex, where he did well for Loughton. In August 2005 he won his first one-day cap, and hit 105 against Bangladesh in only his fifth match – he celebrated modestly, aware that stiffer challenges lay ahead – then pummelled 165 against them in his third Test. Another one-day hundred followed at Christchurch in January 2006, then he lit up Lord's with 120 in the first of what became five successive defeats of England: he added 109 in the fifth of those, at Headingley, sharing an ODI record opening stand with Sanath Jayasuriya. The feature of those innings was the way he made room to drive through the off side. Other opponents might not be so accommodating, but a bright future beckoned for Tharanga, who can also keep wicket. He scored consistently during 2006-07, playing throughout the World Cup and scoring 73 in the semi-final against New Zealand, but struggled the following season and lost his place. But Tharanga is too talented to fade away, and should be back soon.

THE FACTS Tharanga and Sanath Jayasuriya put on 286 in 31.5 overs against England at Leeds in July 2006, a new first-wicket record for all ODIs: Tharanga made 109, his fourth one-day century ... He averages 47.60 in ODIs against England, but 11 v Australia (and 0 v Ireland) ... Tharanga made 165 and 71 not out in the ten-wicket defeat of Bangladesh at Bogra in March 2006 ... His record includes one ODI for the Asia XI ...

THE FIGURES *to 12.9.08*   www.cricinfo.com

Batting & Fielding	M	Inns	NO	Runs	HS	Avge	S/R	100	50	4s	6s	Ct	St
Tests	15	26	1	713	165	28.52	49.51	1	3	99	5	11	0
ODIs	69	65	0	2055	120	31.61	71.57	6	9	243	5	11	0
T20 Ints	8	8	0	114	37	14.25	116.32	0	0	10	3	1	0
First-class	59	102	3	3047	169	30.77	–	5	15	–	–	53	1

Bowling	M	Balls	Runs	Wkts	BB	Avge	RpO	S/R	5i	10m
Tests	15	0	–	–	–	–	–	–	–	–
ODIs	69	0	–	–	–	–	–	–	–	–
T20 Ints	8	0	–	–	–	–	–	–	–	–
First-class	59	18	4	0	–	–	1.33	–	0	0

CHRIS **TREMLETT**

Full name	**Christopher Timothy Tremlett**
Born	**September 2, 1981, Southampton, Hampshire**
Teams	**Hampshire**
Style	**Right-hand bat, right-arm fast bowler**
Test debut	**England v India at Lord's 2007**
ODI debut	**England v Bangladesh at Nottingham 2005**

THE PROFILE Chris Tremlett has the silent, simmering looks – and impressive sideburns – of a baddie in a spaghetti western, and bangs the ball down from an impressive height at an impressive speed. He has a fine cricket pedigree: his grandfather captained Somerset and played for England, while his father also played for Hampshire and is now their coach. But this Tremlett needed no nepotism: he took 4 for 16 on his first-class debut in 2000, and has rarely looked back since, halted only occasionally by niggling injuries (growing pains, perhaps – he's now 6ft 7ins). As he matured he was one of the first chosen for the England Academy, and narrowly missed selection for the 2004 Champions Trophy. The following year he almost marked his ODI debut at Trent Bridge with a hat-trick – the vital ball fell on the stumps without dislodging a bail – then was 12th man in the first four Tests of the epic Ashes series before loss of rhythm led to loss of form. As England's pacemen hit the treatment table in 2007 Tremlett finally got the call. He used his height well, and collected 13 wickets in three Tests against India, including Laxman three times, Dravid and Tendulkar. A side strain forced him home early from New Zealand that winter, after which, amid whispers about his temperament, Tremlett became something of a back number, playing only one ODI in 2008. He was surprisingly overlooked as Ryan Sidebottom's replacement for the Headingley Test against South Africa, when the unknown Darren Pattinson was preferred. Tremlett is also a handy batsman, although he looked a little overplaced at No. 8 for England and bagged a pair on debut.

THE FACTS Tremlett's grandfather, Maurice, played three Tests for England in 1948: his father, Tim, also played for Hampshire ... He took two wickets in successive balls on his ODI debut, against Bangladesh in June 2005: the hat-trick ball bounced on top of the stumps but didn't dislodge the bails ... He bagged a pair on his Test debut in July 2007, the first person ever to do this at Lord's ... Tremlett took 6 for 44 for Hampshire v Sussex at Hove in April 2005 ...

THE FIGURES to 12.9.08   www.cricinfo.com

Batting & Fielding	M	Inns	NO	Runs	HS	Avge	S/R	100	50	4s	6s	Ct	St
Tests	3	5	1	50	25*	12.50	43.85	0	0	5	0	1	0
ODIs	9	6	2	38	19*	9.50	58.46	0	0	2	1	2	0
T20 Ints	1	0	–	–	–	–	–	–	–	–	–	0	0
First-class	84	113	31	1559	64*	19.01	–	0	6	–	–	24	0

Bowling	M	Balls	Runs	Wkts	BB	Avge	RpO	S/R	5i	10m
Tests	3	859	386	13	3–12	29.69	2.69	66.07	0	0
ODIs	9	479	419	9	4–32	46.55	5.24	53.22	0	0
T20 Ints	1	24	45	2	2–45	22.50	11.25	12.00	0	0
First-class	84	14222	7643	274	6–44	27.89	3.22	51.90	7	0

SRI LANKA

MAHELA **UDAWATTE**

Full name **Mahela Lakmal Udawatte**
Born **July 19, 1986, Colombo**
Teams **Chilaw Marians, Wayamba**
Style **Left-hand bat, occasional offspinner**
Test debut **No Tests yet**
ODI debut **Sri Lanka v West Indies at Port-of-Spain 2007-08**

THE PROFILE Mahela Udawatte was a prolific runmaker for Ananda College, but his talents were initially overlooked by the Sri Lankan selectors, who ignored him when they chose the national Under-19 team in 2003, even though he had made more than 1000 runs at school level that season. Undaunted, Udawatte joined Chilaw Marians straight from school, and was soon opening the batting (he'd usually gone in at No. 3 before). He reeled off three hundreds in five matches in the national under-23 tournament in 2004-05: the powers-that-be could ignore him no longer, and gave him a place in the development squad. He progressed to the A team for the tour of England in 2007, after top-scoring for Chilaw Marians in the Premier Championship final against Sinhalese Sports Club in March 2006, with 67 out of 172 against an attack which included the Test fast bowlers Dilhara Fernando and Nuwan Zoysa. A powerful and attacking left-hander who likes to take on the quicks, Udawatte is seen as a future prospect for the Sri Lankan one-day side, perhaps as the eventual replacement for Sanath Jayasuriya. Udawatte is highly rated, not least by Sri Lanka's captain Mahela Jayawardene, and earned a place on the tour of West Indies early in 2008, where he made 73 in his third one-day international. An innings of 67 followed in his only outing in the Asia Cup, then he made a mature 43 against India at the Premadasa Stadium in Colombo to help set up a winning total in a rain-affected match.

THE FACTS Udawatte hit 168, the higher of his two first-class centuries, for Chilaw Marians against Bloomfield in Colombo in February 2008 ... He was out for a duck in his first ODI, against West Indies in Trinidad in April 2008, but made 73 in his third, in St Lucia, and 67 in his fourth, against the UAE in the Asia Cup in June ...

THE FIGURES *to 12.9.08*   www.cricinfo.com

Batting & Fielding	M	Inns	NO	Runs	HS	Avge	S/R	100	50	4s	6s	Ct	St
Tests	0	0	–	–	–	–	–	–	–	–	–	–	–
ODIs	5	5	0	197	73	39.40	71.63	0	2	20	1	0	0
T20 Ints	0	0	–	–	–	–	–	–	–	–	–	–	–
First-class	41	78	4	2239	168	30.25	–	2	15	–	–	23	0

Bowling	M	Balls	Runs	Wkts	BB	Avge	RpO	S/R	5i	10m
Tests	0	0	–	–	–	–	–	–	–	–
ODIs	5	0	–	–	–	–	–	–	–	–
T20 Ints	0	0	–	–	–	–	–	–	–	–
First-class	41	96	76	3	2–31	25.33	4.75	32.00	0	0

UMAR GUL

Full name	**Umar Gul**
Born	**April 14, 1984, Peshawar, North-Western Frontier Province**
Teams	**Peshawar, Habib Bank, Kolkata Knight Riders**
Style	**Right-hand bat, right-arm fast-medium bowler**
Test debut	**Pakistan v Bangladesh at Karachi 2003-04**
ODI debut	**Pakistan v Zimbabwe at Sharjah 2002-03**

THE PROFILE Umar Gul had played only nine first-class games when he was drafted into the Pakistan side at 19, in the wake of a miserable 2003 World Cup campaign. He performed admirably on Sharjah's flat tracks, maintaining good discipline and obtaining appreciable outswing with the new ball. He can also nip the ball back from outside off. He had a gentle introduction to Test cricket, collecting 15 wickets against Bangladesh later in 2003, including four in each innings at Multan. Sterner challenges followed, but he starred in his only Test of India's historic "comeback" tour of Pakistan, at Lahore in April 2004. Gul, who had been disparaged by some as the "Peshawar Rickshaw" to Shoaib Akhtar's "Rawalpindi Express", tore through India's imposing top order, moving the ball both ways off the seam at a sharp pace. His 5 for 31 in the first innings gave Pakistan the early initiative, which they drove home to level the series. Stress fractures in the back kept him out of the third Test, and it was two years before he returned. He managed only two wickets in the Tests in Sri Lanka, but was retained for the subsequent tour of England – where, in the absence of several senior seamers, he looked the best of the rest, particularly enjoying the conditions at Headingley, taking five wickets in the first innings as the others struggled. He maintained his progress in 2006-07, taking nine wickets in the first Test against West Indies at Lahore before missing the series in South Africa with a knee injury. He was back for the World Cup, and was one of the few to return with reputation intact. Back trouble, then a rib injury, restricted him in 2008.

THE FACTS Umar Gul took 6 for 96 in his only Test against India, but averages 106.00 with the ball against Sri Lanka ... His best bowling figures are 8 for 78, for Peshawar v Karachi Urban at Peshawar in October 2005 ... Gul claimed 5 for 46 on his first-class debut, for Pakistan International Airlines v ADBP at Karachi in his only match in 2000-01, then took 45 wickets at 18.62 in 2001-02, his first full season of domestic cricket ...

THE FIGURES to 12.9.08   www.cricinfo.com

Batting & Fielding	M	Inns	NO	Runs	HS	Avge	S/R	100	50	4s	6s	Ct	St
Tests	16	20	2	136	26	7.55	38.09	0	0	19	3	4	0
ODIs	48	16	7	73	17*	8.11	59.83	0	0	6	2	6	0
T20 Ints	9	2	1	0	0*	0.00	0.00	0	0	0	0	4	0
First-class	41	46	7	424	46	10.87	–	0	0	–	–	10	0

Bowling	M	Balls	Runs	Wkts	BB	Avge	RpO	S/R	5i	10m
Tests	16	3612	2114	67	5–31	31.55	3.51	53.91	3	0
ODIs	48	2221	1821	64	5–17	28.45	4.91	34.70	1	0
T20 Ints	9	202	181	13	4–25	13.92	5.37	15.53	0	0
First-class	41	8445	4851	190	8–78	25.53	3.44	44.44	12	1

ROBIN **UTHAPPA**

Full name **Robin Venu Uthappa**
Born **November 11, 1985, Coorg, Karnataka**
Teams **Karnataka, Mumbai Indians**
Style **Right-hand bat, occasional right-arm medium-pacer**
Test debut **No Tests yet**
ODI debut **India v England at Indore 2005-06**

THE PROFILE The tall and robust Robin Uthappa was long spoken of as a batsman with an international future. Although his record in domestic first-class cricket was modest before a stellar 2006-07 season – 1084 runs at 57.05, with five centuries – his limited-overs figures were more imposing. Originally a wicketkeeper-batsman, Uthappa gave up the big gloves to concentrate on batting, and now occasionally bowls some medium-pace. As a batsman he has always been attractive to watch – hard-hitting, with all the shots, and unafraid to hit the ball in the air. He first caught the eye with a brilliant 66 in a losing cause for India B in the Challenger Trophy (trial matches for the national squad) at Mumbai early in 2005, against an attack that included Zaheer Khan, Murali Kartik and RP Singh. But it was in the next edition of the same tournament, at Mohali in October 2005, when he really arrived in the big league. After VVS Laxman had made a century for India A, Uthappa cracked a matchwinning 116 from only 93 balls for the B team. It won him a place instead of Virender Sehwag in the final one-dayer against England early in 2006, and he capitalised with a well-paced 86. His next few outings were less spectacular, apart from a matchwinning half-century at The Oval in September 2007. His first 11 ODI innings produced four fifties, but despite being a regular throughout 2007-08 he managed only one more score above 50 in 23 further attempts, although he did reasonably well in the inaugural IPL season, with 320 runs for Mumbai Indians.

THE FACTS Uthappa's 86 against England at Indore in April 2006 was the highest score by an Indian on ODI debut, beating Brijesh Patel's 82 against England at Leeds in 1974 ... He made 162 for Karnataka v Madhya Pradesh at Bangalore in November 2004: he also thumped 160 in a one-day game against Kerala at Margao in January 2005 ... After only one first-class century in his first four seasons Uthappa hit five in ten weeks in 2006-07 ... For India B v India A at Mohali in October 2005 he sped from 61 to 101 in the space of 14 balls ...

THE FIGURES to 12.9.08   www.cricinfo.com

Batting & Fielding	M	Inns	NO	Runs	HS	Avge	S/R	100	50	4s	6s	Ct	St
Tests	0	0	–	–	–	–	–	–	–	–	–	–	–
ODIs	38	34	5	786	86	27.10	91.92	0	5	94	16	15	0
T20 Ints	9	8	0	149	50	18.62	115.50	0	1	14	6	1	0
First-class	42	69	3	2620	162	39.69	–	6	16	–	–	44	0

Bowling	M	Balls	Runs	Wkts	BB	Avge	RpO	S/R	5i	10m
Tests	0	0	–	–	–	–	–	–	–	–
ODIs	38	0	–	–	–	–	–	–	–	–
T20 Ints	9	0	–	–	–	–	–	–	–	–
First-class	42	156	86	2	1–7	43.00	3.30	78.00	0	0

SRI LANKA

CHAMINDA **VAAS**

Full name	**Warnakulasuriya Patabendige Ushantha Joseph Chaminda Vaas**
Born	**January 27, 1974, Mattumagala**
Teams	**Colts, Basnahira North, Deccan Chargers**
Style	**Left-hand bat, fast-medium left-arm bowler**
Test debut	**Sri Lanka v Pakistan at Kandy 1994-95**
ODI debut	**Sri Lanka v India at Rajkot 1993-94**

THE PROFILE Waspish left-armer Chaminda Vaas – possessor of the most initials and longest name in Test cricket – is easily the most penetrative and successful new-ball bowler Sri Lanka have had. He swings and seams the ball with skill, his trademark delivery being the late indipper. However, he also bowls a well-disguised offcutter, and more recently added reverse-swing to his armoury, a skill that has made him a consistent wicket-taker even on bland subcontinental pitches. As long ago as March 1995 he outbowled New Zealand's seamers on a Napier greentop, taking ten wickets to hasten Sri Lanka to their first Test win overseas. In 2001-02 he made a quantum leap, taking 26 wickets in the 3-0 rout of West Indies, and becoming only the second fast bowler, after Imran Khan, to take 14 in a match on the subcontinent. He's consistent in one-dayers too, and given to spectacular bursts of wicket-taking: he was the first to take eight in an ODI, as Zimbabwe were blown away for 38 in Colombo in December 2001, and also uniquely claimed a hat-trick with the first three balls of the match against Bangladesh in the 2003 World Cup. Vaas has taken over 750 wickets in international cricket, and is easily Sri Lanka's most successful bowler after Muttiah Muralitharan. His approach to his batting is equally whole-hearted: he scored over 2500 runs in Tests before finally making a century in his 97th match, and faced more balls in the Tests in England in 2006 than any of Sri Lanka's specialist batsmen.

THE FACTS Vaas's figures of 8 for 19 against Zimbabwe in Colombo in December 2001 are the best in all ODIs ... That included a hat-trick, and he took another with the first three balls of the match against Bangladesh at Pietermaritzburg in the 2003 World Cup: at the end of the first over they were 5 for 4 ... Vaas finally made a century, in his 97th Test – the longest anyone had had to wait at the time (previously 71 Tests, by Jason Gillespie; Anil Kumble broke the record later in 2007) ... His record includes one ODI for the Asia XI ...

THE FIGURES to 12.9.08   www.cricinfo.com

Batting & Fielding	M	Inns	NO	Runs	HS	Avge	S/R	100	50	4s	6s	Ct	St
Tests	107	156	32	2998	100*	24.17	43.72	1	13	366	15	30	0
ODIs	322	220	72	2025	50*	13.68	72.52	0	1	127	22	60	0
T20 Ints	6	2	1	33	21	33.00	80.48	0	0	1	0	0	0
First-class	185	251	53	5072	134	25.61	–	4	23	–	–	53	0

Bowling	M	Balls	Runs	Wkts	BB	Avge	RpO	S/R	5i	10m
Tests	107	22664	10201	348	7–71	29.31	2.70	65.12	12	2
ODIs	322	15775	11014	400	8–19	27.53	4.18	39.43	4	0
T20 Ints	6	132	128	6	2–14	21.43	5.81	22.00	0	0
First-class	185	35209	16170	648	7–54	24.95	2.75	54.33	27	3

MICHAEL **VANDORT**

Full name **Michael Graydon Vandort**
Born **January 19, 1980, Colombo**
Teams **Colombo Cricket Club, Wayamba**
Style **Left-hand bat, occasional right-arm medium-pacer**
Test debut **Sri Lanka v Bangladesh at Colombo 2001-02**
ODI debut **Sri Lanka v Australia at Melbourne 2005-06**

THE PROFILE Michael Vandort, a 6ft 5ins left-hander fond of the off-drive, emerged in 2001 after a string of impressive performances for Colombo Cricket Club and Sri Lanka A. A late developer, he played only once for his school, St Joseph's College, but nonetheless quickly made an impression in first-class cricket. He was picked for the Board XI against the Indians in August 2001, and earned himself a berth in the Test squad with an impressive 116 against the proven new-ball attack of Javagal Srinath and Venkatesh Prasad. He did not play in that series, but was given a chance against Bangladesh. He duly scored a century in the second Test, but with the Jayasuriya-Atapattu opening combination seemingly unassailable had to wait more than three years before another sniff. An injury to Jayasuriya paved the way for his one-day debut, at Melbourne in February 2006: he top-scored with a gritty 48, but Jayasuriya returned, and Vandort hasn't had an ODI since, although he did play two Tests against Bangladesh shortly afterwards. With Jayasuriya in short-lived retirement Vandort got his chance in England in 2006, and starred in defeat at Edgbaston, last out for a dogged 105 in the second innings. He failed to reach double figures in his other three knocks, though, and missed the one-day demolitions that followed – he's a good slip fielder but is rather ponderous in the field, which counts against him in the one-day arena. When Atapattu sat out the Tests against Bangladesh in mid-2007, Vandort got another chance ... and another century, and added 138 against England at the SSC in December 2007. After that, though, he passed 50 only once in ten attempts in Tests, leaving his position under threat again.

THE FACTS Seven of Vandort's first nine Tests were against Bangladesh: he averages 64.37 against them (but 7.80 v India) ... He scored 100 on his first-class debut, for Colombo Cricket Club v Kurunegala in Colombo in March 1999 ... When still only 18 Vandort made 226 and 225 in successive matches for Colombo in 1998-99, v Panadura and Singha ...

THE FIGURES *to 12.9.08*   www.cricinfo.com

Batting & Fielding	M	Inns	NO	Runs	HS	Avge	S/R	100	50	4s	6s	Ct	St
Tests	19	31	2	1094	140	37.72	48.21	4	4	127	5	6	0
ODIs	1	1	0	48	48	48.00	41.02	0	0	3	0	0	0
T20 Ints	0	0	–	–	–	–	–	–	–	–	–	–	–
First-class	127	214	14	6701	226	33.50	–	15	29	–	–	96	0

Bowling	M	Balls	Runs	Wkts	BB	Avge	RpO	S/R	5i	10m
Tests	19	0	–	–	–	–	–	–	–	–
ODIs	1	0	–	–	–	–	–	–	–	–
T20 Ints	0	0	–	–	–	–	–	–	–	–
First-class	127	61	53	1	1–46	53.00	5.21	61.00	0	0

MICHAEL **VAUGHAN**

ENGLAND

Full name **Michael Paul Vaughan**
Born **October 29, 1974, Manchester, Lancashire**
Teams **Yorkshire**
Style **Right-hand bat, offspinner**
Test debut **England v South Africa at Johannesburg 1999-2000**
ODI debut **England v Sri Lanka at Dambulla 2000-01**

THE PROFILE In September 2005 Michael Vaughan secured his place in English cricket's hall of fame, becoming the first captain to lift the Ashes since Mike Gatting in 1986-87. It was the culmination of a five-year journey for a man whose captaincy had become as classy and composed as the batting technique that briefly carried him to the top of the world rankings. He had faced his first ball in Test cricket with England 2 for 4 on a damp flyer at Johannesburg late in 1999, and drew immediate comparisons with Michael Atherton for his calm aura at the crease. But he soon demonstrated he was more than just a like-for-like replacement. He blossomed magnificently, playing with a freedom Atherton never dared to approach. He conjured 900 runs in seven Tests against Sri Lanka and India in 2002, the prelude to a formidable series in Australia – three tons, 633 runs. He inherited the Test captaincy in 2003 when Nasser Hussain abdicated, having spotted Vaughan's burgeoning man-management abilities. After a stutter in Sri Lanka, he confirmed the arrival of a new era by routing West Indies in the Caribbean. Returning home, England swept seven out of seven Tests in 2004, won in South Africa, then triumphed in the greatest Ashes series of them all. An old injury flared up, wrecking his 2006 season and keeping him out of the Ashes rematch, but he hung doggedly in there. He retired from ODIs after England's lacklustre World Cup, but was back to his silky best in the 2007 home Tests, stroking a superb 103 against West Indies at Leeds and an equally effortless 124 – ended by a freak dismissal – against India at Nottingham. However, the runs dried up in 2008, and after making only 40 in the first three Tests against South Africa – and seeing the series lost – Vaughan stepped down as captain, although he kept his playing contract.

THE FACTS Vaughan was captain in 51 Tests, winning 26: only Mike Atherton (54) led England more often, and no-one has more victories (Peter May is next with 20) ... Vaughan averages 72.57 in Tests against India, but only 14 v Zimbabwe ... He averaged 50.98 before he was captain, and only 36.02 when he was ...

THE FIGURES *to 12.9.08*   www.cricinfo.com

Batting & Fielding	M	Inns	NO	Runs	HS	Avge	S/R	100	50	4s	6s	Ct	St
Tests	82	147	9	5719	197	41.44	51.13	18	18	742	22	44	0
ODIs	86	83	10	1982	90*	27.15	68.39	0	16	204	13	25	0
T20 Ints	2	2	0	27	27	13.50	122.72	0	0	4	0	0	0
First-class	261	459	27	16122	197	37.31	–		42	68	–	–	118	0

Bowling	M	Balls	Runs	Wkts	BB	Avge	RpO	S/R	5i	10m
Tests	82	978	561	6	2–71	93.50	3.44	163.00	0	0
ODIs	86	796	649	16	4–22	40.56	4.89	49.75	0	0
T20 Ints	2	0	–	–	–	–	–	–	–	–
First-class	261	9306	5198	114	4–39	45.59	3.35	81.63	0	0

DANIEL **VETTORI**

Full name	**Daniel Luca Vettori**
Born	**January 27, 1979, Auckland**
Teams	**Northern Districts, Delhi Daredevils**
Style	**Left-hand bat, left-arm orthodox spinner**
Test debut	**New Zealand v England at Wellington 1996-97**
ODI debut	**New Zealand v Sri Lanka at Christchurch 1996-97**

THE PROFILE Daniel Vettori is probably the best left-arm spinner around – an assessment reinforced by his selection in the World XI for the ICC Super Series in Australia late in 2005 – and the only cloud on his horizon is a susceptibility to injury, particularly in the bowler's danger area of the back. He seemed to have recovered from one stress fracture, which led to a dip in form in 2003, but after just a couple of matches in 2006 for Warwickshire, his second English county, Vettori was on the plane home nursing another one. When fit, he still exhibits the enticing flight and guile that made him New Zealand's youngest Test player in 1996-97. There were signs on the 2004 tour of England that he was back to his best after his mini-slump, and he butchered the Bangladeshis shortly afterwards, taking 20 wickets in two Tests. After starting at No. 11, blinking nervously through his glasses, he has improved his batting, to the point that he has made two centuries – one of them New Zealand's fastest in Tests, an 82-ball effort against the admittedly hopeless Zimbabweans at Harare in August 2005. He helped himself to his 200th Test wicket in the same two-day massacre. Vettori atoned for an underwhelming performance at the 2003 World Cup – two wickets for 259 – with 16 in 2007, the most for New Zealand as they marched to the semi-final. He still hasn't passed 14 with the bat in 17 World Cup matches, though. Vettori was confirmed as Stephen Fleming's successor as captain late in 2007, but his early Tests in charge were chastening experiences – he presided over series defeats by South Africa and England (twice), with only two facile victories over Bangladesh to lighten the gloom.

THE FACTS Vettori made his first-class debut in 1996-97, for Northern Districts against the England tourists: his maiden first-class victim was Nasser Hussain ... Three weeks later Vettori made his Test debut, NZ's youngest-ever player at 18 years 10 days: his first wicket was Hussain again ... Vettori has taken 52 Test wickets against Australia, but only four v Pakistan, costing 100.25 each ... His record includes a Test and four ODIs for the World XI ...

THE FIGURES to 12.9.08   www.cricinfo.com

Batting & Fielding	M	Inns	NO	Runs	HS	Avge	S/R	100	50	4s	6s	Ct	St
Tests	83	123	20	2745	137*	26.65	56.75	2	16	360	8	39	0
ODIs	222	136	42	1406	83	14.95	79.56	0	3	107	7	59	0
T20 Ints	9	8	2	52	17*	8.66	123.80	0	0	6	0	3	0
First-class	132	186	27	4388	137*	27.59	–	4	25	–	–	62	0

Bowling	M	Balls	Runs	Wkts	BB	Avge	RpO	S/R	5i	10m
Tests	83	19887	8851	257	7–87	34.43	2.67	77.38	15	3
ODIs	222	10478	7294	230	5–7	31.71	4.17	45.55	2	0
T20 Ints	9	216	203	13	4–20	15.61	5.63	16.61	0	0
First-class	132	29997	13488	420	7–87	32.11	2.69	71.42	25	3

ADAM **VOGES**

Full name	**Adam Charles Voges**
Born	**October 4, 1979, Subiaco, Perth, Western Australia**
Teams	**Western Australia, Nottinghamshire**
Style	**Right-hand bat, slow left-arm unorthodox spinner**
Test debut	**No Tests yet**
ODI debut	**Australia v New Zealand at Hamilton 2006-07**

THE PROFILE Part of Western Australia's big-hitting middle order, Adam Voges (it's pronounced Vo-jes) is most famous for his maiden one-day century in 2004-05, a 62-ball effort against New South Wales – batting at No. 3, he didn't enter until the 30th over – which was the fastest in Australian domestic history at the time. He not only broke a record, but also clattered a sponsor's sign with one of his seven sixes. Voges collected many plaudits for that innings, and a $50,000 bonus for his superb aim ... but was left out for the next Pura Cup match. He did return later in the season, produced his first hundred, and finished with an eye-catching double of 362 four-day runs at 72.40, plus 287 in one-dayers. Next season he passed 600 first-class runs: his prize was a return to the Academy, after captaining them in India in 2004. The only blemish was a brief suspension for missing a training session, but that was forgotten the following season when, after Damien Martyn's unexpected retirement, Voges was called into Australia's squad for the third Ashes Test on his home turf at the WACA. He didn't play – Andrew Symonds got the place instead, and made it his own – but Voges kept his name in the frame by ending the season with 630 runs at 57. He made his ODI debut in New Zealand, but didn't quite do enough to win a World Cup spot. He is a fine fielder, but his left-arm wrist-spin hasn't had much chance yet. He had an unspectacular season with Nottinghamshire in 2008.

THE FACTS Voges's 100 not out in 62 balls for Western Australia against NSW in October 2004 was the fastest century in Australian domestic one-day cricket at the time ... His highest score is 180 for WA against Tasmania at Hobart in December 2007 ... Voges learnt of his call-up to the Australian Test squad in 2006-07 while playing for a Cricket Australia XI against the England tourists: he was tapped on the shoulder and asked to leave the field, and admitted "I thought I was in trouble" ...

THE FIGURES to 12.9.08   www.cricinfo.com

Batting & Fielding	M	Inns	NO	Runs	HS	Avge	S/R	100	50	4s	6s	Ct	St
Tests	0	0	–	–	–	–	–	–	–	–	–	–	–
ODIs	1	1	1	16	16*	–	160.00	0	0	0	1	1	0
T20 Ints	2	1	0	26	26	26.00	130.00	0	0	3	0	1	0
First-class	54	91	13	2986	180	38.28	49.99	7	12	–	–	63	0

Bowling	M	Balls	Runs	Wkts	BB	Avge	RpO	S/R	5i	10m
Tests	0	0	–	–	–	–	–	–	–	–
ODIs	1	18	33	0	–	–	11.00	–	0	0
T20 Ints	2	12	5	2	2–5	2.50	2.50	6.00	0	0
First-class	54	1578	883	22	4–92	40.13	3.35	71.72	0	0

WAHAB RIAZ

Full name	**Wahab Riaz**
Born	**June 28, 1985, Lahore, Punjab**
Teams	**Lahore, National Bank**
Style	**Right-hand bat, left-arm fast-medium bowler**
Test debut	**No Tests yet**
ODI debut	**Pakistan v Zimbabwe at Sheikhupura 2007-08**

THE PROFILE   Left-armer Wahab Riaz has benefited from Pakistan's chronic luck with fast bowlers. With Shoaib Akhtar and Mohammad Asif missing more often than not, for various weird and wonderful reasons, and with Umar Gul prone to injury, Riaz made it into the national squad quicker than he might have reasonably expected. He made a good start early in 2008, taking two good wickets (Tatenda Taibu and Sean Williams) in his first one-day international against Zimbabwe, and adding five more scalps in two outings against Bangladesh, including 3 for 22 in the Kitply Cup at Mirpur. But then reality intruded, in the shape of India's batsmen: two days after he'd beaten up the Banglas, Riaz was knocked about himself, conceding 86 runs in 9.2 overs before being removed from the attack for sending down two beamers. He did have the satisfaction of dismissing both openers, though. Then, in the Asia Cup, the Sri Lankans also took advantage of Riaz's lack of variety. He is a bustling bowler, more conventional in approach than Pakistan's other left-arm newcomer Sohail Tanvir, but he is a bit sharper than he looks. He is a keen learner, and regularly seeks out Wasim Akram for tips and advice, showing that he is a good judge too.

THE FACTS   Wahab Riaz took a wicket (Tatenda Taibu of Zimbabwe) with his third ball in international cricket, in an ODI at Sheikhupura in February 2008 ... Against India at Dhaka in June 2008 Riaz conceded 86 runs in 9.2 overs, the third-most expensive analysis for Pakistan in ODIs ... Riaz took 6 for 76 (11 for 190 in the match) for Hyderabad at Sialkot in April 2004 ... He also took 10 for 149 against Sialkot for National Bank in December 2007 ...

THE FIGURES *to 12.9.08*   www.cricinfo.com

Batting & Fielding	M	Inns	NO	Runs	HS	Avge	S/R	100	50	4s	6s	Ct	St
Tests	0	0	–	–	–	–	–	–	–	–	–	–	–
ODIs	5	4	1	4	3	1.33	28.57	0	0	0	0	1	0
T20 Ints	1	0	–	–	–	–	–	–	–	–	–	0	0
First-class	40	57	9	751	68	15.64	–	0	3	–	–	10	0

Bowling	M	Balls	Runs	Wkts	BB	Avge	RpO	S/R	5i	10m
Tests	0	0	–	–	–	–	–	–	–	–
ODIs	5	241	202	10	3–22	20.20	5.02	24.10	0	0
T20 Ints	1	12	7	1	1–7	7.00	3.50	12.00	0	0
First-class	40	7182	3975	139	6–64	28.59	3.32	51.66	7	2

MALINDA **WARNAPURA**

Full name	**Basnayake Shalith Malinda Warnapura**
Born	**May 26, 1979, Colombo**
Teams	**Colts, Basnahira South**
Style	**Left-hand bat, offspinner**
Test debut	**Sri Lanka v Bangladesh at Colombo 2007**
ODI debut	**Sri Lanka v Pakistan at Abu Dhabi 2007**

THE PROFILE A nuggety left-hander strong on the off side, Malinda Warnapura took his time to make his mark in international cricket, despite an impressive pedigree (his uncle, Bandula Warnapura, captained Sri Lanka). This Warnapura started his first-class career in 1998, but it was not until late in 2006 that he really arrived. Chosen for the Sri Lanka A side that took part in India's Duleep Trophy tournament, he made 421 runs in three matches, including 65 and 149 not out in the final, won by North Zone. Despite this he missed the senior tour of New Zealand that followed, then struggled with illness when the A team visited the West Indies. But when Bangladesh A toured Sri Lanka early in 2007 he was back to his best, stroking a career-best 242 in the first unofficial Test, and followed that with a hundred in one of the one-dayers to show he was adept at the shorter game as well. At 28, he was handed a first Test cap when Bangladesh came calling in June 2007 ... and was dismissed by the only ball he received on his debut. But in the absence of Upul Tharanga (injured foot) and Marvan Atapattu (injured pride, after being kept on the bench throughout the World Cup) Warnapura retained his place, and made an assured 82 in another innings victory in the second Test. Next he made 120 against West Indies in Guyana, and started the Indian series in July 2008 with 115 in Colombo. He is an accumulator of runs, particularly strong square on the off side, but needs to polish his footwork and free up his backlift, which is sometimes too close to his body.

THE FACTS Warnapura scored 242 for Sri Lanka A v Bangladesh A in Colombo in March 2007, sharing a stand of 376 with Thilan Samaraweera ... On his Test debut, against Bangladesh in Colombo three months later, he was out first ball ... In March 2008 Warnapura scored the first Test century at Providence, in Guyana, the 97th ground to stage Test cricket ... His uncle, Bandula Warnapura, captained Sri Lanka in their inaugural Test, against England in 1981-82 ...

THE FIGURES to 12.9.08   www.cricinfo.com

Batting & Fielding	M	Inns	NO	Runs	HS	Avge	S/R	100	50	4s	6s	Ct	St
Tests	7	11	1	542	120	54.20	58.72	2	4	65	1	11	0
ODIs	3	3	0	35	30	11.66	46.05	0	0	5	0	3	0
T20 Ints	0	0	–	–	–	–	–	–	–	–	–	–	–
First-class	127	191	20	6262	242	36.61	–	14	31	–	–	92	0

Bowling	M	Balls	Runs	Wkts	BB	Avge	RpO	S/R	5i	10m
Tests	7	0	–	–	–	–	–	–	–	–
ODIs	3	0	–	–	–	–	–	–	–	–
T20 Ints	0	0	–	–	–	–	–	–	–	–
First-class	127	6636	3090	115	6–22	26.86	2.79	57.70	4	0

SHANE **WATSON**

AUSTRALIA

Full name	**Shane Robert Watson**
Born	**June 17, 1981, Ipswich, Queensland**
Teams	**Queensland, Rajasthan Royals**
Style	**Right-hand bat, right-arm fast-medium bowler**
Test debut	**Australia v Pakistan at Sydney 2004-05**
ODI debut	**Australia v South Africa at Centurion 2001-02**

THE PROFILE Hulking, blond and spiky-haired, Shane Watson should be the shiny embodiment of modern-day Australian cricket ... if only that body didn't keep cracking up. He started young: Queensland Under-17s at 15, the Academy, nipping off at 19 to Tasmania, where he hit his maiden hundred in his fifth match. He missed the 2003 World Cup with stress fractures of the back: until then his batting lacked nothing in swagger, if a little in gap-finding artifice, while his bowling was willing if docile. He bounced back in 2003-04 with four hundreds for Tasmania. Watson remains the cleanest of hitters and, several remodelled actions later, decidedly sharp. Back home in Queensland (Tassie was too cold) he was tipped to become Australia's next champion allrounder by their last one: "A fine physical specimen, good athlete – just give him time," said Alan Davidson in 2002. Watson was overlooked for the 2005 Ashes, but his stock rose anyway as Andrew Flintoff highlighted the benefits of a genuine allrounder. A dislocated shoulder ruined 2005-06, and he watched his mate Andrew Symonds fill in. Watson returned for the one-dayers in South Africa early in 2006, but missed the Tests – although 201 in the Pura Cup final eased the pain. There was more pain later in the year, as a persistent hamstring injury kept him out of the Ashes rematch, but he bounced back to play an allround role in the defence of the World Cup, and announced that he wanted to replace the retired Justin Langer as Australia's Test opener. He hasn't done that (yet), but did score a maiden ODI ton from the top of the order against West Indies in June 2008.

THE FACTS Watson hit 201 in the 2005-06 Pura Cup final demolition of Victoria before retiring hurt; uniquely, four batsmen passed 150 in Queensland's 900 for 6 ... He averaged 145 at the 2007 World Cup, thanks to five not-outs, and scored at a mind-boggling 170.58 runs per 100 balls ... Watson has played for Hampshire, alongside Shane Warne: in 2005 he scored 203 not out for them against Warwickshire at the Rose Bowl ...

THE FIGURES to 12.9.08   www.cricinfo.com

Batting & Fielding	M	Inns	NO	Runs	HS	Avge	S/R	100	50	4s	6s	Ct	St
Tests	3	4	0	81	31	20.25	38.20	0	0	8	0	0	0
ODIs	72	54	18	1263	126	35.08	81.90	1	7	113	17	19	0
T20 Ints	3	2	1	21	17*	21.00	100.00	0	0	1	1	0	0
First-class	62	107	14	4371	203*	47.06	–	12	20	–	–	48	0

Bowling	M	Balls	Runs	Wkts	BB	Avge	RpO	S/R	5i	10m
Tests	3	186	123	2	1–25	61.50	3.96	93.00	0	0
ODIs	72	2809	2247	70	4–39	32.10	4.79	40.12	0	0
T20 Ints	3	51	71	3	1–17	23.66	8.35	17.00	0	0
First-class	62	5757	3379	112	6–32	30.16	3.52	51.40	2	1

CAMERON **WHITE**

Full name	**Cameron Leon White**
Born	**August 18, 1983, Bairnsdale, Victoria**
Teams	**Victoria, Bangalore Royal Challengers**
Style	**Right-hand bat, legspinner**
Test debut	**No Tests yet**
ODI debut	**Australia v World XI at Melbourne 2005-06**

THE PROFILE   Fair-haired and level-headed, Cameron "Bear" White long seemed destined to play a significant role in Australia's future. Only the precise nature of that role baffled his admirers. Nagging legspinner? Solid middle-order bat? Intuitive skipper? Or a bit of all three? The over-eager Shane Warne comparisons that accompanied his arrival have long since died away. Indeed, White is a peculiarly unAustralian leggie – tall and robust, relying on changes of pace and a handy wrong'un rather than prodigious turn or flight. He bowls a good line, and has a neat line in self-deprecation too: "There's no flippers or anything exciting like that," he once admitted. What is not in doubt is his cricket sense, nor his maturity. Victoria's youngest-ever captain at 20, he won rave reviews for his cool head and handling of more experienced colleagues. White played his first ODIs in the Super Series late in 2005. He made little impact, and lost his national contract after a mediocre season. But he had a wonderful time with the bat for Somerset in 2006 (David Hookes, the late Victorian coach, always felt White's best chance of representing Australia was to earn a top-six spot). He feasted on county bowlers, and smashed a Twenty20 ton in 55 balls. That preceded a better home summer, although he was sometimes criticised for not bowling himself enough. He was recalled for the annual one-day triangular at the start of 2007: his bowling lacked control, and batting opportunities were limited. He was overlooked for the World Cup, but there was some good news – he got his national contract back for 2007-08.

THE FACTS   White made 260 not out for Somerset v Derbyshire in August 2006, the highest individual score in the fourth innings of any first-class match, beating a record formerly held by Hansie Cronje and Denis Compton ... White took 6 for 66 (10 for 136 in the match) for Victoria v Western Australia at Melbourne in March 2003 ... Ten of his 13 first-class centuries were scored for Somerset ... In his first Twenty20 international, against England at Sydney in January 2007, White hit 40 not out in 20 balls ...

THE FIGURES to 12.9.08   www.cricinfo.com

Batting & Fielding	M	Inns	NO	Runs	HS	Avge	S/R	100	50	4s	6s	Ct	St
Tests	0	0	–	–	–	–	–	–	–	–	–	–	–
ODIs	21	14	5	236	45	26.22	108.75	0	0	12	10	9	0
T20 Ints	2	2	2	50	40*	–	192.30	0	0	2	4	2	0
First-class	92	153	19	5557	260*	41.47	–	13	24	–	–	87	0

Bowling	M	Balls	Runs	Wkts	BB	Avge	RpO	S/R	5i	10m
Tests	0	0	–	–	–	–	–	–	–	–
ODIs	21	262	277	9	3–5	30.77	6.34	29.11	0	0
T20 Ints	2	18	19	1	1–11	19.00	6.33	18.00	0	0
First-class	92	10506	6158	161	6–66	38.24	3.51	65.25	2	1

LUKE **WRIGHT**

ENGLAND

Full name	**Luke James Wright**
Born	**March 7, 1985, Grantham, Lincolnshire**
Teams	**Sussex**
Style	**Right-hand bat, right-arm fast medium bowler**
Test debut	**No Tests yet**
ODI debut	**England v India at The Oval 2007**

THE PROFILE He's an attacking batsman who can bowl medium-fast, so it's no great surprise that Luke Wright admires Andrew Flintoff, or that he hoped to follow him into the England side. That ambition was realised when Flintoff, among others, was injured, and Wright was called up to play against India in September 2007. Like Freddie, Wright marked his ODI debut by scoring 50, an exciting innings which started with a four and a six. He had a quiet time at the World Twenty20 – 43 runs in five innings and no wickets – and also made little impression during a run in the one-day side, although his strike rate was impressive: he will have to improve to play a major role in the exciting new Pietersen era. Wright actually made his first-class debut for Leicestershire *against* Sussex in 2003, and although Mushtaq Ahmed nabbed him for a duck Sussex signed him up for the following season. He repaid them with a debut century, against his old Loughborough mates, but had played only ten first-class games when he was sent to the West Indies with England A early in 2006. Wright's career really took off the following year, when he was the leading Twenty20 Cup runscorer with 346, including a pyrotechnic 103 in just 45 balls against Kent. That earned him his county cap – and that national call, which he celebrated by hammering 125 in 73 balls in a 40-over game against Gloucestershire. He also made a dramatic start to the 2008 season, with an undefeated 155 for Sussex against MCC. So far his bowling has made less of a mark, and it's probably as a hard-hitting batsman that he will make his name.

THE FACTS Wright made 103 from 45 balls (11 fours, six sixes) in a Twenty20 Cup match against Kent at Canterbury in June 2007 ... He hit 155 not out for Sussex v MCC at Lord's in the first match of the 2008 season ... Wright scored 100 on his debut for Sussex (his second first-class match), v Loughborough UCCE in May 2004 ... He took a hat-trick for England Under-19s v South Africa in a one-day game at Hove in August 2003 ...

THE FIGURES *to 12.9.08* www.cricinfo.com

Batting & Fielding	M	Inns	NO	Runs	HS	Avge	S/R	100	50	4s	6s	Ct	St
Tests	0	0	–	–	–	–	–	–	–	–	–	–	–
ODIs	16	11	1	229	52	22.90	97.86	0	2	22	8	6	0
T20 Ints	8	8	0	98	30	12.25	127.27	0	0	12	3	3	0
First-class	43	60	11	1487	155*	30.34	60.52	3	7	–	–	24	0

Bowling	M	Balls	Runs	Wkts	BB	Avge	RpO	S/R	5i	10m
Tests	0	0	–	–	–	–	–	–	–	–
ODIs	16	186	157	3	2–34	52.33	5.06	62.00	0	0
T20 Ints	8	30	45	1	1–32	45.00	9.00	30.00	0	0
First-class	43	4083	2379	54	3–33	44.05	3.49	75.61	0	0

YASIR ARAFAT

Full name	**Yasir Arafat Satti**
Born	**March 12, 1982, Rawalpindi, Punjab**
Teams	**Rawalpindi, Khan Research Laboratories, Kent**
Style	**Right-hand bat, right-arm fast-medium bowler**
Test debut	**Pakistan v India at Bangalore 2007-08**
ODI debut	**Pakistan v Sri Lanka at Karachi 1999-2000**

THE PROFILE Yasir Arafat is a typical Pakistan allrounder: he's ideal for one-day cricket, but always looked capable of making a contribution in Tests ... and when he finally played in one, at Bangalore in December 2007, he took a five-for and scored a handy 44. He is a useful lower-order plunderer, but his bowling remains much his stronger suit. His straight, full, skiddy bowling, from a slingy action, accounted for Andrew Flintoff in a one-dayer at Karachi in December 2005. It also helped him winkle out nine England wickets in a warm-up game earlier in that tour, and once brought him five wickets in six deliveries (the other one was a no-ball) in a domestic game. How straight he bowls is shown by four of those five being bowled or lbw. Arafat can generate pace and, when conditions are helpful, swing. He has wide experience of cricket in the UK: he took 24 wickets in his first four games for Sussex, and was then called up himself by Pakistan, after injuries to other seamers, and put on standby for the second and third Tests of their England tour in 2006. He earned a national contract for 2007-08 after some fine allround performances for his new county, Kent, despite playing only ODI the previous season (and top-scoring as Pakistan slumped to 89 all out against South Africa). But Pakistan have a lot of allrounders, so Arafat still faces an uphill battle to win a regular place.

THE FACTS Yasir Arafat took five wickets in six balls for Rawalpindi against reigning champions Faisalabad in the Quaid-e-Azam Trophy in December 2004: only three other bowlers had previously done this – Derbyshire's Bill Copson (1937), William Henderson of Orange Free State (1937-38) and Surrey's Pat Pocock (1972) ... Arafat represented Scotland in 2004 and 2005, Sussex in 2006, and Kent in 2007 and 2008 – making 122, his highest score, in his second game for them ...

THE FIGURES *to 12.9.08*   www.cricinfo.com

Batting & Fielding	M	Inns	NO	Runs	HS	Avge	S/R	100	50	4s	6s	Ct	St
Tests	1	2	0	44	44	22.00	61.11	0	0	7	0	0	0
ODIs	8	6	2	48	27	12.00	78.68	0	0	5	0	1	0
T20 Ints	4	4	2	46	17	23.00	176.92	0	0	5	1	1	0
First-class	140	213	33	5049	122	28.05	–	4	28	–	–	44	0

Bowling	M	Balls	Runs	Wkts	BB	Avge	RpO	S/R	5i	10m
Tests	1	315	210	7	5–161	30.00	4.00	45.00	1	0
ODIs	8	294	274	4	1–28	68.50	5.59	73.50	0	0
T20 Ints	4	78	103	2	1–31	51.50	7.92	39.00	0	0
First-class	140	23242	13345	567	7–102	23.53	3.44	40.99	42	3

YASIR HAMEED

Full name	**Yasir Hameed Qureshi**
Born	**Feb 28, 1978, Peshawar, North-West Frontier Province**
Teams	**NWFP, Pakistan International Airlines**
Style	**Right-hand bat, occasional offspinner**
Test debut	**Pakistan v Bangladesh at Karachi 2003-04**
ODI debut	**Pakistan v New Zealand at Dambulla 2002-03**

THE PROFILE Yasir Hameed announced himself in Test cricket with two centuries on debut, against Bangladesh in May 2003. He may look frail, but his game is built on timing and an easy elegance, and a technique more solid than some Pakistan have tried recently. His early one-day exploits were initially equally impressive, and he forged a superb combination with Imran Farhat: against New Zealand at home late in 2003 they put together a record four consecutive three-figure opening stands. But after this promising beginning Yasir developed a worrying tendency to waste his starts, making pretty twenties and then throwing it away, often flailing at wide ones outside off. Selectorial inconsistencies didn't help: he made 58 and 63 against McGrath and Warne at Sydney in January 2005, but was dropped for the next Test (against India) a couple of months later. For a while opportunities were limited to a few scattered ODIs, in most of which he made a contribution with the bat. However, domestic persistence paid off, and he returned to the one-day squad against West Indies at the end of 2006. He made 71 and 41, but still missed out on a World Cup spot (possibly a blessing in disguise). He was recalled for the post-Cup one-dayers against Sri Lanka in Abu Dhabi, but a series of middling scores – and a triple-century in a domestic first-class game early in 2008 – were still not enough to persuade the selectors that he deserved a regular place.

THE FACTS Yasir Hameed made 170 and 105 on his Test debut against Bangladesh at Karachi in August 2003: the only other man to make twin centuries on Test debut is Lawrence Rowe, with 214 and 100 not out for West Indies v New Zealand in 1971-72 ... Yasir made 300 (49 fours) for North West Frontier Province v Baluchistan at Peshawar in March 2008 ... In 2003-04 Yasir and Imran Farhat shared successive opening stands of 115, 142, 134 and 197 in ODIs against New Zealand ... Yasir has played two ODIs against Zimbabwe and was caught behind for a duck in both, lasting a grand total of three balls ...

THE FIGURES to 12.9.08   www.cricinfo.com

Batting & Fielding	M	Inns	NO	Runs	HS	Avge	S/R	100	50	4s	6s	Ct	St
Tests	23	45	3	1450	170	34.52	57.67	2	8	217	3	16	0
ODIs	56	56	1	2028	127*	36.87	66.95	3	12	219	6	14	0
T20 Ints	0	0	–	–	–	–	–	–	–	–	–	–	–
First-class	112	187	12	6492	300	37.09	–	14	29	–	–	82	0

Bowling	M	Balls	Runs	Wkts	BB	Avge	RpO	S/R	5i	10m
Tests	23	72	72	0	–	–	6.00	–	0	0
ODIs	56	18	26	0	–	–	8.66	–	0	0
T20 Ints	0	0	–	–	–	–	–	–	–	–
First-class	112	879	709	7	2–46	101.28	4.83	125.57	0	0

PAKISTAN

YOUNIS KHAN

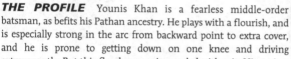

Full name	**Mohammad Younis Khan**
Born	**Nov 29, 1977, Mardan, North-West Frontier Province**
Teams	**NWFP, Habib Bank, Rajasthan Royals**
Style	**Right-hand bat, occasional legspinner**
Test debut	**Pakistan v Sri Lanka at Rawalpindi 1999-2000**
ODI debut	**Pakistan v Sri Lanka at Karachi 1999-2000**

THE PROFILE Younis Khan is a fearless middle-order batsman, as befits his Pathan ancestry. He plays with a flourish, and is especially strong in the arc from backward point to extra cover, and he is prone to getting down on one knee and driving extravagantly. But this flamboyance is coupled with grit. His main weaknesses are playing away from his body and leaving straight balls. He started with 107 on Test debut, against Sri Lanka early in 2000, and scored well in bursts after that, with 153 against West Indies in a Test in Sharjah the highlight. Younis was one of the few batsmen who retained his place after Pakistan's disastrous 2003 World Cup campaign, but he lost it soon afterwards after a string of low scores at home against Bangladesh and South Africa. Another century against Sri Lanka finally cemented that Test place, and he has been a heavy runmaker ever since, especially against India: in March 2005 he made 147 and 267 in successive Tests against them, and continued in that vein early in 2006, with 199, 83, 194, 0 and 77, before scoring consistently in England too, making 173 at Leeds, which became his home ground the following year during a successful spell with Yorkshire. He blotted his copybook by theatrically resigning as captain after being appointed to replace the banned Inzamam-ul-Haq for the Champions Trophy late in 2006 – he then changed his mind and took the job after all. But after another miserable World Cup he announced he was not interested in the position full-time. He is a good fielder, displaying further versatility by keeping wicket – and winning the match award – in a one-dayer against Zimbabwe in October 2004.

THE FACTS Younis Khan averages 88.06 in Tests against India – and more than 31 against everyone else ... He was the seventh of nine Pakistanis to score a century on Test debut, with 107 v Sri Lanka at Rawalpindi in February 2000 ... Against India at home early in 2006 Younis shared successive stands of 319, 142, 242, 0 and 158 with Mohammad Yousuf ... At Lahore in that series he became the sixth batsman to be out for 199 in a Test ...

THE FIGURES *to 12.9.08*   www.cricinfo.com

Batting & Fielding	M	Inns	NO	Runs	HS	Avge	S/R	100	50	4s	6s	Ct	St
Tests	58	105	7	4816	267	49.14	53.76	15	20	599	20	66	0
ODIs	175	169	19	5087	144	33.91	77.07	5	34	409	49	94	0
T20 Ints	12	11	0	223	51	20.27	126.70	0	1	18	9	8	0
First-class	131	212	23	9586	267	50.71	–		32	37	–	–	141	0

Bowling	M	Balls	Runs	Wkts	BB	Avge	RpO	S/R	5i	10m
Tests	58	300	203	2	1–24	101.51	4.06	150.00	0	0
ODIs	175	212	211	2	1–3	105.50	5.97	106.00	0	0
T20 Ints	12	22	18	3	3–18	6.00	4.90	7.33	0	0
First-class	131	1693	1091	20	4–52	54.55	3.86	84.65	0	0

YUVRAJ SINGH

Full name	**Yuvraj Singh**
Born	**December 12, 1981, Chandigarh**
Teams	**Punjab, Kings XI Punjab**
Style	**Left-hand bat, slow left-arm orthodox spinner**
Test debut	**India v New Zealand at Mohali 2003-04**
ODI debut	**India v Kenya at Nairobi 2000-01**

THE PROFILE Generously gifted, Yuvraj Singh made a lordly entry into international cricket when still only 18, toppling Australia in the ICC Knockout of October 2000 with a blistering 84 in his first innings and some scintillating fielding. He supplements those skills with some clever, loopy left-arm spin. While his ability to hit the ball long and clean was instantly recognised, at first he was troubled by quality spin, and also perceived to lack commitment, traits for which he temporarily lost his place. But he returned early in 2002, and swung the series against Zimbabwe India's way with two matchwinning innings, then went to England and played key roles in three one-day runchases, culminating in the Lord's final, where his 69, and stand of 121 with Mohammad Kaif, set up India's memorable victory over England. It still took another 15 months, and an injury to Sourav Ganguly, for Yuvraj to get a Test look-in. But in his third match, against Pakistan on a Lahore greentop, he stroked a stunning first-day century off 110 balls. A troublesome knee injury briefly threatened to keep him out of the 2007 World Cup, but later in the year he smashed Stuart Broad for six sixes in an over during the inaugural World Twenty20 championship. A scintillating 169 against Pakistan at Bangalore in December 2007 seemed to have nailed down a Test place at last – but a string of modest scores followed, and he was out again by the middle of 2008, although he remains marvellously consistent in one-dayers.

THE FACTS Yuvraj played 73 one-day internationals before winning his first Test cap ... He hit England's Stuart Broad for six sixes in an over during the World Twenty20 championships at Durban in September 2007 ... Yuvraj made 209 for North Zone v South Zone in March 2002 ... He averages 63.55 in Tests against Pakistan, but 9.14 v Australia ... His father, fast bowler Yograj Singh, played one Test in 1980-81 ... Yuvraj's record includes three ODIs for the Asia XI ...

THE FIGURES *to 12.9.08*   www.cricinfo.com

Batting & Fielding	M	Inns	NO	Runs	HS	Avge	S/R	100	50	4s	6s	Ct	St
Tests	23	36	4	1050	169	32.81	55.61	3	3	155	6	24	0
ODIs	217	199	28	6141	139	35.91	86.81	8	37	620	100	66	0
T20 Ints	7	6	1	179	70	35.80	177.22	0	2	10	15	1	0
First-class	77	123	15	4636	209	42.92	–	15	20	–	–	80	0

Bowling	M	Balls	Runs	Wkts	BB	Avge	RpO	S/R	5i	10m
Tests	23	282	167	4	2–9	41.75	3.55	70.50	0	0
ODIs	217	2872	2455	59	4–6	41.61	5.12	48.67	0	0
T20 Ints	7	18	38	1	1–38	38.00	12.66	18.00	0	0
First-class	77	1209	668	13	3–25	51.38	3.31	93.00	0	0

MONDE **ZONDEKI**

Full name	**Monde Zondeki**
Born	**July 25, 1982, King William's Town, Cape Province**
Teams	**Cape Cobras, Warwickshire**
Style	**Right-hand bat, right-arm fast-medium bowler**
Test debut	**South Africa v England at Leeds 2003**
ODI debut	**South Africa v Sri Lanka at Bloemfontein 2002-03**

THE PROFILE   Young, raw and quick, Monde Zondeki is cut straight from the modern history of the new South Africa, and spent a year of his childhood in Zambia living with his exiled uncle, the late ANC cabinet minister Steve Tshwete. He eventually returned home and attended Dale College, a fine cricketing nursery which also claims Makhaya Ntini as an old boy. Although he initially tried legspin, Zondeki was soon bowling fast – and later, very fast. He became the latest young fast bowler to attempt to fill Allan Donald's boots, and could hardly have made a more stunning impact, taking a wicket with his first ball in international cricket – Sri Lanka's Marvan Atapattu caught in the slips in a one-dayer at Bloemfontein in 2002. Predictably, Zondeki struggled to make much impression at the 2003 World Cup, but was still selected for that year's England tour. He starred on his Test debut at Headingley ... but with bat not ball. South Africa were struggling at 142 for 7 before Zondeki made 59 and helped Gary Kirsten add 150 for the eighth wicket. However, a side strain restricted him to just 4.5 overs, and bad luck with injuries meant he did not get back into the Test side until March 2005, against Zimbabwe. It was an impressive comeback: nine wickets booked him a place to the Caribbean, but he managed just seven wickets in three Tests there, then injuries impinged again. But he was the leading domestic wicket-taker in 2007-08, with 62 at 19.16, was called up to tour India after Charl Langeveldt pulled out, and also played a few matches for Warwickshire in 2008.

THE FACTS   Zondeki took the wicket of Sri Lanka's Marvan Atapattu with his first ball in ODIs, at Bloemfontein in December 2002: only 14 others have achieved this feat (the only other South African was Martin van Jaarsveld) ... Zondeki took 6 for 39 in a Test against Zimbabwe at Centurion in March 2005 ... He took 6 for 37 in a one-day game for South Africa A against Sri Lanka A at Centurion in October 2003 ...

THE FIGURES to 12.9.08   www.cricinfo.com

Batting & Fielding	M	Inns	NO	Runs	HS	Avge	S/R	100	50	4s	6s	Ct	St
Tests	5	4	0	82	59	20.50	36.60	0	1	12	0	1	0
ODIs	11	3	2	4	3*	4.00	80.00	0	0	0	0	3	0
T20 Ints	1	1	0	0	0	0.00	0.00	0	0	0	0	0	0
First-class	71	98	31	626	59	9.34	–	0	1	–	–	22	0

Bowling	M	Balls	Runs	Wkts	BB	Avge	RpO	S/R	5i	10m
Tests	5	692	438	16	6–39	27.37	3.79	43.25	1	0
ODIs	11	456	414	8	2–46	51.75	5.44	57.00	0	0
T20 Ints	1	18	41	1	1–41	41.00	13.66	18.00	0	0
First-class	71	11900	6371	221	6–39	28.82	3.21	53.84	9	1

IRELAND

Andre Botha

William Porterfield

Kyle McCallan

Cricket in Ireland was once so popular that Oliver Cromwell banned it in 1656. Since then, it has been something of a minority sport, although there have been occasional big days, as in 1969 when the West Indians were skittled for 25 on a boggy pitch at Sion Mills in County Tyrone (rumours that the visitors enjoyed lavish hospitality at a nearby Guinness brewery the night before are thought to be unfounded). Cricket continued as an amateur pastime until the 1990s, when the Irish board left the auspices of the English one and attained independent ICC membership. Ireland became eligible to play in the World Cup, and narrowly missed out on the 1999 tournament, when they lost a playoff to Scotland. They made no mistake for 2007, though, winning the ICC Trophy (handily, it was played in Ireland) to ensure qualification. A change of captain to the Australian-born Trent Johnston ushered in a new, more professional set-up, and Ireland travelled to the Caribbean hopeful of making a mark. No-one, though, was quite prepared for what happened – except maybe Johnston himself, who packed enough for a seven-week stay when most were expecting a quiet return home in a week or two. In their first World Cup match, Ireland tied with Zimbabwe, then went one better on a Sabina Park greentop on St Patrick's Day, hanging on to beat Pakistan and eliminate one of the pre-tournament favourites. Ireland sailed on to the Super Eights, where they beat Bangladesh too. Back home, though, reality set in: the better Irish players are already with English counties (one, Dublin-born Ed Joyce, has already played for England, and others are trying to follow suit), and the others struggle to fit in ever-increasing international commitments around a steady job. It's the same story as in many other associate-member countries: Irish cricket needs a more professional domestic structure if the impression made by Johnston's merry men is to be anything more than a footnote in cricket history.

Ireland's ODI records *as at 12.9.08*

Highest total	308-7	**v Canada at Nairobi 2006-07**
Lowest total	77	**v Sri Lanka at St George's 2006-07**
Most runs	685	**WTS Porterfield (avge. 27.40)**
Highest score	142	**KJ O'Brien v Kenya at Nairobi 2006-07**
Most wickets	33	**AC Botha (avge. 24.39)**
Best bowling	4-19	**AC Botha v Kenya at Belfast 2008**
Most matches	31	**WK McCallan (2006-2008)**
World Cup record		**Reached Super Eight stage in only appearance, 2006-07**
Overall ODI record		**Played 31: Won 9, Lost 18, Tied 1, No result 3**

IRELAND

BOTHA, Andre Cornelius   September 12, 1975, Johannesburg, South Africa
LHB, RM: 27 ODIs, 446 runs at 21.23, HS 56; 33 wickets at 24.39, BB 4-19.
Former South African provincial player: made 186 for Ireland v Scotland in August 2007.

CONNELL, Peter   August 13, 1981, Dannevirke, New Zealand
RHB, RFM: 6 ODIs, 32 runs (no average), HS 22*; 5 wickets at 46.80, BB 2-37.
North Down seamer who took 10 for 69 v Holland in Intercontinental Cup at Rotterdam in July 2008.

CUSACK, Alex Richard   October 29, 1980, Brisbane, Australia
RHB, RFM: 11 ODIs, 161 runs at 26.83, HS 38; 10 wickets at 16.70, BB 3-15.
Man of the Match on ODI debut for 36 and 3-15 v South Africa at Belfast in June 2007.*

FOURIE, Marthinus Jacobus   July 23, 1979, Cape Town, South Africa
RHB, RFM: 7 ODIs, 42 runs at 21.00, HS 19*; 1 wicket for 128, BB 1-33.
Opening bowler from Dublin's Merrion club: took 3-31 v Canada in 2007 Intercontinental Cup final.

JOHNSTON, David Trent   April 29, 1974, Wollongong, NSW, Australia
RHB, RFM: 23 ODIs, 352 runs at 22.00, HS 45*; 11 wickets at 66.36, BB 2-40.
Inspirational captain (and innovative chicken dancer) during Ireland's World Cup run.

KIDD, Gary Edward   September 18, 1985, Craigavon
LHB, SLA: 6 ODIs, 15 runs at 15.00, HS 15; 1 wicket for 172, BB 1-27.
Waringstown spinner who spent some time on the Lord's groundstaff.

McCALLAN, William Kyle   August 27, 1975, Carrickfergus, Co. Antrim
RHB, OB: 31 ODIs, 300 runs at 17.64, HS 50*; 30 wickets at 30.66, BB 4-36.
Tidy offspinner from Ulster club Waringstown: took 10 wickets at 23.30 in the World Cup.

MORGAN, Eoin Joseph Gerard   September 10, 1986, Dublin
LHB: 21 ODIs, 600 runs at 30.00, HS 115, 1×100.
On Middlesex's books: hit 209 (Ireland's first double-century) v UAE in Abu Dhabi in Feb 2007.*

O'BRIEN, Kevin Joseph   March 4, 1984, Dublin
RHB, RFM: 25 ODIs, 642 runs at 29.18, HS 142, 1×100; 15 wickets at 39.80, BB 3-30.
Allrounder with Dublin's Railway Union club: hit 142 (11 fours, six sixes) v Kenya in Feb 2007.

O'BRIEN, Niall John   November 8, 1981, Dublin
LHB, WK: 27 ODIs, 684 runs at 26.30, HS 72; 21 ct, 5 st.
Feisty keeper who has played for Kent and Northants: made 72 in World Cup win over Pakistan.

PORTERFIELD, William Thomas Stuart   September 6, 1984, Londonderry
RHB: 27 ODIs, 685 runs at 27.40, HS 112*, 2×100.
Solid opener: made two ODI hundreds in three days early in 2007; took over as captain in 2008.

RANKIN, William Boyd   July 5, 1984, Derry
LHB, RFM: 12 ODIs, 16 runs at 8.00, HS 7*; 14 wickets at 26.78, BB 3-32.
Tall (6ft 8ins) fast bowler who impressed at the World Cup and later joined Warwickshire.

STRYDOM, Reinhardt   June 16, 1977, Cape Town, South Africa
LHB, LM: 9 ODIs, 83 runs at 13.83, HS 37; 1 wicket for 63, BB 1-63.
Opening batsman from the North County club, the home of Ireland's cricket academy.

WHITE, Andrew Roland   July 3, 1980, Newtownards, Co. Down
RHB, OB: 23 ODIs, 305 runs at 17.94, HS 40; 9 wickets at 36.00, BB 2-17.
Offspinner, formerly with Northants, who hit 152 on first-class debut, for Ireland v Holland in 2004.*

WILSON, Gary Craig   February 5, 1986, Dundonald, Northern Ireland
RHB, WK: 7 ODIs, 132 runs at 18.85, HS 51; 17 ct.
Handy keeper-batsman who is on the Surrey staff; scored 51 against Scotland at Clontarf in 2008.

KENYA

Hiren Varaiya

Steve Tikolo

Alex Obanda

The British Empire spread cricket to Kenya: the first notable match was played there in 1899, and English-style country clubs still flourish in Nairobi, which can claim one cricket record – six different grounds there have staged official one-day internationals, more than any other city. Strong MCC teams have made several visits to East Africa – one of them, in the early 1960s, unearthed Basharat Hassan, who went on to enjoy a long career with Nottinghamshire. Kenyan players formed the backbone of the East African side in the first World Cup, in 1975, but soon after that they struck out on their own, joining the ICC in their own right in 1981. Kenyan cricket continued to improve quietly until they qualified for the World Cup in 1995-96, where they amazed everyone by upsetting West Indies in a group game. Players reared on hard pitches struggled in early-season England at the 1999 Cup, but the 2003 version was different: it was held in Africa, and some of the matches were played in Kenya. Helped by outside events (England refused to go to Zimbabwe, while New Zealand boycotted Nairobi for security reasons), the Kenyans progressed to the semi-finals. It seemed like the start of a golden era: instead it ushered in a depressing time, marked by player strikes and arguments about administration. Peace broke out in time for the 2007 World Cup, but with several players approaching the veteran stage – many of them come from the same Luo tribe, which is why so many of their surnames begin with O – the results were poor. Still, Kenya boast arguably the best batsman outside the Test arena, in their captain Steve Tikolo, while the solidly built allrounder Thomas Odoyo (who played in the 1996 World Cup at 17) was the first bowler from a non-Test nation to take 100 wickets in one-day internationals.

Kenya's ODI records *as at 12.9.08*

Highest total	347-3	v Bangladesh at Nairobi 1997-98
Lowest total	84	v Australia at Nairobi 2002-03
Most runs	2762	SO Tikolo (avge. 31.38)
Highest score	144	KO Otieno v Bangladesh at Nairobi 1997-98
Most wickets	106	TM Odoyo (avge. 30.40)
Best bowling	5-24	CO Obuya v Sri Lanka at Nairobi 2002-03
Most matches	101	SO Tikolo (1996-2008)
World Cup record		Semi-finalists in 2002-03; first phase 1995-96, 1999, 2006-07
Overall ODI record		Played 103: Won 32, Lost 67, No result 4

KENYA

KAMANDE, James Kabatha   December 12, 1978, Muranga
RHB, OB: 51 ODIs, 502 runs at 15.68, HS 68; 29 wickets at 40.48, BB 3-32.
Former medium-pacer who now bowls offspin, after his action was reported to the ICC.

MISHRA, Tanmay   December 22, 1986, Mumbai, India
RHB: 28 ODIs, 698 runs at 31.72, HS 66.
Talented young batsman currently at university in his native India.

OBANDA, Alex Ouma   December 25, 1987, Nairobi
RHB: 8 ODIs, 256 runs at 51.20, HS 85.
Strokeplaying batsman who started his ODI career with innings of 30, 85 and 79*.

OBUYA, Collins Omondi   July 27, 1981, Nairobi
RHB, LB: 57 ODIs, 700 runs at 18.42, HS 68*; 26 wickets at 47.34, BB 5-24.
Tall legspinner who played a few matches for Warwickshire after doing well at the 2003 World Cup.

OBUYA, David Oluoch   August 14, 1979, Nairobi
RHB, WK: 49 ODIs, 838 runs at 18.21, HS 93; 28 ct, 4 st.
Opener, wicketkeeper, and brother of Collins Obuya and Kennedy Otieno.

ODHIAMBO, Nehemiah Ngoche   August 7, 1983, Nairobi, Kenya
RHB, RFM: 25 ODIs, 164 runs at 12.61, HS 66; 17 wickets at 41.70, BB 3-25.
Fast bowler who took 5-54 on first-class debut, v Canada in 2006: brother of Lameck Onyango.

ODOYO, Thomas Migai   May 12, 1978, Nairobi
RHB, RFM: ODIs 104 (5 for Africa), 1945 runs (25.25), HS 111*; 110 wkts (30.72), BB 4-25.
Hard-hitting allrounder: the first bowler from a non-Test nation to take 100 wickets in ODIs.

ONGONDO, Peter Jimmy Carter   February 10, 1977, Nairobi
RHB, RFM: 59 ODIs (1 for Africa), 309 runs at 9.96, HS 36; 65 wkts at 24.69, BB 5-51.
Handy seamer and useful tailender who once top-scored against West Indies with 36 from No. 11.

ONYANGO, Lameck Ngoche   September 22, 1973, Nairobi
RHB, RM: 15 ODIs, 94 runs at 15.66, HS 34*; 10 wickets at 25.80, BB 3-29.
Seamer and late-order blocker who once went in last in an ODI and didn't bowl.

OTIENO, Kennedy Obuya   March 11, 1972, Nairobi
RHB, WK: 80 ODIs, 1723 runs at 22.67, HS 144, 2×100; 41 ct, 14 st.
Veteran of the 1996 World Cup win over West Indies: has made two ODI centuries v Bangladesh.

OUMA, Maurice Akumu   November 8, 1982, Kiambli
RHB, WK: 35 ODIs, 655 runs at 19.84, HS 58; 20 ct, 3 st.
Handy striker who often opens with David Obuya, with whom he vies for the keeper's gloves.

SHAH, Ravindu Dhirajilal   August 28, 1972, Nairobi
RHB, occasional RM: 56 ODIs, 1506 runs at 27.88, HS 113, 1×100; 0 wickets.
Stylish batsman who hit 247 v Pakistan A in 2004: returned after three years for the 2007 World Cup.

SUJI, Otieno Ondik ("Tony")   February 5, 1976, Nairobi
RHB, RM: 60 ODIs, 506 runs at 12.97, HS 67; 21 wickets at 55.95, BB 2-14.
Combative allrounder, who once opened the bowling with his brother Martin in an ODI.

TIKOLO, Stephen Ogonji   June 25, 1971, Nairobi
RHB, OB: 105 ODIs (4 for Africa), 2821 runs at 30.66, HS 111, 2×100; 76 wkts at 32.01, BB 4-41.
Probably the best batsman outside the Test arena: 22 hundreds for Kenya, including two doubles.

VARAIYA, Hiren Ashok   April 9, 1984, Nairobi
RHB, SLA: 26 ODIs, 36 runs at 12.00, HS 10*; 33 wickets at 19.96, BB 4-25.
Young spinner who flights the ball well: took a wicket with first ball in an ODI, v Canada in 2006.

THE NETHERLANDS

Ryan ten Doeschate

Bas Zuiderent

Daan van Bunge

Cricket was brought to The Netherlands by British soldiers during the Napoleonic War: by 1881 there was a Dutch team, and two years later a national board, comprising 18 clubs, four of which still exist. A league system has long flourished, and there has been a tradition of foreign players coming over to coach. Dutch cricket received a boost in 1964 when Australia visited after an Ashes tour and lost by three wickets, and more noses were tweaked in 1989, with a win over England A, captained by Peter Roebuck, which dented his hopes of skippering the full Test side. West Indies (1991) and South Africa (1994) also succumbed – it's safe to say they were more relaxed than they might have been for an official international – and another strongish England side was beaten in 1993. The Netherlands qualified for their first World Cup three years later, and weren't disgraced, and they were there again in 2003, when they beat Namibia. They just scraped in to the 2007 tournament, winning a playoff against the UAE, but again managed a consolation win, this time over Scotland, which made up for being pummelled by South Africa and Australia. Standout performers in recent years have included Roland Lefebvre, who played for Somerset and Glamorgan, and Bas Zuiderent, who had a spell with Sussex. A South African-born newcomer has taken the eye in recent years: Essex's Ryan ten Doeschate hammered four centuries in three ICC Intercontinental Cup games, and soon shot to the top of the national one-day runscoring and wicket-taking lists. The local players are very keen, but there are not that many of them, fans are thin on the ground, and there's really no chance of a proper first-class competition. The future might not be too bright, but for the Dutch one-day team at least, it's certainly orange.

The Netherlands' ODI records as at 12.9.08

Highest total	315-8	v Bermuda at Rotterdam 2007
Lowest total	80	v West Indies at Dublin 2007
Most runs	662	RN ten Doeschate (avge. 50.92)
Highest score	134*	KJJ van Noortwijk v Namibia at Bloemfontein 2002-03
Most wickets	35	RN ten Doeschate (avge. 20.37)
Best bowling	4-31	RN ten Doeschate v Canada at Nairobi 2006-07
Most matches	35	B Zuiderent (1996-2008)
World Cup record	Eliminated in first round 1995-96, 2002-03 and 2006-07	
Overall ODI record	Played 39: Won 13, Lost 24, No result 2	

THE NETHERLANDS

ADEEL RAJA, Mohammad Khalid   August 15, 1980, Lahore, Pakistan
RHB, OB: 10 ODIs, 19 runs at 4.75, HS 8*; 10 wickets at 36.60, BB 4-42.
Big spinner who took 4-42 in the World Cup win over Namibia in 2003.

BORREN, Peter William   August 21, 1983, Christchurch, New Zealand
RHB, RM: 22 ODIs, 265 runs at 14.72, HS 96; 17 wickets at 42.94, BB 3-54.
Combative allrounder who played for NZ Under-19s: made 105 and 96 v Canada in 2006.

BUKHARI, Mudassar   December 26, 1983, Gujrat, Pakistan
RHB, RFM: 10 ODIs, 146 runs at 29.20, HS 71; 10 wickets at 23.00, BB 3-24.
Primarily a bowler, he scored 71 (after opening) and took 3-24 against Ireland in July 2007.

de GROOTH, Tom Nico   May 14, 1979, The Hague
RHB, OB: 12 ODIs, 254 runs at 25.40, HS 97; 1 wicket at 2.00, BB 1-2.
Maturing batsman: hit 98 (v Scotland), 196 and 97 (v Bermuda) in successive matches in Aug 2007.

KERVEZEE, Alexei Nicolaas   September 11, 1989, Walvis Bay, Namibia
RHB, occasional RM: 18 ODIs, 341 runs at 26.23, HS 62; 0 wickets.
Precocious talent: World Cup debut at 17, later made 98 v Canada, and joined Worcestershire in 2007.

MOL, Hendrik-Jan Christiaan   March 29, 1977, The Hague
LHB, LM: 11 ODIs, 67 runs at 8.37, HS 23; 5 wickets at 29.80, BB 2-17.
Allrounder from the Quick Haag club: his brother Geert-Maarten has also played ODIs.

REEKERS, Darron John   May 26, 1973, Christchurch, New Zealand
RHB, RFM: 17 ODIs, 436 runs at 25.64, HS 104, 1×100; 13 wickets at 29.92, BB 3-54.
Has opened the batting and bowling in ODIs, and hit 104 against Ireland in Feb 2007.

SCHIFERLI, Edgar   May 17, 1976, The Hague
RHB, RFM: 21 ODIs, 101 runs at 9.18, HS 22; 15 wickets at 46.20, BB 3-18.
Holland's most experienced fast bowler: was unable to play in the 2007 World Cup after a leg injury.

SEELAAR, Pieter Marinus   July 2, 1987, Schiedam
RHB, SLA: 8 ODIs, 8 runs at 4.00, HS 5*; 10 wickets at 19.80, BB 3-22.
Tidy spinner who took 5 for 57 in Intercontinental Cup match against Kenya at Amstelveen in 2008.

SMITS, Jeroen   June 21, 1972, The Hague
RHB, WK: 32 ODIs, 136 runs at 15.11, HS 26; 29 ct, 6 st.
Steady keeper (and Jamiroquai fan): took over as captain after the 2007 World Cup.

SZWARCZYNSKI, Eric Stefan   February 13, 1983, Vanderbijlpark, South Africa
RHB: 14 ODIs, 394 runs at 32.83, HS 56*.
Student whose favourite player is Allan Donald: made a century for Netherlands A v MCC in 2006.

ten DOESCHATE, Ryan Neil   June 30, 1980, Port Elizabeth, South Africa
RHB, RFM: 19 ODIs, 662 runs at 50.92, HS 109*, 1×100; 35 wickets at 20.37, BB 4-31.
Allrounder who also plays for Essex: took 6-20 (and 3-92) then scored 259 v Canada in 2006.*

van BUNGE, Daan Lodewijk Samuel   October 19, 1982, Voorburg
RHB, LB: 26 ODIs, 434 runs at 20.66, HS 62; 10 wickets at 25.90, BB 3-16.
Talented batsman ... but his legspin was hit for six sixes by Herschelle Gibbs at the 2007 World Cup.

van NIEROP, Maurits Willem Albert   May 11, 1983, Cape Town, South Africa
RHB, RM: 2 ODIs, 35 runs at 35.00, HS 31*.
Middle-order batsman who finished off his first ODI, against Bermuda in 2006, with a six.

ZUIDERENT, Bastiaan   March 3, 1977, Utrecht
RHB: 35 ODIs, 653 runs at 22.51, HS 77*.
Orthodox opener who had a spell with Sussex: has played in all 14 of Holland's World Cup matches.

SCOTLAND

John Blain

Craig Wright

Gavin Hamilton

Cricket crept over the border from England in the mid-18th century: soldiers played it near Perth in 1750, although the first recorded match in Scotland was not till 1785. More recently there has long been a strong amateur league system in the country, although – just as in Ireland – international aspirations have always been handicapped by the absence of a proper professional set-up, which has meant that the better players have always migrated south. One of them, the Ayr-born Mike Denness, captained England, while one of the few bowlers to trouble Don Bradman in 1930 was the Scottish legspinner Ian Peebles. More recently, offspinner Peter Such (born in Helensburgh) played for England, while Gavin Hamilton (born in Broxburn) also won an England Test cap after impressing for Scotland at the 1999 World Cup. Unfortunately, Hamilton bagged a pair, and was soon back playing for Scotland: he hit his maiden ODI century in 2008. At the 2007 World Cup, Hamilton appeared alongside another former England player in Dougie Brown, the combative allrounder who had a long career with Warwickshire and played nine ODIs in 1997-98. Scotland left the auspices of the English board and joined the ICC in 1994, but they failed to win a match – or reach 200 – in any of their World Cup games in 1999 or 2007. They also competed in the English counties' limited-overs league for many years, without managing more than the occasional upset. The main problem lying in the way of Scotland's advancement – apart from the weather – remains the lack of a sound domestic structure which might support first-class cricket; local support is also patchy, despite the sterling efforts of a few diehards. Until this is addressed – if it ever can be – Scotland will continue to suffer from a player drain to English counties.

Scotland's ODI records as at 12.9.08

Highest total	**293-8**	**v Canada at Mombasa 2006-07**
Lowest total	**68**	**v West Indies at Leicester 1999**
Most runs	**882**	**GM Hamilton (avge. 35.28)**
Highest score	**123***	**RR Watson v Canada at Mombasa 2006-07**
Most wickets	**38**	**JAR Blain (avge. 27.94)**
Best bowling	**5-22**	**JAR Blain v Netherlands at Dublin 2008**
Most matches	**31**	**JAR Blain (1999-2008)**
World Cup record		**Eliminated in first round 1999 and 2006-07**
Overall ODI record		**Played 33: Won 9, Lost 21, No result 3**

SCOTLAND

BLAIN, John Angus Rae   January 4, 1979, Edinburgh
RHB, RFM: 31 ODIs, 241 runs at 14.17, HS 30*; 38 wickets at 27.94, BB 5-22.
Reliable seamer who had spells with Northants and Yorkshire: took 5-22 v Holland at Clontarf in 2008.

BROWN, Douglas Robert   October 29, 1969, Stirling
RHB, RFM: 25 ODIs (16 for Scotland), 319 runs at 17.72, HS 50*; 22 wkts at 41.77, BB 3-37.
Long-serving Warwickshire allrounder who played nine ODIs for England in 1997-98.

COETZER, Kyle James   April 14, 1984, Aberdeen
RHB, RM: 1 ODI, 0 runs.
Attractive batsman who is on Durham's books, and scored two first-class hundreds for them in 2007.

HAMILTON, Gavin Mark   September 16, 1974, Broxburn, West Lothian
LHB, RFM: 28 ODIs, 882 runs at 35.28, HS 115, 1×100; 3 wickets at 53.33, BB 2-36.
Played for Yorks & Durham – and once for England, after doing well for Scotland in 1999 World Cup.

HAQ Khan, Rana Majid   February 11, 1983, Paisley
LHB, OB: 18 ODIs, 378 runs at 21.00, HS 71; 25 wickets at 27.48, BB 4-28.
Hard-hitting allrounder, who plays for Ferguslie: took 4-28 v West Indies at Clontarf in 2007.

LYONS, Ross Thomas   December 8, 1984, Greenock
LHB, SLA: 14 ODIs, 80 runs at 40.00, HS 28; 10 wickets at 56.20, BB 2-28.
Promising spinner who dismissed Shahid Afridi in his first ODI.

McCALLUM, Neil Francis Ian   November 22, 1977, Edinburgh
RHB: 26 ODIs, 482 runs at 20.95, HS 100, 1×100.
PE teacher who made 181 v Holland and 100 v Ireland in 2007.

NEL, Johann Dewald   June 6, 1980, Klerksdorp, South Africa
RHB, RFM: 14 ODIs, 10 runs at 5.00, HS 4; 3 wickets at 93.33, BB 1-34.
Fast bowler who dismissed Inzamam-ul-Haq on his ODI debut, and Brendon McCullum in 2008.

POONIA, Naveed Singh   May 11, 1986, Govan, Glasgow
RHB: 16 ODIs, 199 runs at 12.43, HS 67.
Stylish batsman on the Warwickshire staff: he has made eight centuries for their 2nd XI.

ROGERS, Glenn Alan   April 12, 1977, Sydney, New South Wales
RHB, SLA: 13 ODIs, 81 runs at 16.20, HS 26; 8 wickets at 51.12, BB 2-22.
Promising spinner who caught typhoid just before the 2007 World Cup, but recovered in time to play.

SHEIKH, Mohammad Qasim   October 30, 1984, Glasgow
LHB, LM: 5 ODIs, 47 runs at 11.75, HS 23.
Captain of the Clydesdale club, he hit 92 for Scotland v Canada in the Intercontinental Cup in 2008.

SMITH, Colin John Ogilvie   September 27, 1972, Aberdeen
RHB, WK: 24 ODIs, 374 runs at 19.68, HS 59; 21 ct, 10 st.
Policeman and dependable wicketkeeper who has played for Scotland since 1997.

WATSON, Ryan Robert   November 12, 1976, Salisbury (now Harare), Zimbabwe
RHB, RM: 27 ODIs, 819 runs at 34.12, HS 123*, 1×100; 8 wickets at 37.62, BB 3-18.
Chunky batsman, at school with SA's Graeme Smith: captain since 2007 World Cup.

WATTS, David Fraser   June 5, 1979, King's Lynn, Norfolk
RHB: 22 ODIs, 444 runs at 21.14, HS 70.
Banker-turned-batsman who scored 171 in a one-day game against Denmark in 2006.*

WRIGHT, Craig McIntyre   April 28, 1974, Paisley, Renfrewshire
RHB, RFM: 18 ODIs, 216 runs at 16.61, HS 37; 25 wickets at 23.68, BB 4-29.
Scotland's leading wicket-taker in all matches, he stepped down as captain after the 2007 World Cup.

ZIMBABWE

Vusi Sibanda

Ray Price

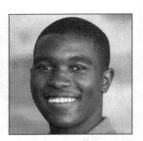

Elton Chigumbura

The decline of cricket in Zimbabwe is one of the game's saddest tales – outranked, of course, by the decline of the country itself from prosperous to dangerous. Cricket was first played in what was then Rhodesia in 1891, and for years the national side took part in South Africa's Currie Cup. Several Rhodesians played for South Africa, notably Colin Bland ... and offspinner John Traicos, in 1970: he was still around 22 years later when Zimbabwe were given Test status themselves. That came after years of consistent performances, including a famous World Cup win over Australia in 1983, inspired by Duncan Fletcher, later England's Ashes-winning coach. Zimbabwe were always hampered by a small player-base, but punched above their weight thanks to a nucleus of world-class players including Dave Houghton, the Flower brothers and Heath Streak. Probably their strongest side was assembled for the 1999 World Cup, following the return of Neil Johnson (previously based in South Africa) and Murray Goodwin (Australia). Zimbabwe qualified for the second phase that year, and six of their eight Test wins came between October 1998 and November 2001. And then it all started to go wrong. At the 2003 World Cup, with the political situation at home worsening, Andy Flower and the black fast bowler Henry Olonga sported black armbands bemoaning the "death of democracy" in Zimbabwe: their reward was to be hounded out of the country. A divisive dispute over payments and selection then tore the rest of the side apart: even Tatenda Taibu, their first black captain, fell out with the board for a while. Zimbabwe pulled out of Test cricket in 2005, just ahead of official ICC action. There was a chink of light late in 2007, when ICC's new president Ray Mali claimed that Zimbabwe's young side could top the world rankings in three years, after witnessing some encouraging performances against South Africa. Sadly, few believe this is really possible in such a poisonous climate.

Zimbabwe's ODI records *as at 12.9.08*

Highest total	340-2	**v Namibia at Harare 2002-03**
Lowest total	35	**v Sri Lanka at Harare 2003-04**
Most runs	6786	**A Flower (avge. 35.34)**
Highest score	172*	**CB Wishart v Namibia at Harare 2002-03**
Most wickets	237	**HH Streak (avge. 29.81)**
Best bowling	6-19	**HK Olonga v England at Cape Town 1999-2000**
Most matches	219	**GW Flower (1992-2004)**
World Cup record		**Second phase 1999 and 2002-03**
Overall ODI record		**Played 333: Won 80, Lost 239, Tied 5, No result 9**

Test records for Zimbabwe can be found in the 2008 Cricinfo Guide

ZIMBABWE

BRENT, Gary Bazil January 13, 1976, Sinoia (now Chinhoyi)
RHB, RFM: 4 Tests, 35 runs (5.83); 7 wkts (44.85). 70 ODIs, 408 runs (12.00), 75 wkts (37.01).
Steady seamer who made ODI debut at 20 in 1996-97: recalled in 2006-07 after three years.

CHIBHABHA, Chamunorwa Justice September 6, 1986, Masvingo
RHB, RM: 0 Tests. 34 ODIs, 820 runs (24.11); 11 wkts (52.81).
Good-looking off-driver, and fine fielder: his sister Julia captains Zimbabwe's women's team.

CHIGUMBURA, Elton March 14, 1986, Kwekwe
RHB, RFM: 6 Tests, 187 runs (15.58), 9 wkts (55.33). 71 ODIs, 1409 runs (24.29), 41 wkts (40.51).
Big-hitting allrounder, and good outfielder, who made his first-class debut before he was 16.

DABENGWA, Keith Mbusi August 17, 1980, Bulawayo
LHB, SLA: 3 Tests, 90 runs (15.00), 5 wkts (49.80). 20 ODIs, 260 runs (23.63), 9 wkts (58.55).
Fitfully brilliant allrounder who scored 161 in 2005 and took 7-1 in a first-class match in 2007.

MASAKADZA, Hamilton August 9, 1983, Harare
RHB, LB: 15 Tests, 785 runs (27.06), 2 wkts (19.50). 51 ODIs, 1037 runs (21.16), 14 wkts (35.35).
Early-flowering batsman who made 119 on Test debut against West Indies in 2001, aged 17.

MATSIKENYERI, Stuart May 3, 1983, Harare
RHB, OB: 8 Tests, 351 runs (23.40), 2 wkts (172.50). 72 ODIs, 1339 runs (20.60), 13 wkts (51.00).
Cheerful, diminutive allrounder who made 150 for Zimbabwe v Bangladesh Board XI in 2005.

MPOFU, Christopher Bobby November 27, 1985, Plumtree
RHB, RFM: 6 Tests, 17 runs (2.83), 8 wkts (69.50). 26 ODIs, 19 runs (2.11), 27 wkts (40.22).
Tall seam bowler, and entertainingly clueless batsman: took 6-8 for Matabeleland in 2006.

MUPARIWA, Tawanda April 16, 1985, Bulawayo
RHB, RFM: 1 Test, 15 runs (15.00), 0 wkts. 23 ODIs, 149 runs (12.41), 40 wkts (26.32).
Fast bowler with a good inswinger, who took 4-46 v Pakistan at Multan in January 2008.

PRICE, Raymond William June 12, 1976, Salisbury (now Harare)
RHB, SLA: 18 Tests, 224 runs (9.73), 69 wkts (39.86). 35 ODIs, 107 runs (10.70), 21 wkts (61.00).
Economical spinner who played for Worcestershire between 2004 and 2007.

RAINSFORD, Edward Charles December 14, 1984, Kadoma
RHB, RFM: 0 Tests. 24 ODIs, 38 runs (4.75), 24 wkts (38.45).
Promising fast bowler, with a good outswinger and yorker: took 6-67 v South Africa A in 2004.

SIBANDA, Vusimuzi October 10, 1983, Highfields, Harare
RHB, RM: 3 Tests, 48 runs (8.00). 63 ODIs, 1440 runs (24.00), 2 wkts (74.00).
Stylish opener who often gets out when set: made 116 in tri-series final v Bermuda in 2006.

TAIBU, Tatenda May 14, 1983, Harare
RHB, WK: 24 Tests, 1273 runs (29.60), 1 wkt (27.00). 96 ODIs, 1791 runs (26.73), 2 wkts (30.50).
Tiny keeper, big-hearted batter: the youngest Test captain at 20, he later fell out with the Board.

TAYLOR, Brendan Ross Murray February 6, 1986, Harare
RHB, OB, WK: 10 Tests, 422 runs (21.10), 0 wkts. 75 ODIs, 1929 runs (28.36), 8 wkts (28.00).
Occasionally brilliant batsman, with a booming cover-drive: has had disciplinary problems.

UTSEYA, Prosper March 26, 1985, Harare
RHB, OB: 1 Test, 45 runs (22.50), 0 wkts. 71 ODIs, 400 runs (10.81), 46 wkts (53.95).
Short offspinner who keeps the runs down: took over as captain in July 2006, when he was 21.

WILLIAMS, Sean Colin September 26, 1986, Bulawayo
LHB, SLA: 0 Tests. 24 ODIs, 606 runs (30.30), 9 wkts (57.55).
Former national Under-19 captain: scored 70 v West Indies in the 2007 World Cup.*

COACHES

MICKEY **ARTHUR**

Full name **John Michael Arthur**
Born **May 17, 1968, Johannesburg, Transvaal**
Country **South Africa**

SOUTH AFRICA

Mickey Arthur was a dedicated batsman for Free State and Griqualand West, scoring over 6000 runs in first-class cricket before turning to coaching. He twice coached the Eastern Cape side to the finals of South Africa's new Twenty20 competition before being the surprise choice to succeed Ray Jennings at the helm of the national side in May 2005. After a tough baptism – home and away series against Australia – he settled down, and in 2007-08 South Africa won series in Pakistan and India, before coming to England in the summer of 2008 and winning the Tests there too, although the wheels fell off in the one-dayers that followed. Throughout, Arthur proved a canny and urbane presence at Graeme Smith's shoulder.

TREVOR **BAYLISS**

Full name **Trevor Harley Bayliss**
Born **December 21, 1962, Goulburn, NSW, Australia**
Country **Sri Lanka**

SRI LANKA

Trevor Bayliss was a strokeplaying middle-order batsman and brilliant cover fielder for New South Wales, and replaced Steve Rixon as their coach in 2004-05. He immediately guided them to the Pura Cup title, and added the one-day cup the following year. In 2007 Bayliss, who never won a Test cap, was named to succeed another Australian, Tom Moody, as Sri Lanka's coach, and although he lost the short Test series in Australia he was then in charge for home victories over England and India, as well as a shared series in the West Indies that included Sri Lanka's first Test win there. For good measure his side won the one-day Asia Cup, too, helped after they unearthed a new spin sensation in Ajantha Mendis.

JOHN **BRACEWELL**

Full name **John Garry Bracewell**
Born **April 15, 1958, Auckland**
Country **New Zealand**

NEW ZEALAND

A resourceful offspinner with a high action, and a useful, hard-hitting batsman, John Bracewell reached both 1000 runs and 100 wickets in his 41st and last Test in 1990 (Richard Hadlee's final Test too). Bracewell's first high-profile coaching job was with the English county Gloucestershire, who became a fine one-day unit under his charge, winning seven limited-overs titles between 1999 and 2004. By the last of those Bracewell was back in New Zealand as national coach. He had a moderately successful time with a limited but workmanlike team, the highlights being winning a limited-overs series against Australia and reaching the semi-finals of the 2007 World Cup, although his tenure was notable for several incidents when his mouth rather ran away with him. After another disappointing tour of England in 2008 Bracewell gave notice that he would be returning to Gloucestershire in April the following year.

JOHN **DYSON**

Full name **John Dyson**
Born **June 11, 1954, Kogarah, Sydney, NSW, Australia**
Country **West Indies**

A correct, hard-working opener, John Dyson played 30 Tests between 1977 and 1984, and did reasonably well for Australia at a time when the West Indian fast bowlers were ruining the careers of a succession of top-order batsmen. At Headingley in 1981 he made a superb century, although it was later rather overshadowed by Ian Botham's heroics. He took over as Sri Lanka's coach in 2003, an appointment which came as a surprise as he had little coaching experience at higher levels at the time. However, the players warmed to his style, and the team arrested a downward slide. His stint lasted nearly two years, before Tom Moody took over. In 2007, Dyson landed the job as West Indies' coach, and started with a bang with a shock Test win in South Africa – although that series was eventually lost, as was the home encounter with Australia.

GARY **KIRSTEN**

Full name **Gary Kirsten**
Born **November 23, 1967, Cape Town, South Africa**
Country **India**

A gritty left-hander, Gary Kirsten worked out his strengths and played to them superbly in a career that brought him 7289 runs in 101 Tests for South Africa, with 21 centuries. His highest score of 275 stretched over 14½ hours, and remains the second-longest innings in Test history. Kirsten was probably the most organised batsman to play for South Africa since their readmission to international cricket, and this methodical approach helped when he turned to coaching, first as a batting consultant for the Warriors franchise, then as director of his own coaching academy in Cape Town. In December 2007 he signed a two-year deal to succeed Greg Chappell as coach of India, and started with a drawn series against his native South Africa before suffering defeat in Sri Lanka.

GEOFF **LAWSON**

Full name **Geoffrey Francis Lawson**
Born **December 7, 1957, Wagga Wagga, NSW, Australia**
Country **Pakistan**

Geoff Lawson, an optometrist by training, suffered from tunnel vision, red mist and blind spots as much as any good fast bowler. He came to the fore in 1978-79 in the then-approved way for a paceman, by hitting Geoff Boycott, and went on to take 180 Test wickets, including 7 for 81 at Lord's in 1981 and 8 for 112 against West Indies at Adelaide in 1984-85. As captain of New South Wales, Lawson insisted on a "get on or get out" philosophy that not only brought the state titles, but also strongly influenced the methods of Mark Taylor and Steve Waugh as Test captains. After a spell as a journalist, Lawson was a slightly surprising choice to take on arguably the hardest coaching job in cricket – the Pakistan national side. And he had a hard act to follow in stepping into the late Bob Woolmer's shoes. He survived losing a Test series in India, although the local press became more and more hostile.

COACHES

ENGLAND

PETER **MOORES**

Full name **Peter Moores**
Born **December 18, 1962, Macclesfield, Cheshire**
Country **England**

Peter Moores had a long, efficient career keeping wicket for Sussex, for whom he made over 500 dismissals. He moved to Hove from Worcester in 1985, initially as understudy to Ian Gould. In 1998, a year after taking over as captain, Moores became first a player-coach and then, after retiring mid-season, concentrated solely on his coaching role. He quickly established a good reputation, and under him Sussex won the second division in 2001, and the first division itself two years later, the first County Championship title in Sussex's 164-year history. He was appointed as director of the ECB's academy in 2005, and landed the top job when Duncan Fletcher resigned after the 2007 World Cup. Initially Moores did not appear to enjoy the rapport with Michael Vaughan that Fletcher seemed to have, and may be more in synch with his own appointee Kevin Pietersen.

AUSTRALIA

TIM **NIELSEN**

Full name **Timothy John Nielsen**
Born **May 5, 1968, Forest Gate, London, England**
Country **Australia**

Tim Nielsen had a hard act to follow, replacing John Buchanan after his incredibly successful stint as Australia's coach, which ended in 2007 after two World Cup titles and countless Test victories. Nielsen, a talented wicketkeeper-batsman for South Australia whose international hopes were stymied by the perpetual presence under the Baggy Green of Ian Healy, had been around for part of the Buchanan era as the assistant coach and computer analyst, although he left to take charge of the national Centre of Excellence in Brisbane in 2005. "Working with 'Buck' was great," said Nielsen. "He's almost a mentor for me and we bounced ideas off each other." Nielsen's tenure started in familiar fashion, with lots more victories, although India ran Australia close in the home Tests of 2007-08 and also won the Aussie tri-series.

BANGLADESH

JAMIE **SIDDONS**

Full name **James Darren Siddons**
Born **April 25, 1964, Robinvale, Victoria, Australia**
Country **Bangladesh**

A stylish, attacking batsman and a superb fielder, Jamie Siddons scored more than 10,000 runs in the Sheffield Shield (later Pura Cup), a record when he retired in 1999-2000. But he never played a Test, at a time of plenty for Australian batting, and made a solitary one-day international appearance in Pakistan in 1988-89. A severe stomach bug he picked up on that tour in Pakistan didn't help his Test prospects, and nor did a fractured cheekbone, courtesy of Merv Hughes, in 1991-92: "It ruined my chances of playing for Australia," said Siddons. After retiring he coached at Australia's Centre of Excellence, then in October 2007 accepted an offer to coach Bangladesh. The size of his task, if he didn't realise it before, was hammered home when they lost his first four Tests in charge, and all his first 20 ODIs against Test-playing opposition.

UMPIRES AND REFEREES

ALEEM DAR

Full name **Aleem Sarwar Dar**
Born **June 6, 1968, Jhang, Punjab**
Country **Pakistan**

Tests **50 since 2003-04**
ODIs **108 since 1999-2000**
T20Is **none yet**

Aleem Dar played 17 first-class matches as an offspinning allrounder, but never surpassed the 39 he scored in his first innings, for Railways in February 1987. He took up umpiring in 1998-99, and stood in his first ODI the following season. He officiated at the 2003 World Cup, and a year later was the first Pakistani to join the ICC's elite panel. Calm and unobtrusive, he soon established a good reputation, and it was no surprise when he was chosen to stand in the 2007 World Cup final. What was a surprise was his part in the chaos in the dark at the end, for which all the officials were excluded from the World Twenty20 championships later in the year. Unlike most of his colleagues, he continues to play, and made 82 in a club game the day after umpiring a Test in Mumbai in November 2004.

ASAD RAUF

Full name **Asad Rauf**
Born **May 12, 1956, Lahore, Punjab**
Country **Pakistan**

Tests **19 since 2004-05**
ODIs **56 since 1999-2000**
T20Is **8 since 2007-08**

Asad Rauf was a right-hand batsman who enjoyed a solid if unspectacular first-class career in Pakistan in the 1980s, four times making more than 600 runs in a season and scoring three centuries, the highest 130 for Railways against National Bank in November 1981. He umpired his first first-class match in 1998-99, and stood in his first ODI early in 2000. It took a bit longer to crack the Test scene, but he advanced rapidly once he did, joining the ICC's elite panel in April 2006. A former offspinner himself, he is more prepared than some to give spinners lbws when batsmen prop forward hiding bat behind pad.

MARK **BENSON**

Full name **Mark Richard Benson**
Born **July 6, 1958, Shoreham-by-Sea, Sussex**
Country **England**

Tests **25 since 2004-05**
ODIs **65 since 2004**
T20Is **8 since 2007-08**

A gritty left-hander, Mark Benson won his only Test cap against India in June 1986, and played his solitary ODI a week later. He played on for almost a decade without catching the selectors' eyes again, making 18,387 runs, with 48 hundreds, the highest 257 against Hampshire on his first day as Kent's captain in 1991. He became a fulltime umpire in 2000, and his star rose rapidly: he was the TV official for an ODI the following season. He stood in an ODI for the first time in 2004, and joined the elite panel in April 2006. Later that year he had to have minor heart surgery after a turn during a Test in South Africa, but returned in time for the 2007 World Cup, in which six of his eight matches involved the South Africans.

UMPIRES AND REFEREES

BILLY **BOWDEN**

UMPIRE

Full name	**Brent Fraser Bowden**	
Born	**April 11, 1963, Henderson, Auckland**	
Country	**New Zealand**	

Tests	**48 since 1999-2000**
ODIs	**127 since 1994-95**
T20Is	**5 since 2004-05**

Some eccentrics are born. Others thrust eccentricity upon themselves. Brent "Billy" Bowden shot to fame with a zany array of embellished signals and a preposterous eye for showmanship. Bowden turned to umpiring after the onset of arthritis in his early twenties, and earned a reputation for giving batsmen out with a curiously bent finger. The most celebrated of his antics is the hop-on-one-leg-and-reach-for-Jesus signal for six. For all the embellishments, his decision-making is usually spot-on, although in 2007 he was suspended from standing in the inaugural World Twenty20 championship following his role (as fourth umpire) in the farcical conclusion of the World Cup final in Barbados.

CHRIS **BROAD**

REFEREE

Full name	**Brian Christopher Broad**	
Born	**Sept 29, 1957, Knowle, Somerset**	
Country	**England**	

Tests	**27 since 2003-04**
ODIs	**133 since 2003-04**
T20Is	**25 since 2005-06**

It was a classic case of poacher turned gamekeeper when Chris Broad became a match referee: he had several jousts with authority during a largely successful 25-Test career in the 1980s, refusing to walk after being given out in a Test in Pakistan, and smashing down the stumps after being bowled for 139 in the Bicentennial Test at Sydney in 1987-88. A tall, angular left-hander, Broad did well in Australia, scoring three more Test hundreds there in the 1986-87 Ashes series. After a back injury hastened his retirement, he tried his hand at TV commentary, then in 2003 became a match referee keen on enforcing the Code of Conduct. His son, Stuart, made his England debut in 2006.

STEVE **BUCKNOR**

UMPIRE

Full name	**Stephen Anthony Bucknor**	
Born	**May 31, 1946, Montego Bay, Jamaica**	
Country	**West Indies**	

Tests	**124 since 1988-89**
ODIs	**174 since 1988-89**
T20Is	**none yet**

Steve Bucknor, whose trademark is nodding gently before raising the dreaded finger, was the first man to umpire 100 Tests. He also stood in five successive World Cup finals. He is not due to retire until 2011, although recently a few errors have crept in – notably his part in the farcical finish of the 2007 World Cup final, and some odd decisions which fuelled the mutual dislike between Australia and India early in 2008, after which he was "rested" for the next Test. Bucknor originally started umpiring after repeated duff decisions in his Jamaican club games. His rise to star status was rapid: he stood in the 1992 World Cup final after just four Tests and a handful of ODIs. He is a man of routine, going through a morning ritual – exercises, a verse from the Bible, and the morning papers – before arriving at the ground. He is also a qualified football referee, who once handled a World Cup qualifier.

UMPIRES AND REFEREES

REFEREE

JEFF **CROWE**

Full name **Jeffrey John Crowe**
Born **September 14, 1958, Auckland**
Country **New Zealand**

Tests **20 since 2004-05**
ODIs **79 since 2003-04**
T20Is **2 since 2005**

Jeff Crowe might have played for Australia – he had several successful Sheffield Shield seasons in Adelaide – but he eventually returned to New Zealand, winning 39 Test caps, six as captain. Although he was often overshadowed by his younger brother Martin, Jeff managed three Test centuries of his own. After retirement he had a spell as New Zealand's manager, before becoming a referee in 2003. He was in charge for the 2007 World Cup final, where he presided over the embarrassing finale, which led to him and the umpires being suspended from the inaugural World Twenty20 championship later in the year, but he was back for England's series in Sri Lanka a couple of months later.

UMPIRE

STEVE **DAVIS**

Full name **Stephen James Davis**
Born **April 9, 1952, London, England**
Country **Australia**

Tests **13 since 1997-98**
ODIs **79 since 1992-93**
T20Is **3 since 2007-08**

Steve Davis played club cricket for the Adelaide club West Torrens before turning to umpiring. He had a rapid rise: appointed to the Australian first-class list in 1990-91, he joined the national panel two years later and stood in his first ODI the same season. Test cricket took a little longer, but in 1997-98 he made his debut at Hobart, when New Zealand's last pair hung on to deny Australia victory. Since then he has been a familiar face on the international scene. He stood in three matches in the 2007 World Cup, then officiated in the final two Tests in his native England in 2008, against South Africa, shortly after being elevated to the elite panel. "I have worked hard for this," he said on hearing of his promotion, "and now I look forward to concentrating on umpiring on a full-time basis."

UMPIRE

ASOKA **DE SILVA**

Full name **Ellawalakankanamge Asoka Ranjit de Silva**
Born **March 28, 1956, Kalutara**
Country **Sri Lanka**

Tests **33 since 2000**
ODIs **82 since 1999-2000**
T20Is **none yet**

Asoka de Silva played 10 Tests and 28 one-day internationals for Sri Lanka between 1985 and 1992 as a legspinner, although he found it hard to replicate his good domestic form on the international stage. He took up umpiring after retiring from first-class cricket in 1996-97, and soon became Sri Lanka's best-regarded official. He first stood in an ODI against Pakistan at Galle in August 1999, and umpired a Test the following year (Aravinda de Silva and Sanath Jayasuriya, who were both in de Silva's last Test as a player, were still playing for his umpiring debut). He had a spell on the ICC's elite panel before being dropped from it in 2004. But he was back for the 2007 World Cup – he also officiated in the 2003 tournament – and was restored to the elite panel in the middle of 2008. No Sri Lankan has umpired in more Tests or ODIs.

UMPIRES AND REFEREES

BILLY **DOCTROVE**

Full name	**Billy Raymond Doctrove**	
Born	**July 3, 1955, Marigot, Dominica**	
Country	**West Indies**	

Tests **19 since 1999-2000**
ODIs **79 since 1997-98**
T20Is **7 since 2007-08**

Billy Doctrove played club cricket in Dominica for a number of years, but his first love was football, particularly Liverpool, which explains his odd nickname "Toshack". In 1995 he became Dominica's first FIFA referee, and officiated in a number of internationals in the Caribbean, including a World Cup qualifier between Guyana and Grenada. In 1997 he quit football to concentrate on umpiring, and stood in his first Test in 2000. He joined the international panel in 2004 and the elite one in 2006, but his first forays at the highest level were uninspiring, and he found himself embroiled in the Pakistan ball-tampering furore at The Oval in 2006, as the "other umpire" to Darrell Hair.

DARYL **HARPER**

Full name	**Daryl John Harper**	
Born	**October 23, 1951, Adelaide**	
Country	**Australia**	

Tests **73 since 1998-99**
ODIs **150 since 1993-94**
T20Is **6 since 2007-08**

Daryl Harper played club cricket in Adelaide for many years before turning to umpiring. He stood in his first first-class match in 1987-88, and joined Australia's international panel six years later. Quiet and undemonstrative, he was Australia's first representative on the ICC's international panel when it was set up in 2002, being chosen ahead of Darrell Hair and Simon Taufel, and is one of only three survivors (with Steve Bucknor and Rudi Koertzen) from that original intake. He likes most sports, particularly Aussie Rules football and basketball, and writes an entertaining online blog about his travels at www.cricketump.com.

ALAN **HURST**

Full name	**Alan George Hurst**	
Born	**July 15, 1950, Altona, Melbourne**	
Country	**Australia**	

Tests **20 since 2004-05**
ODIs **62 since 2004-05**
T20Is **2 since 2007-08**

A strapping fast bowler, Alan Hurst won all but one of his dozen Test caps during the World Series Cricket era, after Australia's leading players had been poached by Kerry Packer. He nonetheless took 25 wickets in the 1978-79 Ashes series, which Australia lost 5-1, before the return of Lillee and Co., and a serious back injury, put paid to his future prospects. He was also a notably bad batsman, collecting ducks in exactly half his 20 Test innings. After a spell as a teacher he joined the ICC's panel of referees in 2004.

UMPIRES AND REFEREES

UMPIRE

RUDI **KOERTZEN**

Full name	**Rudolf Eric Koertzen**	*Tests*	**92 since 1992-93**
Born	**March 26, 1949, Knysna, Cape Province**	*ODIs*	**190 since 1992-93**
Country	**South Africa**	*T20Is*	**2 since 2006-07**

Rudi Koertzen is a modern umpire in the traditional mould, a curious blend of old and new – his flat white cap is usually offset by a pair of wraparound shades, while his trademark is a dalek-like super-slo-mo raise of the fatal finger to exterminate a batsman's innings. A lifelong cricket fan, he played league cricket while working as a railway clerk, but turned to umpiring in 1981. He first stood in a Test in 1992-93, in South Africa's first home series after readmission, and has been a fixture ever since: he has now umpired more ODIs than anyone else. An original member of the elite panel, he leaves little to chance, putting in regular sessions in the gym as well as long hours in front of the TV studying the techniques – and previous dismissals – of the batsmen at his mercy. He was one of the support officials for the 2007 World Cup final, but his lead role in the farcical finale cost him a place at the inaugural World Twenty20 championship later in the year.

REFEREE

RANJAN **MADUGALLE**

Full name	**Ranjan Serenath Madugalle**	*Tests*	**107 since 1993-94**
Born	**April 22, 1959, Kandy**	*ODIs*	**219 since 1993-94**
Country	**Sri Lanka**	*T20Is*	**14 since 2006-07**

A stylish right-hander, Ranjan Madugalle won 21 Test caps, the first of them in Sri Lanka's inaugural Test, against England in 1981-82, when he top-scored with 65 in the first innings. He also made 103 against India in Colombo in 1985, and captained Sri Lanka twice. Not long after retiring, and trying his hand at marketing, he became one of the first match refs, and was appointed the ICC's chief referee in 2001. His easy-going exterior and charming personality are a mask for someone who has a reputation as a strict disciplinarian.

REFEREE

ROSHAN **MAHANAMA**

Full name	**Roshan Siriwardene Mahanama**	*Tests*	**24 since 2003-04**
Born	**May 31, 1966, Colombo**	*ODIs*	**95 since 2003-04**
Country	**Sri Lanka**	*T20Is*	**2 since 2007-08**

Roshan Mahanama's playing career had two major highlights: he was part of the winning team in the 1996 World Cup, and the following year made 225 (the highest score in his 52 Tests) as he and Sanath Jayasuriya put on 576, then a record Test partnership, as Sri Lanka ran up 952 for 6 (another record) against India in Colombo. An attacking right-hander who made four Test centuries in all (three in nine months in 1992-93), he was also a fine fielder. He was jettisoned after the 1999 World Cup and quit not long afterwards, blaming the selectors for their shabby treatment of him in a book he called *Retired Hurt*. He joined the ICC's referees panel in 2003.

UMPIRES AND REFEREES

MIKE **PROCTER**

REFEREE

Full name	**Michael John Procter**	*Tests*	**47 since 2001-02**	
Born	**September 15, 1946, Durban, Natal**	*ODIs*	**154 since 2001-02**	
Country	**South Africa**	*T20Is*	**15 since 2005-06**	

The world's greatest allrounder for a while in the 1970s, Mike Procter did marvels with the bat (once scoring six successive first-class hundreds) and ball (hurtling in and bowling furiously quick using a peculiar wrong-footed action) for a variety of teams, especially Gloucestershire where he was a folk hero. He was restricted to seven Tests as a player, as he peaked just as South Africa were being ostracised from world sport: he still took 41 wickets at just 15.02. When South Africa were readmitted he was their first coach, then went upstairs to the referee's room. There, he exudes calm – although many thought he should have made more noise at The Oval in 2006, when he oversaw what became the first forfeited Test match after Pakistan were penalised for ball-tampering.

JAVAGAL **SRINATH**

REFEREE

Full name	**Javagal Srinath**	*Tests*	**9 since 2006**
Born	**August 31, 1969, Mysore, Karnataka**	*ODIs*	**43 since 2006-07**
Country	**India**	*T20Is*	**5 since 2006-07**

Arguably the fastest bowler India has ever produced, Javagal Srinath took 236 wickets in Tests, and 315 more in ODIs. He was tall, and usually slanted the ball in. Unusually for a quick bowler, he did better in India than overseas, his bowling average of 26 at home being four runs lower than his overall one. He went out at the top: his last international match was the 2003 World Cup final. Sadly, there was no fairytale farewell – Srinath was caned (0 for 87) as Australia ran out easy winners. He was not long away from the international arena, though: after a spell as a commentator he joined the referees' panel in 2006. "I'll have to concentrate more than I did during my playing days," he observed.

SIMON **TAUFEL**

UMPIRE

Full name	**Simon James Arnold Taufel**	*Tests*	**53 since 2000-01**
Born	**Jan 21, 1971, St Leonards, Sydney**	*ODIs*	**138 since 1999-2000**
Country	**Australia**	*T20Is*	**11 since 2007-08**

Simon Taufel came young to umpiring: he was only 24 when he stood in his first Sheffield Shield match, and still under 30 – and younger than some of the players – when he made his Test debut on Boxing Day 2000. He took up umpiring after being forced to retire from Sydney club cricket with a back injury. Calm and collected on the field, he leaves little to chance, regularly running laps of the ground to keep fit and often standing in the practice nets to familiarise himself with players' techniques. And it has paid off: he joined the ICC's elite panel in 2003, and won the award as the world's leading umpire (voted on by the Test captains and referees) five times running from 2004.

UMPIRES AND REFEREES

As well as its "elite" panel of umpires, the ICC also has an "international" panel, who fill in when gaps arise in the rota. This reserve list includes:

Barbour, Kevan Christopher (Zimbabwe)   b. October 23, 1949, Bulawayo
Has stood in 4 Tests and 41 ODIs.

Baxter, Gary Arthur Vincent (New Zealand)   b. March 5, 1953, Christchurch
Has stood in 19 ODIs and 2 Twenty20 internationals.

Duncan, Clyde Rory (West Indies)   b. January 7, 1954, Vreed-En-Hoop, Guyana
Has stood in 2 Tests, 13 ODIs and 2 Twenty20 internationals.

Enamul Haque (Bangladesh)   b. February 27, 1966, Comilla, Chittagong
Played 10 Tests and 29 ODIs: has stood in 9 ODIs and 2 Twenty20 internationals.

Gould, Ian James (England),   b. August 19, 1957, Taplow, Bucks
Played 18 ODIs: has stood in 26 ODIs and 3 Twenty20 internationals.

Hill, Anthony Lloyd (New Zealand)   b. June 26, 1951, Auckland
Has stood in 7 Tests, 59 ODIs and 9 Twenty20 internationals.

Howell, Ian Lester (South Africa)   b. May 20, 1958, Port Elizabeth, Cape Province
Has stood in 9 Tests, 63 ODIs and 8 Twenty20 internationals.

Jerling, Brian George (South Africa)   b. August 13, 1958, Port Elizabeth, Cape Province
Has stood in 4 Tests, 68 ODIs and 6 Twenty20 internationals.

Llong, Nigel James (England)   b. February 11, 1969, Ashford, Kent
Has stood in 2 Tests, 17 ODIs and 10 Twenty20 internationals.

Malcolm, Norman Alexander (West Indies)   b. March 19, 1955, Manchester, Jamaica
Has stood in 2 ODIs.

Nadeem Ghauri, Mohammad (Pakistan)   b. October 12, 1962, Lahore, Punjab.
Played 1 Test and 6 ODIs: has stood in 5 Tests, 37 ODIs and 1 Twenty20 international.

Nadir Shah (Bangladesh)   b. February 7, 1964, Dacca (now Dhaka)
Has stood in 18 ODIs and 1 Twenty20 international.

Parker, Peter Douglas (Australia)   b. July 20, 1959, Herston, Brisbane, Queensland
Has stood in 10 Tests, 65 ODIs and 2 Twenty20 internationals.

Saheba, Amiesh Maheshbhai (India)   b. November 15, 1959, Ahmedabad, Gujarat
Has stood in 21 ODIs and 2 Twenty20 internationals.

Shastri, Suresh Lalchand (India)   b. September 15, 1955, Jodhpur, Rajasthan
Has stood in 2 Tests, 19 ODIs and 1 Twenty20 international.

Tiffin, Russell Blair (Zimbabwe)   b. June 4, 1959, Salisbury (now Harare)
Has stood in 42 Tests and 100 ODIs.

Wijewardene, Tyron Hirantha (Sri Lanka)   b. August 29, 1961, Maradana
Has stood in 4 Tests and 42 ODIs.

Zameer Haider (Pakistan)   b. September 30, 1962, Lahore
Has stood in 4 ODIs and 1 Twenty20 international.

OVERALL RECORDS

Test Matches

Most appearances

168	SR Waugh	A
156	AR Border	A
150	SR Tendulkar	I
145	SK Warne	A
133	AJ Stewart	E
132	CA Walsh	WI
131	Kapil Dev	I
131	BC Lara	WI*
130	A Kumble	I
128	ME Waugh	A

Lara's record includes one Test for the World XI

Most runs

			Avge
11953	BC Lara	WI*	52.88
11877	SR Tendulkar	I	54.23
11174	AR Border	A	50.56
10927	SR Waugh	A	51.06
10246	R Dravid	I*	53.92
10122	SM Gavaskar	I	51.12
10099	RT Ponting	A	58.37
9761	JH Kallis	SA*	55.46
8900	GA Gooch	E	42.58
8832	Javed Miandad	P	52.57

The records for Lara, Dravid and Kallis include one Test for the World XI

Most wickets

			Avge
756	M Muralitharan	SL*	21.96
708	SK Warne	A	25.41
616	A Kumble	I	29.33
563	GD McGrath	A	21.64
519	CA Walsh	WI	24.44
434	Kapil Dev	I	29.64
431	RJ Hadlee	NZ	22.29
421	SM Pollock	SA	23.11
414	Wasim Akram	P	23.62
405	CEL Ambrose	WI	20.99

Muralitharan's record includes one Test for the World XI

Highest scores

400*	BC Lara	WI v Eng at St John's	2003-04
380	ML Hayden	Aust v Zim at Perth	2003-04
375	BC Lara	WI v Eng at St John's	1993-94
374	DPMD Jayawardene	SL v SA at Colombo	2006
365*	GS Sobers	WI v Pak at Kingston	1957-58
364	L Hutton	Eng v Aust at The Oval	1938
340	ST Jayasuriya	SL v India at Colombo	1997-98
337	Hanif Mohammad	Pak v WI at Bridgetown	1957-58
336*	WR Hammond	Eng v NZ at Auckland	1932-33
334*	MA Taylor	Aust v Pak at Peshawar	1998-99
334	DG Bradman	Aust v Eng at Leeds	1930

In all 22 scores of 300 or more have been made in Tests

Best innings bowling

10-53	JC Laker	Eng v Aust at Manchester	1956
10-74	A Kumble	India v Pak at Delhi	1998-99
9-28	GA Lohmann	Eng v SA at Jo'burg	1895-96
9-37	JC Laker	Eng v Aust at Manchester	1956
9-51	M Muralitharan	SL v Zim at Kandy	2001-02
9-52	RJ Hadlee	NZ v Aust at Brisbane	1985-86
9-56	Abdul Qadir	Pak v Eng at Lahore	1987-88
9-57	DE Malcolm	Eng v SA at The Oval	1994
9-65	M Muralitharan	SL v Eng at The Oval	1998
9-69	JM Patel	India v Aust at Kanpur	1959-60

There have been seven further instances of a bowler taking nine wickets in an innings

Record wicket partnerships

1st	415	ND McKenzie (226) and GC Smith (232)	South Africa v Bangladesh at Chittagong	2007-08
2nd	576	ST Jayasuriya (340) and RS Mahanama (225)	Sri Lanka v India at Colombo	1997-98
3rd	624	KC Sangakkara (287) and DPMD Jayawardene (374)	Sri Lanka v South Africa at Colombo	2006
4th	411	PBH May (285*) and MC Cowdrey (154)	England v West Indies at Birmingham	1957
5th	405	SG Barnes (234) and DG Bradman (234)	Australia v England at Sydney	1946-47
6th	346	JHW Fingleton (136) and DG Bradman (270)	Australia v England at Melbourne	1936-37
7th	347	DS Atkinson (219) and CC Depeiaza (122)	West Indies v Australia at Bridgetown	1954-55
8th	313	Wasim Akram (257*) and Saqlain Mushtaq (79)	Pakistan v Zimbabwe at Sheikhupura	1996-97
9th	195	MV Boucher (78) and PL Symcox (108)	South Africa v Pakistan at Johannesburg	1997-98
10th	151	BF Hastings (110) and RO Collinge (68*)	New Zealand v Pakistan at Auckland	1972-73
	151	Azhar Mahmood (128*) and Mushtaq Ahmed (59)	Pakistan v South Africa at Rawalpindi	1997-98

*Figures to 12.9.08. Updated records can be found at **www.cricinfo.com/ci/engine/records***

Most catches

Fielders

181	**ME Waugh** *A*	
176	**R Dravid** *I/World*	
171	**SP Fleming** *NZ*	
164	**BC Lara** *WI/World*	
157	**MA Taylor** *A*	

Most dismissals

Wicketkeepers   *Ct/St*

449	**MV Boucher**	
	SA/World	429/20
416	**AC Gilchrist** *A*	379/37
395	**IA Healy** *A*	366/29
355	**RW Marsh** *A*	343/12
270	**PJL Dujon** *WI*	265/5

Highest team totals

952-6d	**Sri Lanka** v India at Colombo	1997-98
903-7d	**Eng** v Australia at The Oval	1938
849	**Eng** v WI at Kingston	1929-30
790-3d	**WI** v Pakistan at Kingston	1957-58
758-8d	**Aust** v WI at Kingston	1954-55
756-5d	**Sri Lanka** v SA at Colombo	2006
751-5d	**WI** v England at St John's	2003-04
747	**WI** v SA at St John's	2004-05
735-6d	**Aust** v Zimbabwe at Perth	2003-04
729-6d	**Aust** v England at Lord's	1930

There have been four further totals of more than 700, one each day by Australia, India, Pakistan and Sri Lanka

Lowest team totals

Completed innings

26	**NZ** v Eng at Auckland	1954-55
30	**SA** v Eng at Pt Elizabeth	1895-96
30	**SA** v Eng at Birmingham	1924
35	**SA** v Eng at Cape Town	1898-99
36	**Aust** v Eng at B'ham	1902
36	**SA** v Aust at M'bourne	1931-32
42	**Aust** v Eng at Sydney	1887-88
42	**NZ** v Aust at W'ton	1945-46
42*	**India** v England at Lord's	1974
43	**SA** v Eng at Cape Town	1888-89

* One batsmen absent hurt. There have been seven further totals of less than 50, the most recent West Indies' 47 v England at Kingston in 2003-04

Best match bowling

19-90	**JC Laker**	Eng v Aust at Manchester	1956
17-159	**SF Barnes**	Eng v SA at Jo'burg	1913-14
16-136	**ND Hirwani**	India v WI at Madras	1987-88
16-137	**RAL Massie**	Aust v England at Lord's	1972
16-220	**M Muralitharan**	SL v England at The Oval	1998
15-28	**J Briggs**	Eng v SA at Cape Town	1888-89
15-45	**GA Lohmann**	Eng v SA at Pt Elizabeth	1895-96
15-99	**C Blythe**	Eng v SA at Leeds	1907
15-104	**H Verity**	England v Aust at Lord's	1934
15-123	**RJ Hadlee**	NZ v Aust at Brisbane	1985-86

Hirwani and Massie were making their Test debuts. W Rhodes (15-124) and Harbhajan Singh (15-217) also took 15 wickets in a match

Most centuries

		Tests
39	**SR Tendulkar** *India*	150
35	**RT Ponting** *Australia*	119
34	**SM Gavaskar** *India*	125
34	**BC Lara** *West Indies/World XI*	131
32	**SR Waugh** *Australia*	168
30	**ML Hayden** *Australia*	94
30	**JH Kallis** *South Africa/World XI*	123
29	**DG Bradman** *Australia*	52
27	**AR Border** *Australia*	156
26	**GS Sobers** *West Indies*	93

Bradman (12) hit the most double-centuries, ahead of Lara (9) and WR Hammond (7)

Test match results

	Played	Won	Lost	Drawn	Tied	% win
Australia	696	326	179	189	2	46.83
Bangladesh	53	1	47	5	0	1.88
England	877	305	255	317	0	34.77
India	421	95	136	189	1	22.56
New Zealand	342	65	137	140	0	19.00
Pakistan	335	103	88	144	0	30.74
South Africa	336	115	118	103	0	34.22
Sri Lanka	180	54	67	59	0	30.00
West Indies	448	151	146	150	1	33.70
Zimbabwe	83	8	49	26	0	9.63
World XI	1	0	1	0	0	0.00
TOTAL	**1886**	**1223**	**1223**	**661**	**2**	

OVERALL RECORDS *One-day Internationals*

Most appearances

421	ST Jayasuriya *SL/Asia*
417	SR Tendulkar *I*
378	Inzamam-ul-Haq *P/Asia*
356	Wasim Akram *P*
334	M Azharuddin *I*
333	R Dravid *I/Asia/World*
325	SR Waugh *A*
322	WPUJC Vaas *SL/Asia*
314	M Muralitharan *SL/Asia/World*
311	SC Ganguly *I/Asia*

A further 20 men have played in 250 or more ODIs

Most runs

		Avge
16361	SR Tendulkar *I*	44.33
12785	ST Jayasuriya *SL/Asia*	32.69
11739	Inzamam-ul-Haq *P/Asia*	39.52
11363	SC Ganguly *I/Asia*	41.02
11113	RT Ponting *A/World*	43.24
10585	R Dravid *I/Asia/World*	39.49
10405	BC Lara *WI/World*	40.48
9619	AC Gilchrist *A/World*	35.89
9609	JH Kallis *SA/Af/World*	44.69
9378	M Azharuddin *I*	36.92

PA de Silva (9284) and Mohammad Yousuf (9242) have also reached 9000 runs in ODIs

Most wickets

		Avge
502	Wasim Akram *P*	23.52
479	M Muralitharan *SL/World*	23.02
416	Waqar Younis *P*	23.84
400	WPUJC Vaas *SL/Asia*	27.53
393	SM Pollock *SA/Af/World*	24.50
381	GD McGrath *A/World*	22.02
337	A Kumble *I/Asia*	30.89
315	J Srinath *I*	28.08
310	ST Jayasuriya *SL/Asia*	36.55
303	B Lee *A*	22.95

Six other bowlers have passed 250 wickets in ODIs, and 13 more have reached 200

Highest scores

194	Saeed Anwar	Pakistan v India at Chennai	1996-97
189*	IVA Richards	W Indies v England at Manchester	1984
189	ST Jayasuriya	Sri Lanka v India at Sharjah	2000-01
188*	G Kirsten	SA v UAE at Rawalpindi	1995-96
186*	SR Tendulkar	India v NZ at Hyderabad	1999-2000
183*	MS Dhoni	India v Sri Lanka at Jaipur	2005-06
183	SC Ganguly	India v Sri Lanka at Taunton	1999
181*	ML Hayden	Aust v N Zealand at Hamilton	2006-07
181	IVA Richards	WI v Sri Lanka at Karachi	1987-88
175*	Kapil Dev	India v Zim at Tunbridge Wells	1983
175	HH Gibbs	SA v Aust at Johannesburg	2005-06

SR Tendulkar has scored 42 ODI centuries, ST Jayasuriya 27, RT Ponting 26, SC Ganguly 22, HH Gibbs and Saeed Anwar 20

Best innings bowling

8-19	WPUJC Vaas	SL v Zimbabwe at Colombo	2001-02
7-15	GD McGrath	Aust v Namibia at P'stroom	2002-03
7-20	AJ Bichel	Aust v Eng at Port Elizabeth	2002-03
7-30	M Muralitharan	Sri Lanka v India at Sharjah	2000-01
7-36	Waqar Younis	Pakistan v England at Leeds	2001
7-37	Aqib Javed	Pakistan v India at Sharjah	1991-92
7-51	WW Davis	West Indies v Australia at Leeds	1983
6-12	A Kumble	India v West Indies at Calcutta	1993-94
6-13	BAW Mendis	Sri Lanka v India at Karachi	2008
6-14	GJ Gilmour	Australia v England at Leeds	1975
6-14	Imran Khan	Pakistan v India at Sharjah	1984-85
6-14	MF Maharoof	Sri Lanka v W Indies at Mumbai	2006-07

Waqar Younis took five in an innings 13 times and Muralitharan 8

Record wicket partnerships

1st	286	WU Tharanga (109) and ST Jayasuriya (152)	Sri Lanka v England at Leeds	2006
2nd	331	SR Tendulkar (186*) and R Dravid (153)	India v New Zealand at Hyderabad	1999-2000
3rd	237*	R Dravid (104*) and SR Tendulkar (140*)	India v Kenya at Bristol	1999
4th	275*	M Azharuddin (153*) and A Jadeja (116*)	India v Zimbabwe at Cuttack	1997-98
5th	223	M Azharuddin (111*) and A Jadeja (119)	India v Sri Lanka at Colombo	1997-98
6th	218	DPMD Jayawardene (107) and MS Dhoni (139*)	Asia XI v Africa XI at Chennai	2007
7th	130	A Flower (142*) and HH Streak (56)	Zimbabwe v England at Harare	2001-02
8th	138*	JM Kemp (110*) and AJ Hall (56*)	South Africa v India at Cape Town	2006-07
9th	126*	Kapil Dev (175*) and SMH Kirmani (24*)	India v Zimbabwe at Tunbridge Wells	1983
10th	106*	IVA Richards (189*) and MA Holding (12*)	West Indies v England at Manchester	1984

Figures to 12.9.08. Updated records can be found at **www.cricinfo.com/ci/engine/records**

One-day Internationals **OVERALL RECORDS**

Most catches

Fielders

156	M Azharuddin	*I*
151	DPMD Jayawardene	*SL/Asia*
135	RT Ponting	*A/World*
133	SP Fleming	*NZ/World*
127	AR Border	*A*

Most dismissals

Wicketkeepers — *Ct/St*

472	AC Gilchrist	*A/World*	417/55
389	MV Boucher	*SA/Africa*	371/18
287	Moin Khan	*P*	214/73
249	KC Sangakkara	*SL*	190/59
233	IA Healy	*A*	194/39

Highest team totals

443-9	**SL** v N'lands at Amstelveen	2006
438-9	**SA** v Aust at Johannesburg	2005-06
434-4	**Australia** v SA at Jo'burg	2005-06
418-5	**SA** v Zim at P'stroom	2006-07
413-5	**Ind** v Bermuda at P-o-Spain	2006-07
402-2	**NZ** v Ireland at Aberdeen	2008
398-5	**SL** v Kenya at Kandy	1995-96
397-5	**NZ** v Zimbabwe at Bulawayo	2005-06
392-6	**SA** v Pakistan at Centurion	2006-07
391-4	**Eng** v B'desh at Nottingham	2005

NZ's 397-5 was made in 44 overs, all the other totals in 50 except SA's 438-9, when the winning run came off the fifth ball of the 50th over

Lowest team totals

Completed innings

35	**Zim** v SL at Harare	2003-04
36	**Canada** v SL at Paarl	2002-03
38	**Zim** v SL at Colombo	2001-02
43	**Pak** v WI at Cape Town	1992-93
45	**Can** v Eng at Manchester	1979
45	**Nam** v Aust at P'stroom	2002-03
54	**India** v SL at Sharjah	2000-01
54	**WI** v SA at Cape Town	2003-04
55	**SL** v WI at Sharjah	1986-87
63	**India** v Aust at Sydney	1980-81

The lowest total successfully defended in a non-rain-affected ODI is 125, by India v Pakistan (87) at Sharjah in 1984-85

Most sixes

265	ST Jayasuriya	*SL/Asia*
247	Shahid Afridi	*Pak/Asia/World*
190	SC Ganguly	*I/Asia*
166	SR Tendulkar	*I*
153	CL Cairns	*NZ/World*
149	AC Gilchrist	*A/World*
144	Inzamam-ul-Haq	*P/Asia*
136	RT Ponting	*A/World*
133	BC Lara	*WI/World*
126	IVA Richards	*WI*

Eight other men have hit 100 sixes

Best strike rate

Runs per 100 balls		*Runs*
111.22	Shahid Afridi *P/Asia/World*	5479
99.43	IDS Smith *NZ*	1055
99.14	V Sehwag *I/Asia/World*	5810
96.94	AC Gilchrist *A/World*	9619
96.66	RL Powell *WI*	2085
95.07	Kapil Dev *I*	3783
92.78	A Symonds *A*	5006
91.30	MS Dhoni *I/Asia*	3793
91.03	ST Jayasuriya *SL/Asia*	12785
90.64	BB McCullum *NZ*	2605

Qualification: 1000 runs

Most economical bowlers

Runs per over		*Wkts*
3.09	J Garner *WI*	146
3.28	RGD Willis *E*	80
3.30	RJ Hadlee *NZ*	158
3.32	MA Holding *WI*	142
3.37	SP Davis *A*	44
3.40	AME Roberts *WI*	87
3.48	CEL Ambrose *WI*	225
3.53	MD Marshall *WI*	157
3.54	ARC Fraser *E*	47
3.55	MR Whitney *A*	46

Qualification: 2000 balls bowled

One-day international results

	Played	Won	Lost	Tied	No result	% win
Australia	687	425	233	8	21	64.41
Bangladesh	187	40	145	0	2	21.62
England	498	240	235	5	18	50.52
India	696	332	331	3	30	50.07
Kenya	103	32	67	0	4	32.32
New Zealand	548	238	279	5	26	46.07
Pakistan	687	371	295	6	15	55.65
South Africa	409	252	140	5	12	64.10
Sri Lanka	561	256	280	3	22	47.77
West Indies	595	325	246	5	19	56.85
Zimbabwe	333	80	239	5	9	25.46
Others (see below)	220	54	155	1	10	24.77
TOTAL	**2762**	**2645**	**2645**	**23**	**94**	

Other teams: Africa XI (P6, W1, L4, NR1), Asia XI (P7, W4, L2, NR1), Bermuda (P33, W7, L26), Canada (P41, W9, L32), East Africa (P3, L3), Hong Kong (P4, L4), Ireland (P31, W9, L18, T1, NR3), Namibia (P6, L6), Netherlands (P39, W13, L24, NR2), Scotland (P33, W9, L21, NR3), United Arab Emirates (P11, W1, L10), USA (P2, L2), World XI (P4, W1, L3).

Most appearances

16	BB McCullum	NZ
14	MJ Clarke	A
14	PD Collingwood	E
14	KP Pietersen	E
14	SB Styris	NZ
13	AC Gilchrist	A
13	MEK Hussey	A
13	B Lee	A
13	A Symonds	A
13	LRPL Taylor	NZ

New Zealand have so far played 16 matches, Australia 15 and England 14

Most runs

			Avge
364	GC Smith	SA	36.40
363	KP Pietersen	E	27.92
338	Misbah-ul-Haq	P	67.60
337	A Symonds	A	56.16
330	PD Collingwood	E	25.38
323	BB McCullum	NZ	23.07
315	RT Ponting	A	39.37
313	Shoaib Malik	P	31.30
308	ML Hayden	A	51.33
299	G Gambhir	I	37.37

The highest batting average for anyone who has played more than 5 matches is 96.00, by RG Sharma of India

Most wickets

			Avge
15	NW Bracken	A	16.86
15	SM Pollock	SA	20.60
15	Shahid Afridi	P	18.66
14	Abdur Razzaq	B	16.00
13	SCJ Broad	E	27.30
13	SR Clark	A	18.23
13	PD Collingwood	E	18.23
13	RP Singh	I	14.69
13	Umar Gul	P	13.92
13	DL Vettori	NZ	15.61

Five further bowlers have taken 12 wickets

Highest Scores

117	CH Gayle	WI v SA at Johannesburg	2007-08
98*	RT Ponting	Australia v NZ at Auckland	2004-05
96	DR Martyn	Australia v SA at Brisbane	2005-06
90*	HH Gibbs	SA v WI at Johannesburg	2007-08
89*	GC Smith	SA v Aust at Johannesburg	2005-06
89*	JM Kemp	SA v New Zealand at Durban	2007-08
88	ST Jayasuriya	SL v Kenya at Johannesburg	2007-08
87*	Misbah-ul-Haq	Pak v Bangladesh at Karachi	2007-08
85*	A Symonds	Aust v New Zealand at Perth	2007-08
81	Nazimuddin	B'desh v Pakistan at Nairobi	2007-08

Ponting's innings, in the very first such international, is the highest score on T20I debut

Best innings bowling

4-7	MR Gillespie	NZ v Kenya at Durban	2007-08
4-9	DW Steyn	SA v WI at Port Elizabeth	2007-08
4-13	RP Singh	India v SA at Durban	2007-08
4-17	M Morkel	South Africa v NZ at Durban	2007-08
4-18	Moh'd Asif	Pakistan v India at Durban	2007-08
4-19	Shahid Afridi	Pak v Scotland at Durban	2007-08
4-19	HS Baidwan	Canada v N'lands at Belfast	2008
4-20	DL Vettori	NZ v India at Johannesburg	2007-08
4-20	SR Clark	Australia v SL at Cape Town	2007-08
4-21	AR Cusack	Ireland v Scotland at Belfast	2008

There have been 6 further instances of a bowler taking 4 wickets in an innings

Record wicket partnerships

1st	145	CH Gayle (117) and DS Smith (35)	West Indies v South Africa at Johannesburg	2007-08
2nd	111	GC Smith (89*) and HH Gibbs (56)	South Africa v Australia at Johannesburg	2005-06
3rd	120*	HH Gibbs (90*) and JM Kemp (46*)	South Africa v West Indies at Johannesburg	2007-08
4th	101	Younis Khan (51) and Shoaib Malik (57)	Pakistan v Sri Lanka at Johannesburg	2007-08
5th	119*	Shoaib Malik (52*) and Misbah-ul-Haq (66*)	Pakistan v Australia at Johannesburg	2007-08
6th	77*	RT Ponting (98*) and MEK Hussey (31*)	Australia v New Zealand at Auckland	2004-05
7th	91	PD Collingwood (79) and MH Yardy (23*)	England v West Indies at The Oval	2007
8th	40	SB Styris (66) and JW Wilson (18)	New Zealand v Australia at Auckland	2004-05
	40	J Mubarak (28) and WPUJC Vaas (21)	Sri Lanka v Australia at Cape Town	2007-08
9th	44	SL Malinga (27) and CRD Fernando (21)	Sri Lanka v New Zealand at Auckland	2006-07
10th	28	JDP Oram (66*) and JS Patel (4)	New Zealand v Australia at Perth	2007-08

Figures to 12.9.08. Updated records can be found at www.cricinfo.com/ci/engine/records

Twenty20 Internationals **OVERALL RECORDS**

Most catches

Fielders

11	LRPL Taylor	*NZ*
8	AB de Villiers	*SA*
8	MEK Hussey	*A*
8	GC Smith	*SA*
8	Younis Khan	*P*

Most dismissals

Wicketkeepers			*Ct/St*
17	AC Gilchrist	*A*	17/0
12	BB McCullum	*NZ*	9/3
11	Mushfiqur Rahim	*B*	4/7
11	Kamran Akmal	*P*	6/5
9	MV Boucher	*SA*	9/0

Highest team totals

260-6	**Sri Lanka** v Kenya at Jo'burg	2007-08
221-5	**Aust** v England at Sydney	2006-07
218-4	**India** v England at Durban	2007-08
214-5	**Australia** v NZ at Auckland	2004-05
209-3	**Australia** v SA at Brisbane	2005-06
208-2	**South Africa** v WI at Jo'burg	2007-08
208-8	**WI** v England at The Oval	2007
205-6	**West Indies** v SA at Jo'burg	2007-08
203-5	**Pakistan** v B'desh at Karachi	2007-08
201-4	**SA** v Australia at Jo'burg	2005-06

The only other score of 200 or more is England's 200-6 v India at Durban in 2007-08

Lowest team totals

Completed innings

67	**Kenya** v Ireland at Belfast	2008
70	**Bermuda** v Can at Belfast	2008
73	**Kenya** v NZ at Durban	2007-08
74	**India** v Aust at M'bourne	2007-08
79	**Aust** v Eng at Southampton	2005
83	**B'desh** v SL at Jo'burg	2007-08
88	**Kenya** v SL at Jo'burg	2007-08
91	**Canada** v Kenya at Belfast	2008
92	**Kenya** v Pak at Nairobi	2007-08
97	**N'lands** v Canada at Belfast	2008

Bermuda made 99-7 in their 20 overs v Scotland at Belfast in 2008

Most sixes

15	PD Collingwood	*E*
15	Misbah-ul-Haq	*P*
15	JDP Oram	*NZ*
15	Yuvraj Singh	*I*
14	CD McMillan	*NZ*
14	JA Morkel	*SA*
13	AC Gilchrist	*A*
13	ML Hayden	*A*
13	Imran Nazir	*P*
13	BB McCullum	*NZ*

Yuvraj's sixes included 6 in one over

Best strike rate

Runs per 100 balls		*Runs*
177.22	Yuvraj Singh *I*	179
170.20	A Symonds *A*	337
169.69	Shahid Afridi *P*	168
165.75	JDP Oram *NZ*	242
165.10	ST Jayasuriya *SL*	246
164.95	CH Gayle *WI*	193
159.82	CD McMillan *NZ*	187
150.00	Imran Nazir *P*	201
149.12	DPMD Jayawardene *SL*	170
148.77	KP Pietersen *E*	363

Qualification: 90 balls faced

Meanest bowlers

Runs per over		*Wkts*
4.88	TM Odoyo *Kenya*	6
5.37	Umar Gul *P*	13
5.40	JAR Blain *Scot*	6
5.63	DL Vettori *NZ*	13
5.81	WPUJC Vaas *SL*	6
5.91	M Morkel *SA*	10
6.26	JA Morkel *SA*	6
6.40	Abdur Razzak *B'desh*	14
6.44	A Flintoff *E*	5
6.46	CRD Fernando *SL*	10

Qualification: 120 balls bowled

Twenty20 international results

	Played	Won	Lost	Drawn	Tied	% win
Australia	15	8	7	0	0	53.33
Bangladesh	9	3	6	0	0	33.33
England	14	6	8	0	0	42.85
India	10	6	2	1	1	72.22
New Zealand	16	5	10	1	0	34.37
Pakistan	12	9	2	1	0	79.16
South Africa	13	8	5	0	0	61.53
Sri Lanka	8	5	3	0	0	62.50
West Indies	8	3	4	1	0	43.75
Others (see below)	31	11	17	0	3	37.93
TOTAL	68	64	64	2	2	

Other teams: Bermuda (P3, L3), Canada (P3, W2, L1), Ireland (P4, W3, NR1), Kenya (P8, W1, L7), Netherlands (P4, W2, L1, NR1), Scotland (P6, W2, L3, NR1), Zimbabwe (P3, W1, L2).

AUSTRALIA *Test Match Records*

Most appearances

168	SR Waugh
156	AR Border
145	SK Warne
128	ME Waugh
124	GD McGrath
119	IA Healy
119	RT Ponting
107	DC Boon
105	JL Langer
104	MA Taylor

10 of the 45 players with 100 or more Test caps are Australian

Most runs

		Avge
11174	AR Border	50.56
10927	SR Waugh	51.06
10099	RT Ponting	58.37
8242	ML Hayden	53.51
8029	ME Waugh	41.81
7696	JL Langer	45.27
7525	MA Taylor	43.49
7422	DC Boon	43.65
7110	GS Chappell	53.86
6996	DG Bradman	99.94

RN Harvey (6149) also reached 6000 Test runs

Most wickets

		Avge
708	SK Warne	25.41
563	GD McGrath	21.64
355	DK Lillee	23.92
291	CJ McDermott	28.63
289	B Lee	29.58
259	JN Gillespie	26.13
248	R Benaud	27.03
246	GD McKenzie	29.78
228	RR Lindwall	23.03
216	CV Grimmett	24.21

MG Hughes (212), SCG MacGill (208) and JR Thomson (200) also reached 200 Test wickets

Highest scores

380	ML Hayden	v Zimbabwe at Perth	2003-04
334*	MA Taylor	v Pakistan at Peshawar	1998-99
334	DG Bradman	v England at Leeds	1930
311	RB Simpson	v England at Manchester	1964
307	RM Cowper	v England at Melbourne	1965-66
304	DG Bradman	v England at Leeds	1934
299*	DG Bradman	v South Africa at Adelaide	1931-32
270	DG Bradman	v England at Melbourne	1936-37
268	GN Yallop	v Pakistan at Melbourne	1983-84
266	WH Ponsford	v England at The Oval	1934

At the time of his retirement in 1948 DG Bradman had made eight of Australia's highest ten Test scores

Best innings bowling

9-121	AA Mailey	v England at Melbourne	1920-21
8-24	GD McGrath	v Pakistan at Perth	2004-05
8-31	FJ Laver	v England at Manchester	1909
8-38	GD McGrath	v England at Lord's	1997
8-43	AE Trott	v England at Adelaide	1894-95
8-53	RAL Massie	v England at Lord's	1972
8-59	AA Mallett	v Pakistan at Adelaide	1972-73
8-65	H Trumble	v England at The Oval	1902
8-71	GD McKenzie	v West Indies at Melbourne	1968-69
8-71	SK Warne	v England at Brisbane	1994-95

Trott and Massie were making their Test debuts. Massie took 8-84 – Australia's 11th-best analysis – in the first innings of the same match

Record wicket partnerships

1st	382	WM Lawry (210) and RB Simpson (205)	v West Indies at Bridgetown	1964-65
2nd	451	WH Ponsford (266) and DG Bradman (244)	v England at The Oval	1934
3rd	315	RT Ponting (206) and DS Lehmann (160)	v West Indies at Port-of-Spain	2002-03
4th	388	WH Ponsford (181) and DG Bradman (304)	v England at Leeds	1934
5th	405	SG Barnes (234) and DG Bradman (234)	v England at Sydney	1946-47
6th	346	JHW Fingleton (136) and DG Bradman (270)	v England at Melbourne	1936-37
7th	217	KD Walters (250) and GJ Gilmour (101)	v New Zealand at Christchurch	1976-77
8th	243	MJ Hartigan (116) and C Hill (160)	v England at Adelaide	1907-08
9th	154	SE Gregory (201) and JM Blackham (74)	v England at Sydney	1894-95
10th	127	JM Taylor (108) and AA Mailey (46*)	v England at Sydney	1924-25

Figures to 12.9.08. Updated records can be found at www.cricinfo.com/ci/engine/records

Test Match Records — **AUSTRALIA**

Most catches

Fielders

181	ME Waugh
157	MA Taylor
156	AR Border
134	RT Ponting
125	SK Warne

Most dismissals

Wicketkeepers		Ct/St
416	AC Gilchrist	379/37
395	IA Healy	366/29
355	RW Marsh	343/12
187	ATW Grout	163/24
130	WAS Oldfield	78/52

Highest team totals

758-8d	v West Indies at Kingston	1954-55
735-6d	v Zimbabwe at Perth	2003-04
729-6d	v England at Lord's	1930
701	v England at The Oval	1934
695	v England at The Oval	1930
674	v India at Adelaide	1947-48
668	v West Indies at Bridgetown	1954-55
659-8d	v England at Sydney	1946-47
656-8d	v England at Manchester	1964
653-4d	v England at Leeds	1993

Australia have reached 600 on 28 occasions, 15 of them against England

Lowest team totals

Completed innings

36	v England at Birmingham	1902
42	v England at Sydney	1887-88
44	v England at The Oval	1896
53	v England at Lord's	1896
58*	v England at Brisbane	1936-37
60	v England at Lord's	1888
63	v England at The Oval	1882
65	v England at The Oval	1912
66*	v England at Brisbane	1928-29
68	v England at The Oval	1886

*One or more batsmen absent. Australia's lowest total against anyone other than England is 75, v South Africa at Durban in 1949-50

Best match bowling

16-137	RAL Massie	v England at Lord's	1972
14-90	FR Spofforth	v England at The Oval	1882
14-199	CV Grimmett	v South Africa at Adelaide	1931-32
13-77	MA Noble	v England at Melbourne	1901-02
13-110	FR Spofforth	v England at Melbourne	1878-79
13-148	BA Reid	v England at Melbourne	1990-91
13-173	CV Grimmett	v South Africa at Durban	1935-36
13-217	MG Hughes	v West Indies at Perth	1988-89
13-236	AA Mailey	v England at Melbourne	1920-21
12-87	CTB Turner	v England at Sydney	1887-88

Massie was playing in his first Test, Grimmett (1935-36) in his last – he took 10 or more wickets in each of his last three

Hat-tricks

FR Spofforth	v England at Melbourne	1878-79
H Trumble	v England at Melbourne	1901-02
H Trumble	v England at Melbourne	1903-04
TJ Matthews	v South Africa at Manchester	1912
TJ Matthews	v South Africa at Manchester	1912
LF Kline	v South Africa at Cape Town	1957-58
MG Hughes	v West Indies at Perth	1988-89
DW Fleming	v Pakistan at Rawalpindi	1994-95
SK Warne	v England at Melbourne	1994-95
GD McGrath	v West Indies at Perth	2000-01

Fleming was playing in his first Test, Trumble (1903-04) in his last. Matthews, a legspinner, uniquely took a hat-trick in both innings of the same Test

Australia's Test match results

	Played	Won	Lost	Drawn	Tied	% win
v Bangladesh	4	4	0	0	0	100.00
v England	316	131	97	88	0	41.45
v India	72	34	16	21	1	47.22
v New Zealand	46	22	7	17	0	47.82
v Pakistan	52	24	11	17	0	46.15
v South Africa	77	44	15	18	0	57.14
v Sri Lanka	20	13	1	6	0	65.00
v West Indies	105	50	32	22	1	47.61
v Zimbabwe	3	3	0	0	0	100.00
v World XI	1	1	0	0	0	100.00
TOTAL	**696**	**326**	**179**	**189**	**2**	**46.83**

*Figures to 12.9.08. Updated records can be found at **www.cricinfo.com/ci/engine/records***

AUSTRALIA *One-day International Records*

Most appearances

325	SR Waugh
300	RT Ponting
286	AC Gilchrist
273	AR Border
249	GD McGrath
244	ME Waugh
232	MG Bevan
208	DR Martyn
193	A Symonds
193	SK Warne

A total of 21 Australians have played in more than 100 ODIs

Most runs

		Avge
10998	RT Ponting	42.96
9595	AC Gilchrist	35.93
8500	ME Waugh	39.35
7569	SR Waugh	32.90
6912	MG Bevan	53.58
6524	AR Border	30.62
6131	ML Hayden	44.10
6068	DM Jones	44.61
5964	DC Boon	37.04
5346	DR Martyn	40.80

A Symonds (5006), GR Marsh (4357) and MJ Clarke (4077) also reached 4000 runs

Most wickets

		Avge
380	GD McGrath	21.98
303	B Lee	22.95
291	SK Warne	25.82
203	CJ McDermott	24.71
195	SR Waugh	34.67
156	GB Hogg	26.84
148	NW Bracken	21.87
142	JN Gillespie	25.42
134	DW Fleming	25.38
129	A Symonds	37.68

SP O'Donnell (108), PR Reiffel (106) and DK Lillee (103) also reached 100 wickets

Highest scores

181*	ML Hayden	v New Zealand at Hamilton	2006-07
173	ME Waugh	v West Indies at Melbourne	2000-01
172	AC Gilchrist	v Zimbabwe at Hobart	2003-04
164	RT Ponting	v South Africa at Johannesburg	2005-06
158	ML Hayden	v West Indies at North Sound	2006-07
156	A Symonds	v New Zealand at Wellington	2005-06
154	AC Gilchrist	v Sri Lanka at Melbourne	1998-99
151	A Symonds	v Sri Lanka at Sydney	2005-06
149	AC Gilchrist	v Sri Lanka at Bridgetown	2006-07
146	ML Hayden	v Pakistan at Nairobi	2002-03

Gilchrist's 149 against Sri Lanka is the highest score in a World Cup final

Best innings bowling

7-15	GD McGrath	v Namibia at Potchefstroom	2002-03
7-20	AJ Bichel	v England at Port Elizabeth	2002-03
6-14	GJ Gilmour	v England at Leeds	1975
6-39	KH MacLeay	v India at Nottingham	1983
5-13	SP O'Donnell	v New Zealand at Christchurch	1989-90
5-14	GD McGrath	v West Indies at Manchester	1999
5-15	GS Chappell	v India at Sydney	1980-81
5-16	CG Rackemann	v Pakistan at Adelaide	1983-84
5-17	TM Alderman	v New Zealand at Wellington	1981-82
5-18	GJ Cosier	v England at Birmingham	1977
5-18	A Symonds	v Bangladesh at Manchester	2005

DK Lillee took 5-34 against Pakistan at Leeds in the 1975 World Cup, the first five-wicket haul in ODIs

Record wicket partnerships

1st	212	GR Marsh (104) and DC Boon (111)	v India at Jaipur	1986-87
2nd	225	AC Gilchrist (124) and RT Ponting (119)	v England at Melbourne	2002-03
3rd	234*	RT Ponting (140*) and DR Martyn (88*)	v India at Johannesburg	2002-03
4th	237	RT Ponting (124) and A Symonds (151)	v Sri Lanka at Sydney	2005-06
5th	220	A Symonds (156) and MJ Clarke (82*)	v New Zealand at Wellington	2005-06
6th	165	MEK Hussey (109*) and BJ Haddin (70)	v West Indies at Kuala Lumpur	2006-07
7th	123	MEK Hussey (73) and B Lee (57)	v South Africa at Brisbane	2005-06
8th	119	PR Reiffel (58) and SK Warne (55)	v South Africa at Port Elizabeth	1993-94
9th	77	MG Bevan (59*) and SK Warne (29)	v West Indies at Port-of-Spain	1998-99
10th	63	SR Watson (35*) and AJ Bichel (28)	v Sri Lanka at Sydney	2002-03

Figures to 12.9.08. Updated records can be found at **www.cricinfo.com/ci/engine/records**

One-day International Records — **AUSTRALIA**

Most catches

Fielders

134	RT Ponting	
127	AR Border	
111	SR Waugh	
108	ME Waugh	
80	A Symonds/SK Warne	

Most dismissals

Wicketkeepers		Ct/St
470	AC Gilchrist	416/54
233	IA Healy	194/39
124	RW Marsh	120/4
49	WB Phillips	42/7
41	BJ Haddin	37/4

Highest team totals

434-4	v South Africa at Johannesburg	2005-06
377-6	v South Africa at Basseterre	2006-07
368-5	v Sri Lanka at Sydney	2005-06
359-2†	v India at Johannesburg	2002-03
359-5	v India at Sydney	2003-04
358-5	v Netherlands at Basseterre	2006-07
349-6	v New Zealand at St George's	2006-07
348-6	v New Zealand at C'church	1999-2000
347-2	v India at Bangalore	2003-04
347-5	v New Zealand at Napier	2004-05

† In World Cup final. All scores made in 50 overs

Lowest team totals

Completed innings

70	v England at Birmingham	1977
70	v New Zealand at Adelaide	1985-86
91	v West Indies at Perth	1986-87
93	v S Africa at Cape Town	2005-06
101	v England at Melbourne	1978-79
101	v India at Perth	1991-92
107	v W Indies at Melbourne	1981-82
109	v England at Sydney	1982-83
120	v Pakistan at Hobart	1996-97
124	v New Zealand at Sydney	1982-83

Australia scored 101-9 in a 30-overs match against West Indies at Sydney in 1992-93 – and won

Most sixes

148	AC Gilchrist
133	RT Ponting
102	A Symonds
87	ML Hayden
68	SR Waugh
64	DM Jones
57	ME Waugh
43	AR Border
41	MEK Hussey
28	SP O'Donnell

Gilchrist (1) and Ponting (3) also hit sixes for the World XI

Best strike rate

Runs per 100 balls		Runs
96.89	AC Gilchrist	9595
92.70	A Symonds	5006
88.16	IJ Harvey	715
87.51	BJ Hodge	516
85.71	WB Phillips	852
85.52	MEK Hussey	2457
83.84	IA Healy	1764
82.26	RW Marsh	1225
81.90	SR Watson	1263
81.34	DS Lehmann	3078

Qualification: 500 runs

Most economical bowlers

Runs per over		Wkts
3.37	SP Davis	44
3.55	MR Whitney	46
3.58	DK Lillee	103
3.65	GF Lawson	88
3.65	TM Alderman	88
3.87	GD McGrath	380
3.92	PR Reiffel	106
3.94	CG Rackemann	82
3.94	RM Hogg	85
4.03	CJ McDermott	203

Qualification: 2000 balls bowled

Australia's one-day international results

	Played	Won	Lost	Tied	No Result	% win
v Bangladesh	16	15	1	0	0	93.75
v England	93	52	37	2	2	58.24
v India	96	57	32	0	7	64.04
v New Zealand	112	78	30	0	4	72.22
v Pakistan	74	43	27	1	3	61.26
v South Africa	67	36	28	3	0	55.97
v Sri Lanka	68	46	20	0	2	69.69
v West Indies	119	58	57	2	2	50.42
v Zimbabwe	27	25	1	0	1	96.15
v others (see below)	15	15	0	0	0	100.00
TOTAL	**687**	**425**	**233**	**8**	**21**	**64.41**

Other teams: Canada (P1, W1), Ireland (P1, W1), Kenya (P4, W4), Namibia (P1, W1), Netherlands (P2, W2), Scotland (P2, W2), USA (P1, W1), World XI (P3, W3).

BANGLADESH *Test Match Records*

Most appearances

50	Habibul Bashar
44	Khaled Mashud
42	Mohammad Ashraful
40	Javed Omar
33	Mohammad Rafique
29	Mashrafe Mortaza
22	Rajin Saleh
21	Tapash Baisya
17	Alok Kapali
17	Hannan Sarkar
17	Manjural Islam

Habibul Bashar missed only two of Bangladesh's first 52 Tests

Most runs

		Avge
3026	Habibul Bashar	30.87
1922	Mohammad Ashraful	24.64
1720	Javed Omar	22.05
1409	Khaled Mashud	19.04
1115	Rajin Saleh	27.19
1059	Mohammad Rafique	18.57
810	Shahriar Nafees	27.00
683	Al Sahariar	22.76
662	Hannan Sarkar	20.06
584	Alok Kapali	17.69

Habibul Bashar reached 2000 runs for Bangladesh before anyone else had made 1000

Most wickets

		Avge
100	Mohammad Rafique	40.76
66	Mashrafe Mortaza	41.63
42	Shahadat Hossain	36.69
36	Tapash Baisya	59.36
32	Enamul Haque jnr	39.46
28	Manjural Islam	57.32
18	Enamul Haque snr	57.05
14	Mohammad Sharif	79.00
14	Talha Jubair	55.07
13	Khaled Mahmud	64.00
13	Mushfiqur Rahman	63.30

Mohammad Ashraful, Naimur Rahman and Syed Rasel have all taken 12 wickets

Highest scores

158*	Moh'd Ashraful	v India at Chittagong	2004-05
145†	Aminul Islam	v India at Dhaka	2000-01
138	Shahriar Nafees	v Australia at Fatullah	2005-06
136	Moh'd Ashraful	v Sri Lanka at Chittagong	2005-06
129*	Moh'd Ashraful	v Sri Lanka at Colombo	2007
121	Nafees Iqbal	v Zimbabwe at Dhaka	2004-05
119	Javed Omar	v Pakistan at Peshawar	2003-04
114†	Aminul Islam	v Sri Lanka at Colombo	2001-02
113	Habibul Bashar	v West Indies at Gros Islet	2004
111	Moh'd Rafique	v West Indies at Gros Islet	2004

† On debut. There have only been three other centuries for Bangladesh, two by Habibul Bashar and one by Khaled Mashud

Best innings bowling

7-95	Enamul Haque jnr	v Zimbabwe at Dhaka	2004-05
6-27	Shahadat Hossain	v South Africa at Dhaka	2007-08
6-45	Enamul Haque jnr	v Zim at Chittagong	2004-05
6-77	Moh'd Rafique	v South Africa at Dhaka	2002-03
6-81	Manjural Islam	v Zim at Bulawayo	2000-01
6-122	Moh'd Rafique	v New Zealand at Dhaka	2004-05
6-132	Naimur Rahman	v India at Dhaka	2000-01
5-36	Moh'd Rafique	v Pakistan at Multan	2003-04
5-62	Moh'd Rafique	v Australia at Fatulla	2005-06
5-65	Moh'd Rafique	v Zim at Chittagong	2004-05

Other five-wicket hauls have been recorded by Mohammad Rafique (2), Shahadat Hossain and Enamul Haque jnr

Record wicket partnerships

1st	161	Tamim Iqbal (84) and Junaid Siddique (74)	v New Zealand at Dunedin	2007-08
2nd	187	Shahriar Nafees (138) and Habibul Bashar (76)	v Australia at Fatullah	2005-06
3rd	130	Javed Omar (119) and Mohammad Ashraful (77)	v Pakistan at Peshawar	2003-04
4th	120	Habibul Bashar (77) and Manjural Islam Rana (35)	v West Indies at Kingston	2004
5th	126	Aminul Islam (56) and Mohammad Ashraful (114)	v Sri Lanka at Colombo	2001-02
6th	191	Mohammad Ashraful (129*) and Mushfiqur Rahim (80)	v Sri Lanka at Colombo	2007
7th	93	Aminul Islam (145) and Khaled Mashud (32)	v India at Dhaka	2001-02
8th	87	Mohammad Ashraful (81) and Mohammad Rafique (111)	v West Indies at Gros Islet	2004
9th	77	Mashrafe Mortaza (79) and Shahadat Hossain (31)	v India at Chittagong	2006-07
10th	69	Mohammad Rafique (65) and Shahadat Hossain (3*)	v Australia at Chittagong	2005-06

Figures to 12.9.08. Updated records can be found at **www.cricinfo.com/ci/engine/records**

Most catches

Fielders

22	Habibul Bashar
14	Mohammad Ashraful
12	Rajin Saleh
11	Shahriar Nafees
10	Al Sahariar
10	Javed Omar

Most dismissals

Wicketkeepers		*Ct/St*
87	Khaled Mashud	78/9
7	Mushfiqur Rahim	7/0
4	Mohammad Salim	3/1
2	Mehrab Hossain	2/0

Highest team totals

488	v Zimbabwe at Chittagong	2004-05
427	v Australia at Fatullah	2005-06
416	v West Indies at Gros Islet	2004
400	v India at Dhaka	2000-01
361	v Pakistan at Peshawar	2003-04
333	v India at Chittagong	2004-05
331	v Zimbabwe at Harare	2003-04
328	v Sri Lanka at Colombo	2001-02
319	v Sri Lanka at Chittagong	2005-06
316	v England at Chester-le-Street	2005

The 400 against India came in Bangladesh's inaugural Test

Lowest team totals

Completed innings

62	v Sri Lanka at Colombo	2007
86	v Sri Lanka at Colombo	2005-06
87	v West Indies at Dhaka	2002-03
89	v Sri Lanka at Colombo	2007
90	v Sri Lanka at Colombo	2001-02
91	v India at Dhaka	2000-01
96	v Pakistan at Peshawar	2003-04
97	v Australia at Darwin	2003
102	v South Africa at Dhaka	2002-03
104	v Eng at Chester-le-Street	2005

The lowest all-out total by the opposition is 154, by Zimbabwe at Chittagong in 2004-05 (Bangladesh's only Test victory)

Best match bowling

12-200	Enamul Haque jr	v Zimbabwe at Dhaka	2004-05
9-97	Shahadat Hossain	v South Africa at Dhaka	2007-08
9-160	Moh'd Rafique	v Australia at Fatullah	2005-06
7-105	Khaled Mahmud	v Pakistan at Multan	2003-04
7-116	Moh'd Rafique	v Pakistan at Multan	2003-04
6-77	Moh'd Rafique	v South Africa at Dhaka	2002-03
6-81	Manjural Islam	v Zimbabwe at Bulawayo	2000-01
6-100	Enamul Haque jr	v Zim at Chittagong	2004-05
6-117	Tapash Baisya	v W Indies at Chittagong	2002-03
6-122	Moh'd Rafique	v New Zealand at Dhaka	2004-05

Khaled Mahmud took only six other wickets in 11 more Tests

Hat-tricks

Alok Kapali	v Pakistan at Peshawar	2003-04

Alok Kapali's figures were 2.1-1-3-3; he ended Pakistan's innings by dismissing Shabbir Ahmed, Danish Kaneria and Umar Gul. He took only three other Test wickets.

Two bowlers have taken hat-tricks against Bangladesh: AM Blignaut for Zimbabwe at Harare in 2003-04, and JEC Franklin for New Zealand at Dhaka in 2004-05.

Shahadat Hossain took an ODI hat-trick for Bangladesh against Zimbabwe at Harare in 2006

Bangladesh's Test match results

	Played	Won	Lost	Drawn	Tied	% win
v Australia	4	0	4	0	0	0.00
v England	4	0	4	0	0	0.00
v India	5	0	4	1	0	0.00
v New Zealand	6	0	6	0	0	0.00
v Pakistan	6	0	6	0	0	0.00
v South Africa	6	0	6	0	0	0.00
v Sri Lanka	10	0	10	0	0	0.00
v West Indies	4	0	3	1	0	0.00
v Zimbabwe	8	1	4	3	0	12.50
TOTAL	**53**	**1**	**47**	**5**	**0**	**1.88**

Figures to 12.9.08. Updated records can be found at **www.cricinfo.com/ci/engine/records**

BANGLADESH One-day International Records

Most appearances

126	Khaled Mashud
126	Mohammad Ashraful
123	Mohammad Rafique
111	Habibul Bashar
90	Mashrafe Mortaza
80	Aftab Ahmed
77	Khaled Mahmud
76	Abdur Razzak
65	Alok Kapali
60	Shahriar Nafees

Habibul Bashar captained in 69 ODIs, Khaled Mashud in 30, Mohmmad Ashraful in 27

Most runs

		Avge
2506	Moh'd Ashraful	22.99
2168	Habibul Bashar	21.68
1874	Aftab Ahmed	25.32
1857	Shahriar Nafees	33.76
1818	Khaled Mashud	21.90
1312	Javed Omar	23.85
1292	Shakib Al Hasan	32.30
1190	Moh'd Rafique	13.52
1170	Alok Kapali	19.83
1150	Tamim Iqbal	27.38

Rajin Saleh (1005) also passed 1000 runs

Most wickets

		Avge
119	Mohammad Rafique	38.75
111	Mashrafe Mortaza	31.84
106	Abdur Razzak	26.44
67	Khaled Mahmud	42.76
59	Tapash Baisya	41.55
50	Shakib Al Hasan	34.38
44	Syed Rasel	25.88
40	Shahadat Hossain	40.22
29	Hasibul Hossain	46.13
24	Alok Kapali	49.75
24	Manjural Islam	53.50

Mohammad Rafique completed the 1000-run/100-wicket double in ODIs

Highest scores

134*	Shakib Al Hasan	v Canada at St John's	2006-07
129	Tamim Iqbal	v Ireland at Dhaka	2007-08
123*	Shahriar Nafees	v Zimbabwe at Jaipur	2006
118*	Shahriar Nafees	v Zimbabwe at Harare	2006-07
115	Alok Kapali	v India at Karachi	2008
109	Moh'd Ashraful	v UAE at Lahore	2008
108*	Rajin Saleh	v Kenya at Fatullah	2005-06
108	Shakib Al Hasan	v Pakistan at Multan	2007-08
105*	Shahriar Nafees	v Zimbabwe at Khulna	2006-07
104*	Shahriar Nafees	v Bermuda at St John's	2006-07

Two other countries have been scored for Bangladesh, by Mehrab Hossain (101) and Mohammad Ashraful (100)

Best bowling figures

6-26	Mashrafe Mortaza	v Kenya at Nairobi	2006
5-31	Aftab Ahmed	v NZ at Dhaka	2004-05
5-33	Abdur Razzak	v Zimbabwe at Bogra	2006-07
5-42	Farhad Reza	v Ireland at Dhaka	2007-08
5-47	Moh'd Rafique	v Kenya at Fatullah	2005-06
4-16	Tapash Baisya	v West Indies at Kingstown	2004
4-16	Rajin Saleh	v Zimbabwe at Harare	2006
4-19	Khaled Mahmud	v Zimbabwe at Harare	2003-04
4-22	Syed Rasel	v Kenya at Nairobi	2006
4-23	Abdur Razzak	v Scotland at Dhaka	2006-07

Aftab Ahmed has taken only seven more wickets in 79 other matches

Record wicket partnerships

1st	170	Shahriar Hossain (68) and Mehrab Hossain (101)	v Zimbabwe at Dhaka	1998-99
2nd	150	Mohammad Rafique (72) and Aftab Ahmed (81*)	v Zimbabwe at Dhaka	2004-05
3rd	141	Mohammad Ashraful (109) and Raqibul Hassan (83)	v United Arab Emirates at Lahore	2008
4th	175*	Rajin Saleh (108*) and Habibul Bashar (64*)	v Kenya at Fatullah	2005-06
5th	119	Shakib Al Hasan (52) and Raqibul Hassan (63)	v South Africa at Dhaka	2007-08
6th	123*	Al Sahariar (62*) and Khaled Mashud (53*)	v West Indies at Dhaka	1999-2000
7th	89	Alok Kapali (55) and Khaled Mashud (39)	v Kenya at Fatullah	2005-06
8th	70*	Khaled Mashud (35*) and Mohammad Rafique (41*)	v New Zealand at Kimberley	2002-03
9th	97	Shakib Al Hasan (108) and Mashrafe Mortaza (38)	v Pakistan at Multan	2007-08
10th	54*	Khaled Mashud (39*) and Tapash Baisya (22*)	v Sri Lanka at Colombo	2005-06

Figures to 12.9.08. Updated records can be found at **www.cricinfo.com/ci/engine/records**

Most catches

Fielders

29	Mashrafe Mortaza	
28	Mohammad Rafique	
27	Aftab Ahmed	
26	Habibul Bashar	
25	Alok Kapali	

Highest team totals

301-7	v Kenya at Bogra	2005-06
300-8	v UAE at Lahore	2008
293-7	v Ireland at Dhaka	2007-08
285-7	v Pakistan at Lahore	2007-08
283-6	v India at Karachi	2008
278-5	v Canada at St John's	2006-07
278-6	v Scotland at Dhaka	2006-07
272-8	v Zimbabwe at Bulawayo	2000-01
267-9	v Zimbabwe at Dhaka	2001-02
265-9	v Sri Lanka at Mohali	2006-07

Bangladesh passed 300 for the first time in their 119th one-day international

Lowest team totals

Completed innings

74	v Australia at Darwin	2008
76	v Sri Lanka at Colombo	2002
76	v India at Dhaka	2002-03
77	v NZ at Colombo	2002-03
86	v NZ at Chittagong	2004-05
87*	v Pakistan at Dhaka	1999-2000
92	v Zimbabwe at Nairobi	1997-98
93	v S Africa at Birmingham	2004
93	v NZ at Queenstown	2007-08
94	v Pakistan at Moratuwa	1985-86

* One batsman absent hurt

Most dismissals

Wicketkeepers		Ct/St
126	Khaled Mashud	91/35
24	Mushfiqur Rahim	18/6
13	Dhiman Ghosh	9/4

Most sixes

49	Aftab Ahmed
33	Mashrafe Mortaza
29	Mohammad Rafique
22	Mohammad Ashraful
12	Tamim Iqbal
11	Abdur Razzak
10	Alok Kapali
10	Habibul Bashar
8	Farhad Reza
7	Khaled Mahmud
7	Shahriar Nafees

Best strike rate

Runs per 100 balls		Runs
85.94	Mashrafe Mortaza	954
83.54	Aftab Ahmed	1874
72.55	Mohammad Ashraful	2506
71.81	Mohammad Rafique	1190
69.73	Tamim Iqbal	1150
69.68	Shahriar Nafees	1857
68.78	Alok Kapali	1170
68.25	Shakib Al Hasan	1292
67.83	Khaled Mahmud	991
60.45	Habibul Bashar	2168

Qualification: 500 runs

Most economical bowlers

Runs per over		Wkts
4.18	Syed Rasel	44
4.25	Shakib Al Hasan	50
4.26	Abdur Razzak	106
4.39	Mohammad Rafique	119
4.42	Mushfiqur Rahman	19
4.65	Mashrafe Mortaza	111
4.84	Manjural Islam	24
4.95	Naimur Rahman	10
5.07	Khaled Mahmud	67
5.23	Alok Kapali	24

Qualification: 1000 balls bowled

Bangladesh's one-day international results

	Played	Won	Lost	Tied	No Result	% win
v Australia	16	1	15	0	0	6.25
v England	8	0	8	0	0	0.00
v India	19	2	17	0	0	10.52
v New Zealand	11	0	11	0	0	0.00
v Pakistan	25	1	24	0	0	4.00
v South Africa	11	1	10	0	0	9.09
v Sri Lanka	24	1	23	0	0	4.16
v West Indies	13	0	11	0	2	0.00
v Zimbabwe	33	15	18	0	0	45.45
v others (see below)	27	19	8	0	0	70.37
TOTAL	**187**	**40**	**145**	**0**	**2**	**21.62**

Other teams: Bermuda (P2, W2), Canada (P2, W1, L1), Hong Kong (P1, W1), Ireland (P4, W3, L1), Kenya (P14, W8, L6), Scotland (P3, W3), UAE (P1, W1).

ENGLAND
Test Match Records

Most appearances

133	AJ Stewart
118	GA Gooch
117	DI Gower
115	MA Atherton
114	MC Cowdrey
108	G Boycott
102	IT Botham
100	GP Thorpe
96	N Hussain
95	APE Knott

Cowdrey was the first man to reach 100 Tests, in 1968

Most runs

		Avge
8900	GA Gooch	42.58
8463	AJ Stewart	39.54
8231	DI Gower	44.25
8114	G Boycott	47.72
7728	MA Atherton	37.69
7624	MC Cowdrey	44.06
7249	WR Hammond	58.45
6971	L Hutton	56.67
6806	KF Barrington	58.67
6744	GP Thorpe	44.66

ME Trescothick (5825), DCS Compton (5807), N Hussain (5764) and MP Vaughan (5719) also passed 5500 runs

Most wickets

		Avge
383	IT Botham	28.40
325	RGD Willis	25.20
307	FS Trueman	21.57
297	DL Underwood	25.83
252	JB Statham	24.84
248	MJ Hoggard	30.50
236	AV Bedser	24.89
234	AR Caddick	29.91
229	D Gough	28.39
212	SJ Harmison	31.54

JA Snow (202) has also taken more than 200 wickets

Highest scores

364	L Hutton	v Australia at The Oval	1938
336*	WR Hammond	v New Zealand at Auckland	1932-33
333	GA Gooch	v India at Lord's	1990
325	A Sandham	v West Indies at Kingston	1929-30
310*	JH Edrich	v New Zealand at Leeds	1965
287	RE Foster	v Australia at Sydney	1903-04
285*	PBH May	v West Indies at Birmingham	1957
278	DCS Compton	v Pakistan at Nottingham	1954
262*	DL Amiss	v West Indies at Kingston	1973-74
258	TW Graveney	v West Indies at Nottingham	1957

Foster was playing in his first Test, Sandham in his last

Best innings bowling

10-53	JC Laker	v Australia at Manchester	1956
9-28	GA Lohmann	v South Africa at Johannesburg	1895-96
9-37	JC Laker	v Australia at Manchester	1956
9-57	DE Malcolm	v South Africa at The Oval	1994
9-103	SF Barnes	v S Africa at Johannesburg	1913-14
8-7	GA Lohmann	v S Africa at Port Elizabeth	1895-96
8-11	J Briggs	v South Africa at Cape Town	1888-89
8-29	SF Barnes	v South Africa at The Oval	1912
8-31	FS Trueman	v India at Manchester	1952
8-34	IT Botham	v Pakistan at Lord's	1978

Botham also scored 108 in England's innings victory

Record wicket partnerships

1st	359	L Hutton (158) and C Washbrook (195)	v South Africa at Johannesburg	1948-49
2nd	382	L Hutton (364) and M Leyland (187)	v Australia at The Oval	1938
3rd	370	WJ Edrich (189) and DCS Compton (208)	v South Africa at Lord's	1947
4th	411	PBH May (285*) and MC Cowdrey (154)	v West Indies at Birmingham	1957
5th	254	KWR Fletcher (113) and AW Greig (148)	v India at Bombay	1972-73
6th	281	GP Thorpe (200*) and A Flintoff (137)	v New Zealand at Christchurch	2001-02
7th	197	MJK Smith (96) and JM Parks (101*)	v West Indies at Port-of-Spain	1959-60
8th	246	LEG Ames (137) and GOB Allen (122)	v New Zealand at Lord's	1931
9th	163*	MC Cowdrey (128*) and AC Smith (69*)	v New Zealand at Wellington	1962-63
10th	130	RE Foster (287) and W Rhodes (40*)	v Australia at Sydney	1903-04

Figures to 12.9.08. Updated records can be found at www.cricinfo.com/ci/engine/records

ENGLAND

Most catches

Fielders

120	IT Botham	
120	MC Cowdrey	
110	WR Hammond	
105	GP Thorpe	
103	GA Gooch	

Most dismissals

Wicketkeepers		*Ct/St*
269	APE Knott	250/19
241	AJ Stewart	227/14
219	TG Evans	173/46
174	RW Taylor	167/7
165	RC Russell	153/12

Highest team totals

903-7d	v Australia at The Oval	1938
849	v West Indies at Kingston	1929-30
658-8d	v Australia at Nottingham	1938
654-5	v South Africa at Durban	1938-39
653-4d	v India at Lord's	1990
652-7d	v India at Madras	1984-85
636	v Australia at Sydney	1928-29
633-5d	v India at Birmingham	1979
629	v India at Lord's	1974
627-9d	v Australia at Manchester	1934

England have made five other totals of more than 600

Lowest team totals

Completed innings

45	v Australia at Sydney	1886-87
46	v WI at Port-of-Spain	1993-94
52	v Australia at The Oval	1948
53	v Australia at Lord's	1888
61	v Aust at Melbourne	1901-02
61	v Aust at Melbourne	1903-04
62	v Australia at Lord's	1888
64	v NZ at Wellington	1977-78
65*	v Australia at Sydney	1894-95
71	v W Indies at Manchester	1976

*One batsman absent

Best match bowling

19-90	JC Laker	v Australia at Manchester	1956
17-159	SF Barnes	v S Africa at Johannesburg	1913-14
15-28	J Briggs	v S Africa at Cape Town	1888-89
15-45	GA Lohmann	v S Africa at Port Elizabeth	1895-96
15-99	C Blythe	v South Africa at Leeds	1907
15-104	H Verity	v Australia at Lord's	1934
15-124	W Rhodes	v Australia at Melbourne	1903-04
14-99	AV Bedser	v Australia at Nottingham	1953
14-102	W Bates	v Australia at Melbourne	1882-83
14-144	SF Barnes	v South Africa at Durban	1913-14

Barnes took ten or more wickets in a match a record seven times for England

Hat-tricks

W Bates	v Australia at Melbourne	1882-83
J Briggs	v Australia at Sydney	1891-92
GA Lohmann	v S Africa at Port Elizabeth	1895-96
JT Hearne	v Australia at Leeds	1899
MJC Allom	v New Zealand at Christchurch	1929-30
TWJ Goddard	v S Africa at Johannesburg	1938-39
PJ Loader	v West Indies at Leeds	1957
DG Cork	v West Indies at Manchester	1995
D Gough	v Australia at Sydney	1998-99
MJ Hoggard	v West Indies at Bridgetown	2003-04
RJ Sidebottom	v New Zealand at Hamilton	2007-08

Allom was playing in his first match

England's Test match results

	Played	Won	Lost	Drawn	Tied	% win
v Australia	316	97	131	88	0	30.69
v Bangladesh	4	4	0	0	0	100.00
v India	97	34	18	45	0	35.05
v New Zealand	94	45	8	41	0	47.87
v Pakistan	67	18	12	37	0	26.86
v South Africa	134	55	28	51	0	41.04
v Sri Lanka	21	8	6	7	0	38.09
v West Indies	138	41	52	45	0	29.71
v Zimbabwe	6	3	0	3	0	50.00
TOTAL	**877**	**305**	**255**	**317**	**0**	**34.77**

Figures to 12.9.08. Updated records can be found at **www.cricinfo.com/ci/engine/records**

ENGLAND
One-day International Records

Most appearances

170	AJ Stewart
158	D Gough
149	PD Collingwood
130	A Flintoff
125	GA Gooch
123	ME Trescothick
122	AJ Lamb
120	GA Hick
116	IT Botham
114	DI Gower

PAJ DeFreitas (103) and NV Knight (100) also played 100 ODIs for England

Most runs

		Avge
4677	AJ Stewart	31.60
4335	ME Trescothick	37.37
4290	GA Gooch	36.98
4010	AJ Lamb	39.31
3846	GA Hick	37.33
3689	PD Collingwood	35.76
3637	NV Knight	40.41
3176	A Flintoff	31.46
3170	DI Gower	30.77
2804	KP Pietersen	49.19

Eight other batsmen have scored 2000 runs in ODIs for England

Most wickets

		Avge
234	D Gough	26.29
158	A Flintoff	23.17
145	IT Botham	28.54
127	JM Anderson	30.38
115	PAJ DeFreitas	32.82
83	PD Collingwood	38.72
80	RGD Willis	24.60
76	JE Emburey	30.86
69	AR Caddick	28.47
72	SJ Harmison	30.09

Eight further bowlers have taken 50 wickets in ODIs for England

Highest scores

167*	RA Smith	v Australia at Birmingham	1993
158	DI Gower	v New Zealand at Brisbane	1982-83
152	AJ Strauss	v Bangladesh at Nottingham	2005
142*	CWJ Athey	v New Zealand at Manchester	1986
142	GA Gooch	v Pakistan at Karachi	1987-88
137	DL Amiss	v India at Lord's	1975
137	ME Trescothick	v Pakistan at Lord's	2001
136	GA Gooch	v Australia at Lord's	1989
131	KWR Fletcher	v New Zealand at Nottingham	1975
130	DI Gower	v Sri Lanka at Taunton	1983
130	ME Trescothick	v West Indies at Gros Islet	2003-04

Trescothick has scored 12 centuries in ODIs, Gooch 8, Gower 7, KP Pietersen 6, GA Hick and NV Knight

Best innings bowling

6-31	PD Collingwood	v B'desh at Nottingham	2005
5-15	MA Ealham	v Zim at Kimberley	1999-2000
5-20	VJ Marks	v NZ at Wellington	1983-84
5-21	C White	v Zim at Bulawayo	1999-2000
5-23	SCJ Broad	v S Africa at Nottingham	2008
5-26	RC Irani	v India at The Oval	2002
5-31	M Hendrick	v Australia at The Oval	1980
5-32	MA Ealham	v Sri Lanka at Perth	1998-99
5-33	GA Hick	v Zim at Harare	1999-2000
5-33	SJ Harmison	v Australia at Bristol	2005

Collingwood also scored 112 in the same match.*
All Ealham's 5 wickets at Kimberley were lbw, an ODI record

Record wicket partnerships

1st	200	ME Trescothick (114*) and VS Solanki (106)	v South Africa at The Oval	2003
2nd	202	GA Gooch (117*) and DI Gower (102)	v Australia at Lord's	1985
3rd	213	GA Hick (86*) and NH Fairbrother (113)	v West Indies at Lord's	1991
4th	226	AJ Strauss (100) and A Flintoff (123)	v West Indies at Lord's	2004
5th	174	A Flintoff (99) and PD Collingwood (79*)	v India at The Oval	2004
6th	150	MP Vaughan (90*) and GO Jones (80)	v Zimbabwe at Bulawayo	2004-05
7th	110	PD Collingwood (100) and C White (48)	v Sri Lanka at Perth	2002-03
8th	99*	RS Bopara (43*) and SCJ Broad (45*)	v India at Manchester	2007
9th	100	LE Plunkett (56) and VS Solanki (39*)	v Pakistan at Lahore	2005-06
10th	50*	D Gough (46*) and SJ Harmison (11*)	v Australia at Chester-le-Street	2005

Figures to 12.9.08. Updated records can be found at **www.cricinfo.com/ci/engine/records**

One-day International Records

ENGLAND

Most catches

Fielders

86	PD Collingwood	
64	GA Hick	
45	GA Gooch	
45	ME Trescothick	
44	DI Gower/NV Knight	

Most dismissals

Wicketkeepers — Ct/St

163	AJ Stewart	148/15
72	GO Jones	68/4
47	RC Russell	41/6
43	CMW Read	41/2
39	MJ Prior	36/3

Highest team totals

391-4	v Bangladesh at Nottingham	2005
363-7	v Pakistan at Nottingham	1992
340-6	v New Zealand at Napier	2007-08
334-4	v India at Lord's	1975
333-9	v Sri Lanka at Taunton	1983
327-4	v Pakistan at Lahore	2005-06
325-5	v India at Lord's	2002
322-6	v New Zealand at The Oval	1983
321-7	v Sri Lanka at Leeds	2006
320-8	v Australia at Birmingham	1980
320-8	v India at Bristol	2007

England have reached 300 on 10 other occasions

Lowest team totals

Completed innings

86	v Australia at Manchester	2001
88	v SL at Dambulla	2003-04
89	v NZ at Wellington	2001-02
93	v Australia at Leeds	1975
94	v Aust at Melbourne	1978-79
101	v NZ at Chester-le-Street	2004
103	v SA at The Oval	1999
104	v SL at Colombo	2007-08
107	v Zim at Cape Town	1999-2000
110	v Aust at Melbourne	1998-99
110	v Aust at Adelaide	2006-07

The lowest totals against England are 45 by Canada (1979), and 70 by Australia (1977)

Most sixes

88	A Flintoff*	
51	KP Pietersen*	
44	IT Botham	
44	PD Collingwood	
41	GA Hick	
41	ME Trescothick	
30	AJ Lamb	
26	AJ Stewart	
22	DI Gower	
22	RA Smith	

*Also hit one six for the World XI

Best strike rate

Runs per 100 balls — Runs

89.08	A Flintoff	3176
87.70	KP Pietersen	2804
85.21	ME Trescothick	4335
83.83	PAJ DeFreitas	690
79.10	IT Botham	2113
78.21	GO Jones	815
76.31	PD Collingwood	3689
76.12	OA Shah	1052
76.03	MJ Prior	590
75.82	AJ Strauss	2239

Qualification: 500 runs

Most economical bowlers

Runs per over — Wkts

3.28	RGD Willis	80
3.54	ARC Fraser	47
3.79	GR Dilley	48
3.84	AD Mullally	63
3.96	IT Botham	145
3.96	PAJ DeFreitas	115
4.01	AR Caddick	69
4.08	MA Ealham	67
4.10	JE Emburey	76
4.17	GC Small	58

Qualification: 2000 balls bowled

England's one-day international results

	Played	Won	Lost	Tied	No result	% win
v Australia	93	37	52	2	2	41.75
v Bangladesh	8	8	0	0	0	100.00
v India	65	30	33	0	2	47.61
v New Zealand	69	29	34	2	4	46.15
v Pakistan	63	35	26	0	2	57.37
v South Africa	40	15	22	1	2	40.78
v Sri Lanka	43	22	21	0	0	51.16
v West Indies	75	32	39	0	4	45.07
v Zimbabwe	30	21	8	0	1	72.41
v others (see below)	12	11	0	0	1	91.66
TOTAL	498	240	235	5	18	50.52

Other teams: Canada (P2, W2), East Africa (P1, W1), Ireland (P2, W2), Kenya (P2, W2), Namibia (P1, W1), Netherlands (P2, W2), Scotland (P1, NR1), United Arab Emirates (P1, W1).

INDIA
Test Match Records

150	SR Tendulkar
131	Kapil Dev
130	A Kumble
125	SM Gavaskar
124	R Dravid
116	DB Vengsarkar
109	SC Ganguly
99	M Azharuddin
96	VVS Laxman
91	GR Viswanath

Gavaskar played 106 consecutive matches between 1974-75 and 1986-87

Most runs

		Avge
11877	SR Tendulkar	54.23
10223	R Dravid	54.37
10122	SM Gavaskar	51.12
6888	SC Ganguly	41.74
6868	DB Vengsarkar	42.13
6215	M Azharuddin	45.03
6080	GR Viswanath	41.74
6000	VVS Laxman	43.79
5248	Kapil Dev	31.05
5074	V Sehwag	52.85

Tendulkar has scored 39 centuries, Gavaskar 34, Dravid 25, Azharuddin 22

Most wickets

		Avge
616	A Kumble	29.33
434	Kapil Dev	29.64
291	Harbhajan Singh	30.87
266	BS Bedi	29.74
242	BS Chandrasekhar	29.74
236	J Srinath	30.49
189	EAS Prasanna	30.38
162	MH Mankad	32.32
178	Z Khan	34.06
156	S Venkataraghavan	36.11

In all 15 Indians have reached 100 wickets

Highest scores

319	V Sehwag	v South Africa at Chennai	2007-08
309	V Sehwag	v Pakistan at Multan	2003-04
281	VVS Laxman	v Australia at Kolkata	2000-01
270	R Dravid	v Pakistan at Rawalpindi	2003-04
254	V Sehwag	v Pakistan at Lahore	2005-06
248*	SR Tendulkar	v Bangladesh at Dhaka	2004-05
241*	SR Tendulkar	v Australia at Sydney	2003-04
239	SC Ganguly	v Pakistan at Bangalore	2007-08
236*	SM Gavaskar	v West Indies at Madras	1983-84
233	R Dravid	v Australia at Adelaide	2003-04

Dravid has scored five double-centuries, Gavaskar and Tendulkar four

Best innings bowling

10-74	A Kumble	v Pakistan at Delhi	1998-99
9-69	JM Patel	v Australia at Kanpur	1959-60
9-83	Kapil Dev	v WI at Ahmedabad	1983-84
9-102	SP Gupte	v W Indies at Kanpur	1958-59
8-52	MH Mankad	v Pakistan at Delhi	1952-53
8-55	MH Mankad	v England at Madras	1951-52
8-61	ND Hirwani	v W Indies at Madras	1987-88
8-72	S Venkataraghavan	v N Zealand at Delhi	1964-65
8-75	ND Hirwani	v W Indies at Madras	1987-88
8-76	EAS Prasanna	v NZ at Auckland	1975-76

Hirwani's two performances were in the same match, his Test debut

Record wicket partnerships

1st	413	MH Mankad (231) and P Roy (173)	v New Zealand at Madras	1955-56
2nd	344*	SM Gavaskar (182*) and DB Vengsarkar (157*)	v West Indies at Calcutta	1978-79
3rd	336	V Sehwag (309) and SR Tendulkar (194*)	v Pakistan at Multan	2003-04
4th	353	SR Tendulkar (241*) and VVS Laxman (178)	v Australia at Sydney	2003-04
5th	376	VVS Laxman (281) and R Dravid (180)	v Australia at Calcutta	2000-01
6th	298*	DB Vengsarkar (164*) and RJ Shastri (121*)	v Australia at Bombay	1986-87
7th	235	RJ Shastri (142) and SMH Kirmani (102)	v England at Bombay	1984-85
8th	161	M Azharuddin (109) and A Kumble (88)	v South Africa at Calcutta	1996-97
9th	149	PG Joshi (52*) and RB Desai (85)	v Pakistan at Bombay	1960-61
10th	133	SR Tendulkar (248*) and Z Khan (75)	v Bangladesh at Dhaka	2004-05

Figures to 12.9.08. Updated records can be found at www.cricinfo.com/ci/engine/records

Test Match Records   INDIA

Most catches

Fielders

175	R Dravid	
108	SM Gavaskar	
105	M Azharuddin	
102	VVS Laxman	
98	SR Tendulkar	

Most dismissals

Wicketkeepers		Ct/St
198	SMH Kirmani	160/38
130	KS More	110/20
107	NR Mongia	99/8
82	MS Dhoni	68/14
82	FM Engineer	66/16

Highest team totals

705-7d	v Australia at Sydney	2003-04
676-7	v Sri Lanka at Kanpur	1986-87
675-5d	v Pakistan at Multan	2003-04
664	v England at The Oval	2007
657-7d	v Australia at Kolkata	2000-01
644-7d	v West Indies at Kanpur	1978-79
633-5d	v Australia at Kolkata	1997-98
628-8d	v England at Leeds	2002
627	v South Africa at Chennai	2007-08
626	v Pakistan at Bangalore	2007-08

India have reached 600 on seven other occasions

Lowest team totals

Completed innings

42*	v England at Lord's	1974
58	v Australia at Brisbane	1947-48
58	v England at Manchester	1952
66	v S Africa at Durban	1996-97
67	v Aust at Melbourne	1947-48
75	v West Indies at Delhi	1987-88
76	v SA at Ahmedabad	2007-08
81*	v NZ at Wellington	1975-76
81	v W Indies at Bridgetown	1996-97
82	v England at Manchester	1952

*One or more batsmen absent

Best match bowling

16-136	ND Hirwani	v West Indies at Madras	1987-88
15-217	Harbhajan Singh	v Australia at Chennai	2000-01
14-124	JM Patel	v Australia at Kanpur	1959-60
14-149	A Kumble	v Pakistan at Delhi	1998-99
13-131	MH Mankad	v Pakistan at Delhi	1952-53
13-132	J Srinath	v Pakistan at Calcutta	1998-99
13-181	A Kumble	v Australia at Chennai	2004-05
13-196	Harbhajan Singh	v Australia at Kolkata	2000-01
12-104	BS Chandrasekhar	v Australia at Melbourne	1977-78
12-108	MH Mankad	v England at Madras	1951-52

Hirwani's feat was on his Test debut

Hat-tricks

Harbhajan Singh v Australia at Kolkata   2000-01

The wickets of RT Ponting, AC Gilchrist and SK Warne, as India fought back to win after following on.

IK Pathan   v Pakistan at Karachi   2005-06

Salman Butt, Younis Khan and Mohammad Yousuf with the fourth, fifth and sixth balls of the match – Pakistan still won the match by 341 runs.

India have never conceded a hat-trick in a Test match

India's Test match results

	Played	Won	Lost	Drawn	Tied	% win
v Australia	72	16	34	21	1	22.22
v Bangladesh	5	4	0	1	0	80.00
v England	97	18	34	45	0	18.55
v New Zealand	44	14	9	21	0	31.81
v Pakistan	59	9	12	38	0	15.25
v South Africa	22	5	10	7	0	22.72
v Sri Lanka	29	11	5	13	0	37.93
v West Indies	82	11	30	41	0	13.41
v Zimbabwe	11	7	2	2	0	63.63
TOTAL	**421**	**95**	**136**	**189**	**1**	**22.56**

Figures to 12.9.08. Updated records can be found at **www.cricinfo.com/ci/engine/records**

Most appearances

417	SR Tendulkar
334	M Azharuddin
329	R Dravid
308	SC Ganguly
269	A Kumble
229	J Srinath
225	Kapil Dev
214	Yuvraj Singh
196	A Jadeja
191	AB Agarkar

Robin Singh played 136 ODIs for India – but only one Test match

Most runs

		Avge
16361	SR Tendulkar	44.33
11221	SC Ganguly	40.95
10464	R Dravid	39.48
9378	M Azharuddin	36.92
6049	Yuvraj Singh	35.79
5532	V Sehwag	32.73
5359	A Jadeja	37.47
4413	NS Sidhu	37.08
4091	K Srikkanth	29.01
3783	Kapil Dev	23.79

MS Dhoni (3619), DB Vengsarkar (3508), RJ Shastri (3108) and SM Gavaskar (3092) also reached 3000 runs

Most wickets

		Avge
334	A Kumble	30.83
315	J Srinath	28.08
288	AB Agarkar	27.85
253	Kapil Dev	27.45
197	Z Khan	29.72
196	BKV Prasad	32.30
191	Harbhajan Singh	33.23
157	M Prabhakar	28.87
154	SR Tendulkar	44.12
148	IK Pathan	29.57

RJ Shastri (129) and SC Ganguly (100) also reached 100 wickets

Highest scores

186*	SR Tendulkar	v N Zealand at Hyderabad	1999-2000
183*	MS Dhoni	v Sri Lanka at Jaipur	2005-06
183	SC Ganguly	v Sri Lanka at Taunton	1999
175*	Kapil Dev	v Zimbabwe at Tunbridge Wells	1983
159*	D Mongia	v Zimbabwe at Guwahati	2001-02
153*	M Azharuddin	v Zimbabwe at Cuttack	1997-98
153*	SC Ganguly	v New Zealand at Gwalior	1999-2000
153	R Dravid	v N Zealand at Hyderabad	1999-2000
152	SR Tendulkar	v Nam at Pietermaritzburg	2002-03
148	MS Dhoni	v Pakistan at Visakhapatnam	2004-05

Tendulkar has scored 42 centuries (the ODI record), Ganguly 22, Dravid 12, V Sehwag 9 and Yuvraj Singh 8

Best bowling figures

6-12	A Kumble	v West Indies at Calcutta	1993-94
6-23	A Nehra	v England at Durban	2002-03
6-42	AB Agarkar	v Australia at Melbourne	2003-04
6-55	S Sreesanth	v England at Indore	2005-06
6-59	A Nehra	v Sri Lanka at Colombo	2005
5-6	SB Joshi	v South Africa at Nairobi	1999-2000
5-15	RJ Shastri	v Australia at Perth	1991-92
5-16	SC Ganguly	v Pakistan at Toronto	1997-98
5-21	Arshad Ayub	v Pakistan at Dhaka	1988-89
5-21	N Chopra	v West Indies at Toronto	1999-2000

Agarkar has taken four wickets in an ODI innings 12 times, Kumble and J Srinath 10, and Z Khan 8

Record wicket partnerships

1st	258	SC Ganguly (111) and SR Tendulkar (146)	v Kenya at Paarl	2001-02
2nd	331	SR Tendulkar (186*) and R Dravid (153)	v New Zealand at Hyderabad	1999-2000
3rd	237*	R Dravid (104*) and SR Tendulkar (140*)	v Kenya at Bristol	1999
4th	275*	M Azharuddin (153*) and A Jadeja (116*)	v Zimbabwe at Cuttack	1997-98
5th	223	M Azharuddin (111*) and A Jadeja (119)	v Sri Lanka at Colombo	1997-98
6th	158	Yuvraj Singh (120) and MS Dhoni (67*)	v Zimbabwe at Harare	2005-06
7th	102	HK Badani (60*) and AB Agarkar (53)	v Australia at Melbourne	2003-04
8th	82*	Kapil Dev (72*) and KS More (42*)	v New Zealand at Bangalore	1987-88
9th	126*	Kapil Dev (175*) and SMH Kirmani (24*)	v Zimbabwe at Tunbridge Wells	1983
10th	64	Harbhajan Singh (41*) and L Balaji (18)	v England at The Oval	2004

*Figures to 12.9.08. Updated records can be found at **www.cricinfo.com/ci/engine/records***

One-day International Records

INDIA

Most catches

Fielders

156	M Azharuddin	
122	SR Tendulkar	
121	R Dravid	
99	SC Ganguly	
85	A Kumble	

Most dismissals

Wicketkeepers		Ct/St
154	NR Mongia	110/44
151	MS Dhoni	118/33
90	KS More	63/27
86	R Dravid	72/14

Highest team totals

413-5	v Bermuda at Port-of-Spain	2006-07
376-2	v N Zealand at Hyderabad	1999-2000
374-4	v Hong Kong at Karachi	2008
373-6	v Sri Lanka at Taunton	1999
356-9	v Pakistan at Visakhapatnam	2004-05
353-5	v New Zealand at Hyderabad	2003-04
351-3	v Kenya at Paarl	2001-02
350-6	v Sri Lanka at Nagpur	2005-06
349-7	v Pakistan at Karachi	2003-04
348-5	v Bangladesh at Dhaka	2004-05

All scored in 50 overs

Lowest team totals

Completed innings

54	v Sri Lanka at Sharjah	2000-01
63	v Australia at Sydney	1980-81
78	v Sri Lanka at Kanpur	1986-87
79	v Pakistan at Sialkot	1978-79
91	v South Africa at Durban	2006-07
100	v WI at Ahmedabad	1993-94
100	v Australia at Sydney	1999-2000
103	v Sri Lanka at Colombo	2008-09
108	v N Zealand at Auckland	2002-03
108	v NZ at Christchurch	2002-03

*The lowest score against India is
Zimbabwe's 65 at Harare in 2005-06*

Most sixes

189	SC Ganguly	
166	SR Tendulkar	
98	Yuvraj Singh	
85	A Jadeja	
83	MS Dhoni	
83	V Sehwag	
77	M Azharuddin	
67	Kapil Dev	
44	NS Sidhu	
41	Robin Singh	
41	K Srikkanth	

Best strike rate

Runs per 100 balls		*Runs*
99.03	V Sehwag	5532
95.07	Kapil Dev	3783
91.92	RV Uthappa	786
90.13	MS Dhoni	3619
89.43	SB Joshi	584
86.46	Yuvraj Singh	6049
85.49	SR Tendulkar	16361
82.42	SK Raina	1191
82.17	SM Patil	1005
81.73	G Gambhir	1987

Qualification: 500 runs

Most economical bowlers

Runs per over		*Wkts*
3.71	Kapil Dev	253
3.95	Maninder Singh	66
4.05	Madan Lal	73
4.16	Harbhajan Singh	191
4.21	RJ Shastri	129
4.27	M Prabhakar	157
4.29	A Kumble	334
4.33	M Amarnath	46
4.36	SLV Raju	63
4.44	SB Joshi	69
4.44	J Srinath	315

Qualification: 2000 balls bowled

India's one-day international results

	Played	Won	Lost	Tied	No result	% win
v Australia	96	32	57	0	7	35.95
v Bangladesh	19	17	2	0	0	89.47
v England	65	33	30	0	2	52.38
v New Zealand	75	36	35	0	4	50.70
v Pakistan	117	45	68	0	4	39.82
v South Africa	57	20	35	0	2	36.36
v Sri Lanka	106	55	41	0	10	57.29
v West Indies	90	35	53	1	1	39.88
v Zimbabwe	49	39	8	2	0	81.63
v others (see below)	22	20	2	0	0	90.90
TOTAL	**696**	**332**	**331**	**3**	**30**	**50.07**

Other teams: Bermuda (P1, W1), East Africa (P1, W1), Hong Kong (P1, W1), Ireland (P1, W1), Kenya (P13, W11, L2), Namibia (P1, W1), Netherlands (P1, W1), Scotland (P1, W1), United Arab Emirates (P2, W2).

NEW ZEALAND *Test Match Records*

Most appearances

111	SP Fleming
86	RJ Hadlee
82	DL Vettori
82	JG Wright
81	NJ Astle
78	AC Parore
77	MD Crowe
63	IDS Smith
62	CL Cairns
61	BE Congdon

Vettori also played one Test for the World XI against Australia in October 2005

Most runs

		Avge
7172	SP Fleming	40.06
5444	MD Crowe	45.36
5334	JG Wright	37.82
4702	NJ Astle	37.02
3448	BE Congdon	32.22
3428	JR Reid	33.28
3320	CL Cairns	33.53
3124	RJ Hadlee	27.16
3116	CD McMillan	38.46
2991	GM Turner	44.64

Crowe scored 17 Test centuries, Wright 12 and Astle 11

Most wickets

		Avge
431	RJ Hadlee	22.29
256	DL Vettori	34.14
218	CL Cairns	29.40
160	DK Morrison	34.68
140	CS Martin	33.41
130	BL Cairns	32.92
123	EJ Chatfield	32.17
116	RO Collinge	29.25
111	BR Taylor	26.60
102	JG Bracewell	35.81

RC Motz (100) also took 100 Test wickets. Vettori also took one wicket for the World XI

Highest scores

299	MD Crowe	v Sri Lanka at Wellington	1990-91
274*	SP Fleming	v Sri Lanka at Colombo	2002-03
267*	BA Young	v Sri Lanka at Dunedin	1996-97
262	SP Fleming	v South Africa at Cape Town	2005-06
259	GM Turner	v West Indies at Georgetown	1971-72
239	GT Dowling	v India at Christchurch	1967-68
230*	B Sutcliffe	v India at Delhi	1955-56
224	L Vincent	v Sri Lanka at Wellington	2004-05
223*	GM Turner	v West Indies at Kingston	1971-72
222	NJ Astle	v England at Christchurch	2001-02

There have been four other double-centuries, two by MS Sinclair and one each by MP Donnelly and SP Fleming

Best innings bowling

9-52	RJ Hadlee	v Australia at Brisbane	1985-86
7-23	RJ Hadlee	v India at Wellington	1975-76
7-27	CL Cairns	v West Indies at Hamilton	1999-2000
7-52	C Pringle	v Pakistan at Faisalabad	1990-91
7-53	CL Cairns	v Bangladesh at Hamilton	2001-02
7-65	SB Doull	v India at Wellington	1998-99
7-74	BR Taylor	v West Indies at Bridgetown	1971-72
7-74	BL Cairns	v England at Leeds	1983
7-87	SL Boock	v Pakistan at Hyderabad	1984-85
7-87	DL Vettori	v Australia at Auckland	1999-2000

Hadlee took five or more wickets in an innings 36 times: the next-best for NZ is 15, by DL Vettori

Record wicket partnerships

1st	387	GM Turner (259) and TW Jarvis (182)	v West Indies at Georgetown	1971-72
2nd	241	JG Wright (116) and AH Jones (143)	v England at Wellington	1991-92
3rd	467	AH Jones (186) and MD Crowe (299)	v Sri Lanka at Wellington	1990-91
4th	243	MJ Horne (157) and NJ Astle (114)	v Zimbabwe at Auckland	1997-98
5th	222	NJ Astle (141) and CD McMillan (142)	v Zimbabwe at Wellington	2000-01
6th	246*	JJ Crowe (120*) and RJ Hadlee (151*)	v Sri Lanka at Colombo	1986-87
7th	225	CL Cairns (158) and JDP Oram (90)	v South Africa at Auckland	2003-04
8th	256	SP Fleming (262) and JEC Franklin (122*)	v South Africa at Cape Town	2005-06
9th	136	IDS Smith (173) and MC Snedden (22)	v India at Auckland	1989-90
10th	151	BF Hastings (110) and RO Collinge (68*)	v Pakistan at Auckland	1972-73

Figures to 12.9.08. Updated records can be found at **www.cricinfo.com/ci/engine/records**

Test Match Records — NEW ZEALAND

Most catches

Fielders

171	SP Fleming	
71	MD Crowe	
70	NJ Astle	
64	JV Coney	
54	BA Young	

Most dismissals

	Wicketkeepers	Ct/St
201	AC Parore	194/7
176	IDS Smith	168/8
106	BB McCullum	100/6
96	KJ Wadsworth	92/4
59	WK Lees	52/7

Highest team totals

671-4	v Sri Lanka at Wellington	1990-91
630-6d	v India at Chandigarh	2003-04
595	v South Africa at Auckland	2003-04
593-8d	v South Africa at Cape Town	2005-06
586-7d	v Sri Lanka at Dunedin	1996-97
563	v Pakistan at Hamilton	2003-04
561	v Sri Lanka at Napier	2004-05
553-7d	v Australia at Brisbane	1985-86
551-9d	v England at Lord's	1973
545-6d	v Bangladesh at Chittagong	2004-05

671-4 is the record score in any team's second innings in a Test match

Lowest team totals

Completed innings

26	v England at Auckland	1954-55
42	v Australia at Wellington	1945-46
47	v England at Lord's	1958
54	v Australia at Wellington	1945-46
65	v England at Christchurch	1970-71
67	v England at Leeds	1958
67	v England at Lord's	1978
70	v Pakistan at Dacca	1955-56
73	v Pakistan at Lahore	2001-02
74	v W Indies at Dunedin	1955-56
74	v England at Lord's	1958

26 is the lowest total by any team in a Test match

Best match bowling

15-123	RJ Hadlee	v Australia at Brisbane	1985-86
12-149	DL Vettori	v Australia at Auckland	1999-2000
12-170	DL Vettori	v Bangladesh at Chittagong	2004-05
11-58	RJ Hadlee	v India at Wellington	1975-76
11-102	RJ Hadlee	v West Indies at Dunedin	1979-80
11-152	C Pringle	v Pakistan at Faisalabad	1990-91
11-155	RJ Hadlee	v Australia at Perth	1985-86
11-169	DJ Nash	v England at Lord's	1994
11-180	CS Martin	v South Africa at Auckland	2003-04
10-88	RJ Hadlee	v India at Bombay	1988-89

Hadlee took 33 wickets at 12.15 in the three-Test series in Australia in 1985-86

Hat-tricks

PJ Petherick	v Pakistan at Lahore	1976-77
JEC Franklin	v Bangladesh at Dhaka	2004-05

*Petherick's hat-trick was on Test debut: he dismissed Javed Miandad (who had made 163 on **his** debut), Wasim Raja and Intikhab Alam. Petherick won only five more Test caps.*

Franklin is one of only five men to have scored a century and taken a hat-trick in Tests: the others are J Briggs of England, Abdul Razzaq and Wasim Akram of Pakistan, and IK Pathan of India

New Zealand's Test match results

	Played	Won	Lost	Drawn	Tied	% win
v Australia	46	7	22	17	0	15.21
v Bangladesh	6	6	0	0	0	100.00
v England	94	8	45	41	0	8.51
v India	44	9	14	21	0	20.45
v Pakistan	45	6	21	18	0	13.33
v South Africa	35	4	20	11	0	11.42
v Sri Lanka	24	9	5	10	0	37.50
v West Indies	35	9	10	16	0	25.71
v Zimbabwe	13	7	0	6	0	53.84
TOTAL	**342**	**65**	**137**	**140**	**0**	**19.00**

*Figures to 12.9.08. Updated records can be found at **www.cricinfo.com/ci/engine/records***

NEW ZEALAND *One-day International Records*

Most appearances

279	SP Fleming	
250	CZ Harris	
223	NJ Astle	
218	DL Vettori	
214	CL Cairns	
197	CD McMillan	
179	AC Parore	
153	SB Styris	
149	JG Wright	
143	MD Crowe	

Fleming (1), Cairns (1) and Vettori (4) also played in official ODIs for the World XI

Most runs

		Avge
8007	SP Fleming	32.41
7090	NJ Astle	34.92
4881	CL Cairns	29.22
4707	CD McMillan	28.18
4704	MD Crowe	38.55
4379	CZ Harris	29.00
3891	JG Wright	26.46
3699	SB Styris	33.32
3314	AC Parore	25.68
3143	KR Rutherford	29.65

Astle scored 16 centuries: Fleming is next with eight. Fleming also scored 30 runs and Cairns 69 for the World XI

Most wickets

		Avge
222	DL Vettori	32.04
203	CZ Harris	37.50
200	CL Cairns	32.78
158	RJ Hadlee	21.56
140	EJ Chatfield	25.84
126	DK Morrison	27.53
125	SE Bond	19.32
124	JDP Oram	30.70
123	KD Mills	26.75
121	SB Styris	34.40

MC Snedden (114), GR Larsen (113) and C Pringle (103) also took 100 wickets. Vettori also took 8 wickets, and Cairns 1, for the World XI

Highest scores

172	L Vincent	v Zimbabwe at Bulawayo	2005-06
171*	GM Turner	v East Africa at Birmingham	1975
166	BB McCullum	v Ireland at Aberdeen	2008
161	JAH Marshall	v Ireland at Aberdeen	2008
145*	NJ Astle	v USA at The Oval	2004
141	SB Styris	v Sri Lanka at Bloemfontein	2002-03
140	GM Turner	v Sri Lanka at Auckland	1982-83
141	SB Styris	v Sri Lanka at Bloemfontein	2002-03
139	JM How	v England at Napier	2007-08
130	CZ Harris	v Australia at Madras	1995-96

Turner's 171 was the highest score in the first World Cup*

Best bowling figures

6-19	SE Bond	v India at Bulawayo	2005-06
6-23	SE Bond	v Australia at Port Elizabeth	2002-03
6-25	SB Styris	v West Indies at Port-of-Spain	2001-02
5-22	MN Hart	v West Indies at Margao	1994-95
5-22	AR Adams	v India at Queenstown	2002-03
5-23	RO Collinge	v India at Christchurch	1975-76
5-23	SE Bond	v Australia at Wellington	2006-07
5-25	RJ Hadlee	v Sri Lanka at Bristol	1983
5-25	SE Bond	v Australia at Adelaide	2001-02
5-25	KD Mills	v South Africa at Durban	2007-08

In all Hadlee took five wickets in an ODI on five occasions

Record wicket partnerships

1st	266	JAH Marshall (161) and BB McCullum (166)	v Ireland at Aberdeen	2008
2nd	156	L Vincent (102) and NJ Astle (81)	v West Indies at Napier	2005-06
3rd	181	AC Parore (96) and KR Rutherford (108)	v India at Baroda	1994-95
4th	168	LK Germon (89) and CZ Harris (130)	v Australia at Chennai	1995-96
5th	148	RG Twose (80*) and CL Cairns (60)	v Australia at Cardiff	1999
6th	165	CD McMillan (117) and BB McCullum (86*)	v Australia at Hamilton	2006-07
7th	115	AC Parore (78) and LK Germon (52)	v Pakistan at Sharjah	1996-97
8th	79	SB Styris (63) and DL Vettori (47)	v Zimbabwe at Harare	2005-06
9th	74*	BB McCullum (50*) and DL Vettori (23*)	v Australia at Christchurch	2005-06
10th	65	MC Snedden (40) and EJ Chatfield (19*)	v Sri Lanka at Derby	1983

Figures to 12.9.08. Updated records can be found at www.cricinfo.com/ci/engine/records

Most catches

Fielders

132	SP Fleming	
96	CZ Harris	
83	NJ Astle	
66	CL Cairns	
66	MD Crowe	

Most dismissals

Wicketkeepers		*Ct/St*
160	BB McCullum	147/13
136	AC Parore	111/25
85	IDS Smith	80/5
37	TE Blain	36/1
30	LK Germon	21/9
30	WK Lees	28/2

Highest team totals

402-2	v Ireland at Aberdeen	2008
397-5	v Zimbabwe at Bulawayo	2005-06
363-5	v Canada at St Lucia	2006-07
350-9	v Australia at Hamilton	2006-07
349-9	v India at Rajkot	1999-2000
348-8	v India at Nagpur	1995-96
347-4	v USA at The Oval	2004
340-5	v Australia at Auckland	2006-07
340-7	v England at Napier	2007-08
338-4	v Bangladesh at Sharjah	1989-90

The 397-5 came from 44 overs; all the others were from 50, except 350-9 (49.3), and 340-5 (48.4)

Lowest team totals

Completed innings

64	v Pakistan at Sharjah	1985-86
73	v Sri Lanka at Auckland	2006-07
74	v Aust at Wellington	1981-82
74	v Pakistan at Sharjah	1989-90
94	v Aust at Christchurch	1989-90
97	v Aust at Faridabad	2003-04
105	v Aust at Auckland	2005-06
108	v Pakistan at Wellington	1992-93
110	v Pakistan at Auckland	1993-94
112	v Aust at Port Elizabeth	2002-03

The lowest score against New Zealand is 70, by Australia at Adelaide in 1985-86

Most sixes

151	CL Cairns	
86	NJ Astle	
84	CD McMillan	
77	BB McCullum	
63	SP Fleming	
59	SB Styris	
58	JDP Oram	
43	CZ Harris	
41	BL Cairns	
37	MJ Greatbatch	
37	L Vincent	

CL Cairns also hit 2 for the World XI

Best strike rate

Runs per 100 balls		*Runs*
104.88	BL Cairns	987
99.43	IDS Smith	1055
90.64	BB McCullum	2605
84.75	LRPL Taylor	1179
83.76	CL Cairns	4881
83.13	JDP Oram	1854
79.22	DL Vettori	1354
79.20	SB Styris	3699
77.87	CM Spearman	936
75.94	CD McMillan	4707

Qualification: 500 runs

Most economical bowlers

Runs per over		*Wkts*
3.30	RJ Hadlee	158
3.57	EJ Chatfield	140
3.76	GR Larsen	113
4.06	BL Cairns	89
4.14	W Watson	74
4.16	DL Vettori	222
4.17	DN Patel	45
4.17	JV Coney	54
4.20	SE Bond	125
4.28	CZ Harris	203

Qualification: 2000 balls bowled

New Zealand's one-day international results

	Played	Won	Lost	Tied	No result	% win
v Australia	112	30	78	0	4	27.77
v Bangladesh	11	11	0	0	0	100.00
v England	69	34	29	2	4	53.84
v India	75	35	36	0	4	49.29
v Pakistan	78	29	47	1	1	38.31
v South Africa	50	17	29	0	4	36.95
v Sri Lanka	68	34	30	1	3	53.07
v West Indies	46	18	23	0	5	43.90
v Zimbabwe	28	19	7	1	1	72.22
v others (see below)	11	11	0	0	0	100.00
TOTAL	**548**	**238**	**279**	**5**	**26**	**46.07**

Other teams: Canada (P2, W2), East Africa (P1, W1), Ireland (P2, W2), Kenya (P1, W1), Netherlands (P1, W1), Scotland (P2, W2), United Arab Emirates (P1, W1), United States of America (P1, W1).

PAKISTAN — *Test Match Records*

Most appearances

124	Javed Miandad	
119	Inzamam-ul-Haq	
104	Wasim Akram	
103	Salim Malik	
88	Imran Khan	
87	Waqar Younis	
81	Wasim Bari	
79	Mohammad Yousuf	
78	Zaheer Abbas	
76	Mudassar Nazar	

Inzamam-ul-Haq also played one Test for the World XI

Most runs

		Avge
8832	Javed Miandad	52.57
8829	Inzamam-ul-Haq	50.16
6770	Mohammad Yousuf	55.49
5768	Salim Malik	43.69
5062	Zaheer Abbas	44.79
4816	Younis Khan	49.14
4114	Mudassar Nazar	38.09
4052	Saeed Anwar	45.52
3931	Majid Khan	38.92
3915	Hanif Mohammad	43.98

Mohammad Yousuf was known as Yousuf Youhana until September 2005

Most wickets

		Avge
414	Wasim Akram	23.62
373	Waqar Younis	23.56
362	Imran Khan	22.81
236	Abdul Qadir	32.80
220	Danish Kaneria	33.90
208	Saqlain Mushtaq	29.83
185	Mushtaq Ahmed	32.97
178	Shoaib Akhtar	25.69
177	Sarfraz Nawaz	32.75
171	Iqbal Qasim	28.11

Fazal Mahmood (139), Intikhab Alam (125) and Abdul Razzaq (100) also took 100 wkts

Highest scores

337	Hanif Mohammad	v WI at Bridgetown	1957-58
329	Inzamam-ul-Haq	v NZ at Lahore	2001-02
280*	Javed Miandad	v India at Hyderabad	1982-83
274	Zaheer Abbas	v Eng at Birmingham	1971
271	Javed Miandad	v NZ at Auckland	1988-89
267	Younis Khan	v India at Bangalore	2004-05
260	Javed Miandad	v England at The Oval	1987
257*	Wasim Akram	v Zim at Sheikhupura	1996-97
240	Zaheer Abbas	v England at The Oval	1974
237	Salim Malik	v Aust at Rawalpindi	1994-95

Wasim Akram's innings included 12 sixes, a record for any Test innings

Best innings bowling

9-56	Abdul Qadir	v England at Lahore	1987-88
9-86	Sarfraz Nawaz	v Australia at Melbourne	1978-79
8-58	Imran Khan	v Sri Lanka at Lahore	1981-82
8-60	Imran Khan	v India at Karachi	1982-83
8-69	Sikander Bakht	v India at Delhi	1979-80
8-164	Saqlain Mushtaq	v England at Lahore	2000-01
7-40	Imran Khan	v England at Leeds	1987
7-42	Fazal Mahmood	v India at Lucknow	1952-53
7-49	Iqbal Qasim	v Australia at Karachi	1979-80
7-52	Intikhab Alam	v NZ at Dunedin	1972-73
7-52	Imran Khan	v Eng at Birmingham	1982

Wasim Akram took five or more wickets in a Test innings on 25 occasions, Imran Khan 23

Record wicket partnerships

1st	298	Aamer Sohail (160) and Ijaz Ahmed (151)	v West Indies at Karachi	1997-98
2nd	291	Zaheer Abbas (274) and Mushtaq Mohammad (100)	v England at Birmingham	1971
3rd	451	Mudassar Nazar (231) and Javed Miandad (280*)	v India at Hyderabad	1982-83
4th	350	Mushtaq Mohammad (201) and Asif Iqbal (175)	v New Zealand at Dunedin	1972-73
5th	281	Javed Miandad (163) and Asif Iqbal (166)	v New Zealand at Lahore	1976-77
6th	269	Mohammad Yousuf (223) and Kamran Akmal (154)	v England at Lahore	2005-06
7th	308	Waqar Hasan (189) and Imtiaz Ahmed (209)	v New Zealand at Lahore	1955-56
8th	313	Wasim Akram (257*) and Saqlain Mushtaq (79)	v Zimbabwe at Sheikhupura	1996-97
9th	190	Asif Iqbal (146) and Intikhab Alam (51)	v England at The Oval	1967
10th	151	Azhar Mahmood (128*) and Mushtaq Ahmed (59)	v South Africa at Rawalpindi	1997-98

Figures to 12.9.08. Updated records can be found at **www.cricinfo.com/ci/engine/records**

Test Match Records

PAKISTAN

Most catches

Fielders

93	Javed Miandad	
81	Inzamam-ul-Haq	
66	Majid Khan	
66	Younis Khan	
65	Salim Malik	

Most dismissals

Wicketkeepers   Ct/St

228	Wasim Bari	201/27
147	Moin Khan	127/20
142	Kamran Akmal	123/19
130	Rashid Latif	119/11
104	Salim Yousuf	91/13

Highest team totals

708	v England at The Oval	1987
699-5	v India at Lahore	1989-90
679-7d	v India at Lahore	2005-06
674-6	v India at Faisalabad	1984-85
657-8d	v West Indies at Bridgetown	1957-58
652	v India at Faisalabad	1982-83
643	v New Zealand at Lahore	2001-02
636-8d	v England at Lahore	2005-06
624	v Australia at Adelaide	1983-84
616-5d	v New Zealand at Auckland	1988-89

Pakistan have made three other scores of 600 or more, and one of 599-7d

Lowest team totals

Completed innings

53*	v Australia at Sharjah	2002-03
59	v Australia at Sharjah	2002-03
62	v Australia at Perth	1981-82
72	v Australia at Perth	2004-05
77*	v West Indies at Lahore	1986-87
87	v England at Lord's	1954
90	v England at Manchester	1954
92	v S Africa at Faisalabad	1997-98
97*	v Australia at Brisbane	1995-96
100	v England at Lord's	1962

* One batsman retired hurt or absent hurt. The lowest two totals came in the same game

Best match bowling

14-116	Imran Khan	v Sri Lanka at Lahore	1981-82
13-101	Abdul Qadir	v England at Lahore	1987-88
13-114	Fazal Mahmood	v Australia at Karachi	1956-57
13-135	Waqar Younis	v Zimbabwe at Karachi	1993-94
12-94	Fazal Mahmood	v India at Lucknow	1952-53
12-94	Danish Kaneria	v Bangladesh at Multan	2001-02
12-99	Fazal Mahmood	v England at The Oval	1954
12-100	Fazal Mahmood	v West Indies at Dacca	1958-59
12-130	Waqar Younis	v NZ at Faisalabad	1990-91
12-165	Imran Khan	v Australia at Sydney	1976-77

Imran Khan took ten or more wickets in a match six times, Abdul Qadir, Waqar Younis and Wasim Akram five each.

Hat-tricks

Wasim Akram	v Sri Lanka at Lahore	1998-99
Wasim Akram	v Sri Lanka at Dhaka	1998-99
Abdul Razzaq	v Sri Lanka at Galle	1999-2000
Mohammad Sami	v Sri Lanka at Lahore	2001-02

Wasim Akram's hat-tricks came in successive matches: he also took Pakistan's first two hat-tricks in one-day internationals.

RS Kaluwitharana was the first victim in both Wasim Akram's first hat-trick and in Abdul Razzaq's

Pakistan's Test match results

	Played	Won	Lost	Drawn	Tied	% win
v Australia	52	11	24	17	0	21.15
v Bangladesh	6	6	0	0	0	100.00
v England	67	12	18	37	0	17.91
v India	59	12	9	38	0	20.33
v New Zealand	45	21	6	18	0	46.66
v South Africa	16	3	8	5	0	18.75
v Sri Lanka	32	15	7	10	0	46.87
v West Indies	44	15	14	15	0	34.09
v Zimbabwe	14	8	2	4	0	57.14
TOTAL	**335**	**103**	**88**	**144**	**0**	**30.74**

Figures to 12.9.08. Updated records can be found at **www.cricinfo.com/ci/engine/records**

PAKISTAN
One-day International Records

Most appearances

375	Inzamam-ul-Haq	
356	Wasim Akram	
283	Salim Malik	
262	Mohammad Yousuf	
262	Waqar Younis	
260	Shahid Afridi	
250	Ijaz Ahmed	
247	Saeed Anwar	
233	Javed Miandad	
227	Abdul Razzaq	

Moin Khan (219) also played in more than 200 ODIs

Most runs

		Avge
11701	Inzamam-ul-Haq	39.53
9076	Mohammad Yousuf	43.63
8823	Saeed Anwar	39.21
7381	Javed Miandad	41.70
7170	Salim Malik	32.88
6564	Ijaz Ahmed	32.33
5841	Rameez Raja	32.09
5442	Shahid Afridi	23.86
5087	Younis Khan	33.91
4780	Aamer Sohail	31.86

Shoaib Malik (4576) and Abdul Razzaq (4416) also passed 4000 runs

Most wickets

		Avge
502	Wasim Akram	23.52
416	Waqar Younis	23.84
288	Saqlain Mushtaq	21.78
245	Abdul Razzaq	30.80
237	Shahid Afridi	34.94
213	Shoaib Akhtar	22.84
182	Aqib Javed	31.43
182	Imran Khan	26.61
161	Mushtaq Ahmed	33.29
132	Abdul Qadir	26.16

Shoaib Malik (124), Azhar Mahmood (123), Mohammad Sami (118) and Mudassar Nazar (111) also took 100 wickets

Highest scores

194	Saeed Anwar	v India at Chennai	1996-97
160	Imran Nazir	v Zimbabwe at Kingston	2006–07
144	Younis Khan	v Hong Kong at Colombo	2004
143	Shoaib Malik	v India at Colombo	2004
141*	Mohammad Yousuf	v Zim at Bulawayo	2002-03
140	Saeed Anwar	v India at Dhaka	1997-98
139*	Ijaz Ahmed	v India at Lahore	1997-98
137*	Inzamam-ul-Haq	v N Zealand at Sharjah	1993-94
137	Ijaz Ahmed	v England at Sharjah	1998-99
136	Salman Butt	v Bangladesh at Karachi	2007-08

Saeed Anwar scored 20 centuries, Mohammad Yousuf 15, Ijaz Ahmed and Inzamam-ul-Haq 10

Best innings bowling

7-36	Waqar Younis	v England at Leeds	2001
7-37	Aqib Javed	v India at Sharjah	1991-92
6-14	Imran Khan	v India at Sharjah	1984-85
6-16	Shoaib Akhtar	v New Zealand at Karachi	2001-02
6-18	Azhar Mahmood	v W Indies at Sharjah	1999-2000
6-26	Waqar Younis	v Sri Lanka at Sharjah	1989-90
6-27	Naved-ul-Hasan	v India at Jamshedpur	2004-05
6-30	Waqar Younis	v N Zealand at Auckland	1993-94
6-35	Abdul Razzaq	v Bangladesh at Dhaka	2001-02
6-44	Waqar Younis	v New Zealand at Sharjah	1996-97

Waqar Younis took five or more wickets in an innings 13 times (the ODI record), Saqlain Mushtaq and Wasim Akram 6

Record wicket partnerships

1st	204	Saeed Anwar (110) and Rameez Raja (109*)	v Sri Lanka at Sharjah	1992-93
2nd	263	Aamer Sohail (134) and Inzamam-ul-Haq (137*)	v New Zealand at Sharjah	1993-94
3rd	230	Saeed Anwar (140) and Ijaz Ahmed (117)	v India at Dhaka	1997-98
4th	172	Salim Malik (84) and Basit Ali (127*)	v West Indies at Sharjah	1993-94
5th	162	Inzamam-ul-Haq (72) and Mohammad Yousuf (88)	v Australia at Lord's	2004
6th	144	Imran Khan (102*) and Shahid Mahboob (77)	v Sri Lanka at Leeds	1983
7th	124	Mohammad Yousuf (91*) and Rashid Latif (66)	v Australia at Cardiff	2001
8th	100	Fawad Alam (63*) and Sohail Tanvir (59)	v Hong Kong at Karachi	2008
9th	73	Shoaib Malik (52*) and Mohammad Sami (46)	v South Africa at Centurion	2006-07
10th	72	Abdul Razzaq (46*) and Waqar Younis (33)	v South Africa at Durban	1997-98

*Figures to 12.9.08. Updated records can be found at **www.cricinfo.com/ci/engine/records***

One-day International Records — **PAKISTAN**

Most catches

Fielders

113	Inzamam-ul-Haq
92	Wasim Akram
90	Ijaz Ahmed
89	Younis Khan
83	Shahid Afridi

Most dismissals

Wicketkeepers		*Ct/St*
287	Moin Khan	214/73
220	Rashid Latif	182/38
103	Salim Yousuf	81/22
100	Kamran Akmal	86/14
62	Wasim Bari	52/10

Highest team totals

371-9	v Sri Lanka at Nairobi	1996-97
353-6	v England at Karachi	2005-06
351-4	v South Africa at Durban	2006-07
349	v Zimbabwe at Kingston	2006-07
347-5	v Zimbabwe at at Karachi	2007-08
344-5	v Zimbabwe at Bulawayo	2002-03
344-8	v India at Karachi	2003-04
343-5	v Hong Kong at Colombo	2004
338-5	v Sri Lanka at Swansea	1983
335-6	v South Africa at Port Elizabeth	2002-03

Pakistan have reached 300 on 39 further occasions

Lowest team totals

Completed innings

43	v W Indies at Cape Town	1992-93
71	v W Indies at Brisbane	1992-93
74	v England at Adelaide	1991-92
81	v West Indies at Sydney	1992-93
85	v England at Manchester	1978
87	v India at Sharjah	1984-85
89	v S Africa at Mohali	2006-07
107	v S Africa at Cape Town	2006-07
108	v Australia at Nairobi	2002-03
109	v SA at Johannesburg	1994-95

Against India in 1984-85 Pakistan were chasing only 126 to win

Most sixes

245	Shahid Afridi
143	Inzamam-ul-Haq
121	Wasim Akram
103	Abdul Razzaq
97	Saeed Anwar
87	Ijaz Ahmed
84	Mohammad Yousuf
61	Moin Khan
55	Shoaib Malik
49	Younis Khan

Afridi hit 2 other sixes in official ODIs

Best strike rate

Runs per 100 balls		*Runs*
111.10	Shahid Afridi	5442
89.60	Manzoor Elahi	741
88.33	Wasim Akram	3717
88.13	Misbah-ul-Haq	1085
84.80	Zaheer Abbas	2572
83.55	Kamran Akmal	1621
81.30	Moin Khan	3266
80.66	Saeed Anwar	8823
80.40	Abdul Razzaq	4416
80.30	Ijaz Ahmed	6564

Qualification: 500 runs

Most economical bowlers

Runs per over		*Wkts*
3.63	Sarfraz Nawaz	63
3.71	Akram Raza	38
3.89	Imran Khan	182
3.89	Wasim Akram	502
4.06	Abdul Qadir	132
4.14	Arshad Khan	56
4.14	Tauseef Ahmed	55
4.24	Mudassar Nazar	111
4.26	Mushtaq Ahmed	161
4.28	Aqib Javed	182

Qualification: 2000 balls bowled

Pakistan's one-day international results

	Played	Won	Lost	Tied	No result	% win
v Australia	74	27	43	1	3	38.73
v Bangladesh	25	24	1	0	0	96.00
v England	63	26	35	0	2	42.62
v India	117	68	45	0	4	60.17
v New Zealand	78	47	29	1	1	61.68
v South Africa	52	16	35	0	1	31.37
v Sri Lanka	111	67	40	1	3	62.50
v West Indies	110	44	64	2	0	40.90
v Zimbabwe	40	36	2	1	1	93.58
v others (see below)	17	16	1	0	0	94.11
TOTAL	687	371	295	6	15	55.65

Other teams: Canada (P1, W1), Hong Kong (P2, W2), Ireland (P1, L1), Kenya (P5, W5), Namibia (P1, W1), Netherlands (P3, W3), Scotland (P2, W2), United Arab Emirates (P2, W2).

SOUTH AFRICA *Test Match Records*

Most appearances

122	JH Kallis
117	MV Boucher
107	SM Pollock
101	G Kirsten
91	M Ntini
90	HH Gibbs
72	AA Donald
70	DJ Cullinan
69	GC Smith
68	WJ Cronje

Kallis, Boucher and Smith all also played one Test for the World XI against Australia

Most runs

		Avge
9678	JH Kallis	55.30
7289	G Kirsten	45.27
6167	HH Gibbs	41.95
5749	GC Smith	49.99
4554	DJ Cullinan	44.21
4355	MV Boucher	30.24
3781	SM Pollock	32.31
3714	WJ Cronje	36.41
3471	B Mitchell	48.88
2988	ND McKenzie	39.31

Kallis (83 runs), Smith (12) and Boucher (17) also played one Test for the World XI against Australia

Most wickets

		Avge
421	SM Pollock	23.11
358	M Ntini	28.22
330	AA Donald	22.25
239	JH Kallis	31.20
170	HJ Tayfield	25.91
134	PR Adams	32.87
128	DW Steyn	22.51
123	TL Goddard	26.22
123	A Nel	31.86
116	PM Pollock	24.18

NAT Adcock (104) and N Boje (100) also took 100 wickets. Kallis also took one wicket for the World XI

Highest scores

277	GC Smith	v England at Birmingham	2003
275*	DJ Cullinan	v New Zealand at Auckland	1998-99
275	G Kirsten	v England at Durban	1999-2000
274	RG Pollock	v Australia at Durban	1969-70
259	GC Smith	v England at Lord's	2003
255*	DJ McGlew	v New Zealand at Wellington	1952-53
236	EAB Rowan	v England at Leeds	1951
232	GC Smith	v Bangladesh at Chittagong	2007-08
231	AD Nourse	v Australia at Johannesburg	1935-36
228	HH Gibbs	v Pakistan at Cape Town	2002-03

Smith's 277 and 259 were in consecutive matches

Best innings bowling

9-113	HJ Tayfield	v England at Johannesburg	1956-57
8-53	GB Lawrence	v N Zealand at Johannesburg	1961-62
8-64	L Klusener	v India at Calcutta	1996-97
8-69	HJ Tayfield	v England at Durban	1956-57
8-70	SJ Snooke	v England at Johannesburg	1905-06
8-71	AA Donald	v Zimbabwe at Harare	1995-96
7-23	HJ Tayfield	v Australia at Durban	1949-50
7-29	GF Bissett	v England at Durban	1927-28
7-37	M Ntini	v W Indies at Port-of-Spain	2004-05
7-63	AE Hall	v England at Cape Town	1922-23

Klusener and Hall were making their Test debuts

Record wicket partnerships

1st	415	ND McKenzie (226) and GC Smith (232)	v Bangladesh at Chittagong	2007-08
2nd	315*	HH Gibbs (211*) and JH Kallis (148*)	v New Zealand at Christchurch	1998-99
3rd	429*	JA Rudolph (222*) and HH Dippenaar (177*)	v Bangladesh at Chittagong	2002-03
4th	249	JH Kallis (177) and G Kirsten (137)	v West Indies at Durban	2003-04
5th	267	JH Kallis (147) and AG Prince (131)	v West Indies at St John's	2004-05
6th	200	RG Pollock (274) and HR Lance (61)	v Australia at Durban	1969-70
7th	246	DJ McGlew (255*) and ARA Murray (109)	v New Zealand at Wellington	1952-53
8th	150	ND McKenzie (103) and SM Pollock (111)	v Sri Lanka at Centurion	2000-01
	150	G Kirsten (130) and M Zondeki (59)	v England at Leeds	2003
9th	195	MV Boucher (78) and PL Symcox (108)	v Pakistan at Johannesburg	1997-98
10th	103	HG Owen-Smith (129) and AJ Bell (26*)	v England at Leeds	1929

*Figures to 12.9.08. Updated records can be found at **www.cricinfo.com/ci/engine/records***

Test Match Records **SOUTH AFRICA**

Most catches

Fielders

126	JH Kallis	
94	HH Gibbs	
89	GC Smith	
83	G Kirsten	
72	SM Pollock	

Most dismissals

Wicketkeepers		Ct/St
447	MV Boucher	427/20
152	DJ Richardson	150/2
141	JHB Waite	124/17
56	DT Lindsay	54/2
51	HB Cameron	39/12

Highest team totals

682-6d	v England at Lord's	2003
658-9d	v West Indies at Durban	2003-04
622-9d	v Australia at Durban	1969-70
621-5d	v New Zealand at Auckland	1998-99
620-7d	v Pakistan at Cape Town	2002-03
620	v Australia at Johannesburg	1966-67
604-6d	v West Indies at Centurion	2003-04
600-3d	v Zimbabwe at Harare	2001-02
595	v Australia at Adelaide	1963-64
594-5d	v England at Birmingham	2003

The 620 was scored in the second innings of the match

Lowest team totals

Completed innings

30	v Eng at Port Elizabeth	1895-96
30	v Eng at Birmingham	1924
35	v Eng at Cape Town	1898-99
36	v Aust at Melbourne	1931-32
43	v Eng at Cape Town	1888-89
45	v Aust at Melbourne	1931-32
47	v Eng at Cape Town	1888-89
58	v England at Lord's	1912
72	v Eng at Johannesburg	1956-57
72	v Eng at Cape Town	1956-57

South Africa's lowest total since their return to Test cricket in 1991-92 is 84 against India at Johannesburg in 2006-07

Best match bowling

13-132	M Ntini	v W Indies at Port-of-Spain	2004-05
13-165	HJ Tayfield	v Australia at Melbourne	1952-53
13-192	HJ Tayfield	v England at Johannesburg	1956-57
12-127	SJ Snooke	v England at Johannesburg	1905-06
12-139	AA Donald	v India at Port Elizabeth	1992-93
12-181	AEE Vogler	v England at Johannesburg	1909-10
11-112	AE Hall	v England at Cape Town	1922-23
11-113	AA Donald	v Zimbabwe at Harare	1995-96
11-127	AA Donald	v England at Jo'burg	1999-2000
11-150	EP Nupen	v England at Jo'burg	1930-31

Hall was making his Test debut. His performance, and Vogler's, were at the old Wanderers ground in Johannesburg

Hat-tricks

GM Griffin	v England at Lord's	1960

Griffin achieved the feat in his second and final Test (he was no-balled for throwing in the same match).

GA Lohmann (for England at Port Elizabeth in 1895-96), TJ Matthews (twice in the same match for Australia at Manchester in 1912) and TWJ Goddard (for England at Johannesburg in 1938-39) have taken Test hat-tricks against South Africa

South Africa's Test match results

	Played	Won	Lost	Drawn	Tied	% win
v Australia	77	15	44	18	0	19.48
v Bangladesh	6	6	0	0	0	100.00
v England	134	28	55	51	0	20.89
v India	22	10	5	7	0	45.45
v New Zealand	35	20	4	11	0	57.14
v Pakistan	16	8	3	5	0	50.00
v Sri Lanka	17	8	4	5	0	47.05
v West Indies	22	14	3	5	0	63.63
v Zimbabwe	7	6	0	1	0	85.71
TOTAL	**336**	**115**	**118**	**103**	**0**	**34.22**

Figures to 12.9.08. Updated records can be found at **www.cricinfo.com/ci/engine/records**

SOUTH AFRICA *One-day International Records*

Most appearances

294	SM Pollock
274	JH Kallis
263	MV Boucher
245	JN Rhodes
232	HH Gibbs
188	WJ Cronje
185	G Kirsten
171	L Klusener
167	M Ntini
164	AA Donald

*Pollock (9), Kallis (5), Boucher (5)
and Ntini (1) also appeared in
official ODIs for composite teams*

Most runs

		Avge
9580	JH Kallis	45.61
7589	HH Gibbs	36.31
6798	G Kirsten	40.95
5935	JN Rhodes	35.11
5565	WJ Cronje	38.64
5046	GC Smith	41.02
4095	MV Boucher	28.63
3860	DJ Cullinan	32.99
3576	L Klusener	41.10
3300	HH Dippenaar	44.00

*Kallis (29 runs), Smith (0), Boucher
(163) and Dippenaar (91) also appeared
in official ODIs for composite teams*

Most wickets

		Avge
387	SM Pollock	24.31
272	AA Donald	21.78
256	M Ntini	24.41
239	JH Kallis	31.44
192	L Klusener	29.95
114	WJ Cronje	34.78
106	A Nel	27.68
95	N Boje	35.27
95	PS de Villiers	27.74
95	AJ Hall	26.47

*Pollock (6 wickets), Ntini (1), Kallis (4)
and Boje (1) also appeared in official
ODIs for composite teams*

Highest scores

188*	G Kirsten	v UAE at Rawalpindi	1995-96
175	HH Gibbs	v Australia at Johannesburg	2005-06
169*	DJ Callaghan	v N Zealand at Verwoerdburg	1994-95
161	AC Hudson	v Netherlands at Rawalpindi	1995-96
153	HH Gibbs	v B'desh at Potchefstroom	2002-03
147*	MV Boucher	v Zimababwe at Potchefstroom	2006-07
146	AB de Villiers	v West Indies at St George's	2006-07
143	HH Gibbs	v N Zealand at Johannesburg	2002-03
139	JH Kallis	v W Indies at Johannesburg	2003-04
134*	GC Smith	v India at Kolkata	2005-06

*Gibbs has scored 20 one-day hundreds, Kallis 16 and
Kirsten 13*

Best bowling figures

6-22	M Ntini	v Australia at Cape Town	2005-06
6-23	AA Donald	v Kenya at Nairobi	1996-97
6-35	SM Pollock	v W Indies at East London	1998-99
6-49	L Klusener	v Sri Lanka at Lahore	1997-98
5-18	AJ Hall	v England at Bridgetown	2006-07
5-20	SM Pollock	v Eng at Johannesburg	1999-2000
5-21	L Klusener	v Kenya at Amstelveen	1999
5-21	N Boje	v Australia at Cape Town	2001-02
5-21	M Ntini	v Pakistan at Mohali	2006-07
5-23	SM Pollock	v Pakistan at Johannesburg	2006-07

*Klusener has taken five wickets in an ODI innings six times,
Pollock five and Ntini four*

Record wicket partnerships

1st	235	G Kirsten (115) and HH Gibbs (111)	v India at Kochi	1999-2000
2nd	209	G Kirsten (124) and ND McKenzie (131*)	v Kenya at Cape Town	2001-02
3rd	186	JA Morkel (97) and AB de Villiers (107)	v Zimbabwe at Harare	2007
4th	232	DJ Cullinan (124) and JN Rhodes (121)	v Pakistan at Nairobi	1996-97
5th	183*	JH Kallis (109*) and JN Rhodes (94*)	v Pakistan at Durban	1997-98
6th	137	WJ Cronje (70*) and SM Pollock (75)	v Zimbabwe at Johannesburg	1996-97
7th	114	MV Boucher (68) and L Klusener (75*)	v India at Nagpur	1999-2000
8th	138*	JM Kemp (100*) and AJ Hall (56*)	v India at Cape Town	2006-07
9th	61	SM Pollock (46) and J Botha (15*)	v Australia at Melbourne	2005-06
10th	67*	JA Morkel (23*) and M Ntini (42*)	v New Zealand at Napier	2003-04

Figures to 12.9.08. Updated records can be found at **www.cricinfo.com/ci/engine/records**

Most catches

Fielders

105	JN Rhodes
104	SM Pollock
101	JH Kallis
100	HH Gibbs
73	WJ Cronje

Most dismissals

Wicketkeepers		*Ct/St*
380	MV Boucher	363/17
165	DJ Richardson	148/17
15	AB de Villiers	15/0
9	SJ Palframan	9/0

Highest team totals

438-9	v Australia at Johannesburg 2005-06
418-5	v Zimbabwe at Potchefstroom 2006-07
392-6	v Pakistan at Centurion 2006-07
363-3	v Zimbabwe at Bulawayo 2001-02
356-4	v West Indies at St George's 2006-07
354-3	v Kenya at Cape Town 2001-02
353-3	v Netherland at Basseterre 2006-07
329-6	v Zimbabwe at Durban 2004-05
328-3	v Netherlands at Rawalpindi 1995-96
326-3	v Australia at Port Elizabeth 2001-02

438-9 was the highest total in all ODIs, and came from 49.5 overs; all the others above were scored in 50 overs, apart from 353-3 (40)

Lowest team totals

Completed innings

69	v Australia at Sydney 1993-94
83	v England at Nottingham 2008
101*	v Pakistan at Sharjah 1999-2000
106	v Australia at Sydney 2001-02
107	v England at Lord's 2003
107	v England at Lord's 2003
108	v NZ at Mumbai 2006-07
123	v Aust at Wellington 1994-95
129	v Eng at East London 1995-96
149	v England at Jo'burg 1999-2000

* One batsman retired hurt. SA also had 50-overs totals of 140-9 (v WI, 1992-93), 144-9 (v Aust, 1999-2000) and 147-7 (v NZ, 1993-94)

Most sixes

122	HH Gibbs
114	JH Kallis
94	WJ Cronje
76	L Klusener
71	MV Boucher
55	SM Pollock
52	JM Kemp
47	JN Rhodes
35	AB de Villiers
33	DJ Cullinan

Boucher (2), Pollock (3), Kemp (1) and de Villiers (4) also hit sixes for the Africa XI

Best strike rate

Runs per 100 balls		*Runs*
89.91	L Klusener	3576
89.29	N Boje	1410
86.77	AB de Villiers	1476
85.55	SM Pollock	3193
83.79	MV Boucher	4095
83.61	PL Symcox	694
83.14	HH Gibbs	7589
82.78	JM Kemp	1371
81.88	GC Smith	5046
81.41	AP Kuiper	539

Qualification: 500 runs

Most economical bowlers

Runs per over		*Wkts*
3.57	PS de Villiers	95
3.65	SM Pollock	387
3.94	CR Matthews	79
4.15	AA Donald	272
4.15	PL Symcox	72
4.28	BM McMillan	70
4.44	WJ Cronje	114
4.47	M Ntini	256
4.50	RP Snell	44
4.51	N Boje	95
4.51	AJ Hall	95

Qualification: 2000 balls bowled

South Africa's one-day international results

	Played	Won	Lost	Tied	No result	% win
v Australia	67	28	36	3	0	44.02
v Bangladesh	11	10	1	0	0	90.90
v England	40	22	15	1	2	59.21
v India	57	35	20	0	2	63.63
v New Zealand	50	29	17	0	4	63.04
v Pakistan	52	35	16	0	1	68.62
v Sri Lanka	45	22	21	1	1	51.13
v West Indies	45	32	12	0	1	72.72
v Zimbabwe	27	24	2	0	1	92.30
v others (see below)	15	15	0	0	0	100.00
TOTAL	**409**	**252**	**140**	**5**	**12**	**64.10**

Other teams: Canada (P1, W1), Ireland (P2, W2), Kenya (P8, W8), Netherlands (P2, W2), Scotland (P1, W1), United Arab Emirates (P1, W1).

SRI LANKA
Test Match Records

Most appearances

122	M Muralitharan	
110	ST Jayasuriya	
107	WPUJC Vaas	
98	DPMD Jayawardene	
93	PA de Silva	
93	A Ranatunga	
90	MS Atapattu	
83	HP Tillakaratne	
76	KC Sangakkara	
52	RS Mahanama	

Ranatunga uniquely played in his country's first Test, and their 100th

Most runs

		Avge
7757	DPMD Jayawardene	52.41
6973	ST Jayasuriya	40.07
6361	PA de Silva	42.97
6356	KC Sangakkara	54.79
5502	MS Atapattu	39.02
5105	A Ranatunga	35.69
4545	HP Tillakaratne	42.87
2998	WPUJC Vaas	24.17
2576	RS Mahanama	29.27
2552	TT Samaraweera	44.00

TM Dilshan (2533) and AP Gurusinha (2452) also reached 2000 runs

Most wickets

		Avge
751	M Muralitharan	21.90
348	WPUJC Vaas	29.31
98	ST Jayasuriya	34.34
91	SL Malinga	33.80
85	GP Wickremasinghe	41.87
84	CRD Fernando	33.90
73	RJ Ratnayake	35.10
69	HDPK Dharmasena	42.31
64	DNT Zoysa	33.70
59	ALF de Mel	36.94

Muralitharan also took 5 wickets for the World XI

Highest scores

374	DPMD Jayawardene	v SA at Colombo	2006
340	ST Jayasuriya	v India at Colombo	1997-98
287	KC Sangakkara	v SA at Colombo	2006
270	KC Sangakkara	v Zim at Bulawayo	2003-04
267	PA de Silva	v NZ at Wellington	1990-91
253	ST Jayasuriya	v Paki at Faisalabad	2004-05
249	MS Atapattu	v Zim at Bulawayo	2003-04
242	DPMD Jayawardene	v India at Colombo	1998-99
237	DPMD Jayawardene	v SA at Galle	2004-05
232	KC Sangakkara	v SA at Colombo	2004-05

Jayawardene made 23 Test centuries, de Silva 20, and Atapattu 16. Atapattu and Sangakkara both have 6 double-centuries

Best innings bowling

9-51	M Muralitharan	v Zimbabwe at Kandy	2001-02
9-65	M Muralitharan	v England at The Oval	1998
8-46	M Muralitharan	v West Indies at Kandy	2005
8-70	M Muralitharan	v England at Nottingham	2006
8-83	JR Ratnayeke	v Pakistan at Sialkot	1985-86
8-87	M Muralitharan	v India at Colombo	2001-02
7-46	M Muralitharan	v England at Galle	2003-04
7-71	WPUJC Vaas	v West Indies at Colombo	2001-02
7-84	M Muralitharan	v South Africa at Galle	2000-01
7-94	M Muralitharan	v Zimbabwe at Kandy	1997-98

Muralitharan has taken five or more wickets in an innings a record 65 times

Record wicket partnerships

1st	335	MS Atapattu (207*) and ST Jayasuriya (188)	v Pakistan at Kandy	2000
2nd	576	ST Jayasuriya (340) and RS Mahanama (225)	v India at Colombo	1997-98
3rd	624	KC Sangakkara (287) and DPMD Jayawardene (374)	v South Africa at Colombo	2006
4th	240*	AP Gurusinha (116*) and A Ranatunga (135*)	v Pakistan at Colombo	1985-86
5th	280	TT Samaraweera (138) and TM Dilshan (168)	v Bangladesh at Colombo	2005-06
6th	189*	PA de Silva (143*) and A Ranatunga (87*)	v Zimbabwe at Colombo	1997-98
7th	223*	HAPW Jayawardene (120*) and WPUJC Vaas (100*)	v Bangladesh at Colombo	2007
8th	170	DPMD Jayawardene (237) and WPUJC Vaas (69)	v South Africa at Galle	2004-05
9th	105	WPUJC Vaas (50*) and KMDN Kulasekera (64)	v England at Lord's	2006
10th	79	WPUJC Vaas (68*) and M Muralitharan (43)	v Australia at Kandy	2003-04

Figures to 12.9.08. Updated records can be found at www.cricinfo.com/ci/engine/records

Test Match Records — SRI LANKA

Most catches

Fielders

136	DPMD Jayawardene	
89	HP Tillakaratne	
78	ST Jayasuriya	
67	M Muralitharan	
58	MS Atapattu	

Most dismissals

Wicketkeepers		Ct/St
149	KC Sangakkara	129/20
119	RS Kaluwitharana	93/26
56	HAPW Jayawardene	41/15
35	HP Tillakaratne	33/2
34	SAR Silva	33/1

Highest team totals

952-6d	v India at Colombo	1997-98
756-5d	v South Africa at Colombo	2006
713-3d	v Zimbabwe at Bulawayo	2003-04
628-8d	v England at Colombo	2003-04
627-9d	v West Indies at Colombo	2001-02
610-6d	v India at Colombo	2001-02
600-6d	v India at Colombo	2008
591	v England at The Oval	1998
590-9d	v West Indies at Galle	2001-02
586-6d	v Zimbabwe at Colombo	2001-02

952-6d is the highest total in all Tests. In all Sri Lanka have reached 500 on 22 occasions

Lowest team totals

Completed innings

71	v Pakistan at Kandy	1994-95
73*	v Pakistan at Kandy	2005-06
81	v England at Colombo	2000-01
82	v India at Chandigarh	1990-91
93	v NZ at Wellington	1982-83
95	v S Africa at Cape Town	2000-01
97	v N Zealand at Kandy	1983-84
97	v Australia at Darwin	2004
101	v Pakistan at Kandy	1985-86
109	v Pakistan at Kandy	1985-86

* One batsman absent hurt

Best match bowling

16-220	M Muralitharan	v England at The Oval	1998
14-191	WPUJC Vaas	v West Indies at Colombo	2001-02
13-115	M Muralitharan	v Zimbabwe at Kandy	2001-02
13-171	M Muralitharan	v South Africa at Galle	2000
12-82	M Muralitharan	v Bangladesh at Kandy	2007
12-117	M Muralitharan	v Zimbabwe at Kandy	1997-98
12-225	M Muralitharan	v South Africa at Colombo	2006
11-93	M Muralitharan	v England at Galle	2003-04
11-110	M Muralitharan	v India at Colombo	2008
11-132	M Muralitharan	v England at Nottingham	2006

Muralitharan has taken ten or more wickets in a match a record 20 times; the only others to do it for Sri Lanka are Vaas (twice), UDU Chandana and BAW Mendis

Hat-tricks

DNT Zoysa	v Zimbabwe at Harare	1999-2000

He dismissed TR Gripper, MW Goodwin and NC Johnson with the first three balls of his first over, the second of the match.

Four hat-tricks have been taken against Sri Lanka in Tests, all of them for Pakistan: two by Wasim Akram (in successive Tests in the Asian Test Championship at Lahore and Dhaka in 1998-99), Abdul Razzaq (at Galle in 2000-01) and Mohammad Sami (at Lahore in 2001-02)

Sri Lanka's Test match results

	Played	Won	Lost	Drawn	Tied	% win
v Australia	20	1	13	6	0	5.00
v Bangladesh	10	10	0	0	0	100.00
v England	21	6	8	7	0	28.57
v India	29	5	11	13	0	17.24
v New Zealand	24	5	9	10	0	20.83
v Pakistan	32	7	15	10	0	21.87
v South Africa	17	4	8	5	0	23.52
v West Indies	12	6	3	3	0	50.00
v Zimbabwe	15	10	0	5	0	66.66
TOTAL	**180**	**54**	**67**	**59**	**0**	**30.00**

Figures to 12.9.08. Updated records can be found at www.cricinfo.com/ci/engine/records

SRI LANKA
One-day International Records

Most appearances

417	ST Jayasuriya	
321	WPUJC Vaas	
308	PA de Silva	
307	M Muralitharan	
278	DPMD Jayawardene	
269	A Ranatunga	
268	MS Atapattu	
223	KC Sangakkara	
213	RS Mahanama	
200	HP Tillakaratne	

In all 18 Sri Lankans have played more than 100 ODIs

Most runs

		Avge
12719	ST Jayasuriya	32.86
9284	PA de Silva	34.90
8529	MS Atapattu	37.57
7561	DPMD Jayawardene	32.59
7456	A Ranatunga	35.84
6518	KC Sangakkara	35.42
5162	RS Mahanama	29.49
3950	RP Arnold	35.26
3902	AP Gurusinha	28.27
3789	HP Tillakaratne	29.60

RS Kaluwitharana (3711) also reached 3000 runs

Most wickets

		Avge
468	M Muralitharan	23.01
399	WPUJC Vaas	27.45
307	ST Jayasuriya	36.47
159	CRD Fernando	29.74
151	UDU Chandana	31.72
138	HDPK Dharmasena	36.21
109	GP Wickremasinghe	39.64
108	DNT Zoysa	29.75
106	PA de Silva	39.40
104	MF Maharoof	24.39

Muralitharan (11), Vaas (1), Jayasuriya (3) and Fernando (4) all took wickets in ODIs for composite teams

Highest scores

189	ST Jayasuriya	v India at Sharjah	2000-01
157	ST Jayasuriya	v Netherlands at Amstelveen	2006
152	ST Jayasuriya	v England at Leeds	2006
151*	ST Jayasuriya	v India at Mumbai	1996-97
145	PA de Silva	v Kenya at Kandy	1995-96
140	ST Jayasuriya	v N Zealand at Bloemfontein	1994-95
138*	KC Sangakkara	v India at Jaipur	2005-06
134*	ST Jayasuriya	v Pakistan at Lahore	1997-98
134	PA de Silva	v Pakistan at Sharjah	1996-97
134	ST Jayasuriya	v Pakistan at Singapore	1995-96

ST Jayasuriya has scored 27 ODI centuries, MS Atapattu and PA de Silva 11, KC Sangakkara 10

Best bowling figures

8-19	WPUJC Vaas	v Zimbabwe at Colombo	2001-02
7-30	M Muralitharan	v India at Sharjah	2000-01
6-13	BAW Mendis	v India at Karachi	2008
6-14	MF Maharoof	v West Indies at Mumbai	2006-07
6-25	WPUJC Vaas	v B'desh at P'maritzburg	2002-03
6-27	CRD Fernando	v England at Colombo	2007-08
6-29	ST Jayasuriya	v England at Moratuwa	1992-93
5-9	M Muralitharan	v New Zealand at Sharjah	2001-02
5-14	WPUJC Vaas	v India at Sharjah	2000-01
5-17	ST Jayasuriya	v Pakistan at Lahore	2004-05

Vaas's 8-19 are the best bowling figures in all ODIs

Record wicket partnerships

1st	286	WU Tharanga (109) and ST Jayasuriya (152)	v England at Leeds	2006
2nd	170	S Wettimuny (74) and RL Dias (102)	v India at Delhi	1982-83
	170	ST Jayasuriya (120) and HP Tillakaratne (81*)	v New Zealand at Bloemfontein	2002-03
3rd	226	MS Atapattu (102*) and DPMD Jayawardene (128)	v India at Sharjah	2000-01
4th	171*	RS Mahanama (94*) and A Ranatunga (87*)	v West Indies at Lahore	1997-98
5th	166	ST Jayasuriya (189) and RP Arnold (52*)	v India at Sharjah	2000-01
6th	159	LPC Silva (67) and CK Kapugedera (95)	v West Indies at Port-of-Spain	2007-08
7th	126*	DPMD Jayawardene (94*) and UDU Chandana (44*)	v India at Dambulla	2005-06
8th	91	HDPK Dharmasena (51*) and DK Liyanage (43)	v West Indies at Port-of-Spain	1996-97
9th	76	RS Kalpage (44*) and WPUJC Vaas (33)	v Pakistan at Colombo	1994-95
10th	51	RP Arnold (103) and KSC de Silva (2*)	v Zimbabwe at Bulawayo	1999-2000

Figures to 12.9.08. Updated records can be found at **www.cricinfo.com/ci/engine/records**

SRI LANKA

Most catches

Fielders

145	DPMD Jayawardene	
121	M Muralitharan	
118	ST Jayasuriya	
109	RS Mahanama	
95	PA de Silva	

Most dismissals

Wicketkeepers   *Ct/St*

240	KC Sangakkara	184/56
206	RS Kaluwitharana	131/75
45	HP Tillakaratne	39/6
34	DSBP Kuruppu	26/8
30	RG de Alwis	27/3

Highest team totals

443-9	v Netherlands at Amstelveen	2006
398-5	v Kenya at Kandy	1995-96
357-9	v Bangladesh at Lahore	2008
349-9	v Pakistan at Singapore	1995-96
343-5	v Australia at Sydney	2002-03
339-4	v Pakistan at Mohali	1996-97
332-8	v Bangladesh at Karachi	2008
329	v West Indies at Sharjah	1995-96
324-2	v England at Leeds	2006
321-6	v Bermuda at Port-of-Spain	2006-07

The 324-2 was scored in 37.3 overs

Lowest team totals

Completed innings

55	v W Indies at Sharjah	1986-87
78*	v Pakistan at Sharjah	2001-02
86	v W Indies at Manchester	1975
91	v Australia at Adelaide	1984-85
96	v India at Sharjah	1983-84
98	v S Africa at Colombo	1993-94
98	v India at Sharjah	1998-99
99	v England at Perth	1998-99
102	v W Indies at Brisbane	1995-96
105	v SA at Bloemfontein	1997-98

* One batsman absent hurt

Most sixes

263	ST Jayasuriya
102	PA de Silva
64	A Ranatunga
42	AP Gurusinha
40	DPMD Jayawardene
27	KC Sangakkara
22	UDU Chandana
22	WPUJC Vaas
21	RP Arnold
18	MF Maharoof
18	RJ Ratnayake

Best strike rate

Runs per 100 balls   *Runs*

91.09	ST Jayasuriya	12719
86.80	RJ Ratnayake	612
86.18	MF Maharoof	761
81.13	PA de Silva	9284
80.26	TM Dilshan	2944
77.91	A Ranatunga	7456
77.70	RS Kaluwitharana	3711
76.06	DPMD Jayawardene	7561
75.07	LRD Mendis	1527
74.29	KC Sangakkara	6518

Qualification: 500 runs

Most economical bowlers

Runs per over   *Wkts*

3.87	M Muralitharan	468
4.18	WPUJC Vaas	399
4.18	SD Anurasiri	32
4.27	HDPK Dharmasena	138
4.29	CPH Ramanayake	68
4.29	VB John	34
4.50	DS de Silva	32
4.50	RS Kalpage	73
4.52	DNT Zoysa	108
4.53	GP Wickremasinghe	109

Qualification: 2000 balls bowled

Sri Lanka's one-day international results

	Played	Won	Lost	Tied	No result	% win
v Australia	68	20	46	0	2	30.30
v Bangladesh	24	23	1	0	0	95.83
v England	43	21	22	0	0	48.83
v India	106	41	55	0	10	42.70
v New Zealand	68	30	34	1	3	46.92
v Pakistan	111	40	67	1	3	37.50
v South Africa	45	21	22	1	1	48.86
v West Indies	46	18	26	0	2	40.90
v Zimbabwe	37	30	6	0	1	83.33
v others (see below)	13	12	1	0	0	92.30
TOTAL	**561**	**256**	**280**	**3**	**22**	**47.77**

Other teams: Bermuda (P1, W1), Canada (P1, W1), Ireland (P1, W1), Kenya (P5, W4, L1), Netherlands (P3, W3), United Arab Emirates (P2, W2).

WEST INDIES *Test Match Records*

Most appearances

132	CA Walsh
130	BC Lara
121	IVA Richards
116	DL Haynes
112	S Chanderpaul
110	CH Lloyd
108	CG Greenidge
102	CL Hooper
98	CEL Ambrose
93	GS Sobers

Sobers played 85 successive Tests between 1954-55 and 1971-72

Most runs

		Avge
11912	BC Lara	53.17
8540	IVA Richards	50.23
8032	GS Sobers	57.78
8001	S Chanderpaul	49.08
7558	CG Greenidge	44.72
7515	CH Lloyd	46.67
7487	DL Haynes	42.29
6227	RB Kanhai	47.53
5949	RB Richardson	44.39
5762	CL Hooper	36.46

Greenidge and Haynes put on 6482 runs together, the Test record by any pair of batsmen

Most wickets

		Avge
519	CA Walsh	24.44
405	CEL Ambrose	20.99
376	MD Marshall	20.94
309	LR Gibbs	29.09
259	J Garner	20.97
249	MA Holding	23.68
235	GS Sobers	34.03
202	AME Roberts	25.61
192	WW Hall	26.38
161	IR Bishop	24.27

In all 17 West Indians have reached 100 Test wickets

Highest scores

400*	BC Lara	v England at St John's	2003-04
375	BC Lara	v England at St John's	1993-94
365*	GS Sobers	v Pakistan at Kingston	1957-58
317	CH Gayle	v South Africa at St John's	2004-05
302	LG Rowe	v England at Bridgetown	1973-74
291	IVA Richards	v England at The Oval	1976
277	BC Lara	v Australia at Sydney	1992-93
270*	GA Headley	v England at Kingston	1934-35
261*	RR Sarwan	v Bangladesh at Kingston	2003-04
261	FMM Worrell	v England at Nottingham	1950

Lara scored 34 Test centuries, Sobers 26, Richards 24

Best innings bowling

9-95	JM Noreiga	v India at Port-of-Spain	1970-71
8-29	CEH Croft	v Pakistan at Port-of-Spain	1976-77
8-38	LR Gibbs	v India at Bridgetown	1961-62
8-45	CEL Ambrose	v England at Bridgetown	1989-90
8-92	MA Holding	v England at The Oval	1976
8-104	AL Valentine	v England at Manchester	1950
7-22	MD Marshall	v England at Manchester	1988
7-25	CEL Ambrose	v Australia at Perth	1992-93
7-37	CA Walsh	v New Zealand at Wellington	1994-95
7-49	S Ramadhin	v England at Birmingham	1957

Valentine was playing in his first Test, Croft and Noreiga in their second

Record wicket partnerships

1st	298	CG Greenidge (149) and DL Haynes (167)	v England at St John's	1989-90
2nd	446	CC Hunte (260) and GS Sobers (365*)	v Pakistan at Kingston	1957-58
3rd	338	ED Weekes (206) and FMM Worrell (167)	v England at Port-of-Spain	1953-54
4th	399	GS Sobers (226) and FMM Worrell (197*)	v England at Bridgetown	1959-60
5th	322	BC Lara (213) and JC Adams (94)	v Australia at Kingston	1998-99
6th	282*	BC Lara (400*) and RD Jacobs (107*)	v England at St John's	2003-04
7th	347	DS Atkinson (219) and CC Depeiaza (122)	v Australia at Bridgetown	1954-55
8th	148	JC Adams (101*) and FA Rose (69)	v Zimbabwe at Kingston	1999-2000
9th	161	CH Lloyd (161*) and AME Roberts (68)	v India at Calcutta	1983-84
10th	106	CL Hooper (178*) and CA Walsh (30)	v Pakistan at St John's	1992-93

Test Match Records

WEST INDIES

Most catches

Fielders
164	BC Lara	
122	IVA Richards	
115	CL Hooper	
109	GS Sobers	
96	CG Greenidge	

Most dismissals

Wicketkeepers Ct/St
270	PJL Dujon	265/5
219	RD Jacobs	207/12
189	DL Murray	181/8
101	JR Murray	98/3
90	FCM Alexander	85/5

Highest team totals

790-3d	v Pakistan at Kingston	1957-58
751-5d	v England at St John's	2003-04
747	v South Africa at St John's	2004-05
692-8d	v England at The Oval	1995
687-8d	v England at The Oval	1976
681-8d	v England at Port-of-Spain	1953-54
660-5d	v New Zealand at Wellington	1994-95
652-8d	v England at Lord's	1973
644-8d	v India at Delhi	1958-59
631-8d	v India at Kingston	1961-62
631	v India at Delhi	1948-49

West Indies have passed 600 in Tests on seven further occasions

Lowest team totals

Completed innings
47	v England at Kingston	2003-04
51	v Aust at Port-of-Spain	1998-99
53	v Pakistan at Faisalabad	1986-87
54	v England at Lord's	2000
61	v England at Leeds	2000
76	v Pakistan at Dacca	1958-59
77	v NZ at Auckland	1955-56
78	v Australia at Sydney	1951-52
82	v Australia at Brisbane	2000-01
86*	v England at The Oval	1957

*One batsman absent hurt

Best match bowling

14-149	MA Holding	v England at The Oval	1976
13-55	CA Walsh	v N Zealand at Wellington	1994-95
12-121	AME Roberts	v India at Madras	1974-75
11-84	CEL Ambrose	v England at Port-of-Spain	1993-94
11-89	MD Marshall	v India at Port-of-Spain	1988-89
11-107	MA Holding	v Australia at Melbourne	1981-82
11-120	MD Marshall	v N Zealand at Bridgetown	1984-85
11-126	WW Hall	v India at Kanpur	1958-59
11-134	CD Collymore	v Pakistan at Kingston	2004-05
11-147	KD Boyce	v England at The Oval	1973

Marshall took ten or more wickets in a Test four times, Ambrose and Walsh three

Hat-tricks

WW Hall v Pakistan at Lahore 1958-59
The first Test hat-trick not for England or Australia.

LR Gibbs v Australia at Adelaide 1960-61
Gibbs had taken three wickets in four balls in the previous Test, at Sydney.

CA Walsh v Australia at Brisbane 1988-89
The first Test hat-trick to be split over two innings.

JJC Lawson v Australia at Bridgetown 2002-03
Also split over two innings

West Indies' Test match results

	Played	Won	Lost	Drawn	Tied	% win
v Australia	105	32	50	22	1	30.47
v Bangladesh	4	3	0	1	0	75.00
v England	138	52	41	45	0	37.68
v India	82	30	11	41	0	36.58
v New Zealand	35	10	9	16	0	28.57
v Pakistan	44	14	15	15	0	31.81
v South Africa	22	3	14	5	0	13.63
v Sri Lanka	12	3	6	3	0	25.00
v Zimbabwe	6	4	0	2	0	66.66
TOTAL	**448**	**151**	**146**	**150**	**1**	**33.70**

Figures to 12.9.08. Updated records can be found at www.cricinfo.com/ci/engine/records

WEST INDIES One-day International Records

Most appearances

295	BC Lara
238	DL Haynes
235	S Chanderpaul
227	CL Hooper
224	RB Richardson
205	CA Walsh
187	IVA Richards
183	CH Gayle
176	CEL Ambrose
169	PJL Dujon

In all 24 West Indians have played more than 100 ODIs

Most runs

		Avge
10348	BC Lara	40.90
8648	DL Haynes	41.37
7573	S Chanderpaul	40.49
6721	IVA Richards	47.00
6561	CH Gayle	39.76
6248	RB Richardson	33.41
5761	CL Hooper	35.34
5134	CG Greenidge	45.03
4300	RR Sarwan	43.87
3675	PV Simmons	28.93

Lara scored 19 ODI centuries, Haynes 17, Gayle 16, Greenidge and Richards 11

Most wickets

		Avge
227	CA Walsh	30.47
225	CEL Ambrose	24.12
193	CL Hooper	36.05
157	MD Marshall	26.96
149	CH Gayle	32.08
146	J Garner	18.84
142	MA Holding	21.36
130	M Dillon	32.44
118	IR Bishop	26.50
118	IVA Richards	35.83

WKM Benjamin (100) and RA Harper (100) also reached 100 wickets

Highest scores

189*	IVA Richards	v England at Manchester	1984
181	IVA Richards	v Sri Lanka at Karachi	1987-88
169	BC Lara	v Sri Lanka at Sharjah	1995-96
157*	XM Marshall	v Canada at King City	2008-09
156	BC Lara	v Pakistan at Adelaide	2004-05
153*	IVA Richards	v Australia at Melbourne	1979-80
153*	CH Gayle	v Zimbabwe at Bulawayo	2003-04
153	BC Lara	v Pakistan at Sharjah	1993-94
152*	DL Haynes	v India at Georgetown	1988-89
152*	CH Gayle	v S Africa at Johannesburg	2003-04
152	CH Gayle	v Kenya at Nairobi	2001-02

S Chanderpaul scored 150 v SA at East London in 1998-99

Best bowling figures

7-51	WW Davis	v Australia at Leeds	1983
6-15	CEH Croft	v England at Kingstown	1980-81
6-22	FH Edwards	v Zimbabwe at Harare	2003-04
6-29	BP Patterson	v India at Nagpur	1987-88
6-41	IVA Richards	v India at Delhi	1989-90
6-50	AH Gray	v Aust at Port-of-Spain	1990-91
5-1	CA Walsh	v Sri Lanka at Sharjah	1986-87
5-17	CEL Ambrose	v Australia at Melbourne	1988-89
5-22	AME Roberts	v England at Adelaide	1979-80
5-22	WKM Benjamin	v Sri Lanka at Bombay	1993-94

Edwards's feat was in his first ODI; he had earlier taken 5-36 on his Test debut

Record wicket partnerships

1st	200*	SC Williams (78*) and S Chanderpaul (109*)	v India at Bridgetown	1996-97
2nd	221	CG Greenidge (115) and IVA Richards (149)	v India at Jamshedpur	1983-84
3rd	195*	CG Greenidge (105*) and HA Gomes (75*)	v Zimbabwe at Worcester	1983
4th	226	S Chanderpaul (150) and CL Hooper (108)	v South Africa at East London	1998-99
5th	154	CL Hooper (112*) and S Chanderpaul (67)	v Pakistan at Sharjah	2001-02
6th	154	RB Richardson (122) and PJL Dujon (53)	v Pakistan at Sharjah	1991-92
7th	115	PJL Dujon (57*) and MD Marshall (66)	v Pakistan at Gujranwala	1986-87
8th	84	RL Powell (76) and CD Collymore (3)	v India at Toronto	1999-2000
9th	77	RR Sarwan (65) and IDR Bradshaw (37)	v New Zealand at Christchurch	2005-06
10th	106*	IVA Richards (189*) and MA Holding (12*)	v England at Manchester	1984

Figures to 12.9.08. Updated records can be found at www.cricinfo.com/ci/engine/records

One-day International Records — WEST INDIES

Most catches

Fielders

120	CL Hooper	
117	BC Lara	
100	IVA Richards	
84	CH Gayle	
75	RB Richardson	

Most dismissals

Wicketkeepers		*Ct/St*
204	PJL Dujon	183/21
189	RD Jacobs	160/29
77	D Ramdin	73/4
68	CO Browne	59/9
51	JR Murray	44/7

Highest team totals

360-4	v Sri Lanka at Karachi	1987-88
347-6	v Zimbabwe at Bulawayo	2003-04
339-4	v Pakistan at Adelaide	2004-05
333-6	v Zimbabwe at Georgetown	2005-06
333-7	v Sri Lanka at Sharjah	1995-96
333-8	v India at Jamshedpur	1983-84
324-4	v India at Ahmedabad	2002-03
324-8	v India at Nagpur	2006-07
315-4	v Pakistan at Port-of-Spain	1987-88
315-6	v India at Vijayawada	2002-03

All these totals came from 50 overs except 333-8 (45) and 315-4 (47)

Lowest team totals

Completed innings		
54	v S Africa at Cape Town	2003-04
80	v Sri Lanka at Mumbai	2006-07
87	v Australia at Sydney	1992-93
91	v Zimbabwe at Sydney	2000-01
93	v Kenya at Pune	1995-96
103	v Pak at Melbourne	1996-97
110	v Australia at Manchester	1999
111	v Pak at Melbourne	1983-84
113	v Aust at Kuala Lumpur	2006-07
114	v Pak at Pt-of-Spain	1999-2000

The 87 was in a match reduced to 30 overs: Australia made 101-9

Most sixes

133	BC Lara
126	IVA Richards
111	CH Gayle
81	CG Greenidge
75	RL Powell
74	S Chanderpaul
65	CL Hooper
54	RB Richardson
53	DL Haynes
49	WW Hinds

Greenidge and Powell share the West Indian record with 8 sixes in one innings

Best strike rate

Runs per 100 balls		*Runs*
101.54	DR Smith	791
96.66	RL Powell	2085
90.20	IVA Richards	6721
81.22	CH Lloyd	1977
80.72	CH Gayle	6561
80.68	DJ Bravo	1291
79.62	BC Lara	10348
79.25	D Ramdin	554
76.64	MD Marshall	955
76.63	CL Hooper	5761

Qualification: 500 runs

Most economical bowlers

Runs per over		*Wkts*
3.09	J Garner	146
3.32	MA Holding	142
3.40	AME Roberts	87
3.48	CEL Ambrose	225
3.53	MD Marshall	157
3.83	CA Walsh	227
3.97	RA Harper	100
4.00	CE Cuffy	41
4.09	EAE Baptiste	36
4.15	WKM Benjamin	100

Qualification: 2000 balls bowled

West Indies' one-day international results

	Played	Won	Lost	Tied	No result	% win
v Australia	119	57	58	2	2	49.57
v Bangladesh	13	11	0	0	2	100.00
v England	75	39	32	0	4	54.92
v India	90	53	35	1	1	60.11
v New Zealand	46	23	18	0	5	56.09
v Pakistan	110	64	44	2	0	59.09
v South Africa	45	12	32	0	1	27.27
v Sri Lanka	46	26	18	0	2	59.09
v Zimbabwe	36	27	8	0	1	77.14
v others (see below)	15	13	1	0	1	86.66
TOTAL	**595**	**325**	**246**	**5**	**19**	**56.85**

Other teams: Bermuda (P1; W1), Canada (P3, W3), Ireland (P2, W1, NR1), Kenya (P6, W5, L1), Netherlands (P1, W1), Scotland (P2, W2).

INTERNATIONAL SCHEDULE 2008-09

	Tests	ODIs
October 2008		
India v Australia	4	0
Bangladesh v New Zealand	2	3
Kenya v Zimbabwe v Ireland	0	7
South Africa v Kenya	0	2
Stanford Twenty20 Super Series in Antigua	–	–
November 2008		
India v England	2	7
Australia v New Zealand	2	0
South Africa v Bangladesh	2	3
Sri Lanka v Zimbabwe	0	3*
December 2008		
Australia v South Africa	3	5
Pakistan v India	3	5
New Zealand v West Indies	2	5
Bangladesh v Sri Lanka	2	0
January 2009		
Bangladesh v Sri Lanka v Zimbabwe	0	7*
February 2009		
West Indies v England	4	5
Australia v New Zealand	0	5
South Africa v Australia	3	5
Zimbabwe v Sri Lanka	0	3*
March 2009		
New Zealand v India	2	5
April 2009		
Bangladesh v West Indies	2	3

	Tests	ODIs
May 2009		
England v Sri Lanka	2	3
Sri Lanka v India v South Africa	0	7*
June 2009		
ICC World Twenty20 championship in England	–	–
July 2009		
England v Australia	5	7
Sri Lanka v Pakistan	3	5
Zimbabwe v New Zealand	0	3*
August 2009		
Sri Lanka v New Zealand	3	5
Zimbabwe v Bangladesh	2	3*
Scotland v Australia	0	1
September 2009		
ICC Champions Trophy in Pakistan	0	21*
October 2009		
India v Australia	0	7
Bangladesh v Zimbabwe	3	5*
November 2009		
South Africa v England	4	5
Australia v Pakistan	0	3
India v Sri Lanka	3	5
December 2009		
Australia v West Indies	3	0
Bangladesh v India	2	3
Pakistan v New Zealand	3	5

Details subject to change. Home side shown first. Some tours may continue into the month after the one shown above. An asterisk signifies that the number of matches is unconfirmed